A PEOPLE'S GUIDE TO

GREATER BOSTON

UNIVERSITY OF CALIFORNIA PRESS
PEOPLE'S GUIDES

Los Angeles
Greater Boston

Forthcoming

San Francisco Bay Area
New York City
Orange County, California
Richmond and Central Virginia
New Orleans

About the Series

Tourism is one of the largest and most profitable industries in the world today, especially for cities. Yet the vast majority of tourist guidebooks focus on the histories and sites associated with a small, elite segment of the population and encourage consumption and spectacle as the primary way to experience a place. These representations do not reflect the reality of life for most urban residents—including people of color, the working class and poor, immigrants, indigenous people, and LGBTQ communities—nor are they embedded within a systematic analysis of power, privilege, and exploitation. The *People's Guide* series was born from the conviction that we need a different kind of guidebook: one that explains power relations in a way everyone can understand, and that shares stories of struggle and resistance to inspire and educate activists, students, and critical thinkers.

Guidebooks in the series uncover the rich and vibrant stories of political struggle, oppression, and resistance in the everyday landscapes of metropolitan regions. They reveal an alternative view of urban life and history by flipping the script of the conventional tourist guidebook. These books not only tell histories from the bottom up, but also show how *all* landscapes and places are the product of struggle. Each book features a range of sites where the powerful have dominated and exploited other people and resources, as well as places where ordinary people have fought back in order to create a more just world. Each book also includes carefully curated thematic tours through which readers can explore specific urban processes and their relation to metropolitan geographies in greater detail. The photographs model how to read space, place, and landscape critically, while the maps, nearby sites of interest, and additional learning resources create a resource that is highly usable. By mobilizing the conventional format of the tourist guidebook in these strategic ways, books in the series aim to cultivate stronger public understandings of how power operates spatially.

A PEOPLE'S GUIDE TO
GREATER BOSTON

Joseph Nevins   Suren Moodliar   Eleni Macrakis

University of California Press

University of California Press
Oakland, California

The People's Guides are written in the spirit of discovery and we hope they will take readers to a wider range of places across cities. Readers are cautioned to explore and travel at their own risk and obey all local laws. The author and publisher assume no responsibility or liability with respect to personal injury, property damage, loss of time or money, or other loss or damage allegedly caused directly or indirectly from any information or suggestions contained in this book.

Library of Congress Cataloging-in-Publication Data

Names: Nevins, Joseph, author. | Moodliar, Suren, 1962– author. | Macrakis, Eleni, 1991– author.
Title: A people's guide to Greater Boston / Joseph Nevins, Suren Moodliar, Eleni Macrakis.
Description: Oakland, California : University of California Press, [2020] | Includes bibliographical references and index.
Identifiers: LCCN 2019025420 (print) | LCCN 2019025421 (ebook) | ISBN 9780520294523 (cloth) | ISBN 9780520967571 (ebook)
Subjects: LCSH: Boston Region (Mass.)—Guidebooks. | Boston Region (Mass.)—Description and travel.
Classification: LCC F73.18.N48 2020 (print) | LCC F73.18 (ebook) | DDC 917.44/6104—dc23
LC record available at https://lccn.loc.gov/2019025420
LC ebook record available at https://lccn.loc.gov/2019025421

Designer and compositor: Nicole Hayward
Text: 10/14.5 Dante
Display: Museo Sans and Museo Slab
Prepress: Embassy Graphics
Indexer: Jim O'Brien
Cartographer: Neil Horsky
Printer and binder: Imago

Printed in Malaysia

29 28 27 26 25 24 23 22 21 20
10 9 8 7 6 5 4 3 2 1

Contents

Maps

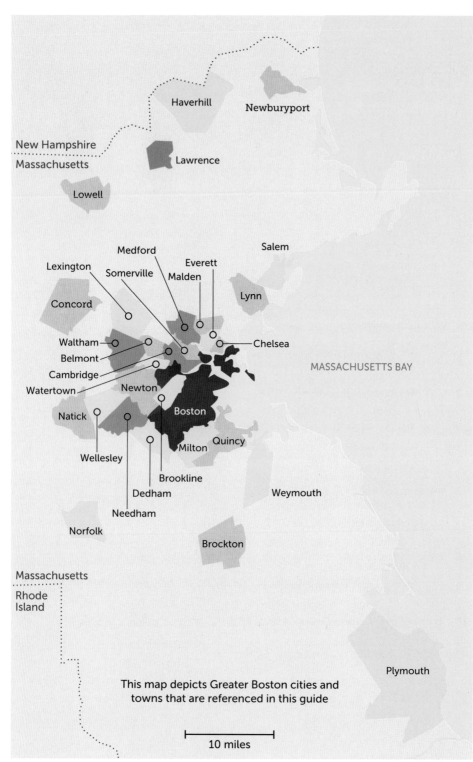

New Hampshire
Massachusetts

Haverhill

Newburyport

Lawrence

Lowell

Salem

Medford

Lexington

Everett

Somerville

Malden

Concord

Lynn

Waltham

Chelsea

Belmont

MASSACHUSETTS BAY

Cambridge

Watertown

Newton

Natick

Boston

Wellesley

Milton

Quincy

Brookline

Dedham

Weymouth

Needham

Norfolk

Brockton

Massachusetts

Rhode
Island

Plymouth

This map depicts Greater Boston cities and
towns that are referenced in this guide

|———————| 10 miles

Greater Boston

Introduction:
Unsettling Greater Boston

Boston, like any particular place, is many things. Among those who have celebrated it, or do so now, it is that "City on the Hill"—a biblical phrase used by the Massachusetts Bay Colony's first governor to highlight the dangers of failure —but now (mis)understood to suggest the promise of great things to come. In addition, as the physician and poet Oliver Wendell Holmes once baptized the city, it is "the Hub" (of the universe), the center of the world. Moreover, it's the "Athens of America" due to Boston's preeminent place in the intellectual and cultural life of the United States, and its leading role in the establishment of educational institutions— from public schools to elite universities. And it is the "Cradle of Liberty" (a title claimed by others, not least Philadelphia) for helping to birth and nurture the American Revolution and subsequent freedom struggles.

But Boston is also a *colonial* enterprise— and has been since its very founding—one with two faces. First, it is a colony in the most literal sense of the word: a place where

people from elsewhere have settled. Indeed, its very name comes from a town in England from where a number of the original Puritan settlers came in the early 1600s. When one speaks of colonial Boston, it is this first face that is typically intended. It is one, particularly in its earliest manifestations, that embodies a colony's most unjust form: one involving a relationship of domination (by a "mother country") and subjugation (of the colonized land and people). Its second face reflects the fact that Boston has also long been a place involved in the colonization of places and peoples. One manifestation is the area's dispossession of the non-European, indigenous inhabitants and the absorption of the Native lands upon which the city and its environs now sit.

Prior to European contact, many Native groups—from the Massachusett and Nipmuc to the Pennacook and the Wampanoag— populated the area. Moreover, there were points during the first several decades of European settlement when relations between settlers and Indians were constructive and respectful—even if often only superficially so—or when dissenting colonists challenged war-making against Indian groups. The potential of these relations was significantly limited, however, by a larger context: the quest—at best, paternalistic—to "civilize" the indigenous population. Such efforts were thus part of a project to "kill the Indian, and save the man," as Richard Henry Pratt, a US Army officer credited with establishing the first Indian boarding school, phrased it in an 1892 speech. These civilizing endeavors are inseparable from the many episodes and various forms of overt violence against Native peoples.

These speak to another project, one that saw Indians and their claims to the land as obstacles to the colonial enterprise, and that thus focused not on "saving" Indians, but instead on "removing" them. It was a project facilitated not only by direct violence—violence intensified by rivalries involving competing European projects in North America and shifting alliances among Native groups—but also by a combination of economic, ecological, and epidemiological forces that led to drastic reductions in Native numbers and far-reaching changes in how they lived. Even before English colonists settled what is today eastern Massachusetts, pathogens introduced by European traders had wreaked havoc on many Indian groups. Between 1616 and 1618, for example, an epidemic or a series of them killed upward of 75 percent of southern New England's coastal Algonquian population, according to one estimate.

And for those who survived the new diseases, as many did, other challenges abounded, which together greatly transformed the area's landscape and the socio-ecological relations of its indigenous peoples. These challenges included new goods and trade networks, as well as novel labor regimes—which involved the enslavement by English settlers of large numbers of Indians as laborers in the emerging colonial economy and for sale in the Caribbean. Also central was the sheer number of arriving colonists with their voracious hunger for land and, with it, for trees to build and fuel their homes, to construct ships, and for export. Moreover, there was the matter of European plants and animals. As they encroached on Indians' traditional lands, the settlers' cows and pigs consumed their food sources, while, like English plants in relation to flora indigenous to the region, crowding out local fauna. And as colonial settlements and agricultural establishments grew, so too did roads and fences, which greatly inhibited the mobility of the Native population and thus their ability to access the land's diversity to provide for themselves as was their custom.

Such developments challenge a dominant perception of nature, one which suggests that the city is nature's antithesis. In fact, urban areas depend upon and embody nature. Hence, the urban and the rural, cities and the countryside, are tightly tied. Indeed, they make each other. Take, for example, the largest inland body of water in present-day Massachusetts, the Quabbin Reservoir. Sixty-five miles east of Boston, it is today the city's primary source of water—as well as that for forty surrounding municipalities. Encircled by forested land and rolling hills, this "natural" body of water and its bucolic environs were built in 1930s. It involved the destruction of four small towns and the relocation of about 3,000 people and 7,613 graves.

The example demonstrates how the commandeering, transformation, and use of environmental resources have been central to the making of Greater Boston, as they have been to any place on the globe, from the time of its founding. As an affluent region of the modern global economy, Greater Boston consumes a grossly outsized slice of the world's resources and similarly produces a disproportionate share of its pollutants. That the region's residents (as a whole) are able to do so is not unconnected to the fact that local actors have played key roles, politically, economically, and intellectually, in giving rise and contributing to, and perpetrating, imperial violence against distant lands and peoples. From the violent annexation of much of what is today the US West as well as the Southwest (and its "taking" from Mexico and the peoples living there) and the colonization of Hawaii in the 1800s to the brutal US wars against the Philippines at the twentieth century's dawn and Vietnam in the 1960s and '70s, and the present-day and seemingly boundless post-9/11 wars, Greater Bostonians have been pivotal figures.

Boston has also been, since its establishment, a place predicated on global trade, and Greater Bostonians have been central to the making of a capitalist and highly unequal world economy. Merchants in Salem, for instance, dominated the world's black pepper trade in the beginning decades of the nineteenth century, and a Boston-based company that focused on bananas came to be the world's largest agricultural enterprise in the early 1900s. Area merchants and industrialists helped to fuel the slave trade through cotton textile production and sale, while some of Greater Boston's leading figures enriched themselves and the local economy by buying and selling enslaved human beings of African origin, as well as by hawking opium in Asia. Even while sermonizing in anticipation of his New England voyage, Puritan leader John Winthrop was contemplating the riches that slavery in the West Indies would produce for his family. Later, in building the city and his personal estate, Winthrop would rob both land and labor from the region's indigenous people.

The hierarchy of humanity applied not only to Native and African-origin peoples. Since the time of its founding, inequality has been at Boston's core. John Winthrop, a member of England's landed gentry, saw poverty and the need for the destitute to submit to the powerful as part of God's plan. He was similarly explicit about his disdain for democracy, calling it "the meanest and worst of all forms of Government."

Responding to a shortage of arable land in England as common holdings were being enclosed and privatized, Winthrop had encouraged settlers to head for the Massachusetts Bay Colony by boasting of the rich availability of low-priced land. The vision of religious freedom was in fact less of a lure than the vision of profit, and, among the twenty-one thousand individuals who arrived in the 1630s, the Puritans were a minority. According to historian Nancy Isenberg, "For every religious dissenter in the exodus of the 1630s, there was one commercially driven emigrant from London or other areas of England." The majority of settlers arrived as extended families, and many of them with servants in tow. While many of the new elite "owned" enslaved people of Indian or African origin, they far more commonly used heavily exploited child laborers and indentured servants (those forced into servitude due to debt or for having been convicted of a crime).

Slavery, child labor, and indentured servitude are, with occasional exceptions, long gone in present-day Greater Boston. Marked inequities and highly exploited labor, however, persist. A 2016 report found that the City of Boston had the greatest income inequality among the one hundred largest cities in the United States. Among metropolitan areas, Boston was the sixth most unequal, with the top 5 percent of households averaging $294,000 in annual income, and the bottom 20 percent averaging $28,000. A 2017 *Boston Globe* "Spotlight" series on race in the Greater Boston area revealed a shocking statistic: the median net worth (meaning half are above, and half below) of African American (nonimmigrant) households was $8. The corresponding figure for whites was $247,500. Immigrant labor, typically very poorly remunerated

and much of it done by individuals who lack basic rights and many of the key protections of citizenship—a significant number of them "undocumented"—provide many of the goods and services consumed and enjoyed by those at the upper end of the income hierarchy.

That the top 5 percent of households in the City of Boston have incomes of at least $266,000 provides insight into who resides in its tony areas. These areas include old-money neighborhoods such as the Back Bay and the new and gentrified high-end residences of the South End, as well as Downtown's Millennium Tower (where the smallest apartments sell for just under $1 million and the "grand penthouse" sold for $35 million in 2016). And then there is the Seaport, Boston's newest area, one that benefited from about $18 billion in public investment and that city planners pledged would be for all Bostonians. This key center of the city's "innovation economy" so celebrated by area elites is, instead, a playground for the affluent. Households in the Seaport have (as of 2017) the highest median income of any of Boston zip codes. It is also one of Boston's least racially diverse areas, with a population that is 3 percent black, and 89 percent white—this is in a city, with a population of almost 700,000, where people of color constitute a slim majority. This is just one manifestation of a metropolitan area that is among the most racially segregated in the United States.

What makes such stark socioeconomic inequality and residential segregation all the more remarkable is that Boston, and the Commonwealth of Massachusetts as a whole, is dominated by the Democratic Party. Author Thomas Frank calls Boston "the real spiritual homeland of the liberal class." It is, he writes, "the city that virtually invented the blue-state economic model, in which prosperity arises from higher education and the knowledge-based industries that surround it." These very strengths, he opines, help explain why Boston and the wealthy areas that surround it embody one of the country's most unequal cities in one of its most unequal states, one composed of many struggling, postindustrial municipalities marked by deep and pervasive poverty. In a state that purports to be progressive, its income tax is a flat one, meaning the rich and poor alike pay at the same rate.

The dominant political-economic narrative is one that embraces meritocracy. The convenient story (convenient for those on the upper ends of the proverbial food chain) is built on the notion that Greater Boston's successful and affluent deserve what they have. The flip side is, of course, that the have-nots get their just rewards as well. In other words, inequality is a result not of how society's resources are organized and allocated—of how political-economic power functions—but of individual (and group) strengths, and failings.

Central drivers of the model are "knowledge industries"—higher education (the City of Boston alone has more than 150,000 college students, and the metropolitan area has eighty-five private colleges and universities), hospitals and medical research, and high technology (with much of it tied to US militarism)—

fueled by federal research funds and venture capital. Also key are the real estate and hospitality sectors.

The outsized influence of these interests helps to explain the seemingly endless construction in recent decades of high-end buildings in and around Boston's downtown and significant gentrification, which is wreaking havoc in many of the city's neighborhoods, as well as in surrounding municipalities. Waterfront development is particularly intense—this in an area greatly threatened by climate change and, relatedly, rising sea levels. A study in 2018 found that 22 percent of Boston's housing stock will be at risk of permanent inundation or chronic flooding by 2050 if greenhouse gas emissions continue to climb. In neighboring Cambridge, the figure is 33 percent. Particularly vulnerable are those who already live at the region's socioeconomic margins.

The focus on such matters speaks to our taking a perspective on Greater Boston that is explicitly one "from below," a perspective of "the people"—while appreciating that who constitutes "the people" is ever changing. A people's perspective privileges the desires, hopes, and struggles of those on the receiving end of unjust forms of power and those who work to challenge such inequities and to realize a Greater Boston, and the larger world of which it is part, that is radically inclusive and democratic and that centers on social and environmental justice. It also privileges spatial justice by focusing on the places "the people" inhabit, work, and claim, and where their memories, hopes, visions, labor, and histories are embedded.

Here we bring you to sites that have been central to the lives of "the people" of Greater Boston over four centuries. You'll visit sites associated with the area's indigenous inhabitants and with the individuals and movements who sought to abolish slavery, to end war, challenge militarism, and bring about a more peaceful world, to achieve racial equity, gender justice, and sexual liberation, and to secure the rights of workers. We take you to some well-known sites, but more often to ones far off the beaten path of the Freedom Trail, to places in Boston's outlying neighborhoods. We also visit sites in other municipalities that make up the Greater Boston region—from Lawrence, Lowell, and Lynn to Concord and Plymouth. Our travels also include homes, because people's struggles, activism, and organizing sometimes are born and unfold in living rooms and kitchens.

A "people's city" is a place not only of struggle, activism, and organizing. It is also one of dreams, ones that envision a fundamentally different world. Insofar as powerful forces and interests stymie the realization of those dreams, they remain deferred. But given the pronounced challenges, and even existential threats (at least for many people and species) faced by Greater Bostonians, the area's denizens no longer have (and of course never did) the benefit of an unlimited future. History's debts, nature's hard limits, and the rift between nature and our political and economic institutions, practices, and relationships necessitate a reckoning. For these reasons and more, we hope that *this* people's project, is suggestive of, and

contributes to, the best of the implicit and explicit futures envisioned by the people's dreamers, agitators, rebels, dissidents, organizers, and movements—those of yesterday and today.

Trying to capture a place as diverse and dynamic as Boston is highly challenging. We thus want to make clear that our goal is not to be comprehensive. Given the constraints of space and time as well as the limitations of knowledge—both our own and what is available in published form—we have not included many important sites, cities, and towns. Our modest goal is to paint a suggestive portrait of the greater urban area that highlights its long-contested nature. In many ways, we merely scratch the region's surface—or many surfaces.

In writing about Greater Boston as a place, we run the risk of suggesting that the city writ large has some sort of essence. Indeed, the very notion of a particular place assumes intrinsic characteristics and an associated delimited space. After all, how can one distinguish one place from another if it has no uniqueness and is not geographically differentiated? Nonetheless, we conceive of places as progressive, as geographer Doreen Massey insists, as flowing over the boundaries of any particular space, time, or society; in other words, we see places as everchanging, as unbounded in that they shape and are shaped by other places and forces from without, and as having multiple identities. In exploring 400 years of Greater Boston from many angles, we embrace this approach. That said, we have to reconcile this with the need to delimit Greater Boston—at least simply to be in a position to name it and thus distinguish it from elsewhere. We likewise also "freeze" the city and its many sites at various points to be able to capture it in time, all while trying to keep in mind that what we're discussing has an ancestry and is helping to lay the foundation for what is yet to come. As geographer Don Mitchell writes, "Place is the stopped frame in the continuous film of change."

Place is also tightly tied to who we are, how we live, and what we know—and do not know. In his acclaimed book *Wisdom Sits in Places: Notes on a Western Apache Landscape*, Keith Basso asks a Western Apache elder by the name of Dudley to define wisdom. Dudley responds by recounting what his grandmother told him: "Wisdom sits in places. It's like water that never dries up. You need to drink water to stay alive, don't you? Well, you also need to drink from places. You must remember everything about them. You must learn their names. You must remember what happened at them long ago. You must think about it and keep on thinking about it. Then your mind will become smoother and smoother. Then you will see danger before it happens. You will walk a long way and live a long time. You will be wise."

This book is about both the stopped frame and the continuous film of the place called Greater Boston—past, present, and future—and many places within. May we all drink from them.

A NOTE TO THE READER

This book has many entry points. We have organized it geographically, grouping our sites by neighborhoods (in the case of the City of Boston), and we conclude the book with a series of tours. Each neighborhood or municipality has a brief introduction and is followed by a selection of site entries.

For each entry, we provide (under "Getting There") directions via public transit. Typically, we also provide the walking distance from the closest MBTA (Massachusetts Bay Transit Authority) station or bus stop, and the amount of time it would take an average walker from that point to reach the destination. A map of the MBTA system is available on page 287.

Within many entries, readers will come across sites and municipalities that are in **bold and italics**; these are discussed elsewhere in the book.

1

Boston's
Historic
Core

Boston Harbor

Boston is a city of the ocean, not simply one along its shores. For thousands of years before English colonization, Native peoples fished in the harbor and traveled across its waters and those of the rivers tied to it. They also visited, settled, foraged, and farmed its islands, transforming landscapes in the process. It was through the harbor that the Puritans first arrived, and it was through its waters that early Bostonians established transatlantic—and, later, worldwide—trade relations. Ocean-born resources, particularly cod, were central to the early development of these ties—manifested by a dense network of wharves along Boston's shore. The resources were also central to the rise of a wealthy class, the so-called cod aristocracy.

Since the 1600s, the islands of Boston Harbor have served multiple purposes. A principal one has been that of social and terri-torial control—control of a heavily regulated, policed, and militarized sort. From military forts and detention camps for official ene-mies to prisons and centers of quarantine, the enterprises of war, "homeland security," and incarceration are embedded in Boston Harbor's ocean-scape and landscapes. So too has been dumping—trash and sewage, as well as unwanted human beings, whether the poor in almshouses or the homeless in shelters.

Boston's rapid development led to heavy pollution of the harbor. In the late 1980s, many came to know it as "the dirtiest harbor in America." Since then, a federal-court-ordered, multibillion-dollar cleanup has made a significantly positive impact on water quality. Today the Harbor Islands are largely sites of recreation, part of a National Recreation Area maintained by the US National Park Service (NPS). In part by

Boston from the harbor, circa 1870–79.

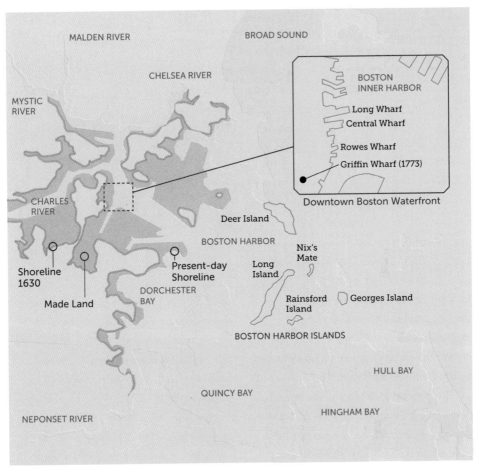

The Waters of Boston

working with the NPS and the Commonwealth of Massachusetts, Native peoples
continue to engage the waters and islands to
protect and maintain sacred sites, as well as
their histories and traditions.

In a time of intensifying climate destabili-
zation and warming temperatures, sea level
rise threatens Boston, particularly those areas
comprising made land (largely filled-in mud
flats)—about one-sixth of the city's total
land area, according to one estimate. It manifests that Boston Harbor is growing.

1.1 Deer Island

BOSTON HARBOR

Before dawn on October 30, 2010, a group
of Native Americans began running twelve
miles from South Natick to Watertown. In
Watertown, the individuals boarded three
mishoonash, traditional wooden dugouts made
by Wampanoag Indians, and a canoe, and
paddled seventeen miles down the Charles
River and three miles across Boston Harbor
to Deer Island, where they and dozens of supporters held a ceremony. The Sacred Run and

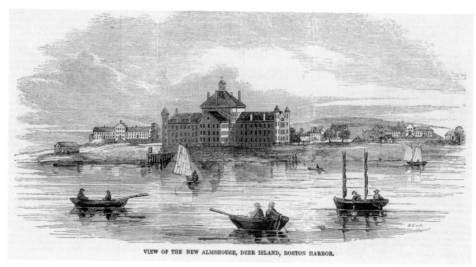

VIEW OF THE NEW ALMSHOUSE, DEER ISLAND, BOSTON HARBOR.

Circa 1850–59.

Paddle's purpose, explained Pam Ellis, one of the organizers and a historian and genealogist for the Natick Nipmuc Council, was "to trace the journey our ancestors took on the forced removal" of Natick's "Praying Indians" in 1675.

The removal took place at the beginning of King Philip's War (1675–78; see *Old Country House/1749 Court House*), when Massachusetts Bay Colony officials determined that they could not trust Christianized Indians living among English settlers. In what is today South Natick, they rounded up what were likely hundreds of Nipmucs from their "praying village" (one established in 1652 by John Elliot when the Native residents of *Nonantum* were compelled to move) and held the majority of them, along with other Eastern Algonquian peoples, on Deer Island—allegedly for their own safety given the potential for indiscriminate retaliatory violence from English settlers. (The rest were held on nearby islands.) Living in what was essentially a concentration camp during the winter of 1675–76, a large number of internees, many of them children, died of cold, malnutrition, and disease, while many others were sold into slavery in the Caribbean, Portugal, or Spain, or were indentured to English families.

Following King Philip's War, authorities used the island for various purposes. In 1677 the British quarantined ships there with passengers suspected of carrying smallpox. During the Irish famine in the 1840s, Boston officials temporarily housed almost five thousand Irish refugees on the island in a quarantine hospital. In the mid-1800s it was the site of an almshouse for the "deserving poor." In 1920 a few hundred individuals were detained there—many for several weeks—in the wake of nationwide raids targeting accused (and largely immigrant) communists, anarchists, and "radicals" with the goal of deporting them (see *Socialist Hall*). And from the late 1800s until 1991, the island hosted a Suffolk County prison.

Prior to European contact, Native Americans lived seasonally on Deer Island. It was so named by English settlers because deer would swim there from the mainland when chased by wolves. When the English first arrived, the island was covered with thick forest, swamps, and thickets.

Since 1938, due to soil erosion, Deer Island has been connected to land, that of the town of Winthrop. The 210-acre island has miles of walking trails, picnic areas, and a modern wastewater treatment plant, a result of the massive cleanup of the Boston Harbor. Plans are also afoot to construct a memorial to Native Americans interned there during King Philip's War.

GETTING THERE

MBTA bus from Orient Heights Station (Blue Line).

TO LEARN MORE

DeLucia, Christine M. *Memory Lands: King Philip's War and the Place of Violence in the Northeast*, New Haven: Yale University Press, 2018.

Lepore, Jill. *The Name of War: King Philip's War and the Origins of American Identity*, New York: Alfred A. Knopf, 1998.

Peterson, Mark. *The City-State of Boston: The Rise and Fall of an Atlantic Power, 1630–1865*, Princeton, NJ: Princeton University Press, 2019.

1.2 Griffin Wharf

Corner of Congress and Purchase Streets

DOWNTOWN

Aged seven or eight, "a slender, frail, female child," according to her "buyer," completed her manacled transatlantic journey aboard the *Phillis* on July 11, 1761, at Griffin Wharf.

An advertisement in the Boston Gazette, July 13, 1761.

The Wheatley family purchased the infirm child in the hope that she would be their caregiver in old age. Taking her name from the ship, she became Phillis Wheatley and, notwithstanding her enslavement, a highly accomplished poet, publishing more than 145 poems.

Although Christianity suffuses her poems, they also exhibit elements of African spirituality. Wheatley's precocious writing and origins led some to question her poems' authenticity. In response, her well-connected "owner" assembled an eighteen-person jury, including the Massachusetts governor and John Hancock, an American Revolution leader. Following a lengthy examination, the jury attested to her authorship. This was not sufficient to win a local publisher, however, leading the family to England, where Phillis found critical acclaim. Even Voltaire, an Enlightenment figure notorious for his contributions to early racist doctrine, praised her poetry. The slave-owning Thomas Jefferson disagreed, complaining that it "kindles the senses only, not the imagination."

Although Wheatley's critique of slavery seems timid, situated in the prerevolutionary Boston, hers was an unambiguous rejection of the institution:

I, young in life, by seeming cruel fate
Was snatch'd from Afric's fancy'd
    happy seat:
What pangs excruciating must molest,
What sorrows labour in my parent's
    breast?
Steel'd was that soul and by no misery
    mov'd
That from a father seiz'd his babe
    belov'd:
Such, such my case. And can I then
    but pray
Others may never feel tyrannic sway?

Not long after her manumission, Wheatley passed away in poverty, barely thirty years old, and after losing three infant children. Of her fate, historian Henry Louis Gates Jr. observed: "Wheatley's freedom enslaved her to a life of hardship." Her travails may be understood in light of Boston's own transition: the Revolutionary War severed many of the elite networks connecting the city to the British empire and, relatedly, her own connections to powerful people, many loyalists, who had championed her work.

Wheatley's journey to Boston was part of an established people-trafficking network. In 1760, the Medford-based Timothy Fitch, owner of the *Phillis*, ordered its captain to sail for Senegal to exchange several thousand gallons of rum for captive Africans. Although most enslaved people usually arrived at well-known Long Wharf, the *Phillis* docked at Griffin Wharf, near the home of a slave auctioneer.

Griffin Wharf, now best known as the site of the Boston Tea Party, no longer exists due to landmaking over the course of the nineteenth century. Phillis Wheatley probably would have disembarked where today's Congress Street is located, just northeast of Purchase Street. A statue of Phillis Wheatley is part of the Boston Women's Memorial on the Commonwealth Avenue Mall in the **Back Bay**.

GETTING THERE

The site is just outside South Station (Red Line).

TO LEARN MORE

Carretta, Vincent. *Phillis Wheatley: Biography of a Genius in Bondage*. Athens: University of Georgia Press, 2011.

Peterson, Mark. *The City-State of Boston: The Rise and Fall of an Atlantic Power, 1630–1865*, Princeton, NJ: Princeton University Press, 2019.

Phillis Wheatley statue, Boston Women's Memorial, Commonwealth Avenue Mall, Back Bay, 2018.

Rainsford's Island, Boston Harbor, painting by Robert Salmon, circa 1840.

1.3 Rainsford Island Hospital

RAINSFORD ISLAND, BOSTON HARBOR

On the morning of May 15, 1855, the ship *Daniel Webster* set sail from Boston to Liverpool, England. On board was Hugh Carr, who had been a patient at a state hospital on Rainsford Island, where officials had transferred him after the East Cambridge resident was diagnosed with mental illness.

Previously used by Native Americans, the eleven-acre island was granted to Edward Rainsford, its first English settler, by the Massachusetts Bay Colony in 1636 for grazing cattle. Between 1737, when Boston first acquired the island, to approximately 1920, it was the site of numerous institutions—including a quarantine hospital, a summer resort for wealthy Bostonians, an almshouse, a Civil War veterans hospital, and a school for delinquent boys. In 1853, Massachusetts established a pauper's colony—in the form of a "hospital"—on the island, part of a much larger effort to house and ghettoize the most destitute of the large numbers of

indigent Irish immigrants arriving on the state's shores during the mid-1800s. Hugh Carr, an immigrant from Ireland, was among them.

During this time, the Commonwealth developed laws for removing foreign paupers residing in the state, an endeavor that intensified with the rise of the "Know-Nothings"—an anti-immigrant movement with a particularly strong animus against Irish Catholics—which swept to power in Massachusetts in the elections of 1854. Massachusetts expelled at least fifty thousand persons between the 1830s and the early 1880s as part of this effort—sending most of them to other US states, Ireland, Canada, and Great Britain (the latter two were deemed appropriate destinations given British colonization of Ireland during the time). While these policies applied to all destitute foreigners and even US Americans originating in other states, the undesirability of the Irish poor was the primary driver of Massachusetts immigration policy.

On board the *Daniel Webster*, Hugh Carr, who had lived in the Boston area for thirteen years prior to being institutionalized, was one of thirty-five Irish "paupers" deported that day in 1855. Although state officials had promised to inform his sisters in East Cambridge of any changes in their brother's condition, his siblings did not learn of his deportation until eight days after the fact.

According to historian Hidetaka Hirota, nineteenth-century efforts by Massachusetts and New York to regulate the mobility of the poor, ones heavily influenced by anti-Irish nativism, helped inspire anti-Chinese immigration politicians and activists in the US West. They also laid the basis for federal immigration control. (Only in the latter part of the century did immigration control become the sole prerogative of the federal government.) Just as Chinese exclusion would later legitimate racism as the basis for the US immigration policing apparatus, the practices of Massachusetts helped to legitimate class as grounds for exclusion.

The City of Boston closed its last institution on Rainsford Island in 1920. Today it is part of the Boston Harbor Islands National Recreation Area.

GETTING THERE

As of now, one can get to Rainsford Island only by way of private boat.

TO LEARN MORE

Hirota, Hidetaka. *Expelling the Poor: Atlantic Seaboard States and the Nineteenth-Century Origins of American Immigration Policy*, New York: Oxford University Press, 2017.

1.4 Central Wharf/James and Thomas H. Perkins and Company

At the intersection of Old Atlantic Avenue and Central and Milk Streets

DOWNTOWN

Now home to the New England Aquarium, Central Wharf was a quarter-mile-long wharf when it opened immediately south of Long Wharf in 1816. With fifty-four four-story warehouses, the wharf was one of Boston's largest and bustled with activity in the nineteenth century.

One contributor to that activity was James and Thomas H. Perkins and Company, a trading company founded by Boston Brahmins in 1792. The company grew out of previous business enterprises by its namesakes, including slave trading in Haiti. First established on Long Wharf, Perkins and Company moved to Foster's Wharf (which no longer exists) within six years and then, by 1820, relocated to 52 Central Wharf, where it would stay for at least two decades before its demise.

Transporting goods across the world in its fleet of ships, Perkins and Company became tremendously wealthy. Largely by smuggling opium from Turkey into China, it earned more from trade with China than any other US company in the first third of the nineteenth century. The illicit opium trade (the Chinese government outlawed the drug) contributed to a social and public health crisis in China as many millions—

including members of the upper class and high-ranking military officials—succumbed to addiction.

In Boston the opium trade enriched many of the city's "leading" families—including the Cabots, Cushings, Forbeses, and Delanos (FDR's grandfather). According to one estimate, Thomas Perkins was Boston's fourth wealthiest individual in 1845, with a net worth of $1.5 million. His nephew, John Perkins Cushing, having served for about twenty-five years as the company's agent in Canton (today Guangzhou), was Boston's second wealthiest with $2 million.

The trade also helped to fuel addiction in Massachusetts as ships would return from China not only with tea, silk, and porcelain, but also with opium. It is unknown how many suffered from opium addiction, but the problem was sufficient in size to merit discussion in the *Boston Medical and Surgical Journal*, forerunner of the *New England Journal of Medicine*, in the 1830s.

Thomas Perkins used his wealth to help fund (and found) some of the city's key institutions—from the Boston Athenaeum to the Massachusetts General Hospital. Thomas Perkins also donated one of his homes (and his name) to what became known as the Perkins School for the Blind (see **South Boston District Courthouse**).

Land reclamation and other projects led to the demolition of much of Central Wharf. Some of its original warehouses still stand, however, at 146–176 Milk Street. They are listed on the National Register of Historic Places.

GETTING THERE

Blue Line to Aquarium Station.

RELATED SITE

E. C. BENTON LIBRARY, 75 Oakley Road, Belmont, where the estate of John Perkins Cushing one stood.

TO LEARN MORE

Haddad, John. *America's First Adventure in China: Trade, Treaties, Opium, and Salvation*, Philadelphia: Temple University Press, 2013.

Seaburg, Carl, and Stanley Paterson, *Merchant Prince of Boston: Colonel T. H. Perkins, 1764–1854*, Cambridge: Harvard University Press, 1971.

1.5 Long Wharf/ Boston Fruit Company

At the intersection of Old Atlantic Avenue and State Street

DOWNTOWN

Built in 1710–1721, during the British colonial period, Long Wharf reflected and projected Boston's dominance as a port city during the eighteenth and nineteenth centuries. Its length at one time was about a half mile, jutting out into the Atlantic Ocean from the eastern end of what was King Street (now State Street). As the harbor's edge east of India Street was gradually filled in, Long Wharf's length decreased markedly.

Many ocean-dependent businesses occupied buildings along the wharf during its heyday. Among them was the Boston Fruit Company. Founded in 1885 by Andrew Preston and Lorenzo Baker with help from Boston investors, it soon came to

Advertisement published in *American Kitchen Magazine*, 1898.

dominate the banana market in the US Northeast. While bananas were by far its main commodity, the company imported a variety of tropical fruits—all, like the banana, relatively new to US palates—such as mangoes and avocados.

Within a decade, the company would own almost forty thousand acres of land, thirty-five plantations, and prime waterfront shipping space in Jamaica. It also had its own line of steamships to transport fruit and to carry tourists between Boston, Philadelphia, and Baltimore and its Jamaican ports. In 1899,

the Boston Fruit Company merged with an entity with banana interests in Central America and Colombia to become the powerful *United Fruit Company*.

Over the course of the late nineteenth and much of the twentieth centuries, the importance of Long Wharf declined—as did Boston's role in international shipping. A hotel and two buildings from the nineteenth century, the Chart House and the Custom House Block, today sit on what remains of the wharf. Public ferries to various Boston Harbor islands depart regularly from Long

Wharf, now a National Historic Landmark, during the warmer months.

GETTING THERE

Blue Line to Aquarium Station, two hundred to three hundred feet away.

TO LEARN MORE

Wilson, Charles Morrow. *Empire in Green and Gold: The Story of the American Banana Trade*, New York: Henry Holt and Company, 1947.

1.6 Fort Strong, Long Island

BOSTON HARBOR

At 225 acres, Long Island is the largest Boston Harbor island. As its name suggests, it is relatively long (three-quarters of a mile) and narrow (a quarter mile). Native Americans likely frequented it during the precolonial period. Later, in the seventeenth and eighteenth centuries, English settlers farmed it. During King Philip's War (see **Old Country House/1749 Court House**) some number of Native people—"prisoners and friendly Indians"—were held there for an undisclosed period. And during the Civil War, it served as training ground for Union soldiers. The island also hosted a resort hotel (Long Island House) during the nineteenth century.

On September 20, 1945, a group of seven German scientists, guests of the Pentagon, arrived at Fort Strong, a US Army installation that had moved to the eastern end of Long Island from Noddle's Island (today part of land-filled **East Boston**) in 1867, but had fallen into disuse after World War I. A whaling vessel had secretly picked them up from a troopship off **Nixes Mate** that had transported them from the Naval Air Station in Quincy. They were some of Nazi Germany's most valuable scientific minds, one of them Wernher von Braun, the Hitler regime's most important rocket engineer. Over the next nine months, scores of German scientists would arrive and stay at Fort Strong—unbeknownst to US immigration authorities or the US State Department—before departing for other destinations within the United

Long Island House, undated.

States. In the mess hall at Fort Strong, the scientists delivered lectures, leading them to call their new place of residence "das Haus der Deutschen Wissenschaft" (the House of German Science).

The scientists were all part of Operation Overcast (later called Operation Paperclip), a Pentagon intelligence program by which more than sixteen hundred scientists who played key roles in the Third Reich's military machine were recruited to work for the United States government. Over subsequent decades, they helped to develop "rockets, chemical and biological weapons, aviation and space medicine (for enhancing military pilot and astronaut performance), and many other armaments at a feverish and paranoid pace that came to define the Cold War"—in the words of investigative journalist Annie Jacobsen.

Apart from its military functions, Long Island housed other activities during the twentieth century, including what was called the Boston Lunatic Hospital and a chronic disease hospital. The latter would subsequently serve as a City of Boston homeless shelter and substance-abuse treatment facility, one where several hundred men and women would stay each night. It included a farm that produced thousands of pounds of organic fruits and vegetables, herbs, eggs, and honey each year to feed the residents, many of whom worked on the farm. In October 2014, the City of Boston suddenly closed down the operations and evacuated the residents when the bridge connecting Long Island to Quincy was condemned. (The bridge did not exist at the time of Operation Paperclip.)

Long Island is currently closed to the public and the remnants of Fort Strong overgrown, its ignominious history of helping to recycle Nazi scientists in the name of US militarism known by few.

GETTING THERE

Some Boston Harbor cruises pass close by.

TO LEARN MORE

Jacobsen, Annie. *Operation Paperclip: The Secret Intelligence Program that Brought Nazi Scientists to America*, New York: Little, Brown and Company, 2014.

1.7 Nixes Mate

BOSTON HARBOR

Greeting new seaborne arrivals to Massachusetts Bay Colony for several years after 1726 were the caged skeletal remains of a pirate, William Fly. Suspended above the tiny island known as Nixes Mate, the grisly public display was intended as a warning to sailors inclined to mutiny.

Such an extreme measure speaks to the strong disposition of eighteenth -century sailors to challenge authority, not least because those manning the huge British fleet were often villagers and newly arrived city dwellers who were press-ganged into service for the Crown. They were also often from outside Britain—seized from West Africa and other places where the British traded. The sailors therefore had little in common with their "gentleman" captains, the British nobility and merchants serviced by the navy. Speaking to this class divide, William Fly complained bitterly at his trial: "Our

Captain and his Mate used us Barbarously. We poor Men can't have Justice done us. There is nothing said to our Commanders, let them never so much abuse us, and use us like Dogs."

Mutineers faced severe penalties, forcing them into piracy. For several decades, the limited reach of governments created space for self-organization that upended the hierarchies the mutineers had challenged and fled, prefiguring an alternative way of organizing work. During the "Golden Age of Piracy" which began in the late 1600s, pirate ships generally elected their captains and quartermasters, made decisions by equal vote, shared their booty on egalitarian lines, and were often multinational, multilingual, and multiracial enterprises.

In pre-Revolution Boston, carefully regulated and taxed trade between the city and the Caribbean was central to the colonial order, and piracy threatened that. Many nevertheless respected pirates—even if begrudgingly. Benjamin Franklin, for example, composed a ditty about the death of Edward Teach (d. 1718), aka Blackbeard, which expressed admiration for the pirate's courage. Similarly, the minister Cotton Mather, despite having failed to have Fly express remorse, described the pirate as a "brave fellow" when recounting Fly's calm instructions to his executioner on how to properly tie the noose from which Fly was to be hanged. His execution signaled the reassertion of state power and the receding fortunes of piracy.

Today Nixes Mate hosts a Coast Guard beacon. The island remains as tiny as it was in Fly's day. Prior to that, it had consisted of several acres rising modestly above the waves until it was quarried for shale for roofing and for shipping ballast.

GETTING THERE

Several Boston Harbor Island ferries departing from near Aquarium Station (Blue Line) pass close by.

TO LEARN MORE

Rediker, Marcus. *Villains of All Nations: Atlantic Pirates in the Golden Age.* Boston: Beacon Press, 2004.

Shawmut Peninsula

English settlers established Boston on the Shawmut Peninsula. Originally consisting of 789 acres, Boston subsequently expanded its historic-geographic core along its wharfs and through in-filling wetlands, and landmaking along its shores. We begin this section by exploring sites in Downtown Boston, and then move to the peninsula's residential neighborhoods: the North End, West End, Beacon Hill, and Chinatown.

South Station with the Atlantic Avenue Elevated in front, 1905.

DOWNTOWN BOSTON

Home to many of Boston's landmarks and historic sites as well as City Hall, Downtown hosts numerous office buildings, department stores, hotels, and bank and corporate headquarters. The area constituted much of Boston proper, a large portion of which was destroyed by a huge fire in 1872, prior to the city's massive growth in the mid- and late 1800s. Bounded by the Back Bay, Beacon Hill, Chinatown, and the North and West Ends, Downtown is also home to two universities—Emerson College and Suffolk University—both of which have played significant roles in the area's transformation in recent years as seen in the growing presence of student residences and luxury condos. As the site of the city's public transit crossroads and its political-economic center, Downtown is also a very diverse space. It is one

marked historically by political activity—from anticolonial riots in the 1700s and Abolitionist organizing in the nineteenth century to civil rights and antiwar protests in the twentieth and #OccupyBoston in 2011.

1.8 The Boston Common

Bounded by Tremont, Beacon, Charles, Park, and Boylston Streets.

DOWNTOWN

The Boston Common is the oldest public park in the United States and the keystone of the city's "Emerald Necklace"—a chain of parks connected by parkways and waterways. It has also long been a contested space, bearing witness to divisions of various sorts, particularly those of class.

For the price of thirty pounds, English colonists purchased the land in 1634 from Anglican minister William Blackstone (or Blaxton) for purposes of pasture and mili-

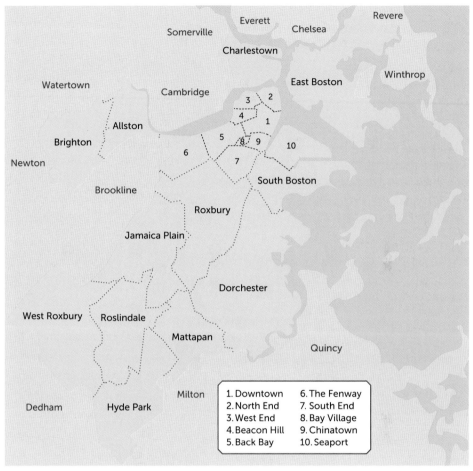

1. Downtown	6. The Fenway
2. North End	7. South End
3. West End	8. Bay Village
4. Beacon Hill	9. Chinatown
5. Back Bay	10. Seaport

City of Boston Neighborhoods

tary training. Blackstone had been part of an earlier but failed settlement at Wessagussett (see **Wessagussett Memorial Garden**). He was the Shawmut Peninsula area's lone European resident when the Puritans first arrived in 1630.

Managed by Boston's "selectmen," the Common was, from its establishment, a site for varied activities—from the regulated grazing of dairy cows ("dry" cattle, sheep, and horses were banned) to, until 1817,

public hangings of religious dissenters, particularly Quakers, alleged pirates, criminal convicts, and witches; there was a mass execution as well—during King Philip's War (see **Old Country House/1749 Court House**) when English authorities killed around forty-five captive Indians. The Common was also the site of everyday activities such as the beating of rugs, gambling, and family picnics. As the area around the Common became increasingly prosperous and bour-

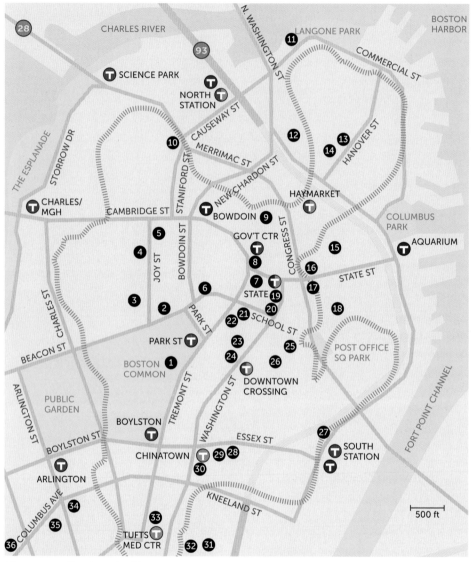

Shawmut Peninsula (Downtown, West End, North End, Beacon Hill, and Chinatown)

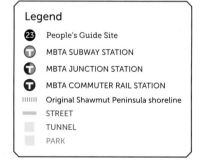

Legend

23	People's Guide Site
T	MBTA SUBWAY STATION
T	MBTA JUNCTION STATION
T	MBTA COMMUTER RAIL STATION
|||||||	Original Shawmut Peninsula shoreline
▬▬▬	STREET
▬▬▬	TUNNEL
▬▬▬	PARK

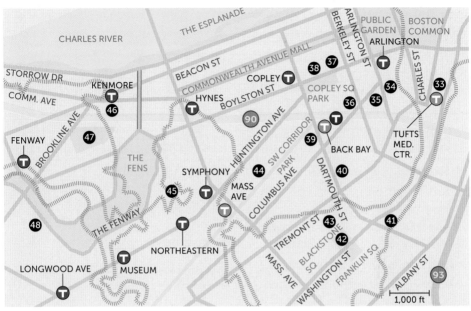

Back Bay, South End, and the Fenway

SHAWMUT / BACK BAY / FENWAY SITES

1   Boston Common
2   Henry Cabot Lodge House
3   Julia Ward Howe Residence
4   Abiel Smith School/Museum of African American History
5   David Walker Home
6   James Bowdoin Home Site
7   Court House Square
8   John P. Jewett & Company
9   American House/John F. Kennedy Federal Building
10 The West End Museum
11 Great Molasses Flood Site
12 Cooper Street Armory
13 Onesimus-Mather House
14 Parmenter Street Chapel
15 Faneuil Hall
16 United Fruit Company
17 The Boston Bellamy Club Immigration Restriction League/Exchange Place
18 Liberty Square
19 Daily Evening Voice
20 Anne Hutchinson House Site
21 The Parker House
22 Tremont Temple
23 Gay Community News
24 Marlboro Hotel and Chapel

25 Odeon Theatre
26 Boston Safe Deposit and Trust Company/ The Vault
27 South Station and Dewey Square
28 New England Telephone Company Exchange/Verizon Building
29 1903 Immigration Raid Site
30 The Naked i
31 Denison House
32 The Metropolitan/Parcel C
33 The Common Cupboard
34 College of Public and Community Service, UMass Boston
35 Armory of the First Corps of Cadets/The Castle
36 The Youth's Companion Building
37 The Newbry
38 Massachusetts Competitive Partnership
39 Tent City
40 Haley House
41 Cathedral of the Holy Cross
42 Blackstone Square
43 Villa Victoria Center for the Arts
44 South End Press
45 Symphony Road Community Garden
46 The Rat
47 Fenway Park
48 Marian Hall, Emmanuel College

geois ideas about nature came to see it as a realm for genteel recreation, however, Boston elites moved to ban activities associated with the lower classes. As environmental historian Michael Rawson observes about Boston, from the time of the city's founding there were conflicts between those (typically associated with the privileged classes) who championed a "culture of privatism" and those whose interests and advocacy were based on community.

In the 1820s the City Council restricted where on the Common one could beat rugs or clean carpets. And in 1830 wealthy area residents succeeded in getting the council to ban cow grazing. What helped make this "victory" possible was the shift from government by town meeting—the democratic nature of which allowed the masses to check the power of the wealthy—to representative government. The shift came about when the Town of Boston became the City of Boston in 1822, which made it easier for the wealthy to impose their interests.

With the end of grazing in 1830, the Boston Common became the largest municipal park in the United States dedicated solely to passive recreation, a place for leisurely strolling and the enjoyment of a highly manufactured nature. In the words of geographer Mona Domosh, the Common functioned as "the front yard of the Boston elite" who lived nearby. It also became a symbol intended for the outside world of Boston's achievements.

That said, the Common has also long been associated with populist rebellion. In 1713, for example, over two hundred people rioted on the Common to protest the high cost of bread and the profiteering merchants whose hoarding of grain was leading to price increases. And in the twentieth century, the Common was the site of many large demonstrations.

Today, the forty-four-acre Common remains a place of leisure—mostly for Boston's working and middle classes. It is also the occasional site of festivals and political gatherings.

GETTING THERE

Park Street Station (Red and Green lines); Boylston Street Station (Green Line).

NEARBY SITES

THE STATEHOUSE; the OLD GRANARY BURIAL GROUND; and the PUBLIC GARDEN.

TO LEARN MORE

Birge-Liberman, Phil. "Landscape and Class: Public Parks as Environmental Amenities in Nineteenth-Century Boston," in Blake Harrison and Richard W. Judd, eds., *A Landscape History of New England*, Cambridge: Massachusetts Institute of Technology Press, 2011: 323–39.

Domosh, Mona. *Invented Cities: The Creation of Landscape in Nineteenth-Century New York and Boston*, New Haven: Yale University Press, 1996.

Rawson, Michael. *Eden on the Charles: The Making of Boston*, Cambridge: Harvard University Press, 2010.

Tager, Jack. *Boston Riots: Three Centuries of Social Violence*. Boston: Northeastern University Press, 2001.

1.9 Anne Hutchinson House Site

283 Washington Street

DOWNTOWN

By late 1637, gatherings at Anne Hutchinson's home in what was then a town of less than two thousand drew dozens of people. The conversations had a political character: They consisted of mixed-gender audiences, were led by a woman, and offered a reading of the Bible that challenged Boston's Puritan establishment. The town's all-male leadership found the meetings to be seditious and brought Hutchinson to trial, one that led to her banishment from the Massachusetts Bay Colony on March 22, 1638.

Although Hutchinson's refusal to embrace Puritan religious doctrine was central to her persecution, also important was the fact that men attending her gatherings had refused to participate in the first major war between the English settlers and an indigenous nation, the so-called Pequot War. Led by veterans of Europe's Thirty Years War, the conflict and especially its final battle, now known as the Mystic massacre (near Mystic, Connecticut), shocked the settlers' indigenous allies with its genocidal character: Colonists killed between four hundred and seven hundred Native persons, mostly noncombatants, wantonly executing many of them.

Following her banishment, Hutchinson and sixty followers moved to the Providence plantation (in present-day Rhode Island). Further migrations followed. Eventually she moved to Dutch-controlled Long Island (New York today), where she died at the hands of an indigenous raiding party challenging settler encroachment.

The original Hutchinson home in Boston burned down in the early 1700s; it was replaced by a brick building, much of which remains. In the mid-1800s it was occupied by the Old Corner Bookstore and later by the Boston Globe Bookstore. The premises now house a fast-food restaurant.

GETTING THERE

Blue and Orange Lines to State Street Station, less than a 0.1 mile (two-minute) walk.

TO LEARN MORE

LaPlante, Eve. *American Jezebel: The Uncommon Life of Anne Hutchinson, the Woman Who Defied the Puritans.* New York: HarperCollins, 2006.

RELATED SITE

MONUMENT OF ANNE HUTCHINSON, erected in 1922, in front of the Massachusetts State House, 24 Beacon Street, Beacon Hill.

1.10 Odeon Theatre

One Federal Street

DOWNTOWN

On Friday evening, January 8, 1836, William Apess, an indigenous minister (Pequot), filled the thirteen-hundred-seat Odeon Theatre. Local bookstores and *The Liberator* (see *William Lloyd Garrison House*) advertised the event at his request. Marking the 160th anniversary of Metacom's execution, Apess delivered his "Eulogy on King Philip." Although attitudes had evolved since the postwar demonization of Metacom/King Philip (see *Old Country House/1749 Court House*), and many had come to see his actions as defensive and even legitimate, Apess had an immediate agenda.

Three years earlier, Apess had come to public attention for helping to lead and chronicle the Mashpee Uprising (1833–34). Giving lie to the notion that the Wampanoags were extinct, the uprising demanded sovereignty and an end to Harvard University's trusteeship over them—one granted by the state. In the uprising's aftermath, which saw Apess imprisoned for thirty days, negotiations produced greater Wampanoag control over their community.

On that January evening, however, Apess was responding to the federal Indian Removal Act and the ethnic cleansing it entailed: The Cherokee, Seminole, Muscogee/Creek, Chickasaw, and Choctaw were slated for removal to the West, leading to the infamous death march of 1838, the Trail of Tears. Although the act enjoyed wide support in the United States, significant opposition was heard in New England; in celebrating Metacom, Apess was fortifying this resistance.

Reprising his contemporary activist, abolitionism's David Walker (see **David Walker Home**) who had called attention to European hypocrisy in relation to slavery, Apess criticized unchristian behavior. Like Walker, Apess nonetheless appealed to common principles of justice: "We want trumpets that sound like thunder, and men to act as though they were going to war with those corrupt and degrading principles that rob one of all rights. . . . Let us have principles that will give everyone

his due; and then shall wars cease, and the weary find rest."

Apess's speech was well received, but it would be his last major project. He had overcome alcohol dependency and become a public intellectual, but it is believed that he relapsed in the face of economic challenges, dying in 1839 at age forty-one.

Between 1835 and 1846, the Odeon served as a lecture and concert hall, hosting the Boston Academy of Music and speakers such as Edgar Allen Poe, Ralph Waldo Emerson, and Angelina Grimke. It was demolished in 1852 and the site redeveloped several times. An office tower occupies the site now.

GETTING THERE

Blue and Orange Lines to State Street Station, 0.2 mile (four-minute) walk.

TO LEARN MORE

O'Connell, Barry. "'Once More Let Us Consider': William Apess in the Writing of New England Native American History," in Colin G. Calloway, ed., *After King Philip's War: Presence and Persistence in Indian New England Reencounters with Colonialism*, Hanover, NH: University Press of New England, 1997.
Gura, Philip F. *The Life of William Apess, Pequot*. Chapel Hill: University of North Carolina Press, 2015.

1.11 Liberty Square

Intersection of Kilby, Water, and Hawes Streets
DOWNTOWN
On the morning of January 24, 1793, large crowds drawn from all social ranks, includ-

ing mixed crowds of men and women, black and white, took to Boston's streets to celebrate events that had taken place five months earlier and across the Atlantic. In September 1792, the French revolutionary army had faced its first military test before Prussian invaders. The revolutionaries prevailed at the Battle of Valmy. International celebrations followed. For President George Washington, John Adams, and the ruling Federalists, however, the French Revolution, with its emphasis on equality, and the ensuing class warfare were suspect and dangerous. Nonetheless, the largest victory celebrations held anywhere outside of France took place in Boston, then Vice President Adams's hometown. For Boston's working people, the celebration provided an opportunity to protest the increasing aloofness of the American political elite.

With parades through State Street, called King's Street before the American Revolution, and through other sites of revolutionary significance, the crowds marched to Oliver's Dock and renamed it Liberty Square. It too recalled one of the Revolution's anteceding events, a 1765 riot against the Stamp Act. This time, however, the theme of social equality permeated the atmosphere. Repeatedly sung throughout the city was the French Revolution's anthem, *Ça Ira*, with its potent declaration:

The one who puts on airs shall be
  brought down
The one who is humble shall be
  elevated

Monument to the Hungarian Uprising, Liberty Square, 2018.

City residents subverted official feasts and carried food away from the sites and into the streets. Contemporary reports documented mixed-race gatherings feasting at the stump (in present-day **Chinatown**) where the British had felled the famed Liberty Tree.

The square itself remained an important site commemorating the Stamp Act riot. In 1986, amid a renewed Cold War, a monument marking the 1956 Hungarian Uprising against Soviet rule was erected. As with the silence about the subversive dimensions of the Battle of Valmy celebration, nothing about the Hungarian rebellion's egalitarian commitments finds its way into the official monument.

GETTING THERE

Orange and Blue Lines to State Street Station, 0.2 mile (three-minute) walk.

TO LEARN MORE

Newman, Simon P. *Parades and the Politics of the Street*, Philadelphia: University of Pennsylvania Press, 1999.

1.12 Marlboro Hotel and Chapel

407 Washington Street

DOWNTOWN

A frequent meeting place of the Massachusetts Anti-Slavery Society, the Marlboro Hotel and Chapel's history is closely tied to the abolitionist movement. It was owned by an abolitionist (and a founder of Boston's publicly funded fire department), Willard Sears. In accordance with their owner's beliefs, what were two adjacent buildings housed the first temperance hotel in the United States and a Christian chapel. William Lloyd Garrison and Frederick Douglass considered its meeting space a truly free-speech alternative to *Faneuil Hall*. Nonetheless, anti-abolitionist mobs frequently threatened to disrupt meetings and attack the movement's speakers outside the hotel.

The hotel and chapel was a hub of organizing and controversy for many issues, including those pertaining to the evolving mid-nineteenth-century Transcendentalist movement. Additionally, it served as an important antiwar movement space, especially for those opposed to the invasion of Mexico (1846–48), one participant being Henry David Thoreau, who frequently mingled at the hotel with other reform-

ers. Future suffragists who would lead nineteenth-century feminism were also active there on matters related to abolition and temperance, the latter issue motivated by a progressive concern with the excessive consumption of alcohol and its deleterious impact, particularly on women and children.

The original temperance hotel, in operation from 1838 through 1852, no longer exists. The site was associated with a succession of businesses in the jewelry trade, and for many years in the late twentieth century was home to a corporate-owned bookstore.

GETTING THERE

Orange and Red Lines to Downtown Crossing station.

1.13 Boston Court House

26 Court Street

DOWNTOWN

Three hundred activists gathered on the steps of the Boston Court House on October 19, 1842. They were there to protect the rights of George Latimer, who had been detained the day before and held in the nearby Leverett Street Jail. Although only a small fraction of the city's population, African Americans, many living nearby on Beacon Hill, made up most of the protestors.

Latimer's arrest came at the request of a Virginia-based enslaver, James Gray. He had traveled to Boston to reassert his ownership of Latimer under the federal Fugitive Slave Act of 1793, which required local authorities to assist in the recapture of enslaved individuals. Earlier that month, Latimer and his pregnant wife, Rebecca, had fled Norfolk,

Virginia. Soon after their arrival in Boston, a former employee of Gray's recognized Latimer and wired Gray. It is estimated that each year during slavery, some fifty thousand individuals escaped their captors, if only briefly. The large number of these escapes suggests why the Fugitive Slave Act was integral to the institution of slavery.

The case resuscitated a movement favoring direct action over purely litigious tactics to free slaves. In Boston's first known case of direct action to challenge the federal legislation, abolitionists, black and white, had seized two enslaved women detained under the same law used to arrest Latimer from a courtroom, and quickly spirited the pair to Nova Scotia on a ship.

Boston Court House and its surrounding scenery during the Latimer trial, undated.

The Latimer version of the direct action movement was led by people like the historian and educator William C. Nell of the New England Freedom Association, an African American organization that grew out of an early "vigilance committee." Those protesting his imprisonment were active organizers and spokespeople who acted in the face of racial abuse and the threat of violence. Their actions spurred a larger multiracial mobilization as well as the publication of a newspaper, the *Latimer and North Star Journal*.

Although the George Latimer case ended with abolitionists *buying* his freedom, the response to his arrest brought about signifi-

cant cooperation between different strands of the abolitionist movement, making for a powerful multiclass coalition. In 1843, less than a year later, sixty-five thousand signatures were gathered in support of a petition "separating the people of Massachusetts from connections with slavery." It also inspired a legislative tactic—the passing of "personal liberty" or "Latimer laws"—that required a jury trial to determine the applicability of the Fugitive Slave Act.

A later version of the act preempted these laws. The Latimer case nonetheless foreshadowed similar efforts by the Boston Vigilance Committee in the 1850s. Despite mixed results, the cases helped to aggravate national tensions over slavery and to draw the lines dividing the future Civil War antagonists.

Court Square was the site of Boston's first jail, and later a courthouse was erected on the site. The pirate William Fly (see **Nixes**

American House,
by Lewis Rice,
circa 1855.

Mate) was detained here in the early 1700s. In 1830 a "New Court House" replaced that building. It too would be superseded by the present structure, which has housed City of Boston agencies for many years.

GETTING THERE

The site is close to both Government Center (Blue and Green Lines) and State (Orange and Blue Lines) stations.

TO LEARN MORE

Gac, Scott. "Slave or Free? White or Black? The Representation of George Latimer," *New England Quarterly* 88, no. 1 (2015): 73–103.

Kantrowitz, Stephen. *More Than Freedom: Fighting for Black Citizenship in a White Republic, 1829–1889*, New York: Penguin Books, 2013.

1.14 American House/John F. Kennedy Federal Building

City Hall Plaza (formerly 50–62 Hanover Street)

DOWNTOWN

American House was one of Boston's leading hotels. Opened in 1835, it was the first hotel in the United States to have a passenger elevator. One of its most famous guests checked in on March 4, 1858. His name was John Brown. Brown was there to meet with his closest supporters, those who would come to be known as the "Secret Six."

The next evening, Friday, March 5, the six abolitionists—Thomas Wentworth Higginson, Samuel Gridley Howe, Theodore Parker, Franklin Benjamin Sanborn, Gerrit Smith, and George Luther Stearns—met with Brown in his room at American House. There they hatched the plan that would culminate in Brown's ill-fated attack on a federal armory at Harpers Ferry, Virginia (now West Virginia). In the following days, the six supporters would form a secret committee to advise Brown and raise the funds needed to undertake the raid, one that aimed to incite an armed uprising among the enslaved. The October 16, 1859, raid and

Boston City Hall Plaza, looking toward the John F. Kennedy Federal Building, 2019.

subsequent trial, conviction, and execution of Brown and his fellow raiders polarized the national conversation over slavery and contributed to the Civil War's outbreak.

American House permanently shut its doors in 1935, one hundred years after its founding, and was torn down shortly thereafter. The section of Hanover Street on which the hotel was located exists no longer. Along with the rest of Scollay Square, it fell victim to urban renewal in the early 1960s. Today the John F. Kennedy Federal Building stands on the site.

GETTING THERE

Blue or Green Line to Government Center Station. The JFK Federal Building stands on the northern side of City Hall Plaza.

TO LEARN MORE

Renehan. Edward J. Jr. *The Secret Six: The True Tale of the Men Who Conspired with John Brown*, New York: Crown Publishers, 1995.

1.15 John P. Jewett and Company

17 and 19 Cornhill

DOWNTOWN

John P. Jewett and Company was a publisher and seller of books. The company's namesake was a member of the Boston Vigilance Committee (see *Court House Square*), an abolitionist organization that helped to protect fugitive slaves from those who sought to return them to the South. In 1846 Jewett, who had worked as a bookseller in *Salem*, opened a business in Boston on a street called Cornhill, the center of the city's publishing, book-selling, and literary establishment. Cornhill was frequented by the likes of Ralph Waldo Emerson and John Greenleaf Whittier; William Lloyd Garrison also published *The Liberator* there for a time.

From its founding Jewett and Company published religious book and textbooks, but soon it also began to publish fiction and antislavery works. By Boston standards, it

Cornhill looking
east—toward the harbor—
from near Tremont Street.
The Sears Crescent Building
is on the right, 1962.

was not a large publishing house. This changed radically when Jewett published Harriet Beecher Stowe's *Uncle Tom's Cabin*, an antislavery story that first appeared in serial form in the Washington, DC–based *The National Era* in 1851. A number of New York and Boston houses had declined to publish it in book form, fearful that it would not sell many copies and that its publication might offend Southern audiences upon whom they relied for sales. About the first concern, they could not have been more wrong: Within the first two days of its publication in 1852, the book sold five thousand copies; by the end of the year, three hundred thousand. Abroad, particularly in Britain and it colonies, the book also did amazingly well; it was translated into many languages. It would become the first US novel to sell over a million copies.

The abolitionist minister Theodore Parker said that the novel "excited more attention than any book since the invention of printing." Indeed, it had a huge impact on public opinion. By powerfully illuminating slavery's evils, *Uncle Tom's Cabin* played a pivotal role in fueling pro-Lincoln sentiment in the North and hardening resistance to abolition in the South, thus contributing significantly to the tensions that led to the Civil War.

In 1854 John P. Jewett and Company opened a large bookstore at what was then 117 Washington Street (roughly where number 263 now stands, underneath the parking garage), diagonally across from Water Street. John Jewett, at least in 1852, lived at 116 Harrison Avenue in today's Chinatown; the Tufts University Health Sciences Bookstore now occupies the site. As for Cornhill, most of it was lost with Scollay Square's demolition in the 1960s. The location of John P. Jewett and Company would have been a few buildings east of where the Sears Crescent Building—part of the little that remains of what was Cornhill—still stands.

GETTING THERE

Blue or Green Line to Government Center. Look south across Government Center to the Sears Crescent Building.

TO LEARN MORE

Parfait, Claire. *The Publishing History of 'Uncle Tom's Cabin,' 1852–2002*, Burlington, VT: Ashgate, 2007

Reynolds, David S. *Mightier Than the Sword: 'Uncle Tom's Cabin' and the Battle for America*, New York: W. W. Norton and Company, 2011.

1.16 *Daily Evening Voice*

91 (243) Washington Street

DOWNTOWN

In the midst of the Civil War, the trade union movement experienced a revival. A key manifestation was the emergence of over a hundred pro-worker newspapers during the war. One, Boston's *Daily Evening Voice*, stood out among US labor newspapers as the only publication that championed the inclusion of former slaves in the labor movement. From its first issue on December 2, 1864, the *Voice* consistently argued for a movement that united all laborers—including women—as the only way to ensure justice for the working class.

Founded by the Boston Typographical Union during a printers strike, the *Voice* championed the eight-hour day, the labor movement's central demand. It also called for labor schools, courses in political economy, libraries, and reading rooms given the necessity of educated workers to ensure a vibrant democracy. It even advocated free college education.

Most striking was the *Voice*'s rejection of "distinction of sex, complexion or birthplace" among workers—particularly as it related to black laborers. With some four million African American workers added to the labor supply after Emancipation, the paper's call for black-white unity was one of principle and pragmatism. Unless white workers abandoned their traditional antipathy toward black workers, the *Voice* argued, the formerly enslaved would have no option but to serve as strikebreakers and thus undermine the cause of all laborers. Consistent with this position, the *Voice*, which enjoyed strong relations with many of Greater Boston's leading abolitionists, also campaigned for Radical Reconstruction—full civil rights and land redistribution for former slaves.

Masthead of *Daily Evening Voice*.

The *Voice*'s explicit and consistent anti-racism incurred opposition and led many workers not to renew their subscriptions. The declining readership combined with an economic downturn in 1866–67 ultimately led to the newspaper's demise, its last issue published on October 16, 1867. Well over a century later, its message of worker unity irrespective "of sex, complexion or birthplace" is as valuable as ever.

GETTING THERE

Red or Orange Line to Downtown Crossing Station. Number 91 Washington Street was located roughly where number 243 now stands, underneath the parking garage, 0.2 mile (four-minute) walk.

TO LEARN MORE

Foner, Philip S. "A Labor Voice for Black Equality: The Boston Daily Evening Voice, 1864–1867," *Science and Society* 38, no. 3 (1974): 304–25.

1.17 Exchange Place/Boston Bellamy Club/Immigration Restriction League

53 State Street

DOWNTOWN

The so-called Gilded Age (from roughly 1870 to 1900) saw marked economic growth, deep recessions, growing concentrations of wealth and income, intense labor strife, and a heavy influx of European immigrants, many of them quite destitute. Boston's elite were divided about how to perceive these changes and how to respond.

One response was the Boston Bellamy Club. It was launched on Saturday, December 1, 1888, when twenty-five "gentle men"

met at the office of Captain Charles E. Bowers. They pledged to do all that they could to "disseminate the views as set forth in *Looking Backward*" and to "help the cause."

The club's name referred to socialist writer Edward Bellamy, while the pledge invoked his book *Looking Backward: From 2000 to 1887*. A literary work set in Boston in the year 2000, the novel provides a hard-hitting critique of late-nineteenth-century industrial capitalist society and its deep socioeconomic injustices and imagines a utopian society built on cooperation and achieved nonviolently.

The meeting at what was then 61 State Street and the creation of the first "Bellamyite" club in the United States illustrated the great popularity *Looking Backward* enjoyed. The third-largest best seller of the 1800s (after *Uncle Tom's Cabin* and *Ben Hur: A Tale of the Christ*), Bellamy's book sold more than four hundred thousand copies in the United States in its first decade and helped to spawn 162 "Nationalist Clubs" across the country. (Bellamy used the term "Nationalism" instead of socialism to capture his advocacy of the nationalization of industry.)

Looking Backward and a follow-up novel, *Equality*, engendered considerable criticism, and not only from those championing the status quo. Although Bellamy was a strong supporter of women's suffrage, and feminists such as Lucy Stone supported him, many saw his work as reproducing the second-class status of women. Meanwhile, his discussion of the era's profound racial injustice was deeply lacking. In addition, Bellamy saw little role for the working class

Front of 53 Exchange Place, looking toward Old State House, 2019.

of the class of 1889—Prescott F. Hall and Charles Warren, both lawyers, and Robert DeCourcy Ward, a geographer and climatologist—gathered at Warren's law office (428 Exchange Building). There they founded the Immigration Restriction League (IRL), an organization that soon spread to other US cities.

Unlike the Bellamyites, the IRL's founders saw little hope for utopian socialism, perceiving US society at the time to be divided between a greedy plutocratic elite and an ignorant proletariat. Society, they perceived, had deviated from an idealized rural past built on a homogeneous (English) population to a corrupt industrial society plagued by a growing and increasingly diverse immigrant population. This intellectual current was informed by social Darwinism, eugenics, and the accompanying assumption that how well one fared in life was tied to one's racial "stock." In this context, anti-immigrant sentiment—focusing increasingly on differences among peoples of European origin—intensified, and the IRL arose.

The League's founders saw growing threats to "the American race" in the form of rising numbers of "unassimilable," "low quality" immigrants of the "socially inferior class." Allowing large numbers of "undesirable aliens" to enter the United States and concentrate themselves in urban ghettoes, asserted the IRL, constituted a form of "race

in bringing about the social transformation that he envisioned: Men of "culture" (and socioeconomic means) would lead the effort to realize a new order in which they would be part of an "industrial army" dominated by a strong state built on technological improvement.

These criticisms notwithstanding, the great excitement and energy that Bellamy's work helped to generate was a sign of the despair many felt in the late 1800s. It also spoke to the hopes of many to bring about a fundamentally different and far more egalitarian society than the one in which they lived, and a willingness to struggle to achieve it. (Soon after Bellamy's death in 1898, at the age of forty-eight, the Nationalist Clubs disappeared, and their largely middle- and professional-class supporters moved into movements associated with Populism and the Progressive Era.)

On May 31, 1894, less than six years after Boston's Bellamyites' first meeting, three recent Harvard College graduates, members suicide." Boston, which was then experiencing the rapidly rising political influence of Irish Catholics—at the expense of the city's Brahmins—embodied the perceived threats' realization. (Even some of Greater Boston's Bellamyite socialists were not immune to such thinking. See *The Youth's Companion Building*.)

Despite its small membership, the IRL had considerable influence, not least due to many of its members' upper-class status. Through public lectures, the publication of anti-immigrant literature, and the lobbying of federal officials—the organization had a strong relationship with Senator Henry Cabot Lodge, for example—the IRL helped to shape the national discussion on immigration. The League's worldview (one shared by other organizations at the time) underlay the passage of federal immigration legislation in 1921 and 1924. These instituted the first *quantitative* limits on immigration on the basis of national origin, criteria that endured until 1965. The League's headquarters remained in Boston until its demise in 1921 following the death of Prescott Hall, the IRL's secretary.

Both the IRL and the Boston Bellamyite Club were housed in the space now occupied by Exchange Place, which was built in 1896 to house the Boston Stock Exchange. Of the original twelve-story building, only the façade remains, behind which is a skyscraper that houses various corporate offices, including, since 2017, the headquarters of *The Boston Globe*. In December 2018, the building sold for $845 million.

GETTING THERE

Blue or Orange Line to State Street Station, a two-minute walk east (toward the harbor).

NEARBY SITE

CUSTOM HOUSE TOWER. Until 1964 Boston's tallest building, it is now a resort. Weather permitting, at 2:00 p.m. and 6:00 p.m., Monday–Thursday, the public has access to its observation deck on the twenty-sixth floor, which affords 360-degree views of Downtown, Boston Harbor, and the Harbor Islands, 3 McKinley Square (India and State Streets).

TO LEARN MORE

Lavery, Colm. "Situating Eugenics: Robert De-Courcey Ward and the Immigration Restriction League of Boston," *Journal of Historical Geography* 53 (2016): 54–62.

Ludmerer, Kenneth M. "Genetics, Eugenics, and the Immigration Restriction Act of 1924," *Bulletin of the History of Medicine* 46, no. 1 (1972): 59–81.

Solomon, Barbara Miller. "The Intellectual Background of the Immigration Restriction Movement in New England," *New England Quarterly* 25, no. 1 (1952): 47–59.

Strauss, Sylvia. "Gender, Class, and Utopia," in Daphne Patai, ed., *Looking Backward, 1988–1888: Essays on Edward Bellamy*, Amherst: University of Massachusetts Press, 1988, 68–90.

1.18 Faneuil Hall

1 Faneuil Hall Square

DOWNTOWN

In the midst of the brief Spanish-American War, which saw the United States take over and colonize Cuba, the Philippines, and Puerto Rico (among other territories), hundreds of people gathered at Faneuil Hall to lay the foundation for what would become the Anti-Imperialist League. The date was June 15, 1898—the same day on which the House of Representatives voted to annex Hawaii on behalf of US business interests. The gathering's immediate result was the creation of the Anti-Imperialist Committee of Correspondence, which soon became the New England Anti-Imperialist League and later a national organization's most active chapter.

The League helped to shape the national debate about US colonization of former Spanish territories and voiced strong support for their peoples' right to self-determination. Its first membership appeal proclaimed, "We are in full sympathy with the heroic struggles for liberty of the people in the Spanish Islands, and therefore we protest against depriving them of their rights by an exchange of masters." The organization focused much of its efforts on challenging the annexation of the Philippines. Of particular concern was the horrific violence and atrocities perpetrated by US forces during the Philippine-American War. This multiyear undertaking to "pacify" the US colony resulted in several thousand deaths among US troops and hundreds of thousands of Filipino fatalities.

The US imperial project enjoyed broad support among many of the country's most powerful political figures, Boston's Henry Cabot Lodge being one of the most prominent and outspoken. Champions of imperialism often employed Manifest Destiny's logic, of a "white man's burden" to uplift allegedly inferior peoples, and of a

> We hold that the policy known as imperialism is hostile to liberty and tends toward militarism, an evil from which it has been our glory to be free. We regret that it has become necessary in the land of Washington and Lincoln to reaffirm that all men, of whatever race or color, are entitled to life, liberty, and the pursuit of happiness. We maintain that governments derive their just powers from the consent of the governed. We insist that the subjugation of any people is "criminal aggression" and open disloyalty to the distinctive principles of our government.
>
> . . .
>
> Imperialists assume that with the destruction of self-government in the Philippines by American hands, all opposition here will cease. This is a grievous error. Much as we abhor the war of "criminal aggression" in the Philippines, greatly as we regret that the blood of the Filipinos is on American hands, we more deeply resent the betrayal of American institutions at home. The real firing line is not in the suburbs of Manila. The foe is of our own household.
>
> **—Excerpt from the platform of the American Anti-Imperialist League, 1899**

virile masculinity (which the United States supposedly embodied) and an associated "natural" tendency to expand one's realm. Underlying these stories were desires for new markets and sources of raw materials on the part of US industries, the interests of the US military, and increasing competition with other imperialist countries (particularly in Europe).

White, Protestant, and professional men, many of whose political allegiances had been informed by the antislavery movement, dominated the Anti-Imperialist League's membership. Yet it was also a diverse movement, one made up of African Americans, Catholics, labor activists, and women— half of those in attendance at the June 15, 1898, meeting were women (there were no women in the national leadership, however). Among its prominent members were Mark Twain, the philosopher William James, and US Senator George Frisbie Hoar, a Republican from Massachusetts.

That the Anti-Imperialist League's founding meeting took place at Faneuil Hall makes sense in numerous ways. From its opening in 1742 as a public marketplace, what many refer to as the "Cradle of Liberty" was a meeting site for the Sons of Liberty in the years preceding the Revolutionary War and, on occasion, for Boston's large abolitionist community during the mid-1800s. In 1903 the founding of the Women's Trade Union League—an effort to build an alliance between the women's and labor movements—happened there.

Given the nature of such events held at what is today Boston's most popular tourist destination, it might seem ironic that in 1858 US Senator Jefferson Davis, appealing to the Founding Fathers' spirit, used Faneuil Hall's podium to make the case for states' rights and thus the right to enslave. However, the appearance there of the man who would lead the Confederacy in Southern secession was also perversely appropriate: Peter Faneuil, who donated the building to the City of Boston and died six months before its completion, earned much of his enormous wealth from the slave trade.

GETTING THERE

Blue Line or Green Line to Government Center Station, 0.2 mile (four-minute) walk. Orange or Blue Line to State Station, about one block away.

NEARBY SITES

BOSTON PUBLIC MARKET, 100 Hanover Street; and the **NEW ENGLAND HOLOCAUST MEMORIAL**, along Congress and Union Streets.

TO LEARN MORE

Baron, Harold. "Anti-Imperialism and the Democrats," *Science and Society* 21, no. 3 (1957): 222–39.
Hoganson, Kristin L. *Fighting for American Manhood: How Gender Politics Provoked the Spanish-American and Philippine-American Wars*, New Haven: Yale University Press, 1998.
Immerwahr, Daniel. *How to Hide an Empire: A History of the Greater United States*, New York: Farrar, Straus and Giroux, 2019.

1.19 Dewey Square

Atlantic Avenue and Summer Street
DOWNTOWN

Dewey Square, named in honor of US naval admiral George Dewey, whose attack on an obsolete Spanish fleet in Manila Bay initiated the first major battle of the Spanish-American War in 1898, lies across from South Station. In its early years, the square served as an important venue for large gatherings to honor dignitaries alighting from trains at South Station, the world's largest railway station at the time of its opening on January 1, 1899.

#OccupyBoston, first general assembly, Dewey Square, September 30, 2011.

much of Dewey Square's former space was reclaimed.

While the square was a site of celebration of imperial occupation in 1899 (that of the United States over the Philippines), more than a century later, a radically different type of occupation would mark the site: From late September through early December 2011, #OccupyBoston, a youth-oriented movement challenging extreme socioeconomic inequality and injustice, as reflected in the neighboring Financial District, took over Dewey Square. Establishing an encampment of scores of tents and the Audre Lorde to Howard Zinn (A to Z) Library, #Occupy-Boston turned Dewey Square into a vibrant site of political organizing, debate, and celebration over two months. On December 10, 2011—International Human Rights Day—the Boston police, under orders from Mayor Tom Menino, forcefully cleared the area of the occupiers and their tents.

One such dignitary, received by throngs of admirers upon exiting the station in February 1899, was President William McKinley. Initially ambivalent about the brief war that ceded Spain's overseas colonies to the United States, the twenty-fifth president owned the victory and came to celebrate with the imperialist war's local boosters (see *Faneuil Hall* and *Henry Cabot Lodge House*).

In subsequent years, with the building of elevated railway lines and later the Central Artery over, under, and around Dewey Square, the area became much less hospitable. With the demolition of the Central Artery and the opening of the Rose Kennedy Greenway in the 2000s, however,

A plaza at the southern end of the Kennedy Greenway, Dewey Square, public property owned by the Massachusetts Department of Transportation, today shows no signs of this history.

TO LEARN MORE

Kinzer, Stephen. *The True Flag: Theodore Roosevelt, Mark Twain, and the Birth of American Empire*, New York: Henry Holt and Co., 2016.

GETTING THERE

Red and Silver Lines to South Station.

The Parker House, 2018.

1.20 The Parker House

60 School Street

DOWNTOWN

Established in 1855, the (Omni) Parker House is the oldest continuously running hotel in the United States. In 1911 a twenty-one-year-old man named Ho Chi Minh became a pastry chef in the hotel, where he worked until 1913. He had fled what was then called French Indochina, where he faced persecution for his anticolonial activities. Ho Chi Minh would later emerge as the head of the nationalist forces that drove the French out of Vietnam, and he served as the prime minister (1945–55) and president (1945–69) of the Democratic Republic of Vietnam. In 1941 a young Malcolm Little (later known as Malcolm X) worked as a busboy in the hotel.

Despite such radical associations, the Parker House has long had strong ties to Boston's political and intellectual establishment. Soon after its founding, the hotel became the monthly meeting place of the famed "Saturday Club," a group whose members included Ralph Waldo Emerson, Nathaniel Hawthorne, Oliver Wendell Holmes, Charles Sumner, and Henry Wadsworth Longfellow. In 1953 John F. Kennedy proposed to Jacqueline Bouvier while dining at the hotel. The Parker House also claims to be the birthplace (in 1856) of the Boston cream pie, which the hotel still serves.

GETTING THERE

Blue or Green Line to Government Center Station, Red or Green Line to Park Street Station, Orange or Blue Line to State Street Station, 0.2 mile (four-minute) walk from the three stations.

1.21 United Fruit Company

60 State Street

DOWNTOWN

On the side of the thirty-eight-story building that now occupies 60 State Street is a historical marker from the Bostonian Society. It reports that the counting-house (where a business conducts its operations, particularly accounting) of Magoun Thatcher and Son, a merchant ship company, was located on the site during the nineteenth century. What is not memorialized is the far more powerful and influential multinational corporation that established its first headquarters on the site for a brief period (roughly 1900–1903).

Known to its detractors as "the Octopus" due to its extensive reach and ability to bully its way in Caribbean and Central and South American countries, the Boston-based United Fruit Company (1899–1970) was a pioneering force in corporate power's globalization. It also played a key role in exacerbating racial hierarchies and segregation and in spreading US imperial influence in much of the Americas.

Workers from the West Indies and from Boston unloading bananas from a United Fruit Company ship docked at Long Wharf, undated.

Within a little more than a decade of its founding—a result of the marriage between the Boston Fruit Company and Minor C. Keith's Tropical Trading and Transport Company and his operations in Central America and Colombia—United Fruit would be the largest agricultural enterprise in the world. A 1954 article in the *Daily Boston Globe* gushed that "fourteen of its 23 directors are residents of Boston and vicinity. The chairman of its board of directors, T. Jefferson Coolidge, is a Bostonian." Written at the height of the company's power, the article went on to report that the "half billion dollar banana empire" had "100,000 employees, a large fleet of merchant ships and 1500 miles of railroad in Latin America."

The article appeared only two months after the US Central Intelligence Agency, working closely with United Fruit, engineered the violent overthrow of the reformist, democratically elected government of Jacobo Arbenz in Guatemala. The coup put an end to the redistribution of land that so enraged *El Frutero,* as many in Latin America called it. (As of 1942, United Fruit owned 70

percent of Guatemala's private land.) It also ushered in more than three decades of military dictatorship and a brutal counterinsurgency war in which US-backed government forces killed about two hundred thousand Guatemalans, mostly indigenous Mayans.

Soon after the destruction of Guatemala's brief democratic opening, United Fruit would begin to decline in size and power. In 1970 the Octopus was no longer, having been bought out. What became United Brands would go through various incarnations. Today it has morphed into the Cincinnati-based Chiquita Brands International.

GETTING THERE

Blue or Orange Line to State Street. The site is diagonally across the street from the Old State House.

RELATED SITES

BOARD OF TRADE BUILDING, 131 State Street, the United Fruit Company's headquarters from 1903 to the early- to mid-1920s. From at least 1925 until the 1940s, its general offices were located at

1 Federal Street (see **Odeon Theater**). Thereafter they were at 80 Federal Street. Throughout this time, United Fruit also continued to operate out of **Long Wharf**.

TO LEARN MORE

Cohen, Rich. *The Fish That Ate the Whale: The Life and Times of America's Banana King*, New York: Picador, 2012.

Colby, Jason M. *The Business of Empire: United Fruit, Race, and US Expansion in Central America*, Ithaca, NY: Cornell University Press, 2011.

1.22 Boston Safe Deposit and Trust Company/The Vault

100 Franklin Street

DOWNTOWN

In 1959 a new, little-known but very powerful group began meeting in the Boston Safe Deposit and Trust Company's headquarters. Informally known as "the Vault," it comprised the heads of Boston's major corporate and financial entities—from Ropes and Gray (a law firm) and Filene's Department Store to the Gillette Company (the South Boston–based manufacturer) and the First National Bank of Boston. Leading the group was Ralph Lowell (aka Mr. Boston), the board chairman of the Boston Safe Deposit and Trust Company.

Members of the Vault (the formal name of which was the Coordinating Committee) saw themselves as the saviors of Boston, a city, in the 1950s and 1960s, in difficult financial straits. Concerned that Boston was on the verge of municipal bankruptcy, the group sought to gain control over the city's finances. (The Vault exercised considerable leverage given that the banks that dominated the consortium were the City of Boston's major lenders.) The Vault worked closely with Mayor John Collins (1960–68), meeting every other Thursday at 4:00 p.m. in the boardroom at 100 Franklin Street, to bring about "fiscal responsibility" and a "revived downtown." This collaboration was critical to Collins's urban renewal agenda—central to which were City Hall Plaza and the Faneuil Hall Marketplace—and in building what boosters referred to as the "New Boston." A term birthed in the 1950s under Mayor John Hynes, "New Boston" was intended to characterize a city shaped by leading corporate minds and experts rather than a corrupt political machine.

The New Boston would ultimately lead to the Vault's demise (the group disbanded in 1997) as the city's economy became increasingly dominated by national and international capital, which bought out many of the area's biggest companies. The New York–based Shearson Lehman Brothers, Inc., for example, bought the Boston Safe Deposit and Trust Company (which had changed its name to the Boston Company) in 1981 and then sold it to the Mellon Bank Corporation in 1992.

Incorporated in Massachusetts in 1867 as the Boston Safe Deposit Company, the bank was one of the oldest financial institutions in the United States and played an important role in serving the interests of Boston's shipping and merchant interests in the late 1800s and early 1900s. In 1909 the company built and opened the Franklin Street building, the last location of the Boston Stock Exchange.

GETTING THERE

Red and Orange Line to Downtown Crossing, 0.2 mile (five-minute) walk.

TO LEARN MORE

Lukas, J. Anthony. *Common Ground: A Turbulent Decade in the Lives of Three American Families*, New York: Knopf, 1985.

1.23 *Gay Community News*

22 Bromfield Street

DOWNTOWN

"There has been a long-standing need in the Boston gay community for improved communication between the various gay organizations and the gay individual." So opened the inaugural issue of the *Gay Community Newsletter* on June 17, 1973. First published at the Charles Street Meeting House (70 Charles Street, the birthplace of Charles Street AME Church), its declared purpose was "to list all the events and information of interest to the gay community in one publication." In less than a year, the local newsletter upgraded to a sixteen-page newspaper, changed its name, and moved to offices on the second floor of 22 Bromfield Street.

Published by the Bromfield Street Education Foundation, *Gay Community News* quickly grew in its reach, readership, and goals. In early 1975, the small, low-paid, female and male staff and its volunteers— the paper operated as a collective—voted to turn it into a regional newspaper (for the US Northeast), and about three years later it became a national one. While the weekly publication's circulation never numbered more than five thousand, it had a large influence and played a key role in uniting local and regional organizations into a national

Gay Community News contingent, Gay Pride March, Copley Square, June 1980.

movement for gay liberation. It was widely considered the most progressive of national gay and lesbian newspapers. In addition to serving as a forum for debate on issues of importance to the queer community, the content of the paper reflected the much broader political concerns of its collective members—from police brutality and nuclear disarmament to racism and US intervention in Central America. As such, many in progressive and left politics outside of the lesbian and gay community were regular readers. *GCN*, as part of its Prison Project, also provided free subscriptions to lesbian and gay prisoners, among other forms of support.

On July 7, 1982, a seven-alarm blaze—one caused by an arson ring whose members were concerned about decreasing public funds for police and fire departments in Massachusetts (it included a Boston police officer and a city firefighter)—destroyed *GCN*'s offices. The publication then moved to 167 Tremont Street. Due to financial difficulties, *Gay Community News* ceased weekly publication in July 1992 and resumed in 1993 as a bimonthly paper. In 1999, after moving to 25 West Street and then 29 Stanhope Street, the Bromfield Street Educational Foundation closed its doors for good after publishing the paper's last issue.

Built in the late 1840s, the Bromfield Street building (nos. 20–30), which housed *Gay Community News,* still stands. As one of a small number of extant nineteenth-century, granite commercial buildings in Downtown, it is an official Boston landmark.

GETTING THERE

Red Line to Downtown Crossing, 0.1 mile (two-minute) walk.

TO LEARN MORE

Hoffman, Amy. *An Army of Ex-Lovers: My Life at the Gay Community News,* Amherst: University of Massachusetts Press, 2007.

THE NORTH END AND THE WEST END

The North End is one of Boston's oldest residential neighborhoods. Known for its Italian restaurants, bakeries, and pastry shops, it is home to some of the city's most iconic historical landmarks—Paul Revere's house, the Old North Church, and Copp's Hill cemetery.

From the 1600s to the 1800s, the North End had a small African American community. Like much of Boston, the neighborhood's character changed tremendously due to Irish immigration in the mid- to late 1800s. During this time, the densely populated North End was a predominantly working-class Irish area. In the late nineteenth century, a small Jewish community arose there. Around the same time, Italian immigration to the area commenced. By the 1930s, the North End's population was almost exclusively Italian.

The West End, originally separated from the North End by a small bay (known as the Mill Pond), was seen as an alternative to Boston's crowded streets in the late 1700s and early 1800s when wealthy Bostonians began building mansions there. (The Harrison Gray Otis House at 141 Cambridge

Street is the sole surviving example.) In the 1820s, Mill Pond was filled in, significantly increasing the West End's size (adding fifty acres of land to Boston) and effectively merging the West End and the North End. As the well-off departed for Beacon

Eradicating the West End, circa 1950s–1960s.

Hill, the West End became a destination for African Americans and new immigrants—most notably the Irish and, later, Eastern European Jews.

By the 1950s, the West End was a diverse, dynamic area of dense streets inhabited by low-income residents. It was then that Boston's political elites identified the neighborhood as blighted and slated it for demolition. While Massachusetts General Hospital and the Charles Street Jail survived, almost the entire West End was destroyed by 1960, its streets eradicated and twenty-seven hundred working-class families displaced.

Today the North End is a heavily gentrified neighborhood, and the West End is a largely sterile area of residential towers, government offices, and large institutions.

1.24 Onesimus-Mather House

300 Hanover Street

NORTH END

Against a background of devastating smallpox epidemics ravaging colonial Boston, the Reverend Cotton Mather asked Onesimus

whether he had experienced the disease. "Yes and no," responded Onesimus, an enslaved African gifted to the renowned minister by his congregation. Onesimus explained that he had been deliberately infected in Africa with the pox as a matter of custom and this produced a very mild outbreak of the disfiguring disease. On recovery, as his community expected, Onesimus was no longer susceptible to the disease.

Although Mather had read about analogous practices in Turkey, this was the first direct account he had received, one that he then corroborated with other enslaved individuals. Although Africans constituted a small proportion of the colony's population, their numbers had begun to swell as the early-eighteenth-century market economy expanded. This left Mather (who believed in baptizing and educating enslaved Africans but argued that their Christianity did not require their emancipation) with a curious challenge: how to validate the knowledge of Africans whom he believed to be inferior to Europeans.

Mather shared Onesimus's prescription with an English physician and noted his desire to test it the next time smallpox struck. That opportunity came in 1721. Mather convinced Dr. Zabdiel Boylston of the potential to inoculate against the disease. Independently interviewing many more enslaved Africans, Boylston was convinced of the inoculation's efficacy. Experimenting with his son, several enslaved individuals, and servants, Boylston found that everyone whom he vaccinated early in the outbreak survived—and with it came the practice's gradual acceptance.

Boston elites initially resisted inoculation, partly because of Mather's own problems of credibility given his dubious role in the Salem witch trials (see **Proctor's Ledge**) and his use of evidence from Africans. This resulted in threats, assassination attempts, and legal restraints against both Boylston and Mather.

Mike's Pastry, January 2019.

Mather soon published his (and Onesimus's) thoughts about inoculation in a report to the Royal Society in London. Decades later in England, Edward Jenner developed a widely used vaccination based on cowpox, but using the same general principle that Onesimus had shared. Thomas Jefferson hailed Jenner's accomplishment: "You have erased from the calendar of human afflictions one of its greatest." It is unclear if the third president knew of Onesimus's role in the vaccination's development. Regardless, he did not celebrate the contribution of African knowledge.

The Mather home site corresponds roughly to where Mike's Pastry, a well-known North End attraction, is located today. An earlier Mather home that burned down in the late seventeenth century, before Onesimus's presence in the household, was located a few houses north on Hanover Street.

GETTING THERE

Orange and Green Lines to Haymarket Station, 0.2 mile (four-minute) walk.

TO LEARN MORE

Coss, Stephen. *The Fever of 1721: The Epidemic That Revolutionized Medicine and American Politics.* New York: Simon & Schuster, 2016.

Koo, Kathryn S. "Strangers in the House of God: Cotton Mather, Onesimus, and an Experiment in Christian Slaveholding," *Proceedings of the American Antiquarian Society* 114 (2007): 143–75.

1.25 Cooper Street Armory

Cooper Street at North Margin Street

NORTH END

A hostile crowd of five hundred to a thousand individuals—many of them women and children—amassed outside the armory on Cooper Street on the evening of July 14, 1863. Tearing up bricks from the street, they hurled them at the building, smashing windows and splintering pieces off of the large double doors. Some of the rioters bore firearms, in addition to clubs and other homemade weapons. Fearful that the mob would break down the door, the officer commanding the militia members inside had one of the armory's two cannons filled with grapeshot, wheeled to the entrance, and fired through the doors at the crowd in the street outside. At least eight and as many as fourteen people were killed, and many more were wounded.

Although the precise motivation behind what is known as the Boston Draft Riot is uncertain, it was the culmination of a day of violent unrest in the North End and its environs. It began in the morning when women in a residential building on Prince Street rebuffed two provost marshals trying to deliver draft notices and one of the officials threatening to arrest a woman who had assaulted him. It was also a time when much more violent anti-

draft riots were taking place in New York City, of which North Enders were certainly cognizant, the local air rife with predictions that Boston would experience similar unrest.

By 1863, more than 50,000 Irish immigrants lived in Boston (out of a total population of approximately 182,000), with the North End being one of the two largest enclaves. Despite living in often impoverished and squalid quarters and experiencing heavy discrimination from the Yankee establishment, Irish Bostonians played a significant role in the Union war effort. They constituted a large portion of two entirely Irish regiments from Massachusetts and a significant part of a third one from the state. Yet while the Irish supported the war, they did so in the name of the Union's preservation, not for enslaved people's freedom. Indeed, most were strongly opposed to Lincoln's Emancipation Proclamation, fearful that it would prolong the war and result in large-

Endicott School, undated.

scale black migration to the North, hurting the economic prospects of Irish laborers in the process. At the same time, most Irish and the Catholic establishment were unsympathetic to abolitionists' egalitarian claims. *The Pilot*, Boston's Catholic weekly newspaper, for example, railed against "negrophilists" and "nigger-worshippers" trying to convince whites of the equality of blacks.

Such sentiment, combined with the class-based inequities contained in the conscription law passed by Congress in 1863 (it allowed the wealthy to buy their way out of the draft), made the draft very unpopular. Meanwhile, high casualty rates among Boston Irish families, income loss due to the absence of male wage-earners, and war-related price increases in many basic foodstuffs greatly heightened the hardships faced by North End women, making them—and many others in the neighborhood—ripe for rebellion against federal and local authorities.

While New York City's draft riots unfolded over three days, Boston's unrest was relatively short-lived. High-profile deployment of the police and military and efforts by Catholic clergy to calm restive youth and men helped bring an end to the violence.

The armory was located in what was the former Endicott School. Sometime after the Civil War, by the mid-1880s, the building became a school again—Saint Mary's Catholic School. At some point in the mid-1900s, the building, which sat on the southwest corner of Cooper and North Margin streets, was demolished. It is now a parking lot.

GETTING THERE

Green or Blue Line to Haymarket Station, 0.2 mile (four-minute) walk.

NEARBY SITES

PAUL REVERE HOUSE, 19 North Square

OLD NORTH CHURCH, 193 Salem Street

BOVA'S BAKERY (open twenty-four hours, seven days), 134 Salem Street, and **PARZIALE'S BAKERY**, 80 Prince Street (two of the oldest and best-known Italian bakeries in Boston)

TO LEARN MORE

Giesberg, Judith Ann. "'Lawless and Unprincipled': Women in Boston's Civil War Draft Riot," in *Boston's Histories: Essays in Honor of Thomas H. O'Connor*, ed. James M. O'Toole and David Quigley, Boston: Northeastern University Press, 2004, 71–91.
Hanna, William F. "The Boston Draft Riot," *Civil War History* 36, no. 3 (1990): 262–73.
O'Connor, Thomas H. *South Boston, My Home Town: The History of an Ethnic Neighborhood*, Boston: Quinlan Press, 1988.

1.26 Parmenter Street Chapel
20 Parmenter Street
NORTH END

During the summer of 1885, a pile of sand was placed in the yard of the Parmenter Street Chapel. Called a sand garden, the pile constituted the birth of the children's playground movement in the United States. (Several other playgrounds had existed previously but never gained momentum as a model for others).

The North End pile came about after a local doctor saw sand gardens on a visit to Berlin, where children of all economic backgrounds played together in public parks. She presented the idea to the Massachusetts Emergency and Hygiene Association (MEHA), an organization of upper-class women dedicated to social reform. It was a time when Boston's population was rapidly increasing and there were growing concerns that the city's youth did not have spaces for recreation.

An early sand garden in Boston, circa 1885.

Operating out of its North End "mission," and building on existing programming with the Parmenter Street Chapel, MEHA believed that structured play—which the sand garden facilitated—would provide a valuable opportunity to educate working-class, immigrant children in morality and manners and thus help them to become good US citizens. MEHA also thought that structured, protected play would improve hygiene and health habits for children living in low-income immigrant neighborhoods.

Initially, neighborhood mothers volunteered to help run the sand garden, checking in as the children played with shovels and buckets, and sometimes leading more organized activities such as singing and dancing. But soon MEHA began to employ "matrons" to run the rapidly expanding number of sand gardens—within five years there were twenty-one of them throughout Boston, serving forty-three hundred children a day. Women's

involvement in designing, funding, advising, and supervising the playground was in line with the belief that women held exclusive rights to childrearing skills. But it also extended to new social reforms that expanded possibilities of paid work in the public realm.

The pile of sand at Parmenter Street Chapel marked the beginning of a decade of immense growth of playgrounds across the United States. Within ten years, thirty-nine cities had at least one playground.

The Parmenter Street Chapel was an Episcopal institution. In the 1890s, it became the home of the North End Union, which provided various forms of assistance to immigrants. Today the building, called Teatro on Parmenter, is a mixed-used building of condominiums and a performing arts theater.

GETTING THERE

About 0.2 miles (five-minute walk) from Haymarket Station (Orange and Green Lines).

TO LEARN MORE

Dickason, Jerry G. "The Origin of the Play-ground: The Role of the Boston Women's Clubs, 1885–1890," *Leisure Sciences* 6, no. 1 (1983): 83–98.

Marsden, K. Gerald. "Philanthropy and the Boston Playground Movement, 1885–1907," *Social Service Review* 35, no. 1 (1961): 48–58.

1.27 Great Molasses Flood Site

529 Commercial Street

NORTH END

By late summer 1918, Isaac Gonzales was experiencing sleepless nights. Confronting the source of his insomnia, he decided to sleep at work, near the base of a fifty-foot-high by ninety-foot-diameter tank filled with molasses. As the contents fermented, warmed, and cooled, Gonzales heard heaving and growling sounds from the molasses-filled behemoth above him. As the assistant manager and senior most person on site, he was troubled by the tank, concerned that it might collapse and smother the neighborhood. He hoped that his vigils would enable him to sound the alarm should his fears come to pass. His warnings to senior management had elicited charges of insubordination and only cosmetic fixes. The stress proved too much; he resigned and enlisted for World War I.

On the morning of January 15, 1919, the tank ruptured. A roaring thirty-foot-tall wave of molasses broke southward across Commercial Avenue, knocking down the elevated railroad, pancaking a fire house, destroying neighboring buildings, and pushing several off their foundations. Ultimately 21 people died and 150 more were injured as a result. The numbers might have been much worse had a morning train failed to brake in time.

The ensuing civil suit clarified the events leading up to the disaster. Faced with a huge liability, the tank's owners, US Industrial Alcohol Company Inc. (USIAC) suggested that anarchists had sabotaged the tank. Years of litigation, however, determined that structural failure, for which the USIAC was responsible, explained the rupture. USAIC settled out of court with survivors for today's equivalent of $6 million.

Several factors explain the hazardous siting and operation of the tank. One was the World War I arms buildup, a time when corporations were successfully championing government deregulation in the name of stimulating investment. This and the fact that USIAC's molasses, from Cuba and Central America, were a precursor to the alcohol used in munitions, lightened the restrictions on the company. Second, while the North End waterfront was ideal given the weapons manufacturing in nearby Cambridge, the marginal status of Boston's Italian community and the North End, then the most densely populated residential community in the United States, allowed USIAC to site the tank there. As a result, an inadequate tank was rushed to completion, using substandard steel and rivets, towering above a vulnerable community.

In the tragedy's wake, Massachusetts revised regulations and increased inspections. Despite local lore that one can still smell the molasses on hot summer days, the disaster has largely receded from public consciousness. A modest green plaque at Langone Park's edge memorializes the site.

TO LEARN MORE

Puleo, Stephen. *Dark Tide: The Great Boston Molasses Flood of 1919*, Boston: Beacon Press, 2003.

GETTING THERE

Orange and Green Line to North Station, 0.3 (five-minute) walk.

1.28 The West End Museum

150 Staniford Street

WEST END

On Thursday, September 24, 2015, Brian Golden, director of the Boston Redevelopment Authority (BRA), attended a West End Museum reception. While there, he expressed official regret for his agency's razing of the West End in the 1950s. "The BRA of today in no way condones the destruction of neighborhoods and the displacement of residents that happened in urban renewal's wake," he said. "And I want to offer my heartfelt apology on behalf of the agency to the families of the West End that were affected."

A *Boston Magazine* writer reporting the apology suggested that it was offered to gain goodwill at a time when the BRA (now the Boston Planning & Development Agency) was seeking a 10-year extension of its redevelopment authority. Regardless of the motives, that the apology took place at the museum speaks to its importance as the grassroots repository of the neighborhood's history as well as a gathering point for its displaced residents and their descendants.

42 Lomasney Way, the West End's "Last Tenement," 2014.

While the museum opened in 2004, discussions to establish it began in 1989 among the editors of the *West End Newsletter* and members of the West End Historical Association. The museum sits in a street-level space in West End Place, a cooperative, mixed-income residential development that, in addition to having market-rate apartments, provides affordable housing for people displaced by the neighborhood's destruction.

The museum is run by volunteers. It houses several revolving exhibits and a permanent one called "The Last Tenement" about the old neighborhood and its demolition.

TO LEARN MORE

The West End Museum website: http://thewestendmuseum.org/

GETTING THERE

Green or Orange Line to North Station, 0.2-mile (four-minute) walk.

NEARBY SITE

42 LOMASNEY WAY. Diagonally across the street from the museum, it is the only tenement building that survived urban renewal.

BEACON HILL

Beacon Hill's first English resident was William Blackstone (or Blaxton), who settled the south slope (site of the **Boston Common**) in 1625. Five years later, upon the Puritans' arrival, English settlers used the area for grazing livestock and conducting military drills. Post-independence, Massachusetts built its State House in front of what was then Beacon Hill, completing it in 1795.

Development soon followed. Mount Vernon Proprietors, a real estate syndicate, turned the sparsely populated area into a residential neighborhood, first of man-

sions and later of brick townhouses and row houses. The south slope would soon become the home of the city's ruling families and synonymous with the Boston Brahmins, the city's traditional upper class. During the nineteenth century, it also became a focal point of antislavery activism.

Beacon Hill's abolitionism cut across racial lines, a manifestation of a strong African-origin community on the north slope, a seedy area prior to the Revolutionary War due to its popularity with British sailors and soldiers. By the mid-1700s, it already had a population of over one thousand black residents. It would become a place for white and black abolitionists to come together. With the post–Civil War black population's departure, it later became home to Eastern European, including many Jewish, immigrants.

The area known as Beacon Hill was once made up of three hills: its namesake, Pemberton Hill, and Mount Vernon (thus the name of Tremont, or "trimountain," Street). The latter two were cut down, as was Beacon Hill somewhat, to develop the neighborhood (and fill in part of the Charles River). Beacon Hill received its name in 1634 when the Puritans put a beacon on the summit to warn Bostonians of danger.

With areas such as Louisburg Square (Boston's most expensive block in 2015), Beacon Hill remains home to some of the city's wealthiest residents.

Cutting down Beacon Hill, circa 1800.

However, with many buildings divided into apartments and small condos, it also has a significant middle-class population among its approximately nine thousand residents.

1.29 James Bowdoin Home Site

17–21 Beacon Street

BEACON HILL

In the fall of 1786, a popular and armed movement consisting largely of Revolutionary War veterans erupted in and around Springfield. Within days, the movement known as Shays' Rebellion spread to Worcester, southeastern Massachusetts, and even to *Concord*, close to Boston proper. The movement focused its energies on shutting down the courts and the debt proceedings that occupied many of them.

The lightning rod of the rebels' anger was one of Boston's leading citizens, Governor James Bowdoin, who lived in an enormous house at the summit of Beacon Hill, adjacent to the new State House (which opened a year after Bowdoin left office). The rebels' grievances centered on matters that Bowdoin seemed to personify: undemocratic government, land speculation, taxation, and war profiteering. Bowdoin's path to office made matters worse: When Bowdoin was unable to secure a majority through election, the state legislature, dominated by the senate's banking and merchant interests, secured the governorship for him.

The son of a prosperous Boston family whose wealth originated in the "Atlantic trade" (a key component of which was slavery), Bowdoin owned large tracts of land throughout New England, particularly in

Maine. He also had sizable financial investments, including a portfolio of Revolutionary War notes, script issued to soldiers in lieu of hard currency. Almost immediately upon issuance, the impoverished soldiers would exchange them for cash, selling them to speculators at a fraction of face value. Wealthy speculators accumulated 80 percent of the script for which the 1780 state constitution, which Bowdoin helped write, guaranteed repayment at face value (many times market value). Repayment on these terms resulted in the state's levying taxes in silver and in windfall profits for the note holders. For the ex-soldiers, the taxes were a double insult: They had been paid pennies on the pound for their service, and then had to pay taxes that benefited wealthy speculators. For such reasons the Western Massachusetts rebels called for the abolition of the senate, relocating the legislature away from Boston, reorganizing the tax system, and ending the financial privileges granted to the Boston elite.

Eventually state militias suppressed the rebellion and arrested and hanged many of its leaders, while the state pardoned most of the rebels. Nonetheless, the rebellion itself attracted national concern; it affected debates over the US Constitution and led to successful calls for a stronger federal government, shifting power away from the individual states.

Bowdoin was voted out of office in 1787 and turned to scholarly matters while retaining his business interests, investing in early trade with China, just a year before his death in 1790. Bowdoin's home was eventually torn down. The Bellevue Hotel, now the Bellevue Apartments (a luxury condo building), later occupied the site.

GETTING THERE

Park Street Station (Green and Red Lines), 0.1 mile (two-minute) walk.

TO LEARN MORE

Richards, Leonard L. *Shays's Rebellion: The American Revolution's Final Battle,* Philadelphia: University of Pennsylvania Press, 2002.

1.30 David Walker Home

81 Joy Street

BEACON HILL

Walking down Beacon Hill's cobblestone streets today, most visitors would find it hard to imagine the inauspicious moment when David Walker (ca. 1797–1830), an African American abolitionist, slumped down in a doorway as his life slipped away. Although the circumstances of his passing remain unclear and suspicions linger that slave owners poisoned him, Walker was probably the victim of tuberculosis. It likely claimed his life before other plots, including those inspired by the Georgia governor's ten-thousand-dollar bounty for his capture, played out.

The son of a free mother and an enslaved father authored *An Appeal to the Coloured Citizens of the World* (1829), a rousing tract calling for black unity and challenging white supremacy and the institution of slavery. Prefiguring many modern antiracist themes, Walker recognized internalized racism and the need for revolutionary change to start within oppressed individuals themselves.

Racist critics questioned Walker's authorship of the erudite pamphlet, but the *Appeal's* sense of outrage and dignity demonstrated an authenticity that could only have come from someone with Walker's life experience. His ideas influenced a multiracial abolitionist movement, and the work was widely circulated. It clandestinely reached Southern slave states via networks—many organized directly by Walker—of preachers, seafarers, and book distributers, thus sparking the Georgia governor's wrath.

Although Boston's black population was only two thousand to three thousand, Walker was part of an organized community that tapped into national currents. This included his regular participation in the New York–based *Freedom's Journal* (the first African American–owned and –operated newspaper) and in black Freemasonry circles. Walker's and his fellow abolitionists' efforts strengthened African American claims to US citizenship and their resolve to reject the "colonization" of African Americans to Africa that many powerful antislavery advocates (including a young Abraham Lincoln) saw as a solution to the problem of slavery.

A prominent resident of 81 Joy Street (following Walker) was the orator and abolitionist pioneer Maria Stewart. An African American woman, she made history as an early speaker before multiracial and mixed-gender gatherings against slavery and for women's rights.

GETTING THERE

Red Line to Charles/MGH Station. The private home is a 0.2 mile (four-minute) walk.

TO LEARN MORE

Walker, David, and Peter P. Hinks. *David Walker's Appeal to the Coloured Citizens of the World.* University Park: Pennsylvania State University Press, 2003.

Hinks, Peter P. *To Awaken My Afflicted Brethren: David Walker and the Problem of Antebellum Slave Resistance,* University Park: Pennsylvania State University Press, 1997.

The David Walker Memorial Project website: www.davidwalkermemorial.org

1.31 Abiel Smith School/ Museum of African American History

46 Joy Street

BEACON HILL

In 1835 the City of Boston opened the first public school dedicated to the education of African American children. It replaced the privately run African School, founded and run by Boston's black community, in the basement of the African Meeting House next door.

For decades members of Boston's free black community had pressured the state and city governments, protesting that their taxes helped pay for the education of white children while Boston had no school for black children (although some did attend its public schools in the early 1800s). As a result, Bos-

ton officially recognized the African School and began providing some funding in 1812. Due to poor conditions and overcrowding of the facility, however, Boston finally agreed to build the Abiel Smith School, named after a white businessman who willed $4,000 in 1815 to the then–Town of Boston for the education of African American children.

Despite the building's newness, its conditions were inferior to those of Boston's white schools. This led to demands by Boston's black community—which at the time numbered two thousand to three thousand, largely concentrated on Beacon Hill's north slope—for educational equality. In 1849 most parents withdrew their children from the Smith School in protest of segregation. That same year, Benjamin Roberts, on behalf of his daughter Sarah, filed a suit in the Massachusetts state court against the Boston School Committee seeking the right to attend the school nearest her home. (Sarah passed five white schools each day on her walk to the

Abiel Smith School, undated.

Smith School.) Serving as Roberts's attorneys were Robert Morris, the first black lawyer in Massachusetts and the first black lawyer in the United States to win a lawsuit, and Charles Sumner, the white abolitionist and later a US senator from Massachusetts.

The court ruled against Roberts, and its decision served as a precedent for the "separate but equal" doctrine that informed US jurisprudence for more than a century, most infamously in the US Supreme Court's *Plessy v. Ferguson* decision. Nonetheless, Boston's black community and its allies continued to organize, and in 1855 Massachusetts outlawed "separate schools," leading to the closure of the Smith School that same year.

Today the building, a national historic landmark, is home to Boston's Museum of African American History and a site on the city's Black Heritage Trail. The African Meeting House, the oldest site of black worship in the United States, is part of the museum.

TO LEARN MORE

Kendrick, Stephen, and Paul Kendrick. *Sarah's Long Walk: The Free Blacks of Boston and How Their Struggle for Equality Changed America*, Boston: Beacon Hill Press, 2004.

GETTING THERE

Red or Green Line to Park Street Station, or Red Line to Charles/MGH Station, 0.4 mile (nine-minute) walk.

1.32 Julia Ward Howe Residence

32 Mount Vernon Street

BEACON HILL

Julia Ward Howe (1819–1910) was a prominent poet and author as well as an abolitionist and suffragist. Perhaps best known for writing the popular Civil War song "The Battle Hymn of the Republic," she became a pacifist largely in response to the horrific violence of the conflict (along with that of the Franco-Prussian War). In this spirit, she penned "An Appeal to Womanhood throughout the World" in September 1870. More popularly known as the "Mother's Day Proclamation," the antiwar statement called for the holding of "a general congress of women . . . to promote the alliance of different nationalities, the amicable settlement of international questions, the great and general interests of peace."

Out of this initiative grew an effort to bring about an annual Mother's Day—Howe chose the date of June 2—to champion peace. Until 1913 or so, a number of US cities and many of Howe's supporters celebrated the date, but its popularity was limited largely to peace activists, and it never caught on nationally. A separate effort by Anna Jarvis of Philadelphia, one having nothing to do with war and peace, instead won the support of the US Congress and President Woodrow Wilson and led to the holiday's official establishment in 1914. It so happens that Jarvis's mother (also named Anna Jarvis) had promoted a different version of Mother's Day prior to the Civil War, one that overlapped with Julia Ward Howe's effort in its emphasis on global unity and disarmament.

Howe and her husband, Samuel Gridley Howe (who cofounded the Perkins School for the Blind), lived in various houses during their years in Boston. Their home at 13 Chestnut Street on Beacon Hill, from 1863 to 1866, is a national historic landmark. However, it was while living at 32 Mount Vernon, still a private home, that Julia Ward Howe authored the proclamation that would help lay the foundation for what we now know as Mother's Day, a holiday that unfortunately today obscures the concerns she championed.

GETTING THERE

Red or Green Line to Park Street Station, 0.3 mile (seven-minute) walk.

TO LEARN MORE

Antolini, Katharine. *Memorializing Motherhood: Anna Jarvis and the Struggle for Control of Mother's Day*, Morgantown: University of West Virginia Press, 2014.

1.33 Henry Cabot Lodge House

31 Beacon Street

BEACON HILL

Number 31 Beacon Street was the home of Henry Cabot Lodge. As reflected in his middle and last names, he was the son of the union of two of the best-known Boston Brahmin families. One of the first at Harvard to be awarded a PhD, he served as a lecturer at the university before winning a seat in the Massachusetts House of Rep-

Henry Cabot Lodge statue, Massachusetts State House, 2017.

resentatives as a Republican. He later won election to the US House of Representatives (1887–93) and subsequently to the US Senate, where he remained until his death in 1924 at the age of seventy-four.

Lodge played a key role in bringing about an overseas US empire. In a number of ways, he was its chief political architect. Working closely with his friend and confidant Theodore (Teddy) Roosevelt, Lodge was an outspoken cheerleader for the war with Spain that erupted in 1898. Lodge was inspired by the writings of naval historian (and rear admiral) Alfred T. Mahan, who argued that the United States, if it was to achieve to greatness, had to mimic Britain by establishing itself as a global sea power—with naval bases at strategic locations and a large navy. In this spirit, Lodge championed, in the name of expanded commercial opportunities, what he called the Large Policy. It was one that would make the United States the dominant force in the Americas, a naval power with a canal across Central America and military bases in the Caribbean and Pacific. Following Mahan's lead, he called for the annexation of Hawaii and was an outspoken advocate for the invasion of Cuba and the taking of the Philippines.

Like many prominent US Americans, Lodge embraced "American exceptionalism"—the notion that the United States is fundamentally different (and better) than other countries. He thus never spoke of "imperialism" but instead paternalistically saw the role of the United States to "uplift" the colonized and to train them for self-government, for which they were "unfit" without US intervention.

In taking such positions, Lodge helped lay the foundation for the contemporary global footprint of the US military. Among its manifestations are hundreds of military bases and hundreds of thousands of soldiers abroad—and myriad forms of associated violence.

Around 1900, the Lodge family moved out of 31 Beacon Street. The building then housed the Massachusetts Society for the Prevention of Cruelty to Animals. In 1916 or so, with the expansion of the State House and it grounds, the building was torn down. It sat roughly where a statue to Henry

Cabot Lodge now stands on the west lawn's far edge.

TO LEARN MORE

Pratt, Julius W. "The 'Large Policy' of 1898, *The Mississippi Valley Historical Review* 19, no. 2 (1932): 219–42.

Thomas, Evan. *The War Lovers: Roosevelt, Lodge, Hearst, and the Rush to Empire, 1898*, New York: Back Bay Books/Little, Brown and Company, 2010.

GETTING THERE

Red or Green Line to Park Street, 0.1 mile (three-minute) walk.

CHINATOWN/ THE SOUTH COVE

An area of only forty-six acres and five thousand residents, Chinatown is one of Boston's smallest neighborhoods. Originally known as the South Cove, much of it is built on landfill, area reclaimed for railroads, industrial activity, and housing. With the establishment of the area as a railroad hub in the 1840s, ethnic enclaves arose, the population largely of Irish, Italian, German Jewish, and "Syrian" (Lebanese Christian) descent. Chinese began arriving in the neighborhood in the late 1870s. As the Chinese population slowly grew, an area called Chinatown emerged. By 1900, several hundred Chinese, almost all men (many having fled anti-Chinese violence in the US West), resided there. The population increased rapidly and its gender composition changed radically after World War II with the repeal of racist immigration exclusion laws that targeted Chinese (especially women). This growth was tied to the rise of

"Unity-Community: The Chinatown Mural Project" by David Fichter and Wen-ti Tsen, 1986.
Building demolished in 2002.

the area's clothing and hospitality industries. With the Chinese population spreading beyond its original core, Chinatown became synonymous with the South Cove.

Chinatown has long been an embattled community. From the 1903 immigration raid to the building of highways and expansion by the New England Medical Center and Tufts University, the neighborhood has struggled to maintain itself, with adequate and affordable housing for its low-income residents a central concern. Gentrification and real estate speculation in recent decades have only intensified its challenges, leading to growing inequality in the neighborhood. Between 1990 and 2010, Chinatown's Asian residents decreased from 70 percent to 46 percent of the population as affluent, largely white newcomers moved into high-end developments. In 2009, the average income of an Asian household in Chinatown was $13,057, while the average white household's was $84,255. Key to the endurance of the neighborhood's Chinese community is a host of long-standing, local institutions—from activist organizations to benevolent associations.

Amelia Earhart returns to Denison House after her famous transatlantic flight, 1928.

1.34 Denison House

93 Tyler Street

CHINATOWN

Founded in 1892, Denison House was a woman-run settlement house providing social and educational services to area residents. It was modeled after Jane Addams's famed Hull House in Chicago. Settlement houses, explains historian Sarah Deutsch, were "homes purchased by members of the middle class or by middle-class institutions in working class neighborhoods," with the intent "to settle well-educated, middle-class people among the working poor" both to study them and "uplift" them through middle-class example. In the case of

Denison House, the three founders were members of the College Settlement Association and faculty at Wellesley College: English professor and labor activist Vida Scudder; and economics professors Katherine Coman and Emily Greene Balch, a famed peace activist.

Located in a heavily immigrant neighborhood, Denison House provided a meeting space for people of different backgrounds as it sought to break down the barriers of class, residential geography, and ethnicity. It also offered courses on topics such as literature, carpentry, and nursing, organized a summer camp for children, and housed a library and clinic. Given that many of its residents were outspoken activist women of a radical bent, Denison House was linked to the causes of socialism and pacifism as well as to the labor movement, much to the displeasure of its (often male) donors. Among its residents were Mary Kenney O'Sullivan, a labor organizer and one of the founders of the Women's Trade Union League, and Amelia Earhart, the aviator and women's rights advocate, who worked as a social worker and teacher there for three years (1925–28).

As Denison House grew—it eventually encompassed several contiguous row houses on Tyler Street—and became more institutionalized, its existence as a woman-run organization disappeared. In 1942, it moved to Dorchester, eventually merging with three other settlement houses and becoming part of the Federated Dorchester Neighborhood Houses. The Asian American Civic Association (which provides education, training, and social services to immigrants and economically disadvantaged people) and the Kwong Kow Chinese School (founded in 1916, it helps "overseas Chinese" maintain their Chinese heritage) now occupy the Tyler Street site where Denison House once stood.

GETTING THERE

Orange Line to Tufts Medical Center Station, 0.2 mile (five-minute) walk.

TO LEARN MORE

Deutsch, Sarah. *Women and the City: Gender, Space, and Power in Boston, 1870–1940*, New York: Oxford University Press, 2000.

1.35 1903 Immigration Raid Site

19 Harrison Avenue

CHINATOWN

On the evening of October 2, 1903, two assailants shot and killed Wong Yak Chong, age thirty-one, in Chinatown. In the days following, both the Boston police and major newspapers helped to incite fears of "Celestials" (as Chinese were often referred to) by framing the murder as one involving rival Chinese "tongs"—private associations, ones sometimes involved in criminal enterprises. They suggested that further violence was imminent, the funeral of Wong Yak Chong being the likely occasion.

The funeral, the procession to the cemetery, and the burial—attended by an estimated three thousand people—went off quietly on Sunday, October 11. The Boston Police Department and the US Immigration Bureau, however, had conspired to take advantage of the presence of many Chinese from outside of the city, in town for the funeral, to search for and arrest "illegal" immigrants. That night, police and immigration agents raided numerous locations in the eight-block area of Chinatown, "seizing every Chinaman they encountered and forcing him to show his papers under penalty of arrest," reported the *Boston Daily Globe*. (The Geary Act of 1892—an extension of the infamous Chinese Exclusion Act—required that all Chinese residents of the United States carry a resident permit.) The purpose, according to the *Globe*, was "keeping dangerous Chinese out of the city."

The police commandeered the building at 19 Harrison Avenue, the home of a

19 Harrison
Avenue, 2018.

restaurant and the residence of many Chinese, who lived on its upper floors, for their headquarters. Authorities took arrestees to the building, where they were temporarily held. In reporting on the events, various newspapers characterized arrestees in heavily racialized terms. "Chinamen," said the *Boston Herald*, "scampered like rats through the dark alleys" as police pursued them.

Between 250 and 300 individuals were arrested, but authorities soon released most of them as they were in the United States with authorization; some were even US citizens. Still, the raid had far-reaching effects on the city's Chinese population: 50 of the arrestees were ultimately deported and another 150 individuals left Boston. (According to the 1900 US census, there were only 254 Chinese living in Chinatown and 850 in Greater Boston at the time.)

The raids and their aftermath helped to cast Boston's Chinese-descended population as permanent outsiders, as unassimilable. Yet the events also revealed the deep roots that many Bostonians of Chinese ethnicity had in the area, and the cross-cultural relationships they had built. In the multi-ethnic area of which Chinatown was part, at least two Chinese men were married to Irish women. Following the raids, many non-Chinese came to the support of the arrestees. And on October 16 several hundred turned out at Faneuil Hall to protest the raid, with William Lloyd Garrison Jr. (son of the famed abolitionist) one of the featured speakers.

The building at 19 Harrison Avenue still stands. However, it is structurally unsound and unoccupied.

GETTING THERE

Orange Line to Chinatown Station, 0.1 mile (two-minute) walk.

TO LEARN MORE

To, Wing-kai. *Chinese in Boston: 1870–1965*, Charleston, SC: Arcadia, 2008.

Wong, K. Scott. "'The Eagle Seeks a Helpless Quarry': Chinatown, the Police, and the Press. The 1903 Boston Chinatown Raid Revisited," *Amerasia Journal* 22, no. 3 (1996): 81–103.

1.36 New England Telephone Company Exchange/ Verizon Building

8 Harrison Avenue and Oxford Street

CHINATOWN

On April 15, 1919, about four thousand Boston telephone operators went on strike for higher wages and better working conditions. The strikers were almost all young Irish-American women. (Although there were a few Jewish employees, until the 1940s it was the policy of the New England Telephone Company not to hire Jews or African Americans.) In what historian Stephen Norwood calls "probably the most complete response ever to a strike call involving workers across [US] state lines," almost every telephone worker, about eight thousand in total, in five of the six New England states walked off the job. During the six-day work stoppage, there was no telephone service in Maine, Massachusetts, New Hampshire, Rhode Island, and Vermont.

The women, almost all of them in their teens and early twenties, were members of the Telephone Operators' Department. The first US trade union led and controlled by women, it was a self-governing entity within the International Brotherhood of Electrical Workers (IBEW). By 1919, under President Julia O'Connor's leadership, the telephone-operators union had locals in thirty US states, a number of Canadian provinces,

and the Panama Canal Zone. More than a third of the union's members were in New England, primarily in Boston. The Boston local's strength was an outgrowth of, among other elements, the presence in the city of the National Women's Trade Union League, which had helped to organize the union in 1912, as well as the larger women's rights movement in the area.

The operators picketed around the clock at exchanges throughout Greater Boston and opened each day of the strike with mass meetings and singing and dancing to ragtime music. They enjoyed strong support across the city—especially among Boston's largely Irish working class. This ethnic solidarity extended even to Boston's police (who would go on strike five months later) and the city's political leadership. In Chinatown, the site of one of Boston's principal telephone exchanges, neighborhood merchants set up tables behind the building to serve food to the striking workers; meanwhile, Chinese residents helped to picket the building. Such factors help explain why the telephone operators won the strike and gained substantial pay increases despite opposition to the labor stoppage from the IBEW's male leadership and the use of strikebreakers (many of whom were students from Harvard, MIT, and Tufts).

In the aftermath of an unsuccessful strike in 1923—one plagued by factionalism within the union and, more importantly, a strong anti-union climate in the 1920s—the telephone operators union declined rapidly. Changes in telephone technology and, relatedly, a large drop in employment only worsened its prospects and ultimately led to the union's disbandment in 1938. Still, the Telephone Operators' Department and the 1919 strike were vital to helping establish a central role for women in organized labor and to the struggle for equal rights.

Julia O'Connor worked as an operator in what was called the Beach Street Exchange. It is part of what is today the much larger Verizon Building, which was built shortly after the strike. The southern portion of the back of the building, on Oxford Street, was the Exchange.

GETTING THERE

Orange Line to Chinatown Station.

TO LEARN MORE

Deutsch, Sarah. *Women and the City: Gender, Space, and Power in Boston, 1870–1940*, New York: Oxford University Press, 2000.

Norwood, Stephen H. *Labor's Flaming Youth: Telephone Operators and Worker Militancy, 1878–1923*, Urbana and Chicago: University of Illinois Press, 1990.

1.37 The Common Cupboard

11a Common Street

CHINATOWN

According to a document dated April 13, 1918, from Agent Paul O. Curtis of the Bureau of Investigation (the forerunner of the FBI), the Common Cupboard "was a meeting place for socialists and anarchists." The restaurant, located in the basement of a rooming house, he reported, was "frequented by Russians and other foreignors [sic] of suspicious appearance," its two small rooms "lighted by candles only, contained in candlesticks of German design." Another

11 Common Street, shortly before its demolition, 1960s. Mark-ups by Boston Redevelopment Authority, undated.

agent characterized the establishment as "a rendezvous for socialists and malcontents of every class, from the dynamite anarchists to the 'pink tea' socialists." Meanwhile, a brief item in a Boston newspaper from January 1918 implied that "Ye Common Cupboard" had recently opened, reporting that it "is announced to be for 'radicals,'" a place where "talk is carried on briskly on all sorts of subjects. Theorists of all sorts are free to air their pet ideas." While many such establishments existed in Greenwich Village in Manhattan, the unidentified writer asserted, "this is the first of its kind in the Hub, I believe."

Owned by the mother of Rose Sullivan, vice president of the all-woman labor union, the Telephone Operators' Department, many of its leaders frequented the Common Cupboard (see *New England Telephone Company Exchange*). Also, young women in general were among the clientele. As one bureau agent wrote in his surveillance report, "shop girls from the Department stores are being encouraged to frequent this restaurant and are being given cigarettes by the proprietress, who is thus teaching the girls to smoke."

The building in which the Common Cupboard was located no longer exists, nor does Common Street. Along with other adjacent streets, Common Street was eradicated in the mid-1960s to allow for the expansion of Tufts New England Medical Center. It ran between Washington and Tremont Streets, between where the Double Tree Hotel (821 Washington) and a Tufts parking garage now stand.

GETTING THERE

Orange Line to Tufts Medical Center Station. The Tufts parking garage stands on top of the station.

TO LEARN MORE

Norwood, Stephen H. *Labor's Flaming Youth: Telephone Operators and Worker Militancy, 1878–1923*, Urbana and Chicago: University of Illinois Press, 1990.

1.38 The Naked i

670 Washington Street

CHINATOWN

At 2:00 a.m. on Tuesday, November 16, 1976, Andrew Puopolo and fellow members of the Harvard University football team stumbled out of the Naked i, then one of Boston's best-known strip clubs, after a raucous night of alcohol-fueled celebration. Exactly what transpired next is subject to some dis-

Combat Zone, 1974.

agreement, but the largely white group of Harvard men ran into two young women, both black, who worked the Combat Zone's streets. One of the football players ended up losing his wallet; he and his teammates, suspecting one of the women, gave chase. This soon led to a fight with four men, black and Latino, who worked in the zone and later claimed to be defending a pair of women of color threatened by a gang of white men. In the fracas, one of them stabbed Puopolo, age twenty-one, in the chest. A month later, Puopolo, comatose, died in the nearby Tufts–New England Medical Center.

The incident and the death of the Boston-born and -raised Puopolo—a Harvard senior on his way to medical school—received intense and extensive media coverage. For many in Boston, the killing personified all that was wrong with the Combat Zone.

With its origins in the 1800s as Boston's theater district, the Combat Zone began to emerge as a seedy center of vice following World War II and a significant downturn in the city's economy. The destruction of Scollay Square (where Government Center now sits) and its adult-oriented establishments in the 1960s helped to fuel the Combat Zone, whose distinctive name derives perhaps from its ties to the many soldiers and shipyard workers who frequented the area. The Combat Zone was a formally designated area. In 1974, to prevent the spread of what the City saw as the area's ills, the Boston Redevelopment Authority turned to a geographic solution: The agency declared an "adult entertainment district" of five and a half acres squeezed between Downtown and Chinatown—"a kind of neon cage for the bawdy enterprises already operating there" in the words of writer Stephanie Schorow.

The area was plagued by high levels of crime—of the organized and street varieties as well as official (in the form of police corruption). It also embodied, as exemplified by the encounters involving Puopolo and his Harvard teammates, profound inequities in class, race, sexuality and space. Yet the Combat Zone, perhaps the city's most racially diverse area, was a place where people were able to explore sexuality, gender, and desire in ways not permitted elsewhere in Boston.

What was formally called Jerome's Naked i closed down in the mid-1990s. By then, the Combat Zone was quickly disappearing. While many point to Puopolo's killing and a subsequent police crackdown on crime in the district as the beginning of the area's end, other forces were at work. By the early 1980s, significant elements of the Chinatown community began calling for the Combat Zone's elimination. Redevelopment and gentrification of the area, and the emergence of VHS recordings and the Internet (allowing people to view pornography in the privacy of their homes) played even larger roles.

The building in which the Naked i stood is no longer. A luxury apartment building (number 660) now stands at the site.

GETTING THERE

Orange Line to Chinatown Station.

Parcel C protest, 1993.

TO LEARN MORE

Schorow, Stephanie. *Inside the Combat Zone: The Stripped Down Story of Boston's Most Notorious Neighborhood*, Wellesley Hills, MA: Union Park Press, 2017.

1.39 The Metropolitan/Parcel C

1 Nassau Street

CHINATOWN

On August 16, 2004, a ribbon-cutting ceremony celebrated the opening of The Metropolitan, a mixed-income and mixed-use development with 251 residential units and both community and commercial space. Among those in attendance were many Chinatown community members and Boston Mayor Thomas Menino.

What made the opening especially noteworthy was the community struggle out of which the development grew. It began in 1993, when the Boston Redevelopment Authority accepted a $2 million proposal from Tufts University Medical School and New England Medical Center (NEMC) to build a 451-car, eight-story parking garage on a small piece of land known as Parcel C. The BRA had created the parcel in the 1970s by expropriating and demolishing the homes of several Chinese residents and granting Tufts and NEMC the right to buy the land. Community efforts to block NEMC expansion in the 1980s resulted in a BRA pledge to preserve the parcel for a community center.

However, the BRA later reneged on its promise, outraging community members already reeling from the displacement of more than seven hundred residents due to institutional expansion and urban renewal starting in the 1950s. NEMC's planned 1993 addition of a large parking garage next door to what was Chinatown's only day care center and an adjoining playground was not welcome news, particularly in a tiny neighborhood already hemmed in by two highways and stricken with serious air pollution problems.

The opposition came together in the form of the Coalition to Protect Parcel C for Chinatown. Their bilingual (Cantonese and English) organizing effort included rallies, legal advocacy, letter writing, petition gathering, alliance building on the environmental justice front, and the holding of a community referendum that showed an overwhelming rejection of the proposed garage. After eighteen months of community pressure, New England Medical Center gave in and withdrew its proposal. At the same time, the City of Boston committed to preserve Parcel C for residential housing.

Of the 133 rental units in The Metropolitan, 46 are for low-income households and 13 are reserved to assist the homeless. Also housed there is the Chinese Progressive Association, a grassroots community organization that played a key role in the Parcel C struggle.

GETTING THERE

Orange Line to Tufts Medical Center Station.

TO LEARN MORE

Lai, Zenobia, Andrew Leong, and Chi Chi Wu. "The Lessons of the Parcel C Struggle: Reflections on Community Lawyering," *UCLA Asian Pacific American Law Journal* 6, no. 1 (2000): 1–43.

Leong, Andrew. "The Struggle Over Parcel C: How Boston's Chinatown Won a Victory in the Fight against Institutional Expansionism and Environmental Racism," *Amerasia Journal* 21, no. 3 (1995/1996): 99–119.

South End

The construction of the South End neighborhood began in the late 1840s when the City of Boston started filling in the tidal marsh on either side of the Boston Neck—a narrow strip of land (centered on what is today Washington Street) that connected the Shawmut Peninsula to **Roxbury.** Boston aimed to create a well-to-do neighborhood in response to the increasingly crowded conditions on **Beacon Hill** and in the downtown area.

With its tree-lined streets, redbrick townhouses, and small parks, the South End quickly became a fashionable district. By the late 1800s, however, the neighborhood's cachet was on the decline as affluent residents moved to the even newer Back Bay or to the suburbs. What were expensive, private homes soon became rooming houses and tenements, and the neighborhood increasingly working class and immigrant—and perhaps the city's most ethno-racially diverse area. A sizeable African American community emerged and, later, so did a Puerto Rican population. Beginning in the 1940s, the neighborhood also became a popular residential area for gay men.

Such diversity and low rents facilitated the South End's emergence in the mid- to late-1900s as a center of progressive activism on a variety of fronts. Somewhat ironically, many of the gains won by this activism helped to stabilize and gentrify the South End. That, combined with its location—wedged between the **Back Bay**, **Chinatown**, and **Roxbury**—now make it increasingly attractive for relatively wealthy individuals and families. Along with the end of rent control in Boston in the 1990s, this has led to dramatic shifts in the now heavily gentrified neighborhood's composition in recent decades. Still, however, the South enjoys considerable ethno-racial and class diversity because of the presence of public, subsidized, and low-income housing of various sorts.

South End residents protest housing situation. This multiracial community mobilization prefigured the Rainbow Coalition that emerged around the 1983 mayoral campaign of Mel King, in vehicle, a longtime community organizer and future state representative, circa 1968.

The South End is a Boston Landmark District and has the largest number of Victorian buildings of any US neighborhood.

1.40 Tent City

130 Dartmouth Street

SOUTH END

For community activist Mel King, the "steamy, explosive summer of 1968 began early in Boston," leading to a three-day occupation of a parking lot at the corner of Dartmouth Street and Columbus Avenue. Gathering under the slogans "People, Not Cars!" and "This is a Place Where Homes Should Be Built!" residents organized the Community Assembly for a United South End (CAUSE, founded in 1966). Led by King, it initiated one of the first serious fightbacks against the gentrification of the South End. The occupation called attention to the Boston Redevelopment Authority's (BRA) urban renewal demolitions and displacement of longtime residents in favor of speculative building plans benefiting absentee private owners.

In its place, CAUSE demanded new housing options for residents and an elected urban renewal committee. The action backing up these demands was the occupation—the construction of a tent city. In the ensuing months, CAUSE turned out tenants to city council hearings and neighborhood association meetings. Mobilizing tenants, homeowners, and businesses, the community organization created new forms of representation and even co-opted city structures to exert "double barreled," multiracial and multiconstituency pressure on the BRA.

Taking advantage of new organizing opportunities, with a changing roster of organizations, activists seized opportunities to push for low-income housing through, among other grassroots entities, People Organized to Save the South End (POSSE) during the 1970s, and, later, a nonprofit called the Tent City Corporation (TCC). Still with a focus on the Dartmouth Street parking lot, a coalition of groups organized an annual protest rally in April, a community lawsuit, and thirteen marches, rallies, and press conferences to maintain pressure between the early 1970s and early 1980s. In 1982, during a city fiscal crisis, activists blocked the Tent City parking lot for three weeks and moved several squatter families into a row-house building abutting the site. While these actions succeeded in blocking BRA plans to build market-rate housing,

Tent City protestors, 1968.

ultimately it was the 1983 mayoral election that proved decisive. Tent City activists won commitments from both finalists, Mel King and eventual victor Ray Flynn, to support TCC as the developer for affordable housing.

Although the following decades' gentrification of the South End's stately dwellings tempers the success story, a major victory resulted from the 1968 action and successive waves of dogged organizing. In 1988, a 269-unit building opened—the Tent City Apartments with one-quarter of the units reserved for low-income tenants and half for those with moderate incomes.

Reflecting on Tent City, housing activist Michael Kane notes "the success in siting a beautifully designed, racially-diverse, community-controlled, low-income housing in a prime urban land site, across from Back Bay Station and next to Copley Place." The victory "shows what can be achieved when, as Mel King puts it, 'people fight for what they really want, not just settle for what they think they can get.'"

TO LEARN MORE

King, Mel. *Chain of Change.* Boston: South End Press, 1981.

Vrabel, Jim. *A People's History of the New Boston.* Amherst and Boston: University of Massachusetts Press, 2014.

1.41 Haley House

23 Dartmouth Street

SOUTH END

Founded in 1966 by Kathe and John McKenna, Haley House is an intentional live-in community of individuals dedicated to social justice. It emerged out of the Catholic Worker movement, a collection of autonomous communities dedicated to nonviolence and active opposition to war and poverty. Community members operate a daily soup kitchen that provides breakfast for men in need, an afternoon "elder meal" program for older individuals (regardless of gender) three times a week, and a food pantry for neighborhood families and elders every Thursday.

Since its establishment more than fifty years ago, Haley House has expanded its activities. It now owns and/or manages over one hundred affordable housing

Live-in community outside soup kitchen, 1980.

units throughout the South End to enable low-income people to live in the neighborhood; these include twenty-four single-room-occupancy apartments for individuals living in shelters or who are in transitional programs and are waiting to move into permanent housing.

As part of its effort to combat social, racial, and economic injustice, Haley House opened a Bakery Café at 12 Dade Street in *Roxbury*'s Dudley Square (it had been previously in operation in a smaller venue in the South End) in 2005 and runs a catering business. The profit-sharing establishment serves delicious food, much of it made from organic, locally sourced ingredients—some of which come from Haley House's community garden (at 95 Thornton Street in *Roxbury*'s Highland Park)—and pays a living wage to its employees. It provides training and jobs to individuals who, for a variety of reasons, face significant obstacles to employment.

GETTING THERE

HALEY HOUSE: Orange Line to Back Bay Station, 0.3 mile (six-minute) walk.

HALEY HOUSE BAKERY CAFÉ: Silver Line to Dudley Square Station, a two-minute walk.

1.42 Cathedral of the Holy Cross

1400 Washington Street

SOUTH END

Begun in 1866 and completed nine years later, in 1875, the Cathedral of the Holy Cross is almost as large as Notre Dame Cathedral in Paris. At the time, its construction manifested the tremendous growth in the Boston area's Catholic population and the

increasing power of the city's Irish. Today the Archdiocese of Boston (the cathedral serves as its spiritual seat), with an estimated 1.8 million followers, is the fourth largest archdiocese in the United States.

When the construction of the Gothic-style cathedral began, the South End seemed destined to become Boston's fanciest area. But with the making of the Back Bay, elites abandoned the neighborhood, leaving the cathedral, in the words of writer J. Anthony Lukas, "standing in a dreary welter of dank saloons, livery stables, and dilapidated tenements." The decision at the turn of the century to put an elevated train line down the middle of Washington Street further marginalized the cathedral, the frequent trains rumbling by drowning out sections of church services.

In early 2002, soon after the initial installments of the *Boston Globe* series revealing widespread sexual abuse by Catholic clergy in the Boston archdiocese, a weekly vigil began outside the cathedral. The purpose was, and remains, to support survivors, to remember the victimized who have died,

Protest of sexual abuse by Catholic clergy outside of Holy Cross Cathedral, 2012.

and to pressure the Church to hold accountable all priests guilty of abuse. As of mid-2019, the vigil, which begins before the 11:30 a.m. Sunday mass and ends shortly thereafter, had taken place (with minor exceptions due to inclement weather) for over nine hundred consecutive Sundays.

With the tearing down of the old Orange Line in the late 1980s and the gentrification of the South End, the cathedral is now in the fashionable area its original architects envisioned. The weekly vigil serves as a vivid reminder of the high costs of the power, prestige, and immunity the Roman Catholic Church hierarchy once enjoyed.

GETTING THERE

Silver Line buses (SL4 between South Station / Essex Street and Dudley Station; and the SL5 between Downtown Crossing / Temple Place and Dudley Station).

1.43 South End Press

116 Saint Botolph Street

SOUTH END

South End Press was a worker-owned and -run collective, not-for-profit book publisher. Founded in 1977, it published highly influential works by leading radical and Left intellectuals and activists, including Jeremy Brecher, Noam Chomsky, Ward Churchill, bell hooks, Mel King, Manning Marable, Cherríe Moraga, Arundhati Roy, Vandana Shiva, Andrea Smith, and Howard Zinn. In the 1990s, it moved to Central Square in Cambridge and, in 2009, to Brooklyn, New York. In 2014, the press, citing financial difficulties, closed down.

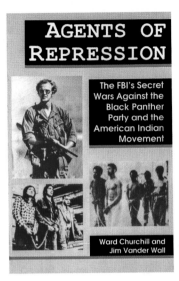

AGENTS OF REPRESSION

The FBI's Secret Wars Against the Black Panther Party and the American Indian Movement

Ward Churchill and Jim Vander Wall

Cover of a South End Press book, published 1990.

Despite the closure, a number of other presses continue to publish South End Press titles. Meanwhile, spinoffs of the press endure, particularly Z *Magazine* and ZNet (established by Michael Albert and Lydia Sargent, two of South End's original founders) as well as Speak Out, a progressive speakers bureau and social justice training institute.

GETTING THERE

Prudential Station (Green Line), 0.1 mile (three-minute) walk. Massachusetts Avenue Station (Orange Line) is also close by. The building is now a private home.

1.44 Villa Victoria Center for the Arts

85 West Newton Street

SOUTH END

Villa Victoria's Center for the Arts is among Boston's premier cultural venues. It hosts an annual Festival Betances, drawing thousands of participants in midsummer; its

Festival Betances, Villa Victoria, circa 1990–2000.

concert series features world-class musicians like Ballaké Sissoko, Richard Ashcroft, and the Miguel Zenon Quartet. Behind the bright lights of success lie five decades of concerted struggle by a Puerto Rican community in the heart of Boston's gentrifying South End.

In 1967, after the Boston Redevelopment Agency's bulldozers had razed the West End and the South End's New York Streets neighborhoods, activists in the South End's largely Puerto Rican enclave coalesced around tenants' rights and launched the Emergency Tenants Coalition (ETC). Israel Feliciano, a charismatic organizer, focused early resistance on City of Boston redevelopment plans by leveraging protest and election turnout to increase the community's bargaining power. Having learned that Parcel 19, an area bound by Washington, West Dedham, Tremont, and West Newton Streets, was slated for redevelopment, the tenants sounded the slogan, one attributed to community activist Doña

Paula Oyola, *No nos mudaremos de la parcela 19* ("We will not move from Parcel 19"). Recognizing that existing housing conditions were unacceptable for the nearly two thousand area residents, ETC adopted a nuanced position with respect to redevelopment by accepting its necessity but demanding community control over the process.

By 1969, the City recognized ETC as the parcel's developer, and over the next seven years, ETC and the community designed, mobilized finance for, and built a neighborhood—what is today Villa Victoria—consisting of a central plaza inspired by Puerto Rican villages, surrounding row houses, parks, and community spaces. It also established a service agency to provide banking services, day-care facilities, a bilingual preschool, and an arts center.

As the initial insurgent generation of activists aged and moved on, the primary nonprofit community formations, ETC and IBA (Inquilinos Boricuas en Acción)

experienced organizational difficulties, and the community solidarity that animated the original project seemed to wane. Meanwhile, the low-income enclave was surrounded by an ever more affluent, largely white and professional South End. Despite these challenges, a new generation of nonprofit leadership has emerged and reinvigorated Villa Victoria. A neighborhood of 435 units of affordable housing, it retains its distinctive, human-scale architecture and village-like sense of community.

TO LEARN MORE

Dominguez Gray, Maria. "The Creation of Villa Victoria" in *ReVista: Harvard Review of Latin America*, Spring 2008. Available from: http://revista.drclas.harvard.edu/book/creation-villa-victoria

GETTING THERE

Orange Line to Back Bay Station, 0.4 mile (eight-minute) walk. The Silver Line (SL4 and SL5 lines) also passes very close by.

1.45 Blackstone Square

Washington Street (between West Newton and West Brookline Streets)

SOUTH END

More than five thousand people, including many families with children, gathered at Blackstone Square, a public park, on Sunday, July 16, 1972, for the Puerto Rican community's fifth annual festival. Around 6:00 p.m., a fistfight broke out in the crowd. Someone soon called the Boston Police Department and reported that an officer was in trouble; meanwhile an unidentified person fired a starter's pistol to break up the fight, leading

BLACKSTONE SQUARE, BOSTON

Blackstone Square with the park in the background, circa 1850.

Mayor White with Blackstone Park Residents, July 18, 1972.

many of those gathered to panic. Boston police arrived on the scene, and the first to do so entered the park aggressively, as if they were facing "a full-scale riot," according to the Reverend Ernesto Serino, director of the nearby Cardinal Cushing Spanish-Speaking Center. Armando Martínez, head of Puente, a local educational organization, reported that police started assaulting innocent people. (Even Catholic priests were not immune: Later that evening, a police officer struck Father William Sharkey of the nearby *Cathedral of the Holy Cross*, causing him to lose consciousness.) Soon projectiles began raining down on the police. Rock throwing intensified as more police arrived and forcefully attempted to clear the park and the surrounding streets. The confrontations in the park led to three nights of conflict in the

area, resulting in at least thirty-six arrests and thirty-three injuries, looting of stores, and the destruction of three police vehicles.

The disturbances spoke to a number of problems for area Puerto Ricans: a lack of Spanish-speaking police officers, high rates of substandard housing, an unemployment rate of 32 percent, and high dropout rates among school-age youth, In this context, community members—progressive residents of the South End, some who had been active in the Puerto Rican Independence Party while living in their homeland, and students who attended local universities and colleges—met in *Villa Victoria* at the home of one of the participants to discuss how to formulate a collective response to the police violence.

Two participants were members of the Puerto Rican Socialist Party (PSP) from the Hartford, Connecticut, chapter. Out of these meetings emerged a Boston *núcleo* (chapter) of the PSP, a Marxist political party that championed independence for the territory. Central to the PSP's activities was the weekly distribution of *Claridad*, the party's newspaper, which served as a regular opportunity to engage community members and to undertake political consciousness-raising.

Over the course of much of the 1970s, the PSP was the leading radical organization in the Boston area's Puerto Rican and Latino communities. Among its achievements, the PSP played a prominent role in protecting bilingual education when the original desegregation/busing plan (see **South Boston Heights Academy**) called for the dispersal of Puerto Rican students from the South End (at the time an already-integrated area) to public schools throughout the city. The PSP also helped to organize Villa Victoria's workers into a labor union, fought against the commercialization of the annual Puerto Rican Festival, and spread its activities to **Cambridge**, **Dorchester**, and **Jamaica Plain**. In addition, the party was also active on the cultural front, organizing a *teatro popular* (people's theater) and a softball team, which became one of the PSP's most effective outreach vehicles.

Various issues led to the chapter's demise by the end of the decade—internal differences over whether to focus on community issues or Puerto Rican independence and international socialism, disagreements with the party in Puerto Rico, and burnout among activists given the all-consuming nature of the political work. Still, the Boston PSP planted many seeds that continued to bear fruit after its passing, not least in the active involvement of former members in Mel King's Rainbow Coalition and his campaigns for mayor in the 1980s.

Opened in 1855, Blackstone Square is now part of a very different South End than what existed in 1972. While gentrification has driven out many Puerto Rican residents from the neighborhood, a strong *Boricua* presence persists in the area, not least because of **Villa Victoria**, the border of which is across the street from the square.

GETTING THERE

Silver Line buses (SL4 and SL5 between Downtown and Dudley Station) pass by the park.

TO LEARN MORE

Matos Rodríguez, Félix V. "Saving the *Parcela*: A Short History of Boston's Puerto Rican Community," in *The Puerto Rican Diaspora: Historical Perspectives*, ed. Carmen Teresa Whalen and Víctor Vásquez-Hernández, Philadelphia: Temple University Press, 1998, 200–26.

Amy Moreno de Toro, Ángel A. "An Oral History of the Puerto Rican Socialist Party in Boston, 1972–1978," in *The Puerto Rican Movement: Voices from the Diaspora*, ed. Andrés Torres and José E. Velásquez, Philadelphia: Temple University Press, 2005, 246–59.

The Back Bay and the Fenway

The Back Bay is Boston's most afflu-ent and architecturally glamorous neighborhood. In addition to some of the city's most expensive com-mercial establishments, it contains many of Boston's landmarks— from Trinity Church in Copley Square to the tree-lined pedestrian mall of Commonwealth Avenue. The result of a huge engineer-ing project from 1857 to 1882, the

Boston Public Library, Copley Square, circa 1930–45.

neighborhood provided stable em-ployment to thousands of Irish immigrant laborers, dozens of whom were killed during its construction. At the proj-ect's height, up to eight hundred railroad cars of gravel, mined in and transported from the towns of Newton and Needham, arrived each workday to provide the mate-rial to fill in what was a large tidal marsh, one that effectively served as Boston's open sewer.

The Back Bay was a response to the city's exploding population. Concentrated at the time on the Shawmut Peninsula, it went from 25,000 in 1800 to 137,000 in 1850, with almost 40,000 of the new inhabitants having arrived within the previous decade. In addi-tion to increasing the city's land area by 450 acres, more than half the size of the original peninsula, the project sought to increase the housing stock for Boston's wealthiest, largely Protestant residents lest they depart for the suburbs in the face of an increasingly crowded (and impoverished) city. The state did not dispense its own funds to pay for it

but financed the project through sales of individual plots, greatly adding to its cof-fers, much of which was used to fund public education.

The Fenway grew out of a combination of the annexation of land from the city of Brookline in the 1870s and landfilling related to the making of the Fenway Parkway and the Fens, part of Frederick Law Olmstead's "Emerald Necklace" of parks, in the 1890s. What is formally called Fenway-Kenmore (it includes the Kenmore Square area) is today home to many educational institutions and has a large student population. It is also home to the Museum of Fine Arts and the Isabella Stewart Gardner Museum.

1.46　The Newbry

501 Boylston Street (lobby), entrance on Newbury Street

BACK BAY

Excavations in the early 1900s revealed that in constructing the Back Bay neighborhood, workers had unwittingly buried evidence of an indigenous community that utilized the

Diorama in the Newbry's lobby, 2018.

bay for at least fifteen hundred years, beginning several millennia ago, as a food source. The construction of an extension of the Boylston subway station in 1913 led to the discovery of a dense collection of wooden stakes driven into the ground. Again in 1939, with excavations for the old New England Mutual Life Insurance Building (now the Newbry), thousands more stakes emerged. Archaeologists believe that the stakes, woven together with brushwork, were effective weirs used to trap fish as the tide receded. Evidence also exists in other New England sites for V-shaped stone dams constricting river flow to trap fish in a similar manner. These sites are the oldest surviving artifacts of precolonial civilizations in New England.

The weirs are brought to life in a diorama exhibited in the lobby of the Newbry, now a mixed-use building of office and retail space. (The lobby has three other dioramas, one of which shows the making of the Back Bay.) Since 2003, the Wampanoag nation and local artists have hosted an annual commemora-tive service that reconstructs the weirs on Boston Common.

GETTING THERE

Green Line to Copley Station, 0.2 mile (five-minute) walk. The dioramas can be accessed only through the building's Newbury Street entrance.

TO LEARN MORE

Décima, Elena B., and Dena F. Dincauze. "The Boston Back Bay Fish Weirs," in *Hidden Dimensions: The Cultural Significance of Wetland Archaeology*, ed. Kathryn Bernick, Vancouver: University of British Columbia Press, 2008, 157–72.

1.47 Armory of the First Corps of Cadets/The Castle

130 Columbus Avenue

BACK BAY

With memories of Civil War draft riots and the short-lived Paris Commune of 1871, fears of class warfare were rampant throughout the United States in the late 1800s. This was particularly the case after the national railroad strike of 1877, which involved widespread rioting, dozens of deaths, and millions of dollars in property destruction. Rather than fruitfully engaging workers, ruling elites in major cities strengthened their repressive capacity by building imposing armory buildings. While the railroad strike did not spread to Boston, the fear and scapegoating of the "dangerous classes," a flexible category that included the poor, the criminal, immigrants, and political radicals, certainly infected the city

In this context, Boston's First Corps of Cadets, a volunteer militia with its origins in the British colonial period, began a campaign in 1880 for its own quarters. Previously the cadets had used rented space for their headquarters and the MIT gym for drills. Invoking the railroad strike and other examples of worker rebellions, the Corps stressed the real possibility of future danger: "The skies might be clear to-day, and the functions of government may run smoothly and peacefully, and no enemy may seem to be lurking at home or abroad, but no man knows when the storm may burst."

Donations from Boston's wealthy and big businesses, in addition to corps-produced theatrical performances, provided the funds to complete the armory in 1897. It was 28,000+-square-foot complex with a four-story Head House, a single-story Drill Hall, a six-story tower, a drawbridge, and windows with "retractable musket-proof steel shutters." A Boston alderman (as city council members were called) explained that "because there is nothing between the mob and the muskets . . . but a door," small, isolated armories would no longer

Armory of the First Corps of Cadets, 2008.

suffice. What were needed were formidable armories that could withstand large-scale civil disturbances. (The new armory would play a significant role in putting down unrest associated with Boston's police strike of 1919. See *Police Station 6/Patriot Homes*.) The Columbus Avenue–Arlington Street site was desirable, according to the corps, because of its "central situation in relation to population, to public buildings and to the termini of the railroads of the City."

Many in Boston were highly critical of the armory. B. O. Flower, for example, an editor of a pro-worker publication, *Arena*, decried the rise of big-city armories, calling them "great storehouses of death." Nothing, he said, was "more contrary to the spirit of republican institutions than permitting the rich men of great centres of wealth to lavish their money upon armories." Meanwhile, one T. W. Curtis penned a poem calling the armory "the Boston Bastille," decrying it as a "moral leper's nest" for the "scions of the wealthy."

The Corps sold the building in 1965. Thereafter it served many functions, including as the site of the University of Massachusetts Boston's library. Today the armory is known as the Castle at Park Plaza. Associated with the nearby Park Plaza Hotel, it is a high-end "unique special event venue" for conferences, gala events, banquets, and the like.

GETTING THERE

Green Line to Arlington Station, 0.2 mile (five-minute) walk.

TO LEARN MORE

Fogelson, Robert M. *America's Armories: Architecture, Society, and Public Order*, Cambridge: Harvard University Press, 1989.

Boston Landmarks Commission. *Study Report of the Boston Landmarks Commission on the Potential Designation of the Armory of the First Corps of Cadets as a Landmark under Chapter 772 of the Acts of 1975*, Boston: Boston Landmarks Commission, 1977.

1.48 The Youth's Companion Building

209 Columbus Avenue

BACK BAY

Shortly after it relocated in 1892 from its office at 41 Temple Place (near Downtown Crossing) to its new, much bigger building on 201 (now 209) Columbus Avenue,

The Youth's Companion, a national children's magazine, published its most famous issue. In response to President Benjamin Harrison's call for the people in the United States to observe "the four hundredth anniversary of the discovery of America," James Upham, a marketer of the magazine, came up with the idea for a "National School Celebration" to cultivate nationalism among the country's youth. Accordingly, the September, 8, 1892, issue of the magazine carried the "official programme" for the celebration. Within the four-page program was the original version of the Pledge of Allegiance. Francis Bellamy, a staffer at the magazine, was its author. The magazine had put him in charge of the program, one timed to coincide with the official dedication of the Chicago World's Fair, also known as the Columbian Exposition.

Bellamy was a Christian socialist preacher critical of excessive materialism and individualism, an advocate of social reform, and a cousin of Edward Bellamy (see **Exchange Place**). He wrote the pledge to promote an active "social citizenry." The words "with liberty and justice for all" reflected his sympathy with the ideals of the French Revolution and his perception that its slogan "Liberty, Equality, and Fraternity," which he desired to incorporate into the pledge, would prove too radical to many in the United States. Bellamy was also, in the words of historian Richard Ellis, "a race-conscious nativist," one anxious about the growing presence of a large, supposedly racially inferior immigrant population, particularly Italians and Central and Eastern European Jews. Widely held views at the time, they were present in *The Youth's Companion*'s pages.

The quest for the Pledge of Allegiance embodied both egalitarian ideals as well as a desire to maintain national order and ignite American patriotism—not least to guard against would-be threats from "new" immigrants. In this regard, it is not surprising that the pledge (slightly amended in later years) would subsequently become associated with US militarism, political conformity, and deference to state authority. The pledge, asserts historian Cecilia O'Leary, "represented a critical step in transforming schools into machines for political socialization."

Founded in 1827, *The Youth's Companion* was originally a small-circulation magazine infused with conservative Christianity. In the late 1800s, it shifted its focus and approach, targeting adults as well as children. The new family-oriented magazine's readership skyrocketed. Writers such as Harriet Beecher Stowe, Willa Cather, Jack London, and Mark Twain appeared in its pages. In 1929, the magazine ceased to exist when it merged with *The American Boy*, a monthly publication.

The Youth's Companion Building is on the National Register of Historic Places. Today it is a mixed-use building.

GETTING THERE

Green Line to Arlington Street Station, 0.3 mile (six-minute) walk.

TO LEARN MORE

Ellis. Richard J. *To the Flag: The Unlikely History of the Pledge of Allegiance*, Lawrence: University of Kansas Press, 2005.

O'Leary, Cecilia. *To Die For: The Paradox of American Patriotism*, Princeton: Princeton University Press, 1999.

O'Leary, Cecilia, and Tony Platt. "Pledging Allegiance: The Revival of Prescriptive Patriotism," *Social Justice* 28, no. 3 (2001): 41–44.

1.49 The Rat

528 Commonwealth Avenue

KENMORE SQUARE

During the 1960s, the Rathskeller was a run-down bar and restaurant in the heart of Kenmore Square that occasionally hosted live music. A new owner bought the establishment (then called T.J.'s) in 1974 and brought back the old name. From then until 1997, the Rat, as it was popularly known, was a live rock music club. In its heyday, it was the center of Boston's punk and alternative rock scene and thus an incubator for music that was often antiestablishment and, at times, politically radical. Among the famed musicians who performed there were the Dead Kennedys, the Ramones, Talking Heads, Metallica, Joan Jett, the Police, the Beastie Boys, and R.E.M. Popular Boston-based bands such as the Cars, the Pixies, the Dropkick Murphys, and Gang Green also played the subterranean club (food was served upstairs).

Its closure in 1997 was both a manifestation of the grungy club's decline as music venues in places like *Cambridge* arose and of dramatic changes in Kenmore Square. During the 1970s and much of the 1980s, it was a gritty area with many low-priced restaurants, bars, and stores, an area open to working-class people exploring countercultural modes of expression. Gentrification,

Aimee Mann playing with her band, the Young Snakes, at the Rathskeller, 1981.

however, driven in part by the expansion of area universities (particularly Boston University), had greatly altered the neighborhood by 1997. Today the building where the Rat stood is gone. A luxury hotel emblematic of the gentrified area stands on the site.

GETTING THERE

Green Line to Kenmore Station.

1.50 Fenway Park

4 Jersey Street

THE FENWAY

Built in 1912, storied Fenway Park is the oldest Major League Baseball stadium in North America and home to the "Green Monster" (the nickname of its leftfield wall). It is also the home of the Boston Red Sox, the last team in baseball to racially integrate. As late as 1958, Tom Yawkey, the team owner at the time, did not employ a single African American at any level of the organization. It would not be until 1959 that the Red Sox fielded a black player, Pumpsie Green. Ironically, perhaps the biggest crowd in Fenway Park's history assembled to protest racism, the type inextricably tied to colonialism. On Sunday, June 30, 1919, at least fifty thousand people—with thousands more denied entry outside the stadium's gates—gathered at Fenway to demand an end to British rule of Ireland. The crowd was three times larger than the number who had seen the Red Sox and Babe Ruth win the World Series the previous year.

The occasion was the visit of Eamon de Valera, president of the Irish Republic, the revolutionary government-in-waiting that had declared independence from the United Kingdom earlier that year. Valera had come to the United States to raise money for nationalist forces and to win diplomatic recognition from the US government. Of the gathering a *Boston Globe* reporter wrote, "To say that it was thrilling is putting it mildly—it was electric." It went on to state, "In that vast audience you sensed this new dignity that has sunk into their consciousness, born of the knowledge that millions of men of Irish blood have been fighting the past four years for democracy as against autocracy and for the self-determination of Nations in the world." Later that evening Valera trav-

Fenway Park, June 30, 1919.

eled to *Lawrence*, which became the first US city to officially recognize the Republic of Ireland, and spoke to a huge crowd there. Valera's visit and the reception he received manifested not only the size of the area's Irish-descended community, but also the massive shift in political power that had taken place throughout much of Greater Boston in the late 1800s as Irish Catholics wrested local political control from Protestant elites.

GETTING THERE

Green Line to Kenmore Square Station, 0.2 mile (five-minute) walk.

TO LEARN MORE

Bryant, Howard. *Shut Out: A Story of Race and Baseball in Boston*, Boston: Beacon Press, 2002.

1.51 Marian Hall, Emmanuel College/Boston Women's Health Book Collective

400 The Fenway

THE FENWAY

On the weekend of May 10–11, 1969, Bread and Roses—a grassroots, feminist and socialist organization—hosted the New England Female Liberation Conference at Emmanuel College, then a Catholic women's college. Alongside workshops on "Working Women," "Black Women in a Caste Society," and the "Liberation of Welfare Mothers," one, called "Women and Their Bodies," aimed to generate a list of "good ob-gyn doctors." Instead, it raised a much more fundamental challenge; according to one participant, workshop goers "realized that

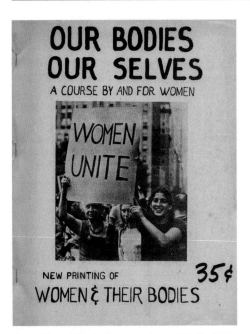

First edition of *Our Bodies, Ourselves*, printed in 1971 by New England Free Press.

[they] did not know what questions to ask to find out whether [the doctors] were good or not." The realization led to the formation of a study group and, later, the Boston Women's Health Book Collective. In 1970, a 138-page newsprint publication called *Women and Their Bodies*, published by the activist-oriented New England Free Press, shared their findings. As demand grew—250,000 copies circulated by 1973—the collective dubbed the work *Our Bodies, Ourselves* (OBOS). It would go on to enjoy worldwide success, outliving the original conference sponsors and political moment.

Representing a militant turn in women's activism and increased self-awareness, the publication signaled an important shift, rebalancing power away from doctors and the medical establishment to women—from the medicalization of health matters toward public-health matters and a concern for general wellness. Realizing that most medical diagnoses and treatments used a biological male as the standard, OBOS also contributed to a reevaluation of research and therapies—a mission that has continued throughout the decades. Moreover, in the cases of birth control, childbirth, postpartum recuperation, hysterectomies, and broad range of other female-specific experiences, OBOS has helped women assume agency over their needs and healing.

As OBOS grew in succeeding decades and across new editions—as feminism itself evolved—it addressed new topics and garnered global readerships, publishing culturally relevant editions in more than two dozen languages.

Emmanuel College is today a coeducational institution with more than two thousand students. Marian Hall, which hosted the original workshop in Room 2, remains a student center, dormitory, and dining hall.

GETTING THERE

Green Line D to Fenway Station.

RELATED SITE

ROCKLEDGE, the former half-acre estate of William Lloyd Garrison and his family, is today part of Emmanuel College's Notre Dame campus. Its roughly thirty residential students focus on community service and social justice. 125 Highland Street, Roxbury.

TO LEARN MORE

Norsigian, Judy. "The Importance of 'Our Bodies, Ourselves.'" *The Big Think* (2011). Available at: https://youtu.be/QwG_JAY4TEY

Seaman, Barbara, and Susan F. Wolf. "The Role of Advocacy Groups in Research on Women's Health," in *Women and Health*, ed. Marlene B. Goldman and Maureen C. Hatch, Cambridge, MA: Academic Press, 2000, 27–36.

1.52 Symphony Road Community Garden

56–72 Symphony Road

THE FENWAY

In the early to mid-1970s, Boston was known as the US arson capital. The small Symphony Road area—with an ethno-racially diverse population made up of the elderly, working-class families, the poor, and students, as well as gay and lesbian residents—was the epicenter. The first fire happened at 40 Symphony Road on January 6, 1974. Over the next three to four years, twenty-three major fires took place in a one-block area, displacing hundreds and killing five, including a four-year-old girl, Jessie Oliver.

Symphony Road Community Garden, 2017.

Neighborhood residents, convinced that the fires represented a pattern of arson perpetrated by outside actors on a vulnerable area suffering from disinvestment, came together to fight the burning of their community, forming STOP, the Symphony Tenants Organizing Project. Efforts to get local authorities to investigate the fires failed; some officials denied that a pattern existed, while others contended that bored teens or neighborhood thugs were responsible; one Boston fire official blamed "angry ethnics,"

while also suggesting that gay men could be the culprits. To counter official inaction at the city level, STOP activists systematically gathered information on housing and fire code violations and researched the sale and resale of properties and insurance coverage.

What the burned buildings shared was that they were owned by absentee landlords, were in a declining state, had vacant units, and had undergone multiple ownership changes in recent years. With the help of Mel King, then a state representative from the neighboring **South End**, STOP was able to gain access to the Massachusetts attorney general's office to present their research findings. This led to a state task force to investigate the fires and, ultimately, to the indictment and conviction of thirty-two individuals. They included lawyers, real estate agents, insurance adjustors, finance executives, accountants, a City of Boston housing inspector, and two police officials—one who led the city's arson squad and the other the state fire marshal's arson unit.

The Symphony Road fires illuminated the ties between capitalist profiteering in real estate and insurance and official corruption, while their resolution demonstrated the power of citizen organizing. Among STOP's legacies are strong tools for the investigation and prosecution of arson-for-profit, ones adopted far beyond Massachusetts.

Another legacy is the Symphony Road Community Garden. It is located on the site of a number of the buildings destroyed by arson in the 1970s. A marker commemorates Jessie Oliver as well as Bertha McCrary, who led the effort to bring about the garden.

GETTING THERE

Green Line (E Branch) to Symphony Station.

NEARBY SITES

SYMPHONY HALL; **NORTHEASTERN UNIVERSITY**; and the **FENS**, part of Boston's "Emerald Necklace."

TO LEARN MORE

Brady, James. "Arson, Urban Economy, and Organized Crime: The Case of Boston," *Social Problems* 31, no. 1 (1983): 1–27.

Brady, James. "The Social Economy of Arson: Vandals, Gangsters, Bankers, and Officials in the Making of an Urban Problem," in *Crime and Capitalism: Readings in Marxist Criminology*, ed. David F. Greenberg, Philadelphia: Temple University Press, 1993, 211–57.

Sonia Weinhaus (producer), *Burning Greed* (documentary film), 2016.

1.53 College of Public and Community Service, UMass Boston

100 Arlington Street

BACK BAY

Sign protesting attempt to relocate CPCS to the Columbia Point campus, circa 1996.

In a September 2006 letter to the *Jamaica Plain Gazette*, a reader noted, "Massachusetts is not an oligarchy. Or is it? The future of one of its best, brightest public colleges hangs on the answer."

The writer was referring to the College of Community and Public Service (CPCS), founded in 1972, at UMass Boston. Chancellor Frank Broderick worried that his faculty, in their "zeal to provide disadvantaged students with the best in higher education," had isolated "large parts of the urban community." Broderick led a university-wide effort to create a new and innovative college, CPCS. Its mission was to provide nontraditional students with access to higher education in a way that respected their life experiences and struggles. Thirty years after its founding, the college had accumulated a powerful cadre of alumnae/i from racially and culturally diverse working-class communities, many already working in public and community service agencies, including then-Boston mayor Thomas Menino.

Threats to the college's well-being emerged in the early 2000s from a changing guard of top administrators who were hostile to CPCS's nontraditional approaches to learning, teaching, and evaluation. They also believed that CPCS was too expensive and wanted it shuttered.

CPCS students, faculty, and staff mounted an intensive campaign of resistance in response, with alumnae/i speaking out about its value. Túbal Padilla-Galiano, a 1989 graduate remarked, "Finding CPCS was finding a treasure. I could receive academic credit for my practical experience, work at my own pace, define a major, work one on one with members of the faculty, and share in a unique, diverse and dynamic community of adult learners." Another activist, Ty de Pass, with roots in the 1960s, explained how CPCS fitted into his life story, "In the midst of all that [sixties] social upheaval, sitting in classes on English Comp . . . seemed particularly self-indulgent, so I chose another road, another life: activism for peace and social justice." Decades later de Pass noted that CPCS enabled him to complete his education. Similarly, alumna Kim Tallbear, who went on to a career in academia, recalled that "CPCS was the best choice for us as students; the classes and the research projects reinforced and improved our responsiveness to community needs, rather

than pulling us away from community." By the end of 2006, despite a talented and acclaimed faculty, successful graduates, and loyal student base, none of the program's dedicated and determined backers were able to prevent the college's elimination. Over ensuing years it was steadily dismantled and "mainstreamed" into other departments.

Although the college moved to the UMass campus at Columbia Point in 1992, it was founded and housed for many years at UMass-Boston's original location in the Back Bay. For many of its backers, the college's relocation foretold its future demise—isolated on Columbia Point and apart from the communities its founders envisioned serving. Today its stalwarts refer to it as "the most interesting College in Boston that you can't visit." Its former site on Arlington Street now houses luxury apartments.

GETTING THERE

Green Line to Arlington Station.

TO LEARN MORE

SaveCPCS.org archive website: https://web .archive.org/web/20051225073841/http://www .cpcs.umb.edu:80/about/mission_statement.htm

1.54 Massachusetts Competitive Partnership

535 Boylston Street

BACK BAY

The top floor of a thirteen-story building on the corner of Boylston and Clarendon Streets is home to what one reporter has described as the "state's most powerful business group, a who's who of Greater Boston's corporate elite." The members of the Massachusetts Competitive Partnership (MACP) include the heads of the Bank of America (Brian Moynihan), Fidelity Investments (Abigail Johnson), and the New England Patriots (owner Robert Kraft). Annual membership in the sixteen-member, secretive group costs $100,000.

Founded in 2008, MACP characterizes itself a "public policy group" whose "goals are to promote job growth and competitiveness in the Commonwealth." Despite labeling itself as "non-profit, non-partisan," its agenda is decidedly focused on expanding the corporate bottom line. Its neoliberal policy advocacy grounded in deregulation, privatization, and austerity favors Greater Boston's One Percent. The MACP's work focuses, for example, on what it calls the high "cost of government," arguing that it "impedes Massachusetts' ability to compete and promote job growth and competitiveness." It thus seeks to "reform" (weaken) the benefits received by public-sector workers. It is also concerned with "the high cost of energy" in the state and thus champions a reexamination of Massachusetts's "green energy policies." In addition, MACP has intervened in the public conversation about the MBTA (Massachusetts Bay Transit Authority), voicing support for "improved

service" but tying this to comingling MBTA activities with those of the private sector, earning the suspicion that it is promoting a piecemeal privatization of public transit.

Some members—John Fish, head of Suffolk Construction, especially—of what is often referred to as "the New Vault" (see **Boston Safe Deposit and Trust Company**) took the lead in founding "Boston 2024," a thinly disguised corporate vehicle to bring the Summer Olympics to Boston. While the effort ultimately fizzled due to significant grassroots opposition, MACP continues its efforts to dominate Greater Boston and Massachusetts as a whole. In 2017–18, it played a key role in preventing a "millionaire's tax" initiative to increase funding for public education and transportation infrastructure from appearing on the state ballot.

GETTING THERE

Green Line to Copley Square Station, 0.1 mile (two-minute) walk.

NEARBY SITE

THE JOHN HANCOCK TOWER (200 Clarendon Street), Boston's tallest building and home to Bain Capital. Founded by former Massachusetts governor and Republican presidential candidate Mitt Romney, Bain is a global investment firm associated with the One Percent that plays a large role in corporate restructuring.

2

Other City of Boston Neighbor- hoods

Charlestown

Bunker Hill Monument and Charlestown, 1923.

Charlestown, which sits on what was once called the Mishawum Peninsula, is best known as the site of the Revolutionary War's Battle of Bunker Hill of June 17, 1775. It is also Boston's oldest neighborhood, the first to be settled by English colonists—who arrived there from Wessagusset (see **Wessagusset Memorial Garden**) in 1629—in the territory now comprised by the city.

Charlestown was the Massachusetts Bay Colony's first capital. Puritan leader John Winthrop lived there for a few months in 1630 in the colony's "Great House"—the community meetinghouse (the foundation of which stands in **City Square Park**)—before moving the government seat across the Charles River to Boston. Until 1874 Charlestown was a distinct political entity, and a geographically large one. What are today **Everett**, Malden, Melrose, **Somerville**, Stoneham, and Woburn were all part of Charlestown, as were areas of Arlington,

Cambridge, and Medford (among other municipalities). The City of Boston agreed to Charlestown's request for annexation out of a desire to gain access to the town's extensive network of wharves.

Long a largely working-class, Irish-Catholic community with a reputation for insularity (and often caricatured as a place of hyperviolent criminality—as in the film *The Town*), Charlestown was a center of opposition to court-ordered desegregation of schools in the 1970s (see **South Boston Heights Academy**). Since the 1990s or so, it has become home to an affluent, gentrifying population. There is still a significant working-class component to the small neighborhood of approximately seventeen thousand inhabitants, but Charlestown today looks and feels very different than it did for most of the twentieth century.

2.1 Charlestown Navy Yard

CHARLESTOWN

Charlestown Navy Yard is part of the Boston National Historical Park (of the National Park Service) and home to the War of 1812–era warship *USS Constitution*. From 1800 to 1974, it was a working shipyard, producing more than two hundred military ships and repairing many more.

Long associated with nationalist wars, the Charlestown Navy Yard served humanity when, on March 28, 1847, the *Jamestown*, a 157-foot sloop, set off for Ireland. On board was humanitarian aid: more than eight thousand barrels of food, clothing, and other supplies for the people of famine-stricken County Cork. The voyage came about in part because a group of Boston businessmen had petitioned Congress to allow the ship to deliver aid to Ireland in the midst of the country's devastating famine.

During what is known as the potato famine (1845–52), Ireland lost about a quarter of its population—more than a million died of starvation and disease and another million emigrated, Boston and its environs being among the principal destinations. At the time, all of Ireland was a colony of the United Kingdom, a significant contributor to many of the famine's underlying causes and the huge death toll.

The *Jamestown* voyage represented a rare instance of Boston's abolitionist community and the city's merchants coming together for a common cause. Together they raised almost $36,000 to buy the provisions—this at a time when many Bostonians, including many "leading" citizens and much of the press, were quite hostile to the tens of thousands of destitute Irish arriving in the city during the famine years.

Today the Navy Yard has a museum dedicated largely to the early decades of the 1800s. It says nothing about the voyage of the *USS Jamestown*.

TO LEARN MORE

Fowler Jr., William M. "Sloop of War / Sloop of Peace: Robert Bennet Forbes and the USS Jamestown,'" *Proceedings of the Massachusetts Historical Society* 98 (1986): 49–59.

Cardinal O'Connell and Governor Cox at Charlestown Navy Yard, circa 1921–25.

Puleo, Stephen. *A City So Grand: The Rise of an American Metropolis, Boston 1850–1900*, Boston: Beacon Press, 2010.

TO GET THERE

Orange Line to Community College Station, 0.9 mile (eighteen-minute) walk.

Green or Orange Line to North Station, 1 mile (nineteen-minute) walk.

RELATED SITE

A monument that is part of the **BOSTON IRISH FAMINE MEMORIAL** (at Washington and School Streets, Downtown) commemorates the *Jamestown*.

2.2 City Square Park

City Square (North Washington and Chelsea Streets)

CHARLESTOWN

Anti-Nazi activists gathered in City Square on May 17, 1934, to protest the *Karlsruhe*, a battleship from Hitler's navy moored in the **Charlestown Navy Yard**. According to the *Daily Boston Globe* in its front-page report, "Clubs were freely used by the police"

Officers of the *Karlsruhe* with Germany's ambassador to the United States, Hans Luther, Charlestown Navy Yard, May 1934.

against the protestors, a "rioting throng of about 2000." In its article, *The Boston Herald* ran photos of protestors Belle Lewis and Alice Burke with the caption "Women Reds Dragged to Charlestown Police Station." The paper cheered a mounted police charge to break up the demonstration. By the end, "more than 150 policeman had arrested 21 communists," it reported, and "battered and bruised heads, bodies and legs were counted by scores."

The protestors opposed the "hospitality shown" to the German ship on an official visit, explained the *Globe*. Police responded to the gathering out of fear that the

crowd "might get out of control" given its proximity to the Charlestown Navy Yard, situated only a few hundred yards away. Although the police claimed to be trying to break up fights between those opposing the *Karlsruhe*'s presence and counterprotestors, all the arrestees were anti-Nazi activists.

The protestors probably numbered a few hundred—largely trade unionists, students, and Communist Party members. Also in attendance was a contingent of pro-Germany students from Harvard who announced their readiness to assist the police. The protestors had marched from the **North End**, their numbers swelled by rush-hour passengers disembarking from what was then the City Square elevated train station. The action reflected broader opposition to the *Karlsruhe*'s ten-day visit as Jewish community leaders from Greater Boston and what the newspapers characterized as "liberal organizations" had strongly objected to plans to welcome the ship.

Such objections illustrate how, despite Hitler's recent rise to power in January 1933, the Nazis' attacks against trade unionists and the political Left, and their virulent anti-Semitism, were already evident to many Greater Bostonians. Nonetheless, media coverage of the *Karlsruhe* and its sailors was typically fawning: The *Herald* gushed, "Each member of the ship has this common denominator—an impeccable appearance, a knowledge of English and a charming, old world courtesy. . . . They were, in short, a joy to the feminine heart, and made that poor fellow, the average American, seem a bit shabby by contrast."

State and society followed suit, holding various events welcoming Hitler's military. They included official visits to City Hall and the State House and a dinner and dance at Boylston Schul Verein—a *Jamaica Plain*–based German-American club—followed by a soccer game the next day. The culmination was a banquet the evening of the City Square protest; nearly a thousand people—among them local German Americans, representatives of the city and of several veterans' organizations—assembled at the *Back Bay*'s Copley Plaza Hotel to fete the *Karlsruhe* officers and sailors. Hanging above the posh gathering were the Nazi swastika,

the Stars and Stripes, and Germany's flag. According to the *Globe*, the speakers "talked of friendly relations between the two countries, defended Germany's economic program, attacked the world boycott against Germany, derided agitation against German-American societies, [and] gave stiff-armed Nazi salutes."

The protest took place in and around City Square Park, the location of the original "Great House"—the community meetinghouse (the foundation of which is visible) and the seat of government—of the Massachusetts Bay Colony, built in 1629. Across the street (3 City Square) the Charlestown Municipal Building still stands, which in 1934 housed the police station and into which the anti-Nazi protestors were violently dragged.

GETTING THERE

Orange Line to Community College Station, 0.6 mile (twelve-minute) walk.

Green or Orange Line to North Station, 0.8 mile (sixteen-minute) walk.

2.3 Charlestown High School football field

Medford Street (at Monument Street)

CHARLESTOWN

On September 28, 1979, Jamaica Plain High School's football team played at Charlestown High School. On the field for Jamaica Plain was fifteen-year-old Darryl Williams of *Roxbury*. While in the end zone, the black teenager was shot in the neck from 301 feet away, paralyzing him for life. Occurring in a neighborhood known for its antibusing mili-

84 Monument Street to the right, looking toward Bunker Hill Monument, with Charlestown High School football field behind, 2019.

tancy, the shooting intensified racial tensions in Boston.

Police charged Steven McGonagle, Joseph Nardone, and Patrick Doe, white teenagers from Charlestown, with the shooting. The three had a rifle at the time of the gunfire on the roof of 84 Monument Street, part of the Bunker Hill housing project, one of the first public housing developments in the United States (built in 1940). The teens claimed they were shooting at pigeons when a bullet went astray and struck Williams. McGonagle admitted to shooting the gun, and he and Nardone eventually pleaded guilty to assault and battery with a deadly weapon, having struck a deal since the Boston Police Department had evidence against them for other crimes. (The official version is that the shooting was not racially motivated.) They both received a sentence of ten years at the state prison in Concord (see **MCI-Concord**). Doe, tried as a juvenile, was not convicted.

Williams, who died in 2010, and his family struggled over his remaining years to meet the high costs of his medical care. The City of Boston did little to help. Despite his many hardships, Darryl Williams eventually received a bachelor's degree from Northeastern University. He also often served as a motivational speaker for young people throughout Greater Boston and emerged as a symbol of racial reconciliation. He forgave the teenagers responsible for his shooting, saying in 2003, "Hate is a useless emotion that takes up too much energy."

GETTING THERE

MBTA Orange Line to Community College Station, 0.7 (fifteen-minute) walk.

East Boston

The land area of what is today East Boston was originally composed of five islands—Noddle's, Hog's, Governor's, Bird, and Apple. Noddle's was the first settled by English colonists, in 1633, three years before Boston's Puritans claimed it. However, in the early 1800s, the island still had only eight residents.

Lovell Street near the intersection of Frankfort Street, East Boston, 1973. Homes later razed for the sake of Logan Airport.

This started to change in the 1830s when the East Boston Company began to develop the area, filling in land, building streets, and constructing houses. By 1837, one year after the City of Boston annexed the neighborhood, there were one thousand residents; by 1865, more than twenty thousand. In the late 1800s and early 1900s, East Boston grew dramatically as many immigrants—Irish, Russian Jews, and Italians—settled there.

Transportation infrastructure has long been central to East Boston's development. During the 1830s, for example, regular ferry service to and from the Boston waterfront began. In 1904 a subway tunnel connected the neighborhood to Downtown Boston. In the 1920s Logan Airport was founded. Such developments, however, have also helped to undermine the community; highway and tunnel construction, and massive airport expansion especially, have led to the destruction of streets and homes and compromised the area's quality of life.

Through much of the 1900s, East Boston was predominantly Italian. This changed in later decades as many Central and South American immigrants moved into the area. By the early 2000s, Latinos—of diverse national origins—made up the majority of East Boston's population.

In more recent years, developers, young professionals, and college students have set their sights on East Boston, helping to gentrify the neighborhood, particularly areas across from Boston's waterfront. This has driven up housing prices and driven out some working-class (largely Latino) residents.

2.4 Maverick Square

EAST BOSTON

Most Boston residents know little about Noddle's Island and its early owner, Samuel Maverick, for whom Maverick Square is named. Such ignorance is perhaps comforting. It turns out that Maverick was the first documented enslaver of Africans in the region. In 1638, some three years before Massachusetts became the first American colony

MAVERICK HOUSE, East Boston, Mass.

Lithograph, 1835.

to legalize slavery, Samuel Maverick bet that slavery would be profitable.

He "purchased" two women and a man from the captain of a **Salem**-based ship named *Desire*. John Josselyn, a seventeenth-century traveler and Maverick houseguest, alleged that his host ordered the enslaved man to mate with one of the two enslaved women regardless of her will because Maverick was "desirous to have a breed of Negroes." Josselyn recorded her ensuing pain as expressed in a "tune sang very loud and shrill."

The original building also spoke to another aspect of the country's founding: The house (which was located where the Lewis Mall, just southwest of the square, now stands) was fortified to fend off anticipated Indian attacks. And so it is that East Boston's best-known square is named after an individual who personifies his nation's original sins, the enslavement of Africans and the genocide of indigenous peoples.

Long after Maverick passed from the scene and Noddle's Island changed ownership, Boston's wealthy honored Maverick, naming a large hotel and a ferry ship after

him in the 1830s. It is unclear how and when the name Maverick Square came to be.

GETTING THERE

MBTA Blue Line to Maverick Station.

TO LEARN MORE

Warren, Wendy Anne. "'The Cause of Her Grief': The Rape of a Slave in Early New England," *Journal of American History* 93, no. 4 (2007): 1031–49.

NEARBY SITE

ALBERT EINSTEIN INSTITUTION, 36 Cottage Street. This organization, founded by Gene Sharp, one of the world's foremost scholars and writers on nonviolent activism, is housed here. The site was also his home until his death in 2018.

2.5 The East Boston Immigration Station/Navy Fuel Pier Airport Edge Buffer

Marginal Street at Jeffries Street,

EAST BOSTON

On May 3, 1932, eleven "hunger marchers" gathered at the East Boston Immigration Station, sometimes dubbed Boston's Ellis Island. Members of a much larger group that had marched to Boston from locations around Massachusetts to call for unemployment relief, they gathered in East Boston to protest the detention and threatened deportation of Edith Berkman, an organizer with the National Textile Workers Union. A Polish immigrant, Berkman had been arrested in **Lawrence**, where she was a key organizer in a textile workers strike in 1931 (see **Schaake's Block**), and ordered deported— reportedly for her membership in an organization with Communist connections. The station served as a detention site for recently arrived immigrants waiting for clearance (because their papers were not in order or because of disease) or for noncitizens deemed as threats to the established order.

The station's most famous detainee was probably Carlo "Charles" Ponzi, the swindler, who spent many years living in Boston. During World War II, it served as a prison for German and Italian soldiers captured at sea, and for German, Italian, and Japanese "enemy aliens," noncitizen residents of the United States.

Opened in 1920 and closed in 1954, the East Boston Immigration Station processed about twenty-three thousand immigrants, about 10 percent of the immigrant arrivals through the port of Boston during that time span. Massport, which eventually acquired the site, tore down the station in 2011 after it deemed the building unsalvageable.

Although the actual site where the Immigration Station stood is inaccessible to the public, one can view it from a small Massport park on the waterfront. The poorly named Navy Fuel Pier Airport Edge Buffer has interpretive panels about the Immigration Station. Looking north, the building stood across from the park, jutting out in the water.

GETTING THERE

Blue Line to Maverick Station, 0.7 mile (fourteen-minute) walk

NEARBY SITE

THE IMMIGRANTS HOME, established in 1881 and rebuilt in 1912, was a refuge for recently arrived European immigrants and was run by the Women's Home Missionary Society of the Methodist Episcopal Church. It is now senior citizen housing. 72 Marginal Street.

TO LEARN MORE

Massport. *The East Boston Immigration Station: A History*, Boston: Massport, 2012.

2.6 Boston Logan International Airport

EAST BOSTON

Traffic came to a standstill at Logan Airport on Friday evening, May 16, 1969, when a motorcade of twenty-three cars deliberately drove five miles per hour in order to tie up traffic. Organized by the East Boston Neighborhood Council, it was one of a series of protests aimed at disrupting business as usual at Logan. Chief among the community's concerns were noise and air pollution associated with the airport—in 1973, for example, aircraft at Logan emitted an average of eighty-four thousand pounds of contaminants each day—dangerous vehicular traffic to and from Logan passing through East Boston's streets, and the airport's seemingly endless growth.

East Boston was especially hard hit by Boston's growing transportation infrastructure in the twentieth century. Between 1934 and 1974, a combination of access roads for tunnels connecting the neighborhood to *Downtown*, the extension of the MBTA Blue Line, a new state highway, and the expansion of Logan cost East Boston a thousand units of housing and seventy acres of public park space. This disruption, coupled with a bureaucracy (in the form of the Massachusetts Port Authority, or Massport) seen as unresponsive to community concerns and the relatively elite composition of the airport's clientele, triggered resentment toward the airport by East Boston's largely working-class and, at the time, mostly Italian-descended residents.

Police arrest Earth Day protestors at Logan, April 22, 1970.

The May 16, 1969, protest included the participation of a multiracial group of residents from *Cambridge*, *Jamaica Plain*, *Mattapan*, *Roxbury*, and the *South End*. All were members of the Greater Boston Committee on the Transportation Crisis, an alliance of community-based groups fighting the proposed Southwest Expressway (see *Southwest Corridor Park*), in addition to airport expansion.

Today Logan is one of the twenty busiest airports in the United States. It occupies about two-thirds of East Boston's total land area, 2,384 acres, the result of large-scale land-making projects, much of it involving joining together former islands.

In addition to improving its communication with East Boston residents, Massport has made efforts in recent years to "green" the airport and to reduce carbon emissions associated with aircraft by making flights more efficient (increasing the percentage of seats occupied on flights, for example). Still, Logan's harmful environmental impact is enormous. With almost 41 million passengers and 424,024 aircraft takeoffs and landings in 2018, flights out of Logan are responsible for millions of metric tons of carbon dioxide emissions each year, more than a number of the world's lowest-income countries, such as Haiti and Niger.

Residents living in the vicinity of the airport pay many of the costs associated with Logan's airborne pollutants. According to a 2014 study by the Massachusetts Executive Office of Health and Human Services, children living nearby are two to four times likelier to have probable asthma than those living farther away. Similarly, adults who have resided in neighboring communities for three or more years are almost twice as likely as others to experience chronic obstructive pulmonary disease.

GETTING THERE

Silver Line bus (SL1 from South Station) to Logan Airport. Also, Blue Line to Airport Station; from there, take a free Massport shuttle to Logan.

TO LEARN MORE

Nelkin, Dorothy. *Jetport: The Boston Airport Controversy*, New Brunswick, NJ: Transaction Books, 1974.

2.7 Lewis Family Home
18 Clipper Ship Lane

EAST BOSTON

On the evening of August 25, 1975, a gang of white teenagers gathered outside the apartment of Annie Mae Lewis in a new public housing development. In a context of rising racial tensions related to the court-ordered desegregation of the Boston public school system (see **South Boston Heights Academy**), the teens hurled rocks and bottles at the home of Ms. Lewis and her five children, one of the few African American families living in the development, and threw a Molotov cocktail into their yard. When the police arrived on the scene, instead of dispersing the teens, they ordered Ms. Lewis to make the members of an organization called People Against Racism, who had responded to her call to protect the apartment, leave, arguing that they were agitating the crowd. When she refused to do so, the police arrested Ms. Lewis.

Soon thereafter the Lewis family, one of many African American families in public housing in East Boston similarly attacked, left their longtime neighborhood and moved into the **Villa Victoria** development in the South End. The incident precipitating the family's departure was part of a process of ethno-racial cleansing that took place in a number of white-majority, but slowly desegregating, public housing developments in Boston during the early years of busing. In East Boston's Maverick Gardens and Orient Heights projects, for example, there were 164 black residents in the 1970s; by 1980 the number was 48. In South Boston's Old

Colony and Old Harbor (now Mary Ellen McCormack) projects, the number of African Americans fell from 155 to zero during the decade.

Today the Heritage Apartments complex (as it is now called) is an ethnically and racially diverse community.

GETTING THERE

Blue Line to Maverick Station. From the exit at the station's southern end, about five hundred feet.

2.8 Neptune Road Edge Buffer Park
Neptune Road (between Frankfurt and Bennington Streets)

EAST BOSTON

On Friday, July 17, 2015, East Boston community members and officials from the Massachusetts Port Authority (Massport) gathered for a ribbon-cutting ceremony to dedicate and open Neptune Road Edge Buffer Park. The 1.7-acre parcel commemorates the vibrant neighborhood of sixty-six houses lost to the expansion of Logan Airport while celebrating—in a series of interpretative panels—the community-based struggle to save it.

In the mid-1960s Massport first bulldozed Wood Island Park, a forty-six-acre park designed by Frederick Law Olmsted located at the end of Neptune Road. Soon thereafter—and following a lengthy court case—Massport evicted eight families from homes on the street that the agency deemed too close to the flight path. The agency destroyed almost all the remaining houses

Original caption: "Children play ball in front of their homes on Neptune Road. Logan Airport is at the end of the street. Many of the children's parents are involved in continuing efforts to halt expansion of the airport."

Airplane coming in for a landing over Neptune Road homes, 1973.

on Neptune Road and many on nearby streets over the next several years.

In the early 1970s, there were about four hundred people living in the largely blue-collar, Italian-American neighborhood, mostly in triple-deckers. Neptune Road was a tree-lined thoroughfare so full of street life that the *Boston Globe* characterized it as a "miniature Commonwealth Avenue." By that time, however, the street and the larger neighborhood were also grappling with major air and noise pollution as they fell victim to urban renewal and their location

in the midst of expanding transportation infrastructure. (The construction of the East Boston Expressway and the MBTA's Blue Line had detrimentally impacted the neighborhood in previous decades.)

In 2007 Massport bought the last remaining house on Neptune Road (no. 18) and razed it. The footprint of the house (and of one on the park's Frankfurt Street side) is marked with cobblestones where it once stood.

GETTING THERE

Blue Line to Wood Island Station. Take the Bennington Street exit. The park is on the left. The East Boston Greenway (for cyclists and pedestrians) passes close by.

NEARBY SITE

TEMPLE OHABEI SHALOM CEMETERY was the first legally established (1844) Jewish cemetery in Massachusetts. 147 Wordsworth Street (about 0.6 miles away).

2.9 Suffolk Downs

525 McClellan Highway

EAST BOSTON

Weekday evenings in fall 2013 brought East Boston parishioners to Our Saviour's Lutheran Church, not for worship but for organizing. The congregation, consisting mostly of recent Central American immigrants, focused its attention on an East Boston referendum concerning the proposed conversion of the Suffolk Downs race track into a casino.

Rally against proposed casino, October 2013. East Boston.

The broad coalition had some unexpected members, including defectors from the political machine of longtime mayor and casino champion Thomas Menino. On the other side, Suffolk Downs' owners "donated generously" to local charities. In the end, with the pro-casino camp spending $2 million and "No Eastie Casino" some $40,000, the latter won a convincing referendum victory, receiving 4,281 votes to the proponents' 3,353.

Although many parishioners could not vote in the referendum because they lacked US citizenship, they canvassed their neighbors who could.

Early concerns about the proposed casino were wide-ranging—concerns about law and order and the casino's impact on the moral climate and the environment. Residents' immediate objections focused on the likely gentrification of the neighborhood, casino-related land uses, and the anticipated tourist traffic. These were seen as leading to higher rents and more competition for community spaces. Our Saviour's parishioners turned to other congregations for allies, among them several Evangelical Christian churches and a predominantly Somali and Muslim congregation led by an Egyptian-born imam, and to Central American governments' local consular staff. The congregations also reached out to more established Italian-American residents who were organizing opposition as well. Soon a campaign called "No Eastie Casino" was born.

In rejecting the casino, the residents considered alternative uses for the former track, including a mixed-use development with affordable housing and retail enterprises. However, no funding sources materialized to realize the community's ambitions.

In March 2017, the HYM Investment Group, a Boston-based real estate company, acquired the land, promising stakeholder consultations, increased community connections, and effective use of the two adjacent subway stops. The community impact of the anticipated large-scale development—plans include the construction of 10,000 condominiums and offices employing 25,000 workers—remains unclear at the time of writing.

GETTING THERE

Blue Line to Suffolk Downs Station.

South Boston

West Broadway, South Boston, 1941.

For many outside of the city, South Boston is often a stand-in for Boston as a whole. Evoking images of working-class toughs of Irish descent suspicious of and hostile to outsiders, Southie (as it is known) is tied to stereotypes, perhaps more so than any other City of Boston neighborhood.

Originally part of the town of *Dorchester*, most of what is today South Boston was known as Dorchester Neck or Great Neck. For many decades following English settlement, the Neck was largely used for the grazing of cows. At the time of the Revolutionary War, there were only twelve families living there. In 1803 some of the individuals involved with Mount Vernon Proprietors, real estate speculators who had developed *Beacon Hill*, began buying land on the Neck. Soon thereafter they petitioned the Town

of Boston to annex the area, arguing that it would allow an increasingly crowded Boston to grow. In March 1804, Boston voted to do as the wealthy investors asked, despite strong opposition from *Dorchester*. While Dorchester received no compensation, the land speculators profited greatly.

South Boston's population exploded in the context of Irish immigration in the mid-1800s. Historically mostly working class, the neighborhood has also always been characterized by significant inequality with middle- and upper-middle class households in the Dorchester Heights and City Point areas. The epicenter of militant (and sometimes violent) white opposition to court-ordered busing in order to desegregate the city's public school system in the 1970s, South Boston has changed radically in recent decades due to gentrification. The area now known as the Seaport District has been especially hard hit by development for the affluent. Largely because it has numerous public housing projects, South Boston today—markedly more racially diverse—retains a significant working-class population.

2.10 L Street Bathhouse/BCYF Curley Community Center

William Day Boulevard at L Street

SOUTH BOSTON

In 1860 the Boston City Council appointed a committee to investigate public health, with a focus on immigrant communities. The major impetus was the large influx of impoverished immigrants from Ireland beginning in the mid-1840s and the lack of sufficient sanitary facilities in their homes. The special committee recommended the construction of a bathhouse, arguing that, in addition to public health benefits, it would provide the

poor "an inducement to self-respect and refinement" and an "elevator in the scale of society."

While the outbreak of the Civil War delayed action on the recommendation, the City Council took up the idea again shortly before the war's end and decided to build six bathhouses across the city. They were constructed in neighborhoods identified as rife with personal hygiene problems and disease.

In mid-1865, the L Street Bathhouse (along with the other five) opened. Offering hot showers and a towel for one penny, the bathhouse proved to be wildly popular—this in a neighborhood where most working-class homes had running water, but few had bathtubs, and almost none had hot water. It was so popular that the City had to build a new, larger facility in 1901. Yet it was also a time when homes in the neighborhood were increasingly being fitted with toilets, bathtubs, and modern plumbing. This eventually

L Street Bathhouse, circa 1917–34.

diminished the need of L Street for bathing and coincided with growing emphasis on its use for physical fitness and recreation.

The current structure, a quarter-mile long, and built during the Depression (1931) under the mayoralty of James Michael Curley, is now called the BCYF Curley Community Center. Primarily a fitness center, it also has programs for active senior citizens and a teen center. It remains the home of the L Street Brownies, famous for their annual New Year's Day swim in the frigid waters of *Boston Harbor*.

GETTING THERE

Red Line to Andrew Station, 1.2 mile (about a twenty-five-minute) walk. An MBTA bus also passes by.

TO LEARN MORE

O'Connor, Thomas H. *South Boston, My Home Town: The History of an Ethnic Neighborhood*, Boston: Quinlan Press, 1988.

2.11 Police Station 6/ Patriot Homes

273 D Street

SOUTH BOSTON

On September 9, 1919, 1,134 Boston police officers—of a total force of 1,544—voted for an immediate strike (only two cast ballots in opposition). The vote was a response to the firing of 19 officers by Boston's police commissioner, Edward Curtis, for organizing a union, one that would be affiliated with the American Federation of Labor.

Large crowds soon gathered outside of police stations in many areas of the city. Some

were there in solidarity with the strikers, while many assembled to voice their anger toward officers whom they saw as abusive and who no longer enjoyed the protection of the badge. In numerous neighborhoods, widespread vandalism and looting occurred, and random passersby were attacked.

South Boston was especially tense, with thousands of people rioting on West Broadway on the strike's first night. When, the following evening (September 10), rioters began pelting National Guardsmen with stones and mud, reinforcements—in the form of the Tenth Regiment's Company G—from Police Station 6 were called. Marching in formation with bayonets drawn and riot guns, the guardsmen formed a line across West Broadway near E Street. With the rioters taunting the soldiers and showering projectiles upon them, they opened fired on the crowd, killing two—sixteen-year-old Robert Sheehan, shot in the back, and Robert Lallie, twenty-one. Several others were wounded.

The next day, the labor stoppage was effectively over—and the threat of a great citywide strike forestalled—with Massachusetts guardsmen deployed across the city and in control, and negotiations between labor leaders and Boston's mayor, Andrew Peters, seemingly making great progress. Governor Calvin Coolidge, however, undercut the mayor by seizing control of Boston's police department and firing all those who had gone on strike.

The effects of the strike and the blow to organized labor would live on for years, not least in terms of the class and communal antagonisms that underlay the labor action. The strike displayed the deep socioeconomic

Faneuil Hall. Headquarters of National Guard during police strike, 1919.

Today Boston's police officers receive solidly middle-class salaries, with many receiving much higher ones. In 1965 they voted to unionize. But like police unions across the country, diverse perspectives among the rank and file notwithstanding, the Boston Police Patrolmen's Association generally champions right-wing politics, opposes efforts aimed at police reform and accountability, and displays little solidarity with the interests of working-class people.

inequities that characterized Boston—and the United States as a whole (the year 1919 saw a fifth of the country's workforce go on strike). It also spoke to the sharp divide between the city's and state's Protestant elite—Calvin Coolidge, the mayor, the police chief and many of the commanders of national guard units were members of long-standing Yankee, upper-class families—and Boston's largely Irish Catholic working class.

These inequities were manifest in the working condition of Boston's police officers. They worked between seventy-three and ninety-eight hours per week, receiving a rest day only every fifteen days, and were required to buy their own uniforms and equipment (a cost of more than $200). They did not receive a raise between 1898 and 1913, a period during which Boston's cost of living doubled; it increased another 79 percent by 1918. Patrolmen's annual wages in 1919 ranged from only $821.25 to $1400 (about $20,000 in 2018) for those with at least six years on the force.

The Division 6 station on D Street opened in 1915 and remained in operation until 1981, when it relocated to a new building on West Broadway. In 2015 the South Boston Neighborhood Development Corporation, as part of its effort to protect housing for low- and moderate-income persons in the rapidly gentrifying neighborhood, refurbished the D Street building and opened Patriot Homes, a twenty-five-unit development for military veterans and their families.

GETTING THERE

MBTA Red Line to Broadway Station.

TO LEARN MORE

O'Connor, Thomas H. *South Boston, My Home Town: The History of an Ethnic Neighborhood*, Boston : Quinlan Press, 1988.

Russell, Francis. *A City in Terror: Calvin Coolidge and the 1919 Boston Police Strike*, Boston: Beacon Press, 2005 (1975).

South Boston High School and Dorchester Heights, circa 1974.

2.12 South Boston High School/Excel High School

95 G Street

SOUTH BOSTON

An estimated crowd of two thousand cheered as Frances Sweeney was escorted out of South Boston High School's auditorium on Sunday evening, March 15, 1942. Sweeney, the head of the American Irish Defense Association, an antifascist organization supportive of President Franklin Delano Roosevelt's foreign policy and US efforts during World War II, was there in opposition to one of the gathering's principal speakers, the Reverend Edward Lodge Curran, an anti-Semitic Catholic priest known as the "Father Coughlin of the East."

The gathering was part of Boston's "Evacuation Day" commemoration, a set of events funded by the city's government. An official holiday in Massachusetts from 1941 to 2010, it memorializes the March 17, 1776 withdrawal of British troops from the city, in response to the amassing of powerful cannons by George Washington's forces on a series of hills known as Dorchester Heights on March 4. The British evacuation ended the siege of Boston and marked the first victory of Washington's forces during the Revolutionary War.

Sweeney's presence at South Boston High School, on Dorchester Heights, for the 1942 Evacuation Day ceremony speaks to the support for civil rights, and opposition to anti-Semitism, among many Irish Catholics at the time. Her expulsion, however, also speaks to the extensive support (active and passive) of many in the Irish community for anti-Semitic causes.

Boston was reputed to have the country's largest concentration of members of Coughlin's Christian Front, an organization that claimed Jews were plotting to take over the world. In 1938 its newspaper (which the Boston archdiocese allowed to be sold outside of Catholic churches), *Social Justice*, reprinted the *Protocols of the Elders of Zion*, a fabricated anti-Semitic text that is supposedly a Jewish plan for global domination. The front's strongest supporters tended to be Irish American. Boston's chapter, led by Francis Moran, who argued that Jewish bankers were responsible for enticing the United States into the war, met regularly at Hibernian Hall, located in the Irish section of *Roxbury*.

The 1930s and 1940s was a time of significant anti-Semitism in cities like Boston and New York. There were numerous violent attacks against Jews and Jewish-owned establishments by gangs of young men from largely Irish neighborhoods that bordered Jewish ones in **Dorchester**, **Mattapan**, and **Roxbury**. Frances Sweeney vociferously blamed the political leadership of the city, state, and the Catholic Church for their silence in the face of the violence.

A combination of factors—growing awareness of the Nazi-perpetrated Holocaust, an improved economic climate, the emigration to the suburbs of many Boston Jews, and the replacement of William O'Connell as cardinal of the Boston archdiocese by the liberal Richard Cushing—contributed to a marked decrease in overt anti-Semitism in Boston in the years following the war.

South Boston High School, an epicenter of often violent antibusing protests during the mid-1970s, is now known as Excel High School.

GETTING THERE

Red Line to Broadway Station, 1 mile (twenty-minute) walk.

NEARBY SITE

DORCHESTER HEIGHTS PARK AND MONUMENT, part of the Boston National Historical Park, located directly behind the high school, has beautiful views of the city.

TO LEARN MORE

Norwood, Stephen H. "Marauding Youth and the Christian Front: Antisemitic Violence in Boston and New York During World War II," *American Jewish History* 91, no. 2 (2003): 233–67.

Hentoff, Nate. *Boston Boy: Growing up with Jazz and Other Rebellious Passions*, Philadelphia: Paul Dry Books, 2001.

O'Connor, Thomas H. *South Boston, My Home Town: The History of an Ethnic Neighborhood*, Boston : Quinlan Press, 1988.

2.13 South Boston District Courthouse

535 East Broadway

SOUTH BOSTON

Formally known today as South Boston Division, Boston Municipal Courthouse, the building occupies the site where the Perkins Institution and Massachusetts School for the Blind stood from 1839 to 1912, as indicated by a prominent stone marker in front. The first school for blind students in the United States, its most famous student was Helen Keller. Anne Sullivan, her teacher, first brought Helen to Boston in May 1888, when she was just shy of eight years old. Each winter, through that of 1891–92, the pair returned to South Boston so Helen could continue her studies.

When the school was torn down (now known as the Perkins School for the Blind, it moved to and remains in Watertown, a small city about eight miles west of Boston), it was eventually replaced by what was originally called the South Boston Municipal Building. It is this building that now serves as the courthouse.

It was there, at 9:00 a.m. on Thursday, March 31, 1966, that eleven, conservatively dressed members, women and men, of the Boston chapter of the Committee for Non-

Violent Action (CNVA), a national pacifist organization, ascended the steps outside the building. Four of the men then proceeded to burn their draft cards.

As the group of anti–Vietnam War activists had publicized their plans, a crowd of a few hundred people, mostly high school students from South Boston, had

Draft card burning, March 31, 1966, South Boston Municipal Building.

gathered in anticipation of the action. As it unfolded, members of the crowd began voicing their hostility, eventually yelling "Shoot them" and "Kill them." In this context, a group of about seventy-five high school boys rushed the courthouse steps and attacked the pacifists, knocking them down and kicking and punching them in their heads and bodies as they tried to flee into the building.

When the police finally arrived, they broke up the crowd but arrested no one. While a woman inside the courthouse apologized to the activists on behalf of South Boston, saying that the attackers were not representative of the community, one of the police officers outside expressed a very different sentiment: "Anyone foolish enough to commit such an unpatriotic gesture in South Boston can only expect what these people got."

Two weeks later, a grand jury in Boston's US District Court indicted the four draft-card burners—David Benson, David O'Brien, John Phillips, and David Reed—

charging them with breaking the federal prohibition (instituted in 1965) against draft-card burning. (A fifth CNVA member, Gary Hicks, who was present at the South Boston courthouse action, was indicted a little later for burning his draft card in April.) All of them were found guilty, receiving sentences ranging from two to five years, and served time in prison. David O'Brien, however, was released after two months when he appealed his conviction.

O'Brien's case eventually went all the way to the US Supreme Court. In *United States v. O'Brien* (1968), the court ruled that a criminal prohibition against burning a draft card was not a violation of free speech rights. Nonetheless, the burning and destruction of draft cards, after a brief hiatus, continued and greatly expanded as domestic opposition to the war in Vietnam intensified. The work of Boston's CNVA played a key role in this opposition.

That a nonviolent antiwar action took place on the site where Helen Keller had

Every modern war has had its root in exploitation. The Civil War was fought to decide whether . . . slaveholders of the South or the capitalists of the North should exploit the West. The Spanish-American War decided that the United States should exploit Cuba and the Philippines. The South African War decided that the British should exploit the diamond mines. The Russo-Japanese War decided that Japan should exploit Korea. The present war [World War I] is to decide who shall exploit the Balkans, Turkey, Persia, Egypt, India, China, Africa. And we are whetting our sword to scare the victors into sharing the spoils with us. Now, the workers are not interested in the spoils; they will not get any of them anyway.

. . .

Strike against all ordinances and laws and institutions that continue the slaughter of peace and the butcheries of war. Strike against war, for without you no battles can be fought. Strike against manufacturing shrapnel and gas bombs and all other tools of murder. Strike against preparedness that means death and misery to millions of human beings. Be not dumb, obedient slaves in an army of destruction. Be heroes in an army of construction.

—Helen Keller, from "Strike against War," a speech given in New York City on January 5, 1916

studied was coincidental. Still, there is little doubt that Keller would have supported it. She was an outspoken radical activist—a member of the Socialist Party and the Industrial Workers of the World (aka the Wobblies), for example. She championed women's suffrage, the rights of workers,

socialism, and pacifism. Whether or not the CNVA activists knew it in 1966, her spirit was within them.

GETTING THERE

Red Line to Broadway Station, 0.9 mile (eighteen-minute) walk.

NEARBY SITE

SOUTH BOSTON HIGH SCHOOL, 95 G Street.

TO LEARN MORE

Foley, Michael S. *Confronting the War Machine: Draft Resistance during the Vietnam War*, Chapel Hill: University of North Carolina Press, 2003.
Website of the Perkins History Museum, Perkins School for the Blind.

2.14 South Boston Heights Academy

486 East Third Street

SOUTH BOSTON

What is popularly known as busing, or forced busing, was a federal-court-ordered program initiated in September 1974 to desegregate the Boston Public Schools. Long a central concern of Boston's African American community, its allies and civil rights activists, the school system was characterized by dozens of racially imbalanced schools, segregation that the Commonwealth of Massachusetts ordered the city's school committee to remedy. In the face of the Boston School Committee's refusal, the federal courts stepped in, with Judge Arthur Garrity mandating a program that bused students between largely white and black schools to achieve integration. While

Police-escorted school buses on the first day of court-ordered busing, South Boston, 1975.

Schoolchildren arrive with police escort at South Boston High School, 1974.

a great majority of white people in Boston opposed the desegregation program, they did so for numerous, often overlapping, reasons. In addition to racism, opposition was fueled by economic class divides, urban-suburban tensions, and loyalties to turf and neighborhood schools. Opposition was often militant, and sometimes violent, but took various forms.

One expression was South Boston Heights Academy. South Boston community members opened it in 1975 to provide an alternative educational venue for neighbor-

hood children boycotting the Boston public school system to protest desegregation and busing. The South Boston Information Center, the propaganda arm of the antibusing group ROAR (Restore Our Alienated Rights), helped to spearhead the effort.

Harkening back to freedom schools set up in the Jim Crow South during the civil rights movement, many people, typically supporters, referred to South Boston Heights Academy as a "white freedom school." Critics often dubbed it a segregation school. When the school first opened, it enrolled 576 students. It closed down in the mid- to late-1980s.

Previously the building had served as the home of the Choate Burnham Elementary School, a public school named after a prominent South Boston coal and wood merchant who served on the Boston School Committee (1891–92). It now houses condominiums.

GETTING THERE

Red Line to Broadway Station, 1 mile (twenty-minute) walk.

TO LEARN MORE

Formisano, Ronald. *Boston against Busing: Race, Class, and Ethnicity in the 1960s and 1970s*, Chapel Hill: University of North Carolina Press, 1991.

2.15 Carson Beach

William A. Day Boulevard

SOUTH BOSTON

When court-ordered desegregation and busing began in the City of Boston in 1974, South Boston's population was 98 percent white. Still, in terms of public facilities along the South Boston waterfront, small numbers of African Americans did frequent them, reportedly without incident. This changed as school desegregation caused racial tensions to skyrocket. Carson Beach emerged as an epicenter.

On July 27, 1975, a group of white youths attacked six African American men, Bible salesmen from out of state who were visiting Boston, sending one to the hospital. While African Americans saw the incident as further proof of the deep racial segregation and associated forms of violence that prevented black residents from accessing large swaths of the city, many in South Boston characterized it an example of black trouble-making, with some alleging that the men had invited the attack by assaulting a white youth with a baseball bat. Others implied that the men had come to Carson Beach to cause political trouble. James Kelly from the South Boston Information Center, an antibusing group, for example, said, "We've always welcomed good colored people to South Boston, but we will not tolerate radical blacks or communists."

On August 10, members of the black community organized a "wade-in" at Carson Beach to assert their right

State troopers and police officers form a human wall during a demonstration at Carson Beach, August 10, 1975.

to the space. Despite a strong police presence and efforts by some in the South Boston community to defuse tensions by organizing a "Southie Pride Day" elsewhere in the neighborhood, violence erupted—with some accusing ultra-leftist groups (particularly the Progressive Labor Party) of helping to provoke white protestors. In the aftermath, retaliatory attacks by black youth against whites in various parts of the city escalated.

Groups of black women and white women separated by Boston police taunt one another in the water at Carson Beach, July 24, 1977.

In the summer of 1977, scores of African American and Latino residents of the nearby **Columbia Point Housing Project** asserted their rights to access Carson Beach by assembling there on occasion. Skirmishes sometimes broke out, but intervention by the police prevented matters from getting worse.

Today Carson Beach is a racially integrated space.

GETTING THERE

Red Line to JFK/UMass Station, 0.5 mile (twelve-minute) walk.

TO LEARN MORE

O'Connor, Thomas H. *South Boston, My Home Town: The History of an Ethnic Neighborhood*, Boston: Quinlan Press, 1988.

Taylor, Steven J. L. *Desegregation in Boston and Buffalo: The Influence of Local Leaders*, Albany: State University of New York Press, 1998.

2.16 South Boston Residents for Peace/Tony Flaherty Home

524 East Broadway

SOUTH BOSTON

The annual Saint Patrick's Day parade in South Boston has long involved controversy. During the 1970s, it included antibusing protests. In subsequent decades it became noteworthy because parade organizers refused to allow gay contingents to participate (a ban not lifted until 2015, when they allowed Out-Vets, a group of LBGTQ military veterans, and Boston Pride, a gay rights organization, to march).

During the 2016, 2017, and 2018 parades, the antiwar group Veterans for Peace held

Veterans for Peace, Saint Patrick's Day vigil, 2018.

silent vigils at 524 East Broadway, the former home of Tony Flaherty. Flaherty, a career Navy veteran, returned from the Vietnam War, as a writer explained in *The Boston Globe*, "a changed man": "One day, he was walking down a dirt road, as a gaggle of Vietnamese kids straggled by, fleeing a village destroyed by American fire." Flaherty, who was born and raised in South Boston, told the journalist, "One of the kids, a boy, had lost a leg. . . . I had an epiphany that day."

After battling posttraumatic stress disorder and alcoholism, Flaherty worked for a program helping vets with housing and substance abuse. He later joined Veterans for Peace; he also played a leading role in the establishment and work of South Boston Residents for Peace, an organization founded soon after the 2003 invasion of Iraq under G. W. Bush's presidency. Flaherty and his fellow Veterans for Peace asked to march in the annual parade, but the organizers, many of them also veterans, denied them—and have continued to do so in recent years.

The vigils began the year after Flaherty passed away in 2015. They commemorate Tony's dedication to peace and social justice activism and serve as a protest of the ongoing ban on antiwar veterans. In recent years many US soldiers marching in the parade have broken ranks to shake hands with the veterans holding the vigil.

GETTING THERE

Red Line to Broadway Station. Tony Flaherty's former home is 0.9 miles away (about an eighteen-minute walk).

2.17 Seaport Common

85 Northern Avenue

SEAPORT

Formally part of South Boston, what is today called the Seaport District has been effectively excised from the larger neighborhood. Until the 1990s, it was mainly an area of parking lots, rotting wharfs, and rundown warehouses. The administration of Mayor Thomas Menino (1993–2014) undertook its redevelopment, turning it into a space dominated by real estate developers and corporate capital, one of office buildings, high-end restaurants and hotels, and luxury residences. Despite Boston's chief planner, in 2000, touting the envisioned neighborhood as one "for all Bostonians," the resulting area is the city's least inclusive. The Seaport is 89 percent white and has the highest household income—$133,000—of any of Boston's zip codes, according to a 2017 *Boston Globe* report.

Seaport Common, opened in 2016, is one of the rare public spaces in the neighborhood. However, it is a privately owned public space. Such spaces result from negotiations between public agencies and real estate developers—in the case of Seaport Common, the Boston Planning & Development Agency and WS Development—desiring zoning variances. Seaport Common hosts myriad activities—free yoga classes, concerts, exercise boot camps, and pop-up retail activities, for instance. While the "Common" is open to all, it is ultimately WS Development that determines what takes place in the less-than-one-acre space. In other words, what is a combination of manicured grass and a concrete plaza is not a common, but, like much of the "green" space in the Seaport (nearby Fan Pier, for instance), less-than-public space that furthers private interests.

Public investment has greatly facilitated these private interests. Billions of public dollars—by cleaning up the harbor, constructing a tunnel under the neighborhood, building a huge convention center and federal courthouse, and routing the MBTA's Silver Line through the area—have created an environment attractive to developers and an upper-class population.

The Seaport Common, like the neighborhood a whole, represents what geographer and urban planner Samuel Stein calls the real estate state—"a political formation in which real estate capital has inordinate influence over the shape of our cities, the parameters of our politics and the lives we lead." While private landowners have long shaped cities, what is new, argues Stein, is the level of power enjoyed by real estate interests.

For the most part, the Seaport is the result of land-making. Built on what used to be tidal marsh, the area is thus highly prone to flooding. The Common's "resilient" design notwithstanding, the overbuilt Seaport is the Boston neighborhood most vulnerable to climate change and associated rising sea levels and intensifying storms.

GETTING THERE

Silver Line from South Station to Courthouse Station, 0.1 mile (two-minute) walk.

TO LEARN MORE

Stein, Samuel. *Capital City: Gentrification and the Real Estate State*, New York: Verso, 2019.

Roxbury and Mission Hill

"Faces of Dudley" by Mike Womble and Mayor's Mural Crew, 1995, restored in 2015.

Roxbury is one of the Massachusetts Bay Colony's six original towns. Settled in 1630, it was an important center of trade and transportation for its first two centuries. Connected to the Shawmut Peninsula by a narrow strip (Boston Neck; today's Washington Street was the main thoroughfare), Roxbury served as the only land route to Boston. The area was also highly desirable to English colonists because of its fertile land, ample supply of timber and stone, as well as Stony Brook, an important water source.

In the early 1800s, Roxbury was largely home to middle- and upper-class Yankees, but that soon changed. Beginning in the mid-1800s, Roxbury's working-class population exploded with the influx of Irish immigrants, particularly in the Dudley Street and Mission Hill areas. In the late 1800s and early 1900s, it became an important center of Jewish life in Boston. In the first decades of the twentieth century, a black population also began to develop in Roxbury as people who had left *Beacon Hill*'s north side and gone to the *South End* moved there. With the arrival of black immigrants from the English-speaking Caribbean and, after World War II, a large inflow of blacks from the US South, and the departure of most whites from the neighborhood, by the 1960s the vast majority of Roxbury's residents were black.

Today Roxbury, a neighborhood of considerable diversity in class, race, and ethno-national origins, maintains its identity as the center of Boston's black community. Important activist organizations and cultural institutions are based there. Among the challenges faced by present-day Roxbury are pressures from university expansion on its periphery, growing student housing, and gentrification due to its proximity to wealthier areas.

Mission Hill—which, like *Jamaica Plain*, *Roslindale*, and *West Roxbury*, was once part of Roxbury—faces the same pressures, but even more intensely. Historically, the ethno-racially diverse neighborhood was largely working class. Mission Hill, less than one square mile in size, now has a large population of young adults, reflecting its importance as a residential area for students and professionals associated with nearby colleges and universities.

2.18 Saint Cyprian's Episcopal Church and Toussaint L'Ouverture Hall

1073 Tremont Street

ROXBURY

Recalling formative aspects of her youth, Ruth Batson, a key leader in the fight to desegregate Boston's public schools, stressed the importance of institutions emphasizing black pride and self-determination. Saint Cyprian's Episcopal Church was such an institution. Another was next door at Toussaint L'Ouverture Hall, named after a leader of the Haitian Revolution, where, in the 1930s and '40s, the local chapter of Marcus Garvey's Universal Negro Improvement Association met regularly. "At these meetings," Batson remembered, "I heard Africa for the Africans at home and abroad. And we heard racial issues constantly being discussed. And so, as I grew up, I was not swayed as much as some people I knew by this business of Boston being such a wonderful place. . . . I knew . . . there were flaws in the Cradle of Liberty."

Saint Cyprian's grew out of a West Indian immigration wave indirectly fostered by the **United Fruit Company** in the early twentieth century. Most immigrants were ticket-paying travelers aboard company vessels, while some were stowaways drawn from workers who loaded those ships.

Many West Indian immigrants to Boston found religious homes in existing African American churches. Others, depending on where they resided, sought to join largely white congregations elsewhere but were often treated disrespectfully and sometimes compelled to sit in segregated pews. In response, some West Indian Episcopalians started meeting in a private home on Northampton Street in the **South End**. With their numbers growing, they began using the building of a predominantly white congregation in 1920, only to discover that that the church would fumigate the facilities after the black Episcopalian service. Congregants thus raised funds to erect a church on Tremont Street in Lower Roxbury. Named after Saint Cyprian of Carthage (North Africa), the church—as did Toussaint

Saint Cyprian's Church, 2018.

L'Ouverture Hall (which closed by the 1950s, its precise relationship to Saint Cyprian's unclear)—symbolized their struggles and affirmed their African heritage.

From the time Saint Cyprian's opened in 1924 well into the 1950s, Lower Roxbury had many thriving small businesses and a large number of single-family homes. By the 1960s, the neighborhood followed the socioeconomic decline of Boston's working class and African American communities that accompanied the region's economic transformation.

In the early 1960s, Saint Cyprian's was active in efforts to desegregate Boston's public schools and served as one of the sites for "Freedom Schools" (see **Saint Mark's Social Center**). While the church remains a home to Boston's Caribbean and African American Episcopalians, in recent decades it has become increasingly physically isolated from the people it serves, in part because the City of Boston has supported Northeastern University's expansion into the area rather than championing community-focused investment.

GETTING THERE

Orange Line to Ruggles Station, 0.1 mile (two-minute) walk.

RELATED SITE

THE MUSEUM OF THE NATIONAL CENTER OF AFRO-AMERICAN ARTISTS (300 Walnut Avenue, Roxbury) was founded by Elma Lewis, a famed arts educator who, like Batson, was a first-generation Caribbean immigrant who attended Saint Cyprian's.

TO LEARN MORE

Shearer, Jackie, and Ruth Batson. "Interview with Ruth Batson," Eyes on the Prize interviews (1988): http://digital.wustl.edu/e/eii/eiiweb/bat5427.0911.011ruthbatson.html

Johnson, Violet Showers. *The Other Black Bostonians: West Indians in Boston, 1900–1950.* Bloomington: Indiana University, 2006.

2.19 Franklin Lynch Peoples' Free Health Center

Tremont Street at Ruggles Street

ROXBURY

Men in front of Franklin Lynch People's Free Health Center pointing to bullet holes after shots were fired at the trailer on the morning of July 5, 1970.

The Boston chapter of the Black Panther Party (BPP) opened the Franklin Lynch Peoples' Free Health Center on May 31, 1970. Building on civil-rights-era efforts to bring about community-based health care delivery, the Panthers insisted on "completely free" government-provided healthcare—both prevention and treatment—"FOR ALL BLACK AND OPPRESSED PEOPLE" (Article 6 of the BPP's "Ten Point Plan"). The BPP argued that poor health was linked to poverty, oppression, and unemployment, as well as to inadequate education and housing. In this

121

Black Panther Party rally, Post Office Square, Downtown, 1970.

sense, the clinic was part of a much broader agenda of political transformation, one that embodied a politics that merged Black Power and the New Left.

Established in May/June 1968 (many of its founders were Boston-born students at Northeastern University), the Boston branch was part of the national Black Panther Party, founded almost two years earlier in Oakland, California. While the Black Panthers originally focused on fighting police brutality, its activities were much broader, growing out of a politics oriented toward revolution, socialism, and Third World-ism.. The Boston chapter worked, for instance, in coalition with Students for a Democratic Society and local efforts to boycott grapes (efforts spurred by the work of the United Farm Workers), and was heavily involved in area efforts to end the US war in Vietnam.

Boston Panthers implemented various programs, including providing free breakfast to children, free clothing to those in need, and transportation to friends and family

members of incarcerated women and men to eastern Massachusetts prisons. The chapter also ran a community library. The clinic, and its public health program, however, was its most successful endeavor.

A trailer served as the clinic's home. It was situated on vacant land that the Panthers and the Black United Front had occupied to block the planned construction of a highway (see **Southwest Corridor Park**). It was land, the BPP stated, that "truly belongs to the people" and not appropriate for a major thoroughfare. "A highway cutting through the Black community will mean air pollution, increased accidents, housing shortages, and excessive noise," the party explained in its newspaper.

Medical professionals—black and white—volunteered at the clinic, as did many lay medical individuals, some of whom received training there in classes on first aid and the use of lab equipment. The clinic, which eventually offered twenty-four-hour service, provided checkups, immunizations, gynecological services, and pregnancy and blood tests. It also offered "people's advocates" and drivers to help those who needed to go to hospitals. On at least once occasion, a successful surgery—to repair the eyes of a fourteen-month-old girl—took place there. Perhaps the clinic's best-known effort was its program that sent volunteers to neighbor-hoods throughout Boston to conduct free tests for sickle cell anemia, a disease that disproportionately impacts people of sub-Saharan African descent.

The Franklin Lynch Peoples' Free Health Center closed down abruptly in July 1972, as did BPP chapters throughout the country, when the BPP's Central Committee ordered the closures and mandated that all Panthers consolidate in Oakland to work on electoral politics. Today the headquarters of the Boston Police Department sits on the clinic's site.

GETTING THERE

Orange Line to Ruggles Station, 0.1 mile (three-minute) walk.

TO LEARN MORE

Bassett, Mary T. "Beyond Berets: The Black Panthers as Health Activists," *American Journal of Public Health* 106, no. 10 (2016): 1741–43.

MacLaury, Duncan Howard. "Silent Guns, Blazing Rhetoric: A Narrative History of the Black Panther Party of Boston," honors thesis, Department of History, Tufts University, 2013.

MacLaury, Duncan, Judson L. Jeffries, and Sarah Nicklas. "The Black Panther Party and Community Development in Boston," in *The Black Panther Party in a City Near You*, ed. Judson L. Jeffries, Athens: University of Georgia Press, 2018, 89–136.

RELATED SITES

375 BLUE HILL AVENUE, Roxbury, is the original site of the Boston chapter's headquarters.

23 WINTHROP STREET, Roxbury, was the chapter's headquarters from February 21, 1970, until its

demise, a site shared with the Malcolm X Community Information Center.

740 TREMONT STREET, South End, formerly the Tremont Street Methodist Episcopal Church, was the site of the Panthers' breakfast program in its early stages.

81 PARKER STREET, Jamaica Plain, a public housing building in a basement of which the Panthers ran a free clothing program.

2.20 Saint Mark's Social Center

216 Townsend Street

ROXBURY

The year 1963 saw brutal violence perpetrated by authorities in Birmingham, Alabama, against youth peacefully protesting Jim Crow segregation. This helped to intensify efforts by Boston's black community and its allies to combat racial injustice. A central concern was the inadequate education received by children in the city's public schools, a problem that disproportionately impacted black students (who numbered approximately fourteen thousand). Chaired by Ruth Batson, the Public Committee of the Boston branch of the NAACP played a leading role in addressing the issue. On June 11, 1963, with the support of forty civil rights, labor, community, and religious groups, it made a presentation to the Boston School Committee on what it characterized as de facto segregation, an assessment the board dismissed.

The following day, Citizens for Human Rights, an entity led by civil rights activists the Reverend James Breeden, an Episcopal priest, and Noel Day, a social worker and director of Saint Mark's Social Center,

Outside Saint Mark's Social Center Freedom School, February 26, 1964.

When we fight about education, we're fighting for our lives. We're fighting for what that education will give us, we're fighting for a job, we're fighting to eat, we're fighting to pay our medical bills; we're fighting for a lot of things. So this is a total fight with us.

—**Ruth Batson**

announced a "Stay Out for Freedom" day on June 18. "Don't go to school," one flyer said. "Instead go to Saint Mark's Social Center . . . for a full day of education for freedom." Explaining the rationale, the flyer declared: "Our schools are segregated. Our schools are inferior. Our school board still hasn't acted to improve the situation."

Despite threats to fine or arrest parents who played a role in youth participation, the boycott—focused on junior high and high school students—went forward. On the appointed day, "Freedom Schools" took place at ten sites in *Dorchester*, Roxbury, and the *South End*, Saint Mark's Social Center among them. Focusing on African American and African history, civil rights, and non-violence, the biracial roster of speakers

included university professors, clergy, and Celtics star Bill Russell. Estimates of the number of participants who attended the "Freedom Schools" varied, ranging between two thousand and five thousand. A WGBH reporter described the showing as "an extraordinary demonstration for one organized within a few days largely by newer, younger leadership."

A second "Stay Out" day involving ten cities in the US "Deep North" unfolded in 1964, part of a national effort inspired by what had transpired in Boston. About 20 percent of Boston's more than ninety thousand students did not attend school on February 26, while around nine thousand youth, black and white, attended Freedom Schools across the city. Together with the first Stay Out day, it reflected and helped to build the organizing capacity of Boston's black community, while strengthening the foundation for efforts aimed at ending racial injustice.

In the mid-1960s, Saint Mark's Social Center and Saint Mark's Congregational Church (United Church of Christ) were torn down. On the same site, church members built a new Saint Mark's, which opened in 1969 and stands at 200 Townsend Street. To the right of the church, on the corner of Hazelwood Street, is where the Social Center stood.

GETTING THERE

MBTA buses pass close by.

TO LEARN MORE

Bundy, Lauren Tess. "'The Schools Are Killing Our Kids!': The African-American Fight for Self-Determination in the Boston Public Schools, 1949–1985, PhD diss., Department of History, University of Maryland, College Park, 2014.

Dunham, Audrea Jones. "Boston's 1963 Stay Out for Freedom: Black Revolt in the 'Deep North,'" WGBH Educational Foundation, 2014; available at http://openvault.wgbh.org/exhibits/boston_civil_rights/article

King, Mel. *Chain of Change: Struggles for Black Community Development*, Boston: South End Press, 1981.

2.21 Dudley Street Neighborhood Initiative

550 Dudley St

ROXBURY

In the 1980s the Dudley Street neighborhood had the lowest incomes in the city and faced disinvestment and many related challenges, including high unemployment, abandoned buildings, out-migration, insurance-related arson, and illegal dumping. In this context, local foundations and community organizations partnered to secure long-term funding for neighborhood development. They confronted an immediate challenge, however: None of the existing organizations spoke for more than a fraction of the diverse residents. To remedy this, they organized meetings to directly engage residents, but soon another

concern surfaced: "How many of you live in this neighborhood?" Che Maydun, an African American resident, asked the organizers. "You always have people from Downtown or somewhere else telling you what you need in your neighborhood."

That question came at the right time. Boston was in ferment: It had recently emerged from an insurgent mayoral campaign challenging the power structure. That had followed struggles over school segregation and campaigns demanding that the City investigate the murders of black women. Moreover, there was a vigorous campaign seeking Roxbury's secession from Boston. In that moment, Maydun's question proved to be a turning point, transforming what may have become a paternalistic exercise in philanthropy into a model for community empowerment. Any future development would be overseen by residents, albeit with outside support.

Today, the Dudley Street Neighborhood Initiative (DSNI) involves more than thirty-six hundred active neighborhood residents as members and has relationships with small businesses, religious institutions, community gardens (including greenhouses operated in collaboration with the Food Project), as well as service agencies. It serves 227 units of resident-owned housing on land that DSNI owns. Some twenty-four thousand residents live in the neighborhood, dubbed the "Dudley Village Campus"—a triangle of more than a thousand acres.

DSNI is a community land trust—a legal entity that owns the land with its residents designated as the beneficiaries of the ownership—

DSNI land on Dudley Street, with Food Project greenhouses in the background, 2017.

and, unique in the United States, it has eminent domain powers delegated to it by the City. This enables DNSI to seize abandoned properties and to make offers on properties within the triangle before they are offered on the open market. As a land trust, DSNI, which continues to expand, has removed housing from the commercial market while stabilizing residents' tenure in their homes, providing credit for critical upgrades and maintenance, and making affordable homes available to the community.

DSNI has a democratic structure: It is governed by a large, elected board in which all community residents have a voice, while also ensuring that all major population groups are equally represented. To further strengthen community involvement, DSNI actively fosters both leadership development and turnover. DSNI has inspired efforts to replicate its land trust model in other Boston neighborhoods.

GETTING THERE

Silver Line to Dudley Station, 1 mile (twenty-minute) walk. MBTA buses also pass close by.

TO LEARN MORE

Medoff, Peter, and Holly Sklar. *Streets of Hope: The Fall and Rise of an Urban Neighborhood*, Boston: South End Press, 1994.

2.22 Mission Main

Saint Alphonsus Street (between Horadan and McGreevey Ways)

MISSION HILL

The Massachusetts State Police received a desperate phone call a little after 8:30 p.m. on October 22, 1989. Charles Stuart reported that both he and his wife had been shot in Roxbury. Because Stuart did not know where he was, police asked him to drive around so he could determine his exact whereabouts. Although the wounded Stuart soon blacked out, police were able

Mission Main site, circa 1940.

height and build—police scoured the Mission Hill area, particularly the housing project, in the shooting's aftermath. Using stop-and-frisk tactics, the police targeted hundreds of young African American and Latino men in and around Mission Main, forcing many of them to drop their pants on the street, as they sought the culprit.

With escalating racial tensions across a city transfixed by the shooting and the hunt for the perpetrator, the police finally identified and arrested a suspect, Willie Bennett, a resident of Mission Main. Days later, Charles Stuart, who had been released from the hospital after six weeks, picked Bennett out of a police lineup.

Within a week, the case fell apart when one of Stuart's brothers came forward and revealed Charles to be the killer. Charles, it seems, was motivated largely by financial reasons and a desired end to a marriage (and future parenthood). With police closing in, Stuart drove to the Tobin Bridge on January 4, 1990, exited his car, and killed himself by plunging into the frigid river below.

The next evening, then-mayor Raymond Flynn, chauffeured under police escort to Mission Main, offered the City's regret to Pauline Bennett, Willie's mother. Before the arrest police had rushed with guns drawn into her apartment, terrorizing her and a young child. Flynn's gesture did little to satisfy

to locate him on the edge of the Mission Main public housing project in Mission Hill. They found his wife, Carol Stuart, who was seven months pregnant, close to death—she passed away after several hours. Their son, Christopher, born by cesarean section, died two-and-a-half weeks later.

The shooting had taken place soon after the Stuarts had left a childbirth class at the Brigham and Women's Hospital. It occurred at a time when many perceived the city to be crime-ridden, with murders and drug-related violence all too frequent. That the shooter had chosen a young, affluent couple from the suburb of Reading, who some in the media dubbed the "Camelot Couple," made the crime all the more sensational. Months later, it was revealed that Charles Stuart himself was the perpetrator of the crime.

With a description of the alleged shooter provided by Stuart—of a black man in his late twenties or early thirties of average the Bennett family: "The mayor came in and spent one hot second in my mother's home, and then flew out the door," stated Ronald Bennett, Willie's brother. "My mother offered him a chair to sit in, but he didn't want to sit down. . . . He acted like my mother's house wasn't good enough for him."

Thirty-eight three-story buildings constructed in 1940, the Mission Main housing project was racially segregated through at least the mid-1960s. According to testimony before the US Commission on Civil Rights in 1966, it was 97 percent white at the time, whereas the project across the street, Mission Extension, was 98 percent black. By the time of what some call the Charles Stuart case, a low point in race and police-community relations in Boston, the racial composition of Mission Main, the epicenter of the case, had changed radically. In the aftermath, nearby prosperous institutions—in the fields of art, education, and medicine—pressured the Boston Housing Authority (BHA) to renovate the development. The BHA did more than that, gradually tearing down the housing project where Mrs. Bennett lived in the 1990s and replacing it in 2002 with a new development, the Mission Main Apartments.

It was built and managed by a private developer (as part of the Hope VI program—see *Laura Ann Ewing home/Columbia Point Housing Project*) and today consists of 535 units, 83 percent of them public housing and 17 percent market-rate units.

In 1990 the family of Carol DiMaiti Stuart set up a foundation in her name to provide college scholarships to Mission Hill–area youth with the goal of promoting "better race relations throughout the city and greater Boston."

GETTING THERE

Longwood (Green Line, E), 0.1 mile (two-minute) walk.

TO LEARN MORE

Sharkey, Joe. *Deadly Greed: The Riveting True Story of the Stuart Murder Case that Rocked Boston and Shocked the Nation*, New York: Prentice Hall Press, 1991.

United States Commission on Civil Rights. *A Time to Listen . . . A Time to Act: Voices from the Ghettos of the Nation's Cities*, Washington, DC: US Government Printing Office, 1967.

Vale, Lawrence J. *From the Puritans to the Projects: Public Housing and Public Neighbors*, Cambridge: Harvard University Press, 2000.

Dorchester, Mattapan, and Hyde Park

Mural on Adams Street at the intersection with Dorchester Avenue, 2014.

first arrived in Dorchester on June 17, 1630, landing at a peninsula then known as Mattaponnock, what is today Columbia Point. Through most of the eighteenth century, Dorchester was a farming community. As it gradually became linked to Boston through roads, and later trolleys and railroads, it became a choice site for wealthy Bostonians to establish their country estates.

Dorchester is home to about 20 percent of Boston's residents. It is also one of its most diverse neighborhoods—with large communities of people of Cape Verdean, Irish, and Vietnamese descent. In more recent years, a significant gay and lesbian population has also established itself. Gentrification and "condo-ization"—especially of multifamily houses—have heavily impacted many areas. Like much of Boston, Dorchester is marked by residential segregation, particularly between its African American and white communities. Ashmont, Codman Square, Fields Corner, Grove Hall (which straddles the border with Roxbury), Savin Hill, and Uphams Corner are among its better-known areas.

Founded a few months before the City of Boston, the Town of Dorchester voted to join its larger neighbor in 1870. Puritans

Mattapan was originally part of Dorchester and became part of Boston when Dorchester was annexed. Now a separate neighborhood, Mattapan, like Dorchester, once had a large Jewish community—in addition to one of Irish descent. Today Mattapan has a large African American population and is the center of Boston's Haitian and (English) Caribbean communities.

Hyde Park was also once part of Dorchester. Its origins lie in the mid-1800s as land companies built housing near railroad stops and manufacturing developed. Formally incorporated as a town of Norfolk County in 1868, Hyde Park voted to join the City of Boston in 1912. It is today a diverse, relatively suburban neighborhood, with large African American and Haitian-descended population and significant Latino and white populations as well.

2.23 Camp Meigs Playground

Hyde Park Avenue in between Stanbro and
Parkson Streets

HYDE PARK

In the early morning of May 28, 1863,
one thousand African American soldiers,
members of the Fifty-Fourth Regiment
Massachusetts Volunteer Infantry, left
Camp Meigs, a military training ground, to
board the 6:30 train from Readville (today
part of Hyde Park) to Downtown Boston.
Thousands of Bostonians lined the streets
to salute the Fifty-Fourth as they marched
past the State House (across from which a
monument to the soldiers now stands) and
directly over the spot where British soldiers
had slain Crispus Attucks, a person of African and Native descent and the first casualty
in the Boston Massacre of 1770. At *Boston*

Recruitment poster for the Fifty-Fourth Regiment,
circa 1863.

Harbor the soldiers boarded a ship that
would take them to South Carolina to take
part in the Civil War, one of the very first
African American units to do so. Among the
soldiers, many of whom Frederick Douglass
himself had recruited, was Douglass's eldest
son, Lewis Henry Douglass. Led by Colonel
Robert Gould Shaw, the son of an abolitionist Brahmin family (African Americans were
not allowed to hold ranks above sergeant
major), the Fifty-Fourth gained fame for
its valor in battle—particularly that at Fort
Wagner near Charleston, South Carolina.
There 272 of the 600 soldiers who charged
the fort were killed, wounded, or captured;
among the slain was Robert Gould Shaw.

Camp Meigs was established in July 1861
after the surrender of Fort Sumter and President Abraham Lincoln's subsequent call for
more volunteers to join the Union effort.
Camp Meigs trained a significant portion of
the Massachusetts Volunteer Militia, including the Fifty-Fifth Infantry Regiment and the
Fifth Regiment Cavalry, also African American
units. It also served as the site of one of the
two Massachusetts US Army general hospitals. After the war ended in 1865, Camp
Meigs served as a discharge site for troops
returning from active duty.

Much of the land on which Camp Meigs
stood is now residential. Today some of it
is the Camp Meigs Playground. Run by the
Massachusetts Department of Conservation
and Recreation as a satellite to the Stony
Brook Reservation, the park hosts a monument (next to the basketball court) that
commemorates the Fifty-Fourth and Fifty-
Fifth Infantries and the Fifth Cavalry.

GETTING THERE

MBTA bus from Forest Hills Station (Orange Line) or Mattapan Station (Red Line) to Wolcott Square, 0.2 mile (four-minute) walk. Alternatively, 0.3 mile (six-minute) walk from Readville Commuter Rail Station (Fairmount and Franklin Lines).

TO LEARN MORE

Kendrick, Paul, and Steven Kendrick. *Douglass and Lincoln: How a Revolutionary Black Leader and a Reluctant Liberator Struggled to End Slavery and Save the Union*, New York: Walker and Company, 2008.

2.24 The William Monroe Trotter House

97 Sawyer Avenue

DORCHESTER

William Monroe Trotter and his family moved to Boston's **South End** when he was seven months old and later to Hyde Park. A graduate of Harvard University and the first person of color elected to its chapter of Phi Beta Kappa (the national academic honor society for university and college undergraduates), Trotter (1872–1934) would emerge as a central figure in the US civil rights movement. He was an outspoken activist and major public intellectual, one strongly opposed to and vociferously critical of the conservative, accommodationist politics of Booker T. Washington and of the segregationist policies of various US presidents, particularly Theodore Roosevelt and Woodrow Wilson.

In 1901, along with George Forbes, Trotter founded the *Boston Guardian*, an influential African American newspaper, which was published for a time in the same building that had once housed William Lloyd Garrison's *The Liberator*. That same year, Trotter helped to establish the Boston Literary and Historical Association, a grouping of radical political thinkers on matters of race that included W.E.B. Du Bois. In 1905 Trotter helped to found the Niagara Movement, a forerunner to the National Association for the Advancement of Colored People (NAACP). Concerned with black representation in popular culture and the media, Trotter also organized boycotts in Boston targeting productions glorifying the Ku

Mural outside the William Monroe Trotter Innovation School in Dorchester, 2018. It opened in 1969 as Boston's first magnet school. A campaign by parents and civic organizations in the black community compelled the Boston School Committee to name it after Trotter.

Klux Klan, including the infamous movie *Birth of a Nation*. In addition, he successfully campaigned to end racial segregation in the city's hospitals, bringing about the integration of Boston City Hospital in 1929.

Trotter moved to the Sawyer Avenue home in the Jones Hill section of Dorchester in 1899 upon marrying Geraldine Louise Pindell. A private home now listed on the National Register of Historic Places, it is marked with a plaque on the outside.

GETTING THERE

Red Line to Savin Hill Station, 0.6 mile (fifteen-minute) walk. A bus from Fields Corner or Andrew Square Stations (Red Line) also pass near the home.

TO LEARN MORE

Fox, Stephen. *The Guardian of Boston: William Monroe Trotter*. New York: Atheneum Press, 1970.

Puttkammer, Charles W., and Ruth Worthy. "William Monroe Trotter, 1872–1934," *Journal of Negro History* 43, no. 4 (1958): 298–316.

Schneider, Mark R. *Boston Confronts Jim Crow, 1890–1920*, Boston: Northeastern University Press, 1997.

2.25 James Reeb House

3 Half Moon Street, Uphams Corner

DORCHESTER

Mrs. Billie Pope and Mrs. Evy King, as reported by *The Boston Globe*, "knelt on the cold pavement" outside the house at 3 Half Moon Street on Friday, March 12, 1965. With "their Winter coats clutched tightly around them" and "tears coursing slowly down their cheeks," the "two Negro women" prayed. They had come from their

Schoolchildren from the Benedict Fenwick School pause to offer prayers at the home of the Rev. James Reeb, March 12, 1965.

Roxbury homes to mourn the death of the Reverend James Reeb, thirty-eight, a white Unitarian Universalist minister who, along with his wife and four children, had lived "in the unimposing gray house with yellow trim" since moving to Boston in September 1974. Reeb was employed by the American Friends Service Committee (AFSC) as its community relations director of the Boston Metropolitan Housing Program. He worked out of the AFSC's storefront office on 350 Blue Hill Avenue, advocating and organizing for housing rights in low-income, predominantly black neighborhoods in Dorchester and *Roxbury*.

In the immediate aftermath of "Bloody Sunday" in Selma, Alabama—when state troopers and local police brutally attacked civil rights activists on the William Pettis bridge—Martin Luther King issued a call for clergy to come to the city for a "ministers' march" two days later. Reeb responded by traveling to Selma on Monday. When leaving a restaurant the next day after the gathering, white segregationists chased him and two other ministers, with one of them hitting Reeb on the head with a pipe or club and knocking him unconscious.

Christopher Gibson School, circa 1920–1960.

Two days later, on March 11, Reeb died in a Selma hospital. His funeral in Selma, March 15, at which Martin Luther King delivered the eulogy, was nationally televised. The previous day in Boston, an interracial, ecumenical crowd of twenty-five thousand to thirty thousand gathered at the **Boston Common** to pay tribute to the slain minister. Meanwhile, about two hundred civil rights activists staged a sit-in, organized by the Student Non-Violent Coordinating Committee (SNCC), at the Federal Building in Downtown Boston to protest the federal government's failure to protect the lives of civil rights activists, particularly black ones, in the South.

GETTING THERE

Commuter Rail or MBTA bus to Uphams Corner Station, 0.3 mile (six-minute) walk.

TO LEARN MORE

Kozol, Jonathan. *Death at an Early Age*, New York: Penguin Books, 1985 (1967).

2.26 Christopher Gibson School

16 Ronald Street

DORCHESTER

In 1965 a Massachusetts Board of Education–commissioned report recommended the closure of numerous Boston schools, the Gibson being one of them. "Thoroughly convinced that that students attending predominantly Negro schools are denied equal educational opportunity," the authors called upon the City to take positive action to create integrated schools. With a student body that was two-thirds "non-white" (largely African American) and a dilapidated building, the Gibson was emblematic of the schools slated for elimination.

Two months after the report's release, in mid-June, the school experienced demonstrations by parents, students, and community members outside of the building as well as two sit-ins within. The immediate catalyst was the firing of teacher Jonathan Kozol for having had his fourth-grade students read Langston Hughes' poem, "Ballad of the Landlord." School administrators cited Kozol's use of the poem as part of a pattern of deviation from the official course of study. Kozol's firing, however, was only one of several grievances put forth by the largely African American mothers who led the protests.

The school department did agree to the sit-in's demand to use racially integrated textbooks and to consider starting a library and having smaller classes. It refused, however, to end the use of the rattan to discipline students and to reinstate Kozol, but promised a full and inclusive investigation of the firing. The promised investigation, coming in the last days of the school year, led to the end of the sit-in. But the events at the Gibson had importance well beyond the school as they marked a significant ratcheting up of the activism of African Americans and their allies to desegregate the city's school system to end racially unjust conditions.

In 1975, the Gibson School was torn down. An overgrown lot for many years, the site is now slated for an affordable housing development for low- and moderate-income seniors.

GETTING THERE

From Columbia Road and Washington Street (MBTA bus lines pass by), 0.1 mile (three-minute) walk.

TO LEARN MORE

Kozol, Jonathan. *Death at an Early Age*, New York: Penguin Books, 1985 (1967).

Massachusetts State Board of Education. *Because It Is Right—Educationally: Report of the Advisory Committee on Racial Imbalance and Education*, Boston, April 1965.

2.27 Boston Welfare Department, Grove Hall Office/ Mother Caroline Academy and Education Center

515 Blue Hill Avenue

DORCHESTER

About 30 women, black and white, entered and occupied the welfare office in the Grove Hall area on Thursday, June 1, 1967, and spent the night there. By Friday, the group had grown to 50 or so, and included men and some students. Organized by Mothers for Adequate Welfare, a Boston-area grass-roots organization of welfare recipients, the protestors chained shut the building's doors, locking themselves and some welfare workers inside, and insisting that they would not leave until City officials met ten demands. (At the time, municipalities in Massachusetts were largely in charge of administering welfare.) They demanded, among other things, that welfare recipients have representation on policy-making boards; that benefits be sufficient to allow them to save money for their children's education; that recipients be able to see social workers more than once a week; and that Boston's welfare director, Daniel Cronin, be removed.

On Friday evening, Boston Police, without negotiating with those inside or community leaders according to witnesses, stormed the building, under the pretext that one of the welfare workers needed hospitalization. The police broke down the doors, shattering their windows, and violently dragged the occupiers out. Community organizer (and later Massachusetts state representative) Byron Rushing saw the police dragging

MAW sit-in, Grove Hall, June 1967.

with a vibrant commercial district connecting Dorchester and **Roxbury**, was the center of Boston's black community. It was one plagued by "deplorable conditions" in housing, education employment—black joblessness was twice that of whites, and half of the city's black population lived in dilapidated housing according to the 1960 census—asserted the Massachusetts Advisory Committee to the United States Commission on Civil Rights. It was also a time of welfare rights organizing across the country, particularly in urban centers.

The Boston Welfare Department, originally known as the "Overseers of the Poor in the Town of Boston," was first established in 1772. The city agency ceased to exist soon after the incident at the Grove Hall office: later in 1967, the state legislature abolished municipal welfare departments, placing them under the control of the Massachusetts Department of Public Welfare.

The Grove Hall building still stands. Purchased from the City of Boston in 1996 for one dollar, it is today the home of the Mother Caroline Academy and Educa-

women over broken glass. While pleading with a police officer to bring him to a supervisor to discuss a way to de-escalate the situation, another officer struck him in the head with a nightstick, and then police arrested him.

Reports of police beating and arresting the protestors—what many referred to as a police riot—quickly spread and neighborhood residents rushed to free them. Some of the demonstrators threw rocks and bottles, leading to the arrival of more police, dressed in riot gear and armed with rifles. Although the police soon achieved control of the building and its environs, the anger of community members quickly spread, leading to three days of rioting and looting along Blue Hill Avenue. While no one was killed, $1.3 million in damage to area businesses resulted.

At the time of the incident, Grove Hall, a neighborhood of about 65,000 residents

MAW spokeswoman, Mrs. Roberts, hands a list of demands to Commissioner Ott, 1968.

tion Center, a Catholic-rooted, tuition-free school for girls in grades 4–8 from families of limited financial means, regardless of religious and ethno-racial background.

GETTING THERE

MBTA buses from Ashmont (Red Line), Dudley Square (Silver Line), and Ruggles (Orange Line) stations pass nearby.

TO LEARN MORE

Sokol, Jason. *All Eyes Are upon Us: Race and Politics from Boston to Brooklyn*, New York: Basic Book, 2014.

2.28 Temple Beth Hillel

800 Morton Street

MATTAPAN

Founded in 1921, Temple Beth Hillel was one of many Jewish establishments in the Mattapan-Dorchester-Roxbury area in the 1900s. As Jews departed neighborhoods such as the **North End** and the **West End** where they had been previously concentrated, the area around Franklin Park became the focal point of Jewish life in Boston, with Blue Hill Avenue its main thoroughfare. In the 1930s, the area's Jewish community numbered approximately eighty thousand individuals, about half of the entire Jewish population of Boston and its environs.

When Temple Beth Hillel completed its new building at 800 Morton Street in 1944, about twelve hundred people attended the opening ceremony. According to the *Globe* report on the event, Rabbi Mordecai Bressler "pledged the Temple to function as a potent force for justice, freedom and peace in this country and community, and

to foster friendship and understanding with non-Jewish neighbors, and work for establishment of a Jewish Commonwealth in Palestine." The new house of worship was one of more than fifty synagogues, Jewish community centers, and Hebrew schools in the area at that time. By the early 1970s, however, all had dissolved or relocated, Temple Beth Hillel among them, with only a small number of Jewish residents left in the area.

What explains the Jewish community's demise in Mattapan is a matter of debate. Sociologist Hillel Levine and journalist Lawrence Harmon put heavy emphasis on the Boston Banks Urban Renewal Group (BBURG), a program established in 1968 to provide mortgages to low-income black families, and the unscrupulous activities of bankers and real estate agents who exploited the opportunity to "block-bust" Jewish neighborhoods in Mattapan. Historian Gerald Gamm, however, shows that the area's Jewish exodus has deeper roots. More affluent Jews had steadily migrated to the suburbs in preceding decades, leaving a largely lower-middle- and working-class (and relatively elderly) Jewish population behind. And the departure of the remaining Jewish residents from Mattapan had intensified in the years before BBURG in the face of large numbers of black and non-Jewish families moving into the neighborhood, block-busting efforts by real estate interests, and rising levels of street crime (a problem in many Boston neighborhoods at the time). Jewish institutions and individuals were sometimes the target. In 1969 two young men attacked Temple Beth Hillel's rabbi at his home, throwing acid in his face and damaging one of his eyes. In 1970 arsonists attacked two nearby synagogues in Dorchester. On a more structural level, Gamm points to the fact that synagogues are not territorially based, that, unlike Catholics and their parishes, synagogues and members of Jewish congregations are not tied to a particular neighborhood. For Gamm this explains why Catholics were likelier than Boston Jews to stay in neighborhoods experiencing demographic change or to fight such change.

Temple Beth Hillel, in effect, followed its congregants and moved in 1970 to West Roxbury, where it merged with Beth Torah to form Temple Hillel Bnai Torah, today a Jewish Reconstructionist congregation. Its former Morton Street home now houses Berea Seventh Day Adventist Academy. Many of its students, reflecting the "new" Mattapan, are of Haitian descent.

GETTING THERE

MBTA buses from Ashmont (Red Line) and Forest Hills (Orange Line) stations pass in front of the site, with stops close by.

TO LEARN MORE

Gamm, Gerald. *Urban Exodus: Why the Jews Left Boston and the Catholics Stayed*, Cambridge: Harvard University Press, 1999.

Levine, Hillel, and Lawrence Harmon. *The Death of an American Jewish Community: A Tragedy of Good Intentions*, New York: Touchstone Books, 1993.

2.29 Laura Ann Ewing Home/ Columbia Point Housing Project

260 Mount Vernon Street

DORCHESTER

It was midday on a Monday—April 25, 1962—when a ten-ton, City of Boston dump truck struck and killed Laura Ann Ewing, a six-year-old African American girl, as she skipped across Mount Vernon Street while doing an errand for her mother. The truck was one of hundreds that each day would rumble down what was locally known as Mile Road, the only thoroughfare into Columbia Point and to the peninsula's two dumps. Rats proliferated as did toxic air due to regular burnings of the refuse. Almost a decade earlier, the City's planning board had warned that dumping would have to end and the dump cleaned up before residents moved into the housing project where the Ewing family lived, but the advice was not heeded.

Laura Ewing's killing was a manifestation of Columbia Point's history as a literal and figurative dumping ground. Beginning in the 1800s, it was the site of a sewage discharge station and a trash dump; during World War II, it housed a prison camp for Italian soldiers; and, in 1954, the Columbia Point Housing Project opened, becoming home for, among others, some **West End** residents displaced by their neighborhood's demolition (see **West End Museum**). (Ironically, much of the refuse from the West End's destruction was dumped as landfill at Columbia Point.)

Immediately following the tragedy, a multiracial group of mothers resident in

Picketing at Columbia Point housing project, April 23, 1962.

Columbia Point organized a picket line across Mount Vernon, blocking the passage of the dump trucks. That, combined with intense engagement with city and state officials—through meetings and protests—led, within a few days, to the dumps' closing.

New England's largest public housing project, Columbia Point was comprised of twenty-seven high-rise buildings and 1,504 apartment units. While the City constructed housing for thousands, it had not built a viable community. When it opened, the neighborhood, isolated physically and socially, had no playgrounds, stores, churches, public transit or schools.

While some amenities eventually came to be, a combination of factors led to a precipitous decline in the neighborhood in the 1960s and 1970s. These included declining financial support from the federal government, decreasing investment by the Boston Housing Authority (BHA), and poor man-

Residents help clean up at Columbia Point housing project in Boston, June 20, 1970.

agement (leading Suffolk County Supreme Court to deem the BHA an unfit landlord in 1975). Together these factors contributed to the deterioration of the actual building stock.

They also led to the departure of the more socioeconomically mobile families, and a broader shift in the makeup of the residents. Initially composed mostly of working class families—largely white, but also black to a significant degree—with stable jobs, the residents became poorer and almost exclusively black and Latino (during this time the Boston Housing Authority pursued practices that enhanced racial segregation between public housing developments). The neighborhood also became increasingly ghettoized and isolated (see **Carson Beach**). In this context, crime and general safety concerns grew markedly—so much so that ambulances and firefighters entered the neighborhood only with a police escort. As conditions worsened, many residents moved out: By 1979 less than a quarter of units were occupied, and many of the buildings were boarded up—resulting in the effective elimination of one thousand units in a city with a substantial shortage of public housing.

After the Boston Housing Authority failed to ameliorate conditions, a federal court took control in 1980 and worked with tenants to find a private company to rectify matters. In the eyes of area powerbrokers, this became all the more necessary in light of developments elsewhere on the Columbia Point peninsula during the 1970s—the openings of the Harbor Campus of the University of Massachusetts Boston and the John F. Kennedy Presidential Library—that made the hitherto unattractive area increasingly desirable. In this context, the demolition of most of the high-rises began in 1986—including the one in which Laura Ann Ewing and her family resided—and the construction of townhouse-style homes, a new neighborhood, came to be.

Today Harbor Point is a mixed-income and racially diverse residential neighborhood. While many applaud the develop-

ment's transformation as a safer and more livable environment, Harbor Point enacted strict policies that led to the expulsion of some of the remaining Columbia Point Housing Project residents. At the same time, it froze the number of low-income units at four hundred, representing a significant loss of such housing and the gentrification of what had been an area dedicated to sheltering the city's neediest residents.

The destruction and replacement of the Columbia Point Housing Project goes well beyond Boston: Harbor Point's public-private partnership served as the model for the federal government's HOPE VI program, which aims to "revitalize" public housing by creating mixed-income developments where private developers play a large role. It is a neoliberal "solution" that represents a marked reduction in the federal government's commitment to housing provision.

The Boys and Girls Club (270 Mount Vernon) in Harbor Point sits roughly where Laura Ann Ewing's building once stood.

GETTING THERE

Red Line to JFK/UMass Station, 0.4 mile (eight-minute) walk.

TO LEARN MORE

Roessner, Jane. *A Decent Place to Live: From Columbia Point to Harbor Point—A Community History*, Boston: Northeastern University Press, 2000.

Kennedy, Marie. "Mixed Messages: A Brief Story of Columbia Point and US Public Housing," an essay accompanying *Columbia Point: Life in the ghetto, USA*, a video slide transfer by Linda Swartz, March 1989.

2.30 Columbia Point Health Center/Geiger-Gibson Health Center

250 Mount Vernon Street

DORCHESTER

Inside the Columbia Point Health Center, undated.

On December 11, 1965, the first community health center in the United States opened in Dorchester's Columbia Point. Two local physician-activists, H. Jack Geiger and Count Gibson, realized that while Boston was a mecca of high-quality medical institutions, it did not have adequate or accessible care for the city's poor residents. The pair intentionally sited the center in Columbia Point in part because of its history as a literal and figurative dumping ground (see *Laura Ann Ewing Home*). Up until that point, residents had to take at last three buses to reach Boston City Hospital and medical care.

After it opened in one of the housing project buildings, the Columbia Point Health Center was quickly overwhelmed with demand, seeing up to two hundred people a day. The center, funded by the federal Office of Economic Opportunity, gained national attention as a successful model of health care, one that reduces health disparities across socioeconomic groups and provides comprehensive, accessible, and affordable health services to historically underserved populations regardless of health insurance coverage. With help from the federal government, the model quickly spread, and by 1971 there were eighteen more community health centers in Boston, many with strong community involvement and services tailored to local needs.

Despite the many problems that unfolded in the Columbia Point area in the years after its founding, the clinic endured. However, it faced financial challenges due to issues with private insurance reimbursements and went into receivership in 1984. It later merged with Neponset Health Center and now operates under Harbor Health Services as the renamed Geiger-Gibson Health Center.

GETTING THERE

Red Line to JFK/UMass Station, 0.4 mile (about eight-minute) walk.

TO LEARN MORE

Lefkowitz, Bonnie. *Community Health Centers: A Movement and the People Who Made It Happen,* Issues in Health and Medicine, New Brunswick, NJ: Rutgers University Press, 2007.

Roessner, Jane. *A Decent Place to Live: From Columbia Point to Harbor Point—A Community History,* Boston: Northeastern University Press, 2000.

Thebaud, Angie, Jeanne Haffner, and Erick Guerra. "Privately-Funded Public Housing Redevelopment: A Study of the Transformation of Columbia Point (Boston, MA)," Institute for International Urban Development, Cambridge, MA, September 2008.

2.31 US Armed Forces Recruiting Station and Dorchester District Courthouse

1306 Dorchester Avenue (Fields Corner) and
510 Washington Street (Codman Square)

DORCHESTER

Nine Vietnam veterans entered a US military recruiting station in Dorchester's Fields Corner area on the afternoon of December 30, 1971. Using desks and filing cabinets, they barricaded themselves in the Air Force recruiter's office; it was part of a coordinated set of actions by Vietnam Veterans against the War at sites across the country during Christmas week. Called "Operation Peace on Earth," its crowning moment was a takeover of the Statue of Liberty and the hanging of an upside-down US flag from Lady Liberty's face.

In Dorchester, members of the Boston Police Department's Tactical Patrol Force arrived at the site within twenty minutes. Deploying tear gas, the police broke down the door and arrested the former soldiers,

charging them with trespassing, property destruction, and injury to a building.

A little more than three weeks later, the veterans appeared for their trial at Dorchester District Court in nearby Codman Square. About 150 protestors organized by VVAW demonstrated in support of the "Dorchester 9" that day outside the building. Their lawyer argued that given that courts played a role in enforcing the draft—during the war Vietnam, a large percentage of court cases dealt with conscientious objector petitions or cases of draft dodging—military veterans opposing recruitment could not get a fair trial. Ultimately the judge decided not to hear the case and sent it to Superior Court.

In April, a Suffolk Superior Court jury found eight of the nine guilty of willful and malicious injury to personal property and trespassing. The judge sentenced them to one year's probation.

Dorchester was an appropriate place for one of the VVAW's actions. As historian Christian Appy has shown, it was the type of community, with its large low-income and working-class population, from which US soldiers in Vietnam came in disproportionate numbers. More than forty years later, Dorchester demonstrates how imperial conflicts often generate significant out-migration to the country of the aggressor. The Fields Corner area is today the home of a large population of Vietnamese descent. Thus, it is more than an irony that the site of the recruit-

Demonstration in support of the Dorchester Nine, Dorchester Courthouse, January 21, 1972.

ing station, at the time of its demolition in late 2016, was home to a flower shop owned by Vietnamese immigrants.

GETTING THERE

(*To the recruiting station site*) Red Line to Fields Corner Station. The building stood on northeast corner with Linden Street, 0.5 mile (ten-minute) walk.

(*To the courthouse*) Red Line to Shawmut Station, 0.5 mile (ten-minute) walk; 0.8 mile walk from Fields Corner Station.

NEARBY SITE

THE MATHER ELEMENTARY SCHOOL, founded in 1639, the oldest public elementary and the first tax-supported school in the United States (1 Parish Street, Meetinghouse Hill, Dorchester).

TO LEARN MORE

Appy, Christian. *Working-Class War: American Combat Soldiers and Vietnam*, Chapel Hill: University of North Carolina Press, 1993.
Foley, Mark S. "Operation Peace on Earth," in *Vietnam Veterans against the War, 40 Years Anniversary Celebration*, Chicago, VVAW, 2007: 22–23; available at http://www.vvaw.org/pdf/VVAW_40th_booklet.pdf
Nicosia, Gerald. *Home to War: A History of the Vietnam Veterans Movement*, New York: Crown Publishers, 2001.

2.32 *The Boston Globe* Headquarters

135 William T. Morrissey Boulevard

DORCHESTER

A little after midnight on Monday, October 7, 1974, a beige sedan parked on Morrissey Boulevard across from the *Globe*'s headquar-

ters. A man got out of the vehicle with a rifle and fired several shots into the building, striking the inside of the lobby and the pressroom, and then fled. The following night, a car speeding by on the Southeast Expressway (behind the *Globe*'s headquarters), fired seven shots at the building.

By the time of the shootings, the *Globe* had emerged at the top of Boston's newspaper pyramid. Associated with the region's liberal political establishment, the paper's editorial page was often on the cutting edge of national politics. In 1968 it ran a "Draft Counselor" column to advise US military draftees of their rights, and in May 1970 it became the second major US newspaper to call on the United States government to withdraw unilaterally from Vietnam. In October 1973, it was the first to demand President Richard Nixon's resignation.

While such positions enjoyed broad support in the region, they also angered many. What especially earned the *Globe* great ire were its liberal positions on social issues ranging from abortion to gay rights. With the leadership of the *Globe*'s sympathy for the court-ordered-desegregation of the Boston Public Schools and its criticisms of the most vocal and militant elements of the antibusing movement, antipathy toward the newspaper rose markedly. It became the focus of much of the frustration of white, working-class Bostonians and their political leaders, many of whom saw the paper as one run by suburban elites out of touch with their concerns and interests as city dwellers.

Globe headquarters, Dorchester, 2018.

ington Street). In December 2017, the *Globe* sold its Dorchester complex, having moved its editorial and business offices to State Street (see **Exchange Place**), not far from the paper's birthplace, earlier that year. Now a newspaper with much more conventional politics than was the case in the 1960s and 1970s, the depth of its international and national news reporting has decreased markedly, like newspapers across the country.

Still, its local investigative news team, "Spotlight," continues to produce strong journalism. As recounted in the Oscar-winning film (2015) by the same name, the team's 2002 series on the pedophilia scandal within Boston's Catholic Church played a huge role in exposing the widespread, long-standing nature of the abuses and the systemic cover-up by the church hierarchy.

As of this writing, the *Globe*'s former headquarters is being redeveloped into "creative office," light industrial, and retail spaces.

As busing began in September 1974, angry crowds in South Boston threatened *Globe* reporters, and the paper's headquarters received almost nightly bomb threats. Meanwhile, individuals threatened newspaper vendors in South Boston with violence if they sold the newspaper, and ROAR, the principal antibusing organization, organized a citywide boycott.

It was in this context that the shootings took place at the *Globe*'s Dorchester headquarters. A longtime associate of Whitey Bulger, the infamous South Boston gangster, admitted to the *Globe* in 2001 to having carried out the shootings in retaliation for what he perceived as the paper's bias against the antibusing movement.

Founded in 1872, the *Globe* moved to Dorchester in 1958 to take advantage of a much larger space and a location that allowed it greater access to its expanding suburban readership. It was the last of Boston's newspapers to abandon "Newspaper Row" in Downtown (the *Globe* was located at 238–240 Wash-

GETTING THERE

Red Line to JFK/UMass Station, 0.4 mile (eight-minute) walk.

TO LEARN MORE

Formisano, Ronald. *Boston against Busing: Race, Class, and Ethnicity in the 1960s and 1970s*, Chapel Hill: University of North Carolina Press, 1991.

Lukas, J. Anthony. *Common Ground: A Turbulent Decade in the Lives of Three American Families*, New York: Knopf, 1985.

2.33 Combahee River Collective

26a Moultrie Street

DORCHESTER

In 1974 a group of black women activists, each with long histories in the antiwar, feminist, and black liberation movements, began to gather in one another's homes in Boston's working-class communities. The first place was Demita Frazier's living room on Moultrie Street, where regular meetings occurred in the early years. In this intimate space, they analyzed their diverse commitments to these movements while lamenting the estrangement they experienced in male-led and/or white-dominated formations. In their conversations, Frazier, the twin sisters Barbara and Beverly Smith, and several others addressed the challenges facing working-class, black women activists, noting the energy and emotional work they invested in various coalitions given the interlocking character of their oppression. Considering matters of gender, class, race, and sexual orientation, they evolved a theory of liberation that has proved to be very influential in academia and among social justice organizers, one based on the insights provided by multiple intersecting oppressions and the resulting coalitions: with black men in the fight against racism, with white women in the struggle against male domination. Acknowledging also their class position, they defined themselves as socialists aiming to overthrow capitalist social relations. In this sense especially, they reflected a very different political orientation from the National Black Feminist Organization in which several of them had participated.

Naming themselves after an 1863 military campaign led by Harriet Tubman that freed 750 enslaved individuals in South Carolina, the collective foregrounded their commitment to action. This was not an abstract choice: The collective was founded in the midst of a Boston "race war" triggered by white opposition to integrated schools. Members of the collective themselves, especially the Smith sisters, had a background in organizing "freedom schools" during the Civil Rights movement.

Although the collective was itself a breakaway from mainstream feminism, its coalitions reached out broadly to address concrete issues of reproductive freedom, forced steriliza-

Members of the Combahee River Collective at an anti-police-brutality rally on January 15, 1980.

We have identified and worked on many issues of particular relevance to Black women. The inclusiveness of our politics makes us concerned with any situation that impinges upon the lives of women, Third World and working people. We are of course particularly committed to working on those struggles in which race, sex, and class are simultaneous factors in oppression.
—**From the Combahee River Collective Statement of April 1977**

tion, and violence against women. They also called attention to a series of murders and violent attacks against black women that were going uninvestigated by the Boston Police Department. Their community-based research and reports engaged both *The Boston Globe* and local African American papers, which had been underreporting these incidents. By the late 1970s, their public demonstrations addressing these attacks had drawn broad public support and produced a strong coalition of feminist and community-based activists. The coalition's organizing work prefigured future Boston coalitions, including most directly the Rainbow Coalition mayoral candidacy of Mel King in 1983.

During their later years, the collective met regularly at the Women's Center in Cambridge. The coalition disbanded in 1981 as its members moved on to other activities, including academic work.

GETTING THERE

Red Line to Shawmut Station. The private residence is a 0.3 mile (three-minute) walk.

TO LEARN MORE

Cobble, Dorothy Sue, Linda Gordon, and Astrid Henry. *Feminism Unfinished: A Short, Surprising History of American Women's Movements,* New York: W.W. Norton, 2015.
Taylor, Keeanga-Yamahtta. *How We Get Free: Black Feminism and the Combahee River Collective,* Chicago: Haymarket Books, 2017.

2.34 State Temple Church of God in Christ

16–18 Fessenden Street

MATTAPAN

After a three-hour service attended by an overflow crowd of approximately two thousand people on September 5, 1987, members of Boston's Haitian community marched for about ninety minutes from the State Temple Church of God in Christ in Mattapan to the Forest Hills Cemetery in Jamaica Plain. They gathered and marched to honor the life and death of Antoine Thurel, fifty-six. Only six days earlier, Thurel, an immigrant to the United States who worked as a cabdriver, had set himself on fire on the steps of the Massachusetts State House to protest US support for the Haitian military and the country's ruling junta.

The Boston Globe described the funeral as "more a testimonial than a religious gathering," with many of the speakers at the funeral mass characterizing Thurel as a hero. "He spent his life so the freedom of Haiti will never be lost," said one. "His spirit will never die." His eldest son asserted that his death was "not a suicide. . . . It was a sacrifice." Boston Mayor Ray Flynn dropped by the service to make a brief speech and offer

Friends of Antoine Thurel hold hands during a procession down Norfolk Street, September 5, 1987.

lization in the community and a tradition of progressive politics. Moreover, it illustrated the significant growth that the community had experienced. By 1987 there were an estimated fifty thousand Haitians in Greater Boston, with Mattapan the community's epicenter, making it one of the three largest Haitian cities in the United States. With its roots in the 1950s, the Haitian diaspora in Greater Boston remains the largest of the area's various West Indian communities.

his sympathies to Antoine Thurel's wife and children as well as, he stated, "to the larger family of Haitians here in Boston."

Accompanied by pallbearers carrying the casket and followed by about a dozen taxis, the march first went to the Thurel family home nearby at 465 Norfolk Street before continuing down Morton Street to his place of burial. Outside the house, mourners and protestors sang songs and chanted in Haitian Creole. Banners had slogans that included "US Imperialism Out of Haiti" and "Support the Revolution from Haiti to South Africa."

The response to Antoine Thurel's death demonstrated the depth of the Haitian community's anger against US backing of Haiti's oligarchy and the country's brutal military establishment. Indeed, Thurel's act of protest came in a context of weekly demonstrations outside the Haitian consulate in Boston. The size and strength of the response also manifested the high level of political mobi-

The State Temple of the Church of God in Christ, a Holiness-Pentecostal denomination, was established on Fessenden Street in the early 1970s. At the time, the two joined buildings (constructed in 1938 and 1954) were the home of Congregation Kehillath Jacob, an Orthodox Jewish congregation. The two religious communities shared the premises until Congregation Kehillath Jacob moved to Randolph in 1979.

GETTING THERE

MBTA buses from Mattapan and Ashmont (Red Line) and Forest Hills (Orange Line) stations pass nearby.

TO LEARN MORE

Jackson, Regine O. "The Uses of Diaspora among Haitians in Boston," in *Geographies of the Haitian Diaspora*, ed. Regine O. Jackson, New York: Routledge, 2011, 135–62.

Jamaica Plain, Roslindale, and West Roxbury

Wake Up the Earth Festival, Jamaica Plain, 2015.

What are now the neighborhoods of Jamaica Plain, Roslindale, and West Roxbury were long part of **Roxbury**. In 1851, five years after Roxbury had successfully petitioned the state of Massachusetts to become its own city, Roxbury's "Jamaica End" became a separate town called West Roxbury. At this time the area was quite rural, with most its small number of residents working as farmers on large land tracts. There was also a concentration of wealthy estates around what is today Jamaica Pond. For reasons of both personal preference and profit, the champions of West Roxbury's secession envisioned a nonurban future where wealthy residents could live in a bucolic setting without the unsightly poor in proximity.

As elsewhere, railroads greatly changed the character of the Town of West Roxbury, allowing middle- and working-class folks to settle the area, as did the desire to have access to urban amenities (plumbing, streetlights, etc.). In 1873 Roslindale became part of the City of Boston. The following year, Jamaica Plain and (what remained of) West Roxbury followed suit.

Today Jamaica Plain, home to a sizable activist community, is the most "urban" of the three neighborhoods given its dense housing stock in areas and significant amount of public housing. It is also the most socioeconomically polarized, with a large working-class community and a considerable population of high-income professionals. Home to the Arnold Arboretum, the Forest Hills Cemetery, and, in part, Franklin Park, it has significant green space.

Like Jamaica Plain, Roslindale enjoys considerable ethno-racial diversity, with a substantial Latino and African American, in addition to working-class, presence.

West Roxbury, the most suburban of Boston's neighborhoods, is largely white and generally the most affluent of the three. In recent years it has been the focus of intense efforts by climate change and environmental justice activists to block the construction of a natural gas pipeline through the neighborhood.

Brook Farm, 2014.

2.35 Brook Farm

670 Baker Street

WEST ROXBURY

A self-sustaining community based on the values of Transcendentalism—a philosophical and social movement that saw the divine in all forms of life, embraced simple living, and supported equal rights for women—Brook Farm was a utopian experiment in communal living. George Ripley, who had recently resigned from his position as a Unitarian minister, and Sophia Dana Ripley founded what was formally called the Brook Farm Institute for Agriculture and Education in 1841. Twenty others joined the Ripleys when the cooperative was first established, all of them living together in the main farmhouse, called the Hive. Soon the community grew to 120 members.

Brook Farm was based on a joint-stock system by which each member paid $500 and received a fixed income regardless of the type of work they performed. In addition to engaging the arts and literature, the community was deeply intellectual and eventually adopted the ideas of the French philosopher Charles Fourier, a utopian socialist. Its residents included some of the area's leading thinkers and writers of the day—Ralph Waldo Emerson, Charles Dana, Margaret Fuller, and Nathaniel Hawthorne among them.

Hawthorne lived on Brook Farm for a little over half a year in 1841. His departure was related to his disillusion with the collectivist endeavor, a sentiment made clear in his novel *The Blithedale Romance* (despite his assurances to the reader that the work of fiction was not a reflection of his time on Brook Farm).

While Hawthorne's assessment is that of only one person, life on the farm was not easy. Food and clothing shortages and disease outbreaks occurred during the winters of 1844–45 and 1845–46. At the same time, the agricultural inexperience of the farms' residents was apparent, Such factors, coupled with a large fire in March 1846 that destroyed an almost-completed new residential building—the loss of which proved quite costly—led to the famous utopian experiment's end. In August 1847 the Brook Farm community disbanded.

Today the site of Brook Farm is both a City of Boston landmark and a national historic landmark. In 1988 the Commonwealth of Massachusetts acquired the property. The state's Department of Conservation and Recreation oversees the site.

GETTING THERE

MBTA buses stop near the site.

2.36 Theodore Parker Unitarian Universalist Church

1859 Centre Street

WEST ROXBURY

Theodore Parker was a renegade Unitarian minister and an influential theologian who became involved in Transcendentalism. Like his fellow Transcendentalists, he strongly opposed the institution of slavery and saw the world and all humans as divine. Unlike many of them, however, he did not reject religion but saw it as fundamental to Transcendentalism.

From 1837 to 1846, Parker, then a recent graduate of the Harvard Divinity School, served as the minister of what would later become the First Church of West Roxbury (in 1854, when West Roxbury seceded from the town of Roxbury). He gradually introduced Transcendentalist ideas to the congregation and was actively involved with the nearby **Brook Farm**.

In 1846, a time when his considerable public influence was growing and he was also becoming increasingly isolated among Unitarians and Evangelicals due to his radi-

A man held against his will as a slave has a natural right to kill every one who seeks to prevent his enjoyment of liberty. This has long been recognized as a self-evident proposition, coming so directly from the Primitive Instincts of Human Nature, that it neither required proofs nor admitted them.

It may be a natural duty for the freeman to help the slaves to the enjoyment of their liberty, and as a means to that end, to aid them in killing all such as oppose their natural freedom.

—From Theodore Parker's letter in defense of John Brown

cal theology and politics, Parker became the head of a new congregation in Downtown Boston organized by his many followers. They included Louisa May Alcott, William Lloyd Garrison, and Elizabeth Cady Stanton. From the pulpit and with thousands in attendance at his Sunday sermons, Parker, a noted orator, championed abolition and women's suffrage (one of the first US clergy to do so). He also argued against the US invasion of Mexico and the subsequent war (1846–48) and was the first clergyman to refer to God as both Father and Mother.

Parker, who died in Rome in 1860 from tuberculosis, was a key intellectual among abolitionists. He was also a leader in the Boston movement to rescue fugitive slaves, sometimes hiding them in his home. A member of the "Secret Six," he helped to plan and

Theodore Parker Unitarian Universalist Church, 2014.

fund John Brown's raid on a federal arsenal in Harpers Ferry, Virginia, in 1859 (see **American House**). In a long letter to a fellow Boston abolitionist (published in 1860), Parker defended Brown and the rights of the enslaved to rise up and slay those who keep them in bondage.

Parker's West Roxbury congregation split into two in the early 1890s, with one moving to Roslindale. In 1962, however, the two congregations decided to consolidate into one due to their dwindling memberships. A historic landmark of the City of Boston, the Theodore Parker Unitarian Universalist Church is located near where the First Church of West Roxbury once stood.

Parker's influence went far beyond the Boston area and his time. Martin Luther King Jr. paraphrased the Unitarian theologian when he famously stated, "The arc of the moral universe is long, but it bends towards justice."

TO LEARN MORE

Parker, Theodore. *John Brown's Expedition Reviewed in a Letter from Rev. Theodore Parker in Rome to Francis Jackson, Boston*, Boston: The Fraternity, 1860.

Renehan, Edward J. Jr. *The Secret Six: The True Tale of the Men Who Conspired with John Brown*, New York: Crown Publishers, 1995.

Website of the Theodore Parker Unitarian Universalist Church: http://www.tparkerchurch.org/

GETTING THERE

MBTA buses from Forest Hills Station (Orange Line) pass close by.

2.37 Science for the People/ Helen Keller Collective

9 Walden Street

JAMAICA PLAIN

Science for the People (SftP) first emerged in 1969–70 as an expression of moral outrage regarding the role of science in the US war in Vietnam, one realized through the national organization Scientists and Engineers for Social and Political Action (SESPA). With the infusion of activist-oriented graduate students from Harvard and MIT and Boston-area scientists and others, the organization began to disrupt scientific meetings and transformed the *SESPA Newsletter* into a magazine, *Science for the People*. The actions and the magazine resulted in media exposure and rapid growth. Soon the organization took on the magazine's name, and active chapters arose in dozens of US cities and towns—typically ones with large university communities—and eventually in other countries as well. The organization's members were not limited to academics but included workers from various sectors and others concerned with the use of science for the narrow ends of war, militarism, and capitalist profit.

First published in 1970, the magazine became an important intellectual and political organ for left-leaning activists and scientists; it endured until 1989. In issues of the magazine in the mid- and late 1970s, it presented its parent organization as one that "opposes the ideologies of sexism, racism, elitism and their practice, and holds an anti-imperialist world-view" while seeking to expose "the class control of science

Cover of *Science for the People*'s first issue. Cover by Elizabeth Fox-Wolfe (aka Alphabet).

collective's members lived on the top two floors of the house, while the ground floor became the SftP office, giving the organization and its flagship publication their first dedicated space.

The collective lasted until 1975, at which point its members gave the house to a family from Bromley-Heath. SftP then briefly had an office at 16 Union Square in *Somerville* before moving to 897 Main Street in *Cambridge*, where it stayed until its demise as a national organization.

An April 2014 conference at UMass Amherst on SftP's history and impact catalyzed a revitalization project that has resulted in new chapters in the United States, including one based at MIT and one in Mexico.

GETTING THERE

Orange Line to Jackson Square Station, 0.4 mile (nine-minute) walk.

TO LEARN MORE

Henig, Robin Marantz. "Radical Group 10 Years Later . . . Science for the People: Revolution's Evolution," *BioScience* 29, no. 6 (1979): 341–44.

Schmalzer, Sigrid, Daniel S. Chard, and Alyssa Botelho. *Science for the People: Documents from America's Movement of Radical Scientists*, Amherst: University of Massachusetts Press, 2018.

and technology." The publication explored myriad issues over the year—ranging from nuclear power, US imperialism, and toxic waste to women in science, biotechnology, and race and racism—while its politics, reflecting shifts within SftP, evolved from radical and revolutionary to broadly progressive.

Because the Boston chapter initiated the magazine, continued its publication, and put out calls for actions and organizing, the Boston-Cambridge area became the epicenter of SftP's activities. In 1971 Britta Fischer, who with Herb Fox published the first issue of *Science for the People*, purchased a house on 9 Walden Street, across from the Bromley-Heath public housing project (today known as the Mildred C. Hailey Apartments) to house the Helen Keller Collective, a small group of like-minded radical activists. The

2.38 Southwest Corridor Park

JAMAICA PLAIN AND SOUTH END

A lively phalanx of green spaces, public art, community gardens, bicycle lanes, springtime festivals, and recreational areas, the Southwest Corridor Park extends 4.1 miles,

Near Roxbury Crossing, 1970s.

connecting the **Back Bay**, **South End**, **the Fenway**, **Roxbury**, and Jamaica Plain. A model of urban design, its relative tranquillity and many virtues belie the park's origins in a high-stakes community struggle.

Beginning in 1948, construction companies, federal and state officials, and even some urban reformers—all united by a vision of an automobile-centered city—advanced a plan to expand Greater Boston's highway network. The original vision had an inner corridor branching off Route 93, running through **Somerville**, Boston, **Cambridge**, and Brookline and then splitting into an eight- to twelve-lane lane highway cutting southwest through Boston to Route 95 while other lanes reconnected to Route 93. The early stages of the project resulted in the clearing of large areas of Roxbury and Jamaica Plain and the tearing down of twelve hundred homes. Had the highway been built, it would have resulted in much more destruction in Boston, as well as in Somerville and Cambridge, as the plan included stripping the impacted cities of the

right to veto the project even where it ran through their jurisdictions.

A regional social movement and broad community mobilization emerged by 1968 to challenge this project, armed with the slogan "A *city*, not a highway." It brought together planners, progressive policy makers, environmentalists, and neighborhood activists. Capping an intense grassroots campaign, the movement organized a demonstration at the State House, rallying two thousand residents in January 1969, to oppose the highway. In 1970 Governor Francis Sargent declared a moratorium on its construction. Having concluded that the two sides were so polarized that he was "compelled to choose one side or another in a clear-cut fashion," he sided with the social movement and formally canceled the project in 1972.

Much as the park today stretches from Boston's mostly white urban core through largely African American Roxbury before coming to rest in multicultural Jamaica Plain, late 1960s organizing encompassed a similarly diverse, albeit more integrated, social movement. The Boston Black United Front, led by Chuck Turner, organized community resistance to land-taking in Roxbury and combined their efforts with activists and clerics in largely white Cambridge. Their movement also worked closely with largely Italian-American activists in **East Boston** fighting **Logan Airport**. Using mass meetings and door-to-door campaigns at the

Right to Remain
Boston Assembly,
Fields Corner,
Dorchester, 2015.

neighborhood level, the movement grew to encompass leading politicians and technocrats, including both major gubernatorial candidates in the 1968 election, the region's major universities, and then-Senator Ted Kennedy. Activists also reflected the rising environmental consciousness of the era.

After ending the highway plans, Massachusetts lawmakers helped change federal policy to enable a modest redirection of federal funds to mass transit and away from highways. Ultimately the movement was a democratizing influence on city planning.

Southwest Corridor Park opened in its entirety in 1990. It sits on a portion of the would-be highway's route.

GETTING THERE

The park is directly off the Orange Line on all outbound stations from Back Bay onward.

TO LEARN MORE

Crockett, Karilyn. *People before Highways.* Amherst: University of Massachusetts Press, 2018.

2.39 City Life/Vida Urbana

284 Amory Street

JAMAICA PLAIN

Representing groups and neighborhoods from across the city, hundreds of individuals attended the "Right to Remain" assembly at the Vietnamese American Community Center on Charles Street in the Fields Corner area of ***Dorchester***, the heart of Boston's flourishing Vietnamese community. Anchoring the October 3, 2015, gathering was a network of organizations representing Asian American, Cape Verdean, and other low-income communities harmed by the gentrification of Boston neighborhoods.

The event responded to processes of displacement intensified by the bursting of the national $8 trillion housing bubble and related 8.4 million job losses of the Great Recession (which began in December 2007). It saw housing foreclosures and evictions rise dramatically in the area. Moreover, Boston's characteristic triple- and quadruple-deck buildings meant that a single foreclosure would impact several households, often involving both tenants and working-class landlords. In 2006–11, financial institutions foreclosed on some forty-three hundred homes in Boston, mostly in communities of color in Dorchester, **Roxbury**, **Mattapan**, and **East Boston**.

In response, City Life/Vida Urbana (CLVU), a main organizer of the 2015 assembly, turned to the 1930s for inspiration. The thirty-five-year-old Jamaica Plain–based housing rights organization used the eviction blockade tactic employed by the National Unemployment Council during the Great Depression. Drawing on its long-standing grassroots work, CLVU mobilized local residents and allies for its first blockade in January 2008, at Melonie Griffiths' family home on 26 Semont Road in Dorchester. The action resulted in the eviction's postponement, but the lender moved to evict again a week later. A second blockade arose, however, that was so fierce that the mortgage holder backed down and agreed to negotiate with the homeowner.

CLVU's actions inspired organizations throughout the area and housing advocates nationwide, leading to the creation of the "Boston model." Dubbed the "Sword, Shield, and Offer," the model weds direct action with a sophisticated combination of self-help, legal actions, negotiations, and eventually ownership transactions designed to keep residents in their homes.

CLVU's organizing focused on the predatory lending practices of large banks. Using careful research into the housing market and federal and state regulations, CLVU pres-

sured lenders, usually the banks that took possession of foreclosed properties, to negotiate in good faith with the tenants of foreclosed homes. It encouraged the bank to sell the properties at their current market value as opposed to the "book value" (the inflated prices obtained during the housing bubble). CLVU's allies in legal aid organizations, community development corporations, and low-income housing assistance groups also provided a framework to assist working-class homeowners in financing their homes at sustainable rates.

CLVU's role in forming the National Right to the City Alliance and participation in other national networks greatly facilitated the national diffusion of its model. Since 2006 CLVU has had its offices in the Jamaica Plain Neighborhood Development Corporation–owned Brewery Complex.

GETTING THERE

Stony Brook Station (Orange Line), 0.2 mile (four-minute) walk.

TO LEARN MORE

City Life/Vida Urbana website: www.clvu.org

2.40 Bikes Not Bombs (The Shop)

18 Bartlett Square

JAMAICA PLAIN

Bikes Not Bombs is a nonprofit organization "using the bicycle as a vehicle for social change"—in Boston and in more than a dozen countries in the global South. In Boston its multiracial staff runs a six-week Earn-

Members of the Bikes Not Bombs youth program, 2016.

a-Bike program (among other activities) in which youth participants learn mechanics on a used bicycle that they get to keep upon completion. They also learn how to ride a bike safely and navigate the city. Abroad, Bikes Not Bombs has partnered with social-justice-oriented bicycle organizations in fourteen different countries—from El Salvador to Uganda—over the years. Since its founding in 1984, the organization has sent more than fifty-five thousand salvaged and donated bikes to its sister organizations in Africa, the Caribbean, and Central America, while collaborating with those organizations to share experiences, strategies, and other resources, and to build capacity. Meanwhile thousands of Boston teens have participated in its local youth programs.

Committed to "sustainable, equitable consumption of resources," the Boston-based organization originally arose in opposition to the Reagan administration's efforts to overthrow the leftist Sandinista government in Nicaragua during the 1980s. It expressed its antiwar, anti-imperial and pro-peace and -environment politics through the provision of material aid to Nicaraguans.

In addition to its store in Bartlett Square, where one can buy a refurbished bicycle (and equipment and accessories), Bikes Not Bombs has a warehouse on 10 Harvard Street in *Dorchester* where bikes destined for abroad are stored. Its international and youth programs are based at The Hub, which is part of the Brewery Complex on Armory Street (located between Stony Brook and Green Street stations on the Orange Line). Numerous graduates of its youth program are employed, or volunteer, at the various Bikes Not Bombs sites.

GETTING THERE

Orange Line to Green Street Station.

2.41 William A. Hinton State Laboratory Institute

305 South Street

JAMAICA PLAIN

In April 2017, Massachusetts state prosecutors announced that they would dismiss 21,587 convictions that involved drug evidence handled by Hinton State Laboratory —perhaps the largest dismissal of convictions in US history. Years of litigation by the ACLU of Massachusetts, and others in defense of people unjustly convicted, led to the announcement.

All the cases involved a chemist by the name of Annie Dookhan, who had begun working at the state Department of Health facility in late 2003. Coworkers in the drug-evidence lab became suspicious of Dookhan when she reported conducting an extraordinarily high number of drug sample tests: almost five times more than other chemists' average. As inappropriate practices came to light, Dookhan resigned in March 2012. Months later, state police arrested her, and in April 2013 she pleaded guilty to tampering with drug samples and fabricating results. She spent three years in prison and in April 2016 was released on parole.

Organizations such as the Jamaica Plain–based Families for Justice as Healing (42 Seaverns Street), an organization of formerly incarcerated women, and Boston's No Drug Arrests Collective (which it helped to found), continue to work for justice for those whose convictions involved malfeasance. Seeing them as the result of the "war on drugs," not the dishonesty of one state employee, they demand full and immediate dismissal of the remaining convictions associated with tainted evidence, as well as "a total transformation of the criminal punishment system: community-based transformative justice alternatives, accessible housing, educational opportunities, dignified employment, and quality mental and physical health care for people and their families."

The Hinton Laboratory Institute, part of the University of Massachusetts Medical School Jamaica Plain campus, continues to operate at the site, but the drug lab was closed down in the wake of the scandal. Its work now takes place at a facility outside of Boston.

GETTING THERE

Orange Line to Forest Hills Station, 0.1 mile (three-minute) walk.

NEARBY SITE

THE ARNOLD ARBORETUM, a 281-acre arboretum run by Harvard University and open free of charge to the public, is across the street from the laboratory.

Allston and Brighton

People's historian Howard Zinn addresses an antiwar rally in Allston outside Harvard Stadium, May 8, 1970.

Upwards of seventy-five thousand people live in the tightly tied neighborhoods of Allston and Brighton. Established as part of the Massachusetts Bay Colony in the 1600s, Brighton always included its Allston neighborhood. In the nineteenth century, Allston and Brighton were areas of farming and meatpacking, as well as working-class residential communities. By the early 1900s, Allston and Brighton were streetcar suburbs, dormitory communities connected to Downtown by mass transit. Public transit has rendered some areas highly walkable, notwithstanding the 1969 loss of the "A" trolley line and the relative inaccessibility via mass transit of some areas of Brighton.

Distinct neighborhoods since Brighton's annexation by Boston in 1874, Allston and

Brighton have developed large student populations and local businesses catering to their lifestyles. With the demographic shift, the neighborhoods' formerly immigrant and working-class housing stock has increasingly come to serve the transient student housing market as well as wealthier, younger workers seeking homes close to Downtown. Another and related source of pressure is the expansion of Harvard University into north Allston. Rising property values and changing land-use patterns to serve higher education and new technology companies and corporate headquarters, including those of New Balance and WGBH Public TV, have generated struggles over affordability.

There is an increasing presence of immigrants from Eastern Europe, Asia, and Latin

America in largely white Allston and Brighton. The neighborhoods are also home to new organizing among more recent Brazilian immigrants.

2.42   Nonantum

Oak Square

BRIGHTON

Magnolia Avenue and Eliot Memorial Road

NEWTON

Nonantum means "rejoicing" in the Algonquin language. It is the name given by John Eliot, the leading Christian missionary of his time to the "praying village" he founded in what is today the borderlands of Boston's Brighton neighborhood and Newton, a neighboring city.

An English colonist from a wealthy, land-owning family, Eliot is reputed to have converted an estimated eleven thousand indigenous people to Christianity in eastern Massachusetts from 1646 to 1674. As part of this endeavor, Eliot learned Algonquian and oversaw the Bible's translation into the language. He then set about establishing villages of Indian "converts," the first one

being Nonantum. (It is unclear the extent to which many alleged converts altered their beliefs. Instead, many of them appear to have made selective behavioral changes.)

On October 28, 1646, the Reverend Eliot, with an interpreter's assistance, met for three hours with a group of Indians led by a sachem named Waban on the southwest slope of what is today known as Nonantum Hill. The meeting included a sermon and a question-and-answer session. Afterward, Waban requested assistance in setting up a Native town. With a land grant from the colony's General Court and funding from the England-based Society for the Propagation of the Gospel, the "Praying Indian" settlement of Nonantum was born. Less than five years later, however, due to the colonists' land-hungry ways and their distrust of Indians, Eliot was compelled to move Nonantum's population to what is today the town of Natick (about seventeen miles west).

So-called praying towns were central to English colonization efforts. Indeed, Native conversion was a primary reason the English Parliament had chartered the Massachusetts Bay Colony. Eliot's praying towns sought to "civilize" Indians by getting them to abandon traditional clothing, rituals, and hunter-gatherer practices and adopt English modes of dress and sedentary agriculture. These efforts—and Native dispossession and dislocation associated with English colonization—led to great resentment among Indians and eventually gave rise to

Nonantum monument, Newton, 2018.

King Philip's War (1675–78—see *Old Country House/1749 Court House*), which put an end to most of Eliot's fourteen praying towns.

Eliot, whom some referred as "the apostle to the Indians," died in 1690. In addition to helping to found Roxbury Latin School, he was also associated with *Harvard Indian College*, established in the 1650s.

There is disagreement about where Eliot first preached to the Indians who would become part of Nonantum. Some say it took place under the shade of an enormous white oak tree in what is today Brighton's Oak Square. Approximately one mile away, in Newton, there is a memorial to Nonantum that claims that Eliot preached "near this spot" on the fateful day in October 1846. The two sites are almost linked by Nonantum Street, reputed to overlay an old Indian trail.

GETTING THERE

MBTA bus to Oak Square. To get to the memorial in Newton, walk west on Nonantum Street. The monument, which borders the Newton Commonwealth Golf Course, is located where Magnolia Avenue intersects with Eliot Memorial Road, 1.1 mile (about twenty-one-minute) walk.

NEARBY SITE

DURANT-KENDRICK HOUSE AND GROUNDS (a historic farmhouse and museum with exhibits on colonial life, the Revolutionary War, slavery and abolitionism, and the history of US horticulture), 86 Waverly Avenue, Newton.

TO LEARN MORE

Cogley, Richard W. *John Eliot's Mission to the Indians before King Philip's War*, Cambridge: Harvard University Press, 1999.

Marchione, William P. *Allston-Brighton in Transition: From Cattle Town to Streetcar Suburb*, Charleston, SC: The History Press, 2007.

Winship, J. P. C. *Historical Brighton: An Illustrated History of Brighton and Its Citizens*, vol. 1, Boston: George A. Warren Publishers, 1899.

2.43 Noah Worcester House

437–439 Washington Street

BRIGHTON

Immediately behind a chain-link fence between the houses at 437 and 439 Washington Street is a small monument with the appearance of a headstone. Installed by the US Post Office Department (the predecessor of the US Postal Service), the monument is dedicated to Noah Worcester, noting that he was the first postmaster of Brighton. The monument marks the site where his home once stood and out of which he operated the local postal service.

Far beyond his work as a postmaster, Noah Worcester is known as one of the founders of the US peace movement. Born in Hollis, New Hampshire, in 1758, Worcester was a Unitarian minister and a preeminent

> Rulers of nations are as liable to be misled by their passions and interests as other men; and when misled, they are very sure to mislead those of their subjects, who have confidence in their wisdom and integrity. Hence it is highly important that the custom of war should be abolished, and some other mode adopted, to settle disputes between nations.
>
> **—Noah Worcester, *A Solemn Review of the Custom of War*, p. 20**

pacifist—a political stance that grew out of his experience as a soldier in the Revolutionary War (he fought in the Battle of Bunker Hill, among others). In December 1814, while the War of 1812 was still unfolding, he published (under the pen name Philo Pacificus) *A Solemn Review of the Custom of War*, a book subsequently published in numerous languages. It is considered by many to be a classic of antiwar literature. In 1815 Worcester founded the Massachusetts Peace Society and served as the editor of its quarterly publication, *The Friend of Peace*, from 1819 to 1828.

Noah Worcester moved to Brighton in 1813, and in 1837 died in his Washington Street home (which was demolished in the early 1900s). His remains are buried in the Mount Auburn Cemetery in **Cambridge**.

GETTING THERE

MBTA bus to Brighton Center, 0.3 mile (five-minute) walk.

NEARBY SITES

BRIGHTON-ALLSTON HISTORICAL SOCIETY AND HERITAGE MUSEUM, 20 Chestnut Hill Avenue (in the basement of the Veronica Smith Senior Center). Former site of the home of **HANNAH WEBSTER FOSTER**, author of *The Coquette, or the History of Eliza Wharton* (1797), one of the most popular books of its time and the first novel written by a native-born woman in the United States, 6–10 Academy Hill Road.

TO LEARN MORE

Marchione, William P. *Allston-Brighton in Transition: From Cattle Town to Streetcar Suburb*, Charleston, SC: The History Press, 2007.

2.44 Barry's Corner

Intersection of North Harvard Street and Western Avenue

ALLSTON

Barry's Corner is a 9.3-acre area of Lower (or North) Allston that embodies the imperial practices of the Boston Redevelopment Authority (BRA) in the 1960s and predatory property acquisition of Harvard University in more recent decades. In 1961 the largely working-class residents of the neighborhood learned on the evening news that the BRA and the City of Boston were planning to raze the area's fifty-two buildings to make way for a luxury apartment complex. They soon formed an organization, Citizens for Private Property, to protest the plan and protect their homes and neighborhood. On Thanksgiving Day 1964, residents received official notice that Boston had seized their homes by eminent domain and that they now had to pay rent to the City. By June 1965 more than half the families had left the neighborhood rather than face eviction. The rest of them, along with allies from across Boston, many of whom had been victimized by urban renewal projects elsewhere, and some Harvard students, engaged in militant resistance to the City's attempts to evict them.

In the face of strong opposition and negative publicity, the BRA ultimately retreated from the luxury development plan and agreed to set up a blue-ribbon commission to make recommendations. The City eventually agreed to allow the Committee for North Harvard, a nonprofit group of five religious congregations, to construct a low- and moderate-income housing complex.

North Harvard Street: Protest on Hefferan Street of BRA's plan to raze buildings in Barry's Corner, August 9, 1965.

Police forcibly remove Barry's Corner protester, August 9, 1965.

After the razing of the homes of the last holdouts in 1969, Charlesview Apartments went up, opening in 1971.

In the decades that followed, Harvard slowly and secretly purchased property in the area, announcing in 1997 that it had obtained 52 acres of land in Allston through a real estate firm. As of 2017, Harvard owned 358 acres in Allston (most associated with longstanding properties—the Harvard Business School campus and Harvard Stadium)—143 acres more than it possessed in *Cambridge*. Among the university's buildings on its "Allston campus" are three "innovation labs," a ceramics studio, and the Harvard Ed Portal. Such developments, along with plans for further expansion, explain why Harvard President Drew Faust in 2016 gushed that "all roads lead to Allston."

Today what was Barry's Corner is a construction site, the future home of a Harvard science and engineering complex, replacing the Charlesview Apartments, which had fallen into disrepair and were torn down in 2015. Harvard and Charlesview engaged in a land swap, with the latter getting a larger piece of land a few blocks away on Western Avenue in Brighton, where the new Charlesview Residences have arisen.

The land swap has allowed the area's low- and moderate-income housing to be maintained (and even increased a bit). However, Harvard's rapid growth in Allston and its ambitious plans for further development raise serious questions about the area's future as a viable neighborhood for working- and middle-class households.

GETTING THERE

Various MBTA buses pass by.

Seminarians at Saint John's Seminary, 1975.

2.45 Saint John's Seminary

127 Lake Street

BRIGHTON

In the 1960s Boston's Catholic Church proved not to be immune to the decade's spirit of protest against established norms, institutions, and authorities. In late March 1966, more than a hundred seminarians picketed outside Saint John Seminary's auditorium while Cardinal Richard Cushing spoke to a gathering of Boston-area priests on Vatican II

The Second Vatican Council (Vatican II)—an assembly (1962–5) of Catholic leaders that reformed much of church doctrine—led to great changes in the religious body. "Almost no aspect of Catholic life, customs, devotion, piety or ritual remained untouched," asserts historian Thomas O'Connor. In Boston these changes unfolded in an environment fraught with intense debate and divisions within parishes and across the archdiocese over theology and church practices.

In this context, students at Saint John's Seminary asked Cushing for a meeting to discuss their grievances regarding what they saw as an absence of personal and academic freedom. The lack of response from Cushing led to the protest. Furious about the seminarians' insubordination, Saint John's expelled eight of the action's leaders. Meanwhile, Cushing forbade *The Pilot,* the Archdiocese's newspaper, from reporting on what had transpired.

In support of the expelled seminarians, who characterized the reigning atmosphere at Saint John's as one of "dusty medievalism," fellow students—with estimates ranging from thirty to two hundred—conducted a "holy fast" to express their "concern for critical problems at the seminary." In addition, lay Catholics and college students from the area held a demonstration outside Cushing's residence on Commonwealth Avenue. Some also organized a four-day Easter prayer vigil to champion the seminarians' cause.

Despite the pressures, Cushing never agreed to reinstate the expelled students. However, reforms did take place in subsequent years at Saint John's, with the institution allowing seminarians greater personal freedoms and instituting new educational mechanisms.

Having opened its doors in Brighton in 1884, Saint John's is the major seminary of the Archdiocese of Boston, preparing men for the Catholic priesthood, and serves many dioceses in New England and even some outside the United States. It also has many lay students. In the 2000s, Saint John's sold much of its land and numerous buildings to Boston College.

GETTING THERE

Green Line, B Branch, to Boston College Station, 0.4 mile (nine-minute) walk.

NEARBY SITE

CARDINAL'S RESIDENCE (2101 Commonwealth Avenue, Brighton), was once the centerpiece of the Archdiocese's "Little Rome." In 2004, the Archdiocese, in need of funds to pay restitution to the victims of sexual abuse, sold Boston College forty-three acres of land and some buildings, including the cardinal's residence, a three-story, ornate, and opulent Italian Renaissance–style palazzo for $99.4 million. Today it houses the college's McMullen Museum of Art.

TO LEARN MORE

O'Connor, Thomas H. *Boston Catholics: A History of the Church and Its People*, Boston: Northeastern University Press, 1998.

2.46 Power-One Corporation Factory Site

20 Linden Street

ALLSTON

In May 2001 the largely Chinese-immigrant workforce of three hundred at the small, electrical-device manufacturer Power-One Corporation had had enough. Not only had the company announced the planned closure of the Allston plant later that year and several rounds of layoffs, but workers discovered that management was unilaterally deciding who among them would receive severance packages. In response, the mostly female workforce organized a one-hour work stoppage. This in turn led the Chinese-speaking management to threaten workers with denial of unemployment assistance. At

Workers demonstrating outside Power-One, June 2001.

this point, the workers turned to community-based allies—a network of organizations, led by the Chinese Progressive Association, that included Greater Boston Legal Services and the Campaign on Contingent Work.

Although ethnic solidarity had helped the workers find their jobs, their relative linguistic isolation had denied them access to education about their rights: "We are ordinary people. When we came to the U.S., we always had to work, never had time to learn English," recalls Jun Ru Wang, one of the employees. In their struggle, the workers overcame these limits by combining traditional protest tactics with community outreach and a multipronged legal and public policy strategy to pressure both the employer and the state to provide compensation for the layoffs and to help them find new jobs.

Over much of May and into June, picket lines organized by the workers and their allies greeted management and informed passersby, including thousands of motorists on the adjacent interstate freeway. A media campaign and the filing of unfair-labor-practice charges against Power-One added to the pressures. As a result, by late June, management apologized to the workers and began negotiating severance packages and overtime benefits for all of them. Moreover, the Commonwealth of Massachusetts, embarrassed by its delay in enforcing regulations that applied to mass layoffs, responded positively to demands for job-retraining benefits and English as a Second Language education for the workers.

Occurring a little more than a year after the massive protests in Seattle against the World Trade Organization and corporate-driven globalization, the struggle at Power-One illustrated the unjust and destabilizing impacts (for workers and communities) of capitalist restructuring. Ironically, Power-One, which had acquired the factory two years earlier from its Chinese-American owners, took advantage of free-trade treaties to outsource work abroad, including to China, from where most of the Allston workers had emigrated in the first place. Over the ensuing decade, the corporation would change ownership several times. Today the actual Allston factory buildings are home to a business and office center, while an adjacent structure hosts a high-end nightclub.

GETTING THERE

Green Line, B Branch to Harvard Avenue, 0.5 mile (ten-minute) walk.

TO LEARN MORE

Mark, Cynthia, and Yvonne Yang. "The Power-One Campaign: Immigrant Worker Empowerment through Law and Organizing," *Clearinghouse Review: Journal of Poverty Law and Policy* 36, nos. 3–4 (2002): 264–74.

2.47 Binland Lee House

87 Linden Street

ALLSTON

In the early morning of April 28, 2013, a fire broke out at 87 Linden Street. All the dozen or so occupants, except one, escaped that morning as the fire quickly engulfed the building. Binland Lee, a twenty-two-year-old student from a Chinese immigrant family in Brooklyn, New York, was not able to get out of her attic room, the one exit blocked by flames. A firefighter would later find her body by a dormer window in her room. According to a medical examiner, the marine science major died of smoke inhalation—two weeks before she was to graduate from Boston University.

The tragedy brought to the fore the huge increase in Boston's student population, and the failure of colleges and universities to provide adequate housing for their rapidly expanding student bodies. The shortfall led students to pursue options in surrounding neighborhoods: From 2006 to 2013, it is conservatively estimated that the undergraduate and graduate student population living off campus in the city grew 36 percent, to forty-five thousand individuals. The tragedy also highlighted the woefully inadequate nature of the City's rental housing inspection regime, the pervasive presence of illegal, substandard, and overcrowded apartments in Boston's college neighborhoods, and gross levels of impunity for landlords who regularly flouted the law.

The rising demand for private rental housing for students during this period led to massive real estate speculation—particularly in *the Fenway*, Allston-Brighton, and *Mission Hill* neighborhoods—given the lucrative income stream available to landlords. In the case of 87 Linden Street, for example, at the time of the fire its owner, Anna Belokurova, was receiving $7,850 in rent per month from the fourteen students living in twelve bedrooms divided between two units—this for a house whose building plan listed six bedrooms and in the face of a City zoning ordinance prohibiting more than four full-time undergraduates from sharing a house or apartment.

In 2015 the Suffolk County district attorney determined that it would not criminally charge Belokurova for what transpired, despite the building's many code violations and the illegality of Binland Lee's apartment, which did not have two proper exits. The DA justified the decision by saying that Belokurova had not received a citation for the missing second exit and that code violations had not contributed to the fire or the death.

One year after the death of Binland Lee, her family and friends returned to Linden Street and set up a memorial to her in front of the condemned building. Within hours, the candles, flowers, framed photos, and other mementos were gone. Today a new building, one housing students, stands in its place—with nothing commemorating Binland Lee.

GETTING THERE

Green Line, B Branch, to Harvard Avenue, 0.2 mile (five-minute) walk.

3

Adjacent Cities

Cambridge and Somerville

Anti-nuclear-power demonstration, Kendall Square, 1974.

Two cities on the Mishawum Peninsula—with the Charles River to the south, the Mystic River to the north—Cambridge and Somerville were sites of the earliest settlement by English colonists.

Cambridge was originally called New(e) Town. Five years after its establishment in 1631, it became home to Newe College. Set up to train Anglican ministers, the institution later renamed itself after a donor, John Harvard.

A city of approximately 110,000 residents, Cambridge has a history as a factory town. Indeed, by the early twentieth century, it was one of New England's largest industrial cities. In the mid-1800s, the city had the largest glassworks in the world. A little later, the world's largest ink producer came to call it home. Well-known Cambridge companies included the Kennedy Biscuit Company,

maker of the famed Fig Newton, and Necco (as in wafer), the confectioner.

Cambridge has long been home to the political-economic establishment as well as rebels, the latter giving rise to its reputation as a center of progressive activism. This was true during the colonial period, just as it is today: The country's first gay marriage took place there; the city champions the right of non-US-citizen residents to vote in school committee elections (but is waiting for state authorization), and hosts an official peace commission. Today's Cambridge is much tamer than in the 1960s, '70s, and '80s, however. Heavily gentrified, its working-class population is small, its student and affluent populations large. The "knowledge economy" (particularly around Kendall Square), heavily capitalized biotech and high-tech companies, along with Harvard and MIT—and its strong ties to military research—dominate the city.

Neighboring Somerville, until 1842 part of *Charlestown*, played an important role in the early stages of the Revolutionary War. In the nineteenth century, it developed a strong industrial base, brickmaking and meat processing among its core activities. It later had a large automobile plant (today the site of the Assembly Square neighborhood and shopping mall). Long a bastion of the working class, Somerville, heavily impacted by gentrification, has changed radically in recent decades. Largely white, it, like Cambridge, also has a considerable immigrant population and diversity. The city's political scene is characterized as increasingly progressive.

3.1 Ten Hills Farm

Governor Winthrop Road and Shore Drive
SOMERVILLE

In 1629, John Winthrop, a shareholder in and future governor of Massachusetts Bay Colony, a corporation chartered by the English monarchy, asked a straightforward question before journeying to present-day Greater Boston: "What right have we to take that land, which is and hath been of long tyme possessed of others of the sons of Adam?" Unable to find a satisfactory answer, according to historian Margaret Ellen Newell, the best that he could offer years later, after settling in New England, was that it was justified by good relations with "the natives." But that answer was a shaky one. By 1636, just a few years after establishing the colony, Winthrop and his fellow settlers were at war with the Pequot nation and were seizing captives.

In fact, Winthrop himself held captive Wincumbone, wife of Mononotto, the defeated Mystic Pequot sachem. Together with other indigenous captives, she formed part of the Puritan's labor force. Although Wincumbone's high status afforded some protection, other Pequot captives provided physical labor, adding to that of the indentured and lower-status members of the household. In stark contrast to the image of the modest New England farmstead and its relative egalitarianism, Winthrop's Ten Hills Farm, at six hundred acres, was too large to be worked by a single family.

Described as the "first keeper of the New England conscience" and sometimes even as "the forgotten founding father," Winthrop facilitated the exchange and export of enslaved Pequot prisoners of war for enslaved Africans, who were less likely to enjoy support from still-free Indian communities. In 1641 the Massachusetts Bay Colony formally enshrined slavery in its constitution, defining the circumstances under which people could be enslaved to include capture in a "just" war.

The Ten Hills Farm changed hands many times over succeeding

Marker for Ten Hills Farm, 2019.

generations. Remaining parts include the Royall House and Slave Quarters (a museum located at 15 George Street in Medford), the former estate of Isaac Royall, a sugar planter in Antigua who moved to Massachusetts in the eighteenth century. His wealth helped to establish Harvard Law School.

Twelve residential city blocks upon a hill bound by Interstate 93, Route 28, and the Mystic River today form Somerville's Ten Hills neighborhood, the southeast corner of the original Ten Hills farm. A historic marker at the intersection of Governor Winthrop Road and Shore Drive indicates the site of Winthrop's home on the farm.

GETTING THERE

Orange Line to Assembly Square Station, 0.5 mile (ten-minute) walk. Also accessible by the Mystic River Reservation Bike Trail.

TO LEARN MORE

Mangold, C. S. *Ten Hills Farm: The Forgotten History of Slavery in the North*, Princeton: Princeton University Press, 2010.

Newell, Margaret Ellen. *Brethren by Nature: New England Indians, Colonists, and the Origins of American Slavery*, Ithaca: Cornell University Press, 2015.

3.2 Harvard Indian College/ Matthew Hall

Harvard Yard

CAMBRIDGE

In the early years after its founding in 1636, Harvard College struggled financially. The English Society for the Propagation of the Gospel in New England helped to sustain it by raising and donating funds to support Indian education at Harvard. This explains why the charter of Harvard College (written in 1650) asserts a promise to promote the "education of English and Indian youth of this Country, in knowledge and godliness." In terms of Native youth, a central goal was that they would serve as missionaries to their home communities and play a large role in conversions to Christianity; relatedly, conversion was seen as a means of containing the perceived threat embodied by Indians. To serve these ends, the institution completed the construction of the Harvard Indian College in 1655. It was a two-story brick building and housed the English colonies' only printing shop. There, Harvard Press published the first Bible in North America, one translated into the Algonquian language and produced by John Eliot and some bilingual Native men.

King Philip's War (see **Old Country House/1749 Court House**) greatly harmed relations between English settlers and Native Americans, leading many Puritans to advocate complete domination of the indigenous population. In a context of declining support for Native education, the Harvard Corporation determined in November 1693 that "the Indian College be taken down, provided the charges of taking it down amount not to more than five pounds." In 1698 the college ceased to exist.

Only five Native American students attended the Indian College. Caleb Cheeshahteaumuck (Wampanoag) was the first to graduate. After the school's closure, it was not until 1970 that Harvard gave renewed attention to Native American issues

Indigenous People's Day, outside Matthews Hall, October 11, 2016.

when it established the American Indian Program. In 1997, what's now called the Native American Program placed a historical marker on Matthew Hall, a student dormitory that occupies the former site of the Indian College.

GETTING THERE

Red Line to Harvard Square Station.

TO LEARN MORE

Brooks, Lisa. *Our Beloved Kin: A New History of King Philip's War*, New Haven: Yale University Press, 2018.

Wilder, Craig Steven. *Ebony and Ivy: Race, Slavery, and the Troubled History of America's Universities*, New York: Bloomsbury Press, 2013.

3.3 Elmwood

33 Elmwood Avenue

CAMBRIDGE

When Lieutenant Governor Thomas Oliver exited his residence on Cambridge's "Tory Row" on Saturday afternoon, September 2, 1774, there were three thousand to four thousand people—common farmers, according to one account—surrounding the home, a quarter of them armed, he reported. A "Committee" of five men met him at his front door. On behalf of "the people," they politely demanded that he resign. The British colonial official resisted the request, however, and the crowd became increasingly agitated. Many threatened to spill his blood if he did not agree to sign a resignation document. Afraid for himself and his family (his wife and six daughters were in the house), Oliver ultimately signed. A few days later, he and his family abandoned the estate.

The impetus for the event was the wildly unpopular Massachusetts Government Act (May 1774) of the British parliament. It effectively overrode the 1691 charter of the Massachusetts Bay Colony and gave the governor (a royal appointee) wide-ranging powers, eliminating meaningful local rule. A response to the Boston Tea Party and other acts of dissent, the act led to rebellion across Massachusetts, particularly outside of Boston, as large groups of citizens rose up and seized power from crown-appointed officials. By October 1774, all such officials throughout Massachusetts had, under coercion, disavowed British authority or had fled to British military–occupied Boston. In the resulting political vacuum, Massachusetts residents began establishing their own government.

Elmwood, 2008.

Historian Ray Raphael characterizes this participatory, democratic, and bloodless uprising as the first American Revolution. The American Revolution that is taught in most schools, the one associated with the battles at Lexington, *Concord*, and Bunker Hill, he contends, was the British attempt "to regain control of a colony they had already lost."

Thomas Oliver built Elmwood, an enormous house on one hundred acres of land, in 1767. Born in Antigua to a sugar-plantation- (and thus slave-) holding family, his parents migrated to Cambridge when he was a young boy. He would go on to study at Harvard College. His considerable wealth inherited, Oliver is known to have purchased enslaved Africans on a trip to Antigua in 1763. It is likely, but not known for certain, that enslaved people lived at Elmwood.

During the Revolutionary War, Elmwood served as a hospital for soldiers of the Continental Army. After the war, the Commonwealth of Massachusetts sold the estate. A. Kingsley Porter, a Harvard professor, was the last private individual to own Elmwood. In 1962 he willed it to the university. The estate, now about 2.6 acres and on the National Register of Historic Places, has served as the home of Harvard's president since 1971.

GETTING THERE

Red Line to Harvard Square Station, about a 1.0 mile (twenty-minute) walk.

TO LEARN MORE

Beckert, Sven, Katherine Stevens, and the students of the Harvard and Slavery Research Seminar. *Harvard and Slavery: Seeking a Forgotten History*, Cambridge: Harvard University Press, 2011.

Kingsley Porter, Lucy. "The Owners of Elmwood: A History and Memoir," *Proceedings of the Cambridge Historical* Society 33 (1949): 58–93.

Raphael, Ray. *The First American Revolution: Before Lexington and Concord*, New York: The New Press, 2002.

3.4 Ursuline Convent

Broadway at Illinois Avenue

SOMERVILLE

In 1834 the Ursuline Convent on top of Mount Benedict (formally known as Ploughed Hill) became a flashpoint in Boston's intensifying anti-Catholic animus. Fueled by unfounded rumors that Ursuline nuns were engaging in forced conversions to Catholicism and holding a young woman against her will, opponents of the growing Irish presence in the region focused their ire on the convent, egged on by the Reverend Lyman Beecher (father of Harriet Beecher Stowe). On Sunday, August 10, he delivered a series of sermons while visiting Boston, calling upon the city's Protestant faithful to repel the Catholic menace.

The next evening, August 11, a mob of several dozen Protestant men, many of them reportedly drunk, assembled at the convent's gate and demanded that the mother superior produce the woman allegedly imprisoned there. When the head nun refused to do so

View of Somerville, Mass., from the ruin of the Ursuline Convent, 1854.

and insisted that the convent was engaging in no wrongdoing, the men's anger only intensified. After retreating for a brief time and starting a bonfire near the Ursuline school (most of the students, ironically, were young women from affluent Protestant families), the mob stormed the convent. They tore down the door, took furniture, musical instruments, personal belongings and religious items and threw them into the fire. The convent and several nearby buildings—the religious community's horse stables and library, for example—were soon engulfed in flames. The rioters also desecrated the convent's mausoleum, tearing open coffins and scattering the bones within.

While the nuns and their students were able to escape the mob's wrath and flee to safety, the Ursuline community on Mount Benedict was destroyed. Leading political figures of Boston condemned the violence, and a mass meeting took place at *Faneuil Hall* in response. Authorities arrested thirteen men, trying eight of them, one of whom was convicted and received a life sentence.

A fortified military post during the Revolutionary War, Ploughed Hill/Mount Benedict was gradually cut down in the decades following the 1834 riot to provide earth for landfill. A monument now marks the site of the hill and the convent.

GETTING THERE

Orange Line to Sullivan Square Station. The monument is on the lot of the East Branch of the Somerville Public Library, 0.5 mile (ten-minute) walk.

TO LEARN MORE

Bruce, Susannah Ural. *The Harp and the Eagle: Irish-American Volunteers and the Union Army, 1861–1865*, New York: New York University Press, 2006.

Handlin, Oscar. *Boston's Immigrants, 1790–1880*, New York: Atheneum, 1975.

Morris, Dee, and Dora St. Martin. *Somerville, Massachusetts: A Brief History*, Charleston, South Carolina: The History Press, 2008.

3.5 Riverside Cycling Club

882–884 (formerly 458) Main Street

CAMBRIDGE

The late nineteenth century saw a national cycling boom. Among the touring and cycling groups founded during this time was the Riverside Cycling Club (1893) in Cambridge. Established by a group of friends as the first all-black cycling club in the United States, it catered to residents of Cambridgeport, an area settled by many former slaves after the Civil War, the city's Riverside section, and Boston's **Allston** neighborhood.

The most famous individual associated with Riverside (it never officially claimed her most likely due to long-standing gender segregation in cycling clubs) was Katherine "Kittie" Knox. A seamstress born in 1874 to a black father and a white mother in Cambridge, Knox garnered attention for her impressive showings in area meets as a century rider (one hundred miles rather than the shorter track races), a pacer, her participation in costume contests, and her self-made and highly fashionable riding outfits. As a young black woman, Knox stuck out at most cycling meets and newspapers often highlighted her participation.

Knox is perhaps best known for directly challenging a racial barrier of the League of American Wheelmen (LAW), the era's largest national cycling group. Despite the Massachusetts delegation's unanimous opposition, the organization passed a resolution in 1894, sponsored by delegates from Southern states, that denied membership to nonwhite cyclists and barred their participation in LAW recreational cycling meets. Nonethe-less, Knox, along with a group of Boston-area cyclists and fellow LAW members, traveled to Asbury Park, New Jersey, in July 1895 for the national LAW meet. While Knox had joined LAW prior to the color ban, the organization initially denied her entrance. In the face of protest led by fellow area cyclists, many Boston newspapers, and LAW executive board member George Perkins, a former member of the Massachusetts House of Representatives, Knox was ultimately able to participate because her membership predated the bar.

By 1896 the Riverside Cycling Club was in decline as interest in cycling shifted from road races to track races. A multi-family home now occupies its former site. Knox died in 1900 of kidney disease. Her tombstone can be found in Mount Auburn Cemetery in Cambridge. In 2019, the City of Cambridge renamed a bike path connecting Broadway and Binney Street in Kendall Square in honor of Kittie Knox.

GETTING THERE

Red Line to Central Square Station, 0.2 mile (five-minute) walk.

TO LEARN MORE

Finison, Lorenz J. *Boston's Cycling Craze, 1880–1900: A Story of Race, Sport, and Society*, Amherst: University of Massachusetts Press, 2014.

3.6 *Old Mole*/The Middle East and Zuzu Restaurant and Nightclub

2 Brookline Street

CAMBRIDGE

Old Mole was an underground newspaper—one associated with the counterculture of the 1960s and 1970s. The publication's politics broadly reflected those of the New Left and its strong presence in and around Cambridge at the time. Calling itself a radical biweekly and characterizing its largely volunteer staff as an "anti-profit institution," the newspaper took its name from the words of Karl Marx: "We recognize our old friend, our old mole, who knows so well how to work underground, suddenly to appear: the revolution."

A sixteen-page, tabloid-style newspaper, it initially sold for 15 cents, and later for a quarter during its two years of existence (September 1968–September 1970). Prisoners and soldiers received free subscriptions. For most of its existence its office operated out of the storefront and basement at 2 Brookline Street. While national and global affairs were central to the newspaper's focus, about half of its coverage was local. Reporting focused on issues ranging from the National Democratic Convention in Chicago and environmental matters to the CIA's links with Harvard and the war in Vietnam.

Old Mole's former space is now part of the Middle East and Zuzu Restaurant and Nightclub (472–480 Massachusetts Avenue). Comprising four distinct dining and performance venues, the Middle East is one of the Cambridge-Boston area's best live-music spaces. It is also a "movement institution." In addition to being a backer of public cultural events in the area, it is supportive of peace, antiwar, and social justice activism and organizing. The Middle East has often

Man selling the *Old Mole* outside the Cambridge Trust Co., 1969.

served as the venue for cause-oriented fundraisers and has frequently provided food to progressive movement events at a loss to the establishment's bottom line.

GETTING THERE

Red Line to Central Square Station, 0.2 mile (four-minute) walk.

RELATED SITE

SGT. BROWN'S MEMORIAL NECKTIE, an antiwar coffeehouse operated by the Boston Draft Resistance Group. *Old Mole*, its office nearby, advertised the coffee house, where counseling was offered to active-duty soldiers and draft resisters. 49 Pleasant Street (the back of the building now occupied by Keezers Classic Clothing at 140 River Street), Cambridge.

3.7 Polaroid/Tech Square

549 Technology Square

CAMBRIDGE

In 1970 Ken Williams, a design photographer for Polaroid, and another African American employee, Caroline Hunter, a chemist, found a sample identification badge for the

South Africa Department of Mines in the company's "Tech Square" headquarters. Through research they discovered that Polaroid, using its local intermediary, had sold the Cambridge-based corporation's ID-2 system to South Africa's apartheid state. The technology enabled South Africa to quickly manufacture identification cards, producing its infamous passbooks, which were used to control the residence and mobility of the country's black population.

When confronted by Williams, Polaroid executives were not forthcoming. In response Hunter, Williams, and others founded the Polaroid Revolutionary Workers Movement (PRWM) to force the company to end its complicity with apartheid. On October 8, 1970, the organization held its first demonstration outside headquarters, attracting hundreds of employees and other supporters. Through such actions, alliances with area students and academics, workers, and community members, and its call for a global boycott of Polaroid products, the PRWM exerted significant pressure on the corporation.

The PRWM, which gave birth to the South Africa divestment movement in the United States, called for a total Polaroid pullout from the country, a public denunciation of apartheid by the company, and the handover of its profits to South Africa's liberation movement. Polaroid responded by announcing a partial ban on the sale of its products in South Africa and implementing what became known as the "Polaroid experiment"—an effort to promote reform through the company's business practices within South Africa. Far from satisfying the

Flyer by Polaroid Revolutionary Workers Movement, March 1971. Design by Ken Williams.

Button by Polaroid Revolutionary Workers Movement. Design by Ken Williams.

PRWM and its growing network of allies in the United States and in South Africa, the campaign against Polaroid only grew. While it took several years, Polaroid eventually withdrew from South Africa, announcing its decision on November 22, 1977, becoming the first US corporation to do so.

In 1998, Polaroid left Kendall Square and moved its headquarters to its building on 784 Memorial Drive building, which it had occupied since 1940. In the face of rapidly changing technologies and plummeting sales, Polaroid declared bankruptcy in 2001, ending its presence in Cambridge. Demolished in 2000, the 549 building stood in the middle of the green space of today's Tech Square. Tech Square is the epicenter of a dense conglomeration in and around Kendall Square of venture capital and high-tech research and production businesses focused on weaponry, big pharma, biotech, and information technology.

TO LEARN MORE

Morgan, Eric J. "The World Is Watching: Polaroid and South Africa," *Enterprise and Society* 7, no. 3 (2006): 520–49.

GETTING THERE

Red Line to Kendall/MIT Station, 0.3 mile (seven-minute) walk.

3.8 888/The Women's Center

888 Memorial Drive

CAMBRIDGE

On March 6, 1971, several hundred women marched from Boston in honor of International Women's Day and the fiftieth anniversary of the Nineteenth Amendment to the US Constitution, which gave women the right to vote. Led by a small group of organizers, the march followed Massachusetts Avenue into Cambridge, took a left onto Pearl Street, and continued until Memorial Drive. There, about 150 marchers broke into and took over a Harvard University–owned building, declaring it the Women's Center.

The action emerged out of a variety of concerns, including Harvard's and MIT's large-scale real estate acquisitions and the resulting loss of residential housing, inade-

888 Memorial Drive during the building takeover, 1971.

quate daycare services in the area, and a general lack of spaces for women—particularly for the lesbian community. The women also connected their discontent to the Vietnam War and the prison-industrial complex's targeting of people of color.

The idea of a women's center came out of a small group of women who belonged to Bread and Roses, a feminist socialist organization founded in Cambridge in 1969. The women targeted 888 Memorial Drive as a symbolic gesture in opposition to Harvard's plan to tear down the building and construct faculty housing in its place instead of low-income housing as demanded by the Riverside neighborhood's residents.

Harvard responded immediately to the takeover by turning off heat and telephone service and declaring the building unsafe for habitation. Harvard then offered an alternative space to serve as a center, but the women deemed the proposed venue inadequate and quickly dismissed the offer. University officials next turned to legal action and served the women an ultimatum that included a temporary restraining order to evict them by force from the building. In response, ten days into the takeover, the women left the building.

Inspired by the action and subsequent organizing efforts, many in the Cambridge-Somerville-Boston area donated money to allow the leaders of the 888 takeover to buy a house nearby at 46 Pleasant Street, one that has served as the Women's Center's home since January 1972. The Women's Center provides resources and services, particularly for low-income women and victims of domestic and sexual violence. It is the longest running women's center in the country.

Built in 1904, 888 Memorial Drive was originally a knitting factory. The building no longer exists. The site is now part of a residential complex for Harvard students and faculty. Across the street, in Riverside City Park, there is a plaque commemorating the takeover.

GETTING THERE

Red Line to Central Square Station, 0.7 mile (fifteen-minute) walk.

TO LEARN MORE

Website of Left on Pearl: http://www.leftonpearl .org; website of the Women's Center: http:// www.cambridgewomenscenter.org.

3.9 Sojourner: The Women's Forum

143 Albany Street

CAMBRIDGE

Sojourner front page, December 1984

Founded in 1975 by female students, staff, and faculty at the Massachusetts Institute of Technology "as the voice of the MIT women's community," *Sojourner* would go on to become one of the most important feminist newspapers in the United States. The chancellor at the male-dominated MIT helped launch the newspaper with a $1,700 grant—enough to fund the first two issues. Thereafter the staff and supporters sustained the newspaper through subscriptions, advertising, sales of individual copies, and donations.

Sojourner quickly moved beyond MIT, its birth and growth a manifestation of campus activism at the time as well as the area's strong feminist and progressive communities. After its first year, it characterized itself as Boston's "Feminist Journal of News, Opinion, and the Arts." Soon the paper went national. On April 22, 1977, to accommodate its growth and its reach well beyond the university, *Sojourner* launched its first off-campus office at 143 Albany Street.

What made *Sojourner* unique was its refusal to adopt any particular feminist theoretical or political position. It saw itself, as asserted by its subtitle, as a forum, one dedicated, as the paper explained to its readers, to "offering a place where feminists (women and men) can explore ideas and events in an attempt to shape their own experience and our collective experience toward changing our lives and society." The newspaper further declared that it would not "exclude opinions because we do not agree with them (unless they are racist, sexist, or homophobic)." Because *Sojourner* had no columnists or staff writers, and relied largely on unsolicited contributions (in later years, it solicited articles to ensure a diverse set of perspectives and authors), thousands of individuals wrote for the publication over its years of existence. *Sojourner* also had a program to provide the monthly newspaper for free to incarcerated women across the United States.

In 1990 the growing staff and newspaper moved to *Jamaica Plain* (42 Seaverns Avenue). In the face of generational shifts, the rise of the Internet, financial difficulties, and declining readership, it closed its doors in 2002.

GETTING THERE

Red Line to Kendall Station, 0.7 mile (fifteen-minute) walk.

TO LEARN MORE

Kahn, Karen, ed. *Front Line Feminism, 1975–1995: Essays from "Sojourner"'s First 20 Years*, San Francisco: Aunt Lute Books, 1995.

3.10 Dollars & Sense

1 Summer Street

SOMERVILLE

March/April 2011 issue.

A growing move to the right in academic economics in the 1970s led a group of leftist economists in the Boston area to publish a sample issue of *Dollars & Sense* in the spring of 1974. As members of the Union for Radical Political Economics, their motivation was to provide "clear and concise interpretations of current economic events from a socialist perspective" that were accessible to readers of all backgrounds.

Given the successful reception enjoyed by the first issue, the Dollars & Sense collective began regularly publishing the magazine in November 1974 out of an office on Somerville Avenue, eventually moving to 1 Summer Street. There it shared offices with the publication *Radical America*, and Resist, then an activist, antiwar organization. The publication, first as a monthly and later as a bimonthly, remained at the address until the early 2000s.

Dollars & Sense was, and continues to be, a nonhierarchical, democratically run, largely volunteer collective. While in the early years it was almost entirely made up of economists, the collective now includes and publishes voices from related fields, including sociology and political science, and from community activists. This is reflected in the magazine's content. While capitalist globalization and labor struggles were topics long at the forefront of the publication, it now covers a much wider array of issues.

In its early years, the collective worked to maintain an equal sex ratio through moratoriums on new male membership. It also worked to increase membership of people of color through the establishment of a task force as part of its effort to counter the mostly white-male economics establishment.

In addition to publishing the magazine, the collective produces its own college-level textbooks to provide instructors with resources that include perspectives and voices typically ignored in standard economics textbooks. It has also helped many progressive economists make their writing accessible while still accurate.

The Dollars & Sense collective currently runs out of an office at the Nonprofit Center of New England (89 South Street) in Boston's Financial District. The building at 1 Summer Street in a gentrifying Somerville is now home to luxury condominiums.

TO LEARN MORE

Dollars & Sense website: http://dollarsandsense.org/

GETTING THERE

A number of MBTA bus lines pass close by.

3.11 Old Cambridge Baptist Church

1151 Massachusetts Avenue and
400 Harvard Street

CAMBRIDGE

"This is for the Sisters": Feminist parade marchers outside church, 1969.

Founded in 1844, the Old Cambridge Baptist Church (OCBC) has a deep tradition of work in support of peace and justice. From its opposition to slavery and protest of the Vietnam War to its early support for LGBTQ rights, OCBC has played a prominent role in a variety of progressive social movements. One area in which the church has been particularly active is sanctuary.

OCBC was the first house of worship in Massachusetts to declare itself a sanctuary for Central American refugees fleeing US government–backed repression in El Salvador, Guatemala, and Honduras during the 1980s. On December 4, 1984, the church received "Estela Ramirez," a Salvadoran trade unionist who had fled her homeland after authorities had murdered her husband and subsequently arrested and tortured her on numerous occasions. Congregants took turns staying with her over the weeks she remained there to prevent arrest by US immigration authorities. (Eventually Magdalena Rivas—her real name—received political asylum and US citizenship.) Because of its activism challenging US policy—OCBC housed numerous antiwar, anti-imperialist, and solidarity organizations in its basement—it came under FBI surveillance and experienced numerous break-ins during the Reagan administration. More than 30 years later, the OCBC continues to support illegalized migrants threatened by US authorities.

Since 1992 OCBC has also championed sanctuary of a different sort—for the area's homeless population. For more than twenty-five years, the church has served as headquarters of the Homeless Empowerment Project and its biweekly newspaper, *Spare Change News*. Sold by about a hundred vendors, who receive 75 percent of the two dollars charged for each copy they sell, the paper is a platform for news and analysis by members of the area's homeless and low-income population, and an income source for economically disadvantaged individuals.

Today the OCBC characterizes itself as a "progressive peace and justice congregation." It strives "to follow the example of Jesus and to work, through active nonviolence, for social, racial, economic and ecological justice, and for peace."

GETTING THERE

Red Line to Harvard Station.

TO LEARN MORE

Surbrug, Robert. *Beyond Vietnam: The Politics of Protest in Massachusetts, 1974–1990*, Amherst: University of Massachusetts Press, 2009.

3.12 Food Not Bombs

195 Harvard Street

CAMBRIDGE

Food Not Bombs is an organization founded in 1980 in Cambridge by eight activists from Greater Boston involved in the effort to shut down New Hampshire's Seabrook nuclear power plant. Insisting on the links between US militarism, war-making, and the profound socioeconomic insecurity experienced by many in the United States, the group held its first action outside of the Federal Reserve Bank across from Boston's South Station on March 26, 1981. While the First National Bank of Boston stockholders' meeting took place inside the Federal Reserve, outside Food Not Bombs did street theater involving the provision of a free meal to those in need. Homeless men from the Pine Street Inn attended the action and suggested that they distribute food on a daily basis. Within days, the eight activists quit their jobs, rented a house at 195 Harvard Street in Cambridge, and dedicated themselves to serving free food (always vegetarian or vegan) as a tactic of antiwar organizing and community building.

Since that time, Food Not Bombs has exploded in size as local chapters have sprung up all over the world. Today there are more than one thousand collectively run, autonomous chapters in cities and towns in sixty-five countries across six continents.

Because of its distribution of free food in public—whether in support of social movements or to feed the homeless and the hungry—Food Not Bombs chapters have often clashed with local governments. In 1993, for example, Boston authorities cited

Food Not Bombs icon.

its activists for trespassing when they refused to stop serving meals on the **Boston Common** and in Copley Square. On at least one occasion, the Boston police officers even seized the organization's table and pot of soup. As one Food Not Bombs member explained in defense of the group's work, "We're serving here in the face of prosperity. We want to bring poverty out in the open, but people don't want to see it. They want to look away."

Food Not Bombs no longer operates out of 195 Harvard Street, which is now a private home.

GETTING THERE

Red Line to Central Square Station, 0.4 mile (nine-minute) walk.

TO LEARN MORE

Heynen, Nik. "Cooking up Non-violent Civil-disobedient Direct Action for the Hungry: 'Food Not Bombs' and the Resurgence of Radical Democracy in the US," *Urban Studies* 47, no. 6 (2010): 1225–40.

Seiter, Alessandra. "Veganism of a Different Nature: How Food Not Bombs Challenged Capitalism, Militarism, and Speciesism in Cambridge, MA," undergraduate senior thesis, Department of Earth Science and Geography, Vassar College, April 2016.

Food Not Bombs cofounders Susan Eaton, Brian Feigenbaum, C.T. Lawrence Butler, and Keith McHenry outside 195 Harvard Street in the summer of 1981. Mira Brown, Jessie Constable, Amy Rothstein, and Jo Swanson are not pictured.

3.13 The John F. Kennedy School of Government at Harvard University

79 John F. Kennedy Street

CAMBRIDGE

On June 6, 1991, Héctor Alejandro Gramajo Morales was walking toward the entrance of Harvard University's John F. Kennedy School of Government for a graduation ceremony to receive his master's degree when a process server stopped him. The individual handed Guatemala's former defense minister a legal document detailing a multimillion-dollar lawsuit filed in the US District Court in Boston by the New York City–based Center for Constitutional Rights. The case sought dam-

Gramajo receives the legal papers outside the Kennedy School, 1991.

program that enrolled Pentagon officials. According to Trumpbour, it brought "droves of CIA agents, admirals, generals, and NSA staffers to Harvard annually." Allison embodies the revolving door between the Kennedy School and the national security establishment. During the Reagan administration, he was special advisor to the secretary of defense; he also served as assistant secretary of defense for policy and plans during the Clinton administration. He then returned to the JFK School, where he headed the Belfer Center for Science and International Affairs for more than twenty years.

ages for Gramajo's involvement in "acts of summary execution, disappearance, torture, cruel, inhumane or degrading treatment, wrongful death, false imprisonment and intentional infliction of emotional distress . . . carried out under his orders against Guatemalan civilians."

That a former military general implicated in horrific crimes was a student at what is perhaps the world's most elite public policy and public administration schools is both shocking and unsurprising. Harvard trustees, professors, and graduates have a long history of taking leading roles in human rights atrocities, particularly in relation to US imperial violence. As historian John Trumpbour notes, "Harvard men . . . helped plan and execute most of the major military, paramilitary, and covert interventions of the postwar period"—from Iran and Guatemala to Vietnam and tiny Grenada. The Kennedy School has been a central player in furthering such activities.

Graham Allison, as the school's dean from 1977 to 1989, for example, oversaw a

Founded in 1936 as the Harvard Graduate School of Public Administration, the Kennedy School has also long been the academic home of an international elite—many top officials in the World Bank, the United Nations, and in numerous national governments have studied there. Yet, despite the internationalist veneer, the school is, as suggested by author Shin Eun-jung, one "where the ideology of *Pax Americana* is maintained and spread."

Hector Gramajo was a beneficiary of the largess associated with that Pax Americana. A graduate of the infamous School of Americas at Fort Benning in Georgia, he also studied at the Pentagon's Command and General Staff College at Fort Leavenworth in Kansas. Recruited by Harvard and sponsored by the US State Department, he was enrolled in the Edward S. Mason Program, the Kennedy School's "flagship international program."

A week after being served with the first lawsuit, Gramajo was served with a second, one concerning his involvement in the kidnapping, repeated rape, and brutal torture of a US Maryknoll nun in Guatemala, Sister Diana Ortiz. This time, Gramajo spat on the process server.

Gramajo eventually fled to Guatemala and never faced his accusers in court. In April 1995, a federal judge in Boston ruled against him in absentia and awarded $47.5 million in damages to the plaintiffs. Gramajo died in 2004 from an attack by a swarm of bees.

As for the Kennedy School, its links to the US national security establishment endure. Ashton Carter and Samantha Power, both professors at the school, served in the Obama administration—Carter as head of the Pentagon, and Power, a key architect of armed intervention in the name of humanitarianism, as UN ambassador.

GETTING THERE

Red Line to Harvard Station, 0.3 mile (six-minute) walk.

TO LEARN MORE

Eu-jung, Shin. *Verita$: Harvard's Hidden History*, Oakland: PM Press, 2015.

Trumpbour, John. "Harvard, the Cold War, and the National Security State," in *How Harvard Rules: Reason in the Service of Empire*, ed. John Trumpbour, Boston: South End Press, 1989, 51–128.

3.14 Ray and Maria Stata Center, Massachusetts Institute of Technology

32 Vassar Street

CAMBRIDGE

Beginning in 1993, members of the Wampanoag nation gathered with Jessie Little Doe Baird of the Mashpee community to think through the challenge of reclaiming the language of their ancestors; they defined the project as part of a "process of finding ourselves." Curiously, their journey would take them to MIT and its Department of Linguistics and Philosophy. The largest obstacle to the resurrection of the spoken language was that its last speakers had passed on more than a century earlier. But there were also surprising written resources available to them: the seventeenth- and eighteenth-century contracts, titles, petitions, and testimonials that documented the colonial encounter between the Wampanoag nation and the settlers. These were often phonetic transcriptions. How then to go from written words removed by centuries to a living, spoken language?

Baird turned to MIT. There she worked with Kenneth Hale, a linguist, who specialized in endangered languages. A polyglot, Hale had studied many aboriginal languages by engaging in collaborative research with indigenous partners. Hale, Baird, and Norvin Richards, then one of Hale's mentees, came to focus on the seventeenth-century Wampanoag Bible, which had been produced at the **Harvard Indian College** and which provided a key for translating Wampanoag words into English. Surviving copies often also contain the handwritten notes of their Wampanoag readers.

As John Eliot (see **Non-antum**) and other Puritans raised funds for their missionary work in England, they provided Wampanoag testimonies as evidence of conversion experiences. These testimonials yielded significant insights into the lives of Baird's ancestors, which also assisted the language's reclamation.

Stata Center, 2014.

The Wampanoag-MIT collaboration has yielded an English-Wampanoag dictionary, now containing more than eleven thousand words. There are also Wampanoag-language courses in the Mashpee High School on Cape Cod. Baird's daughter, Mae, was the first child in several generations to be raised as a first language speaker.

The Department of Linguistics and Philosophy is housed in the Stata Center, an unusual, aesthetically complex building designed by Frank Gehry. It was also home to the famed linguist and leading dissident intellectual Noam Chomsky, who notes the scale of the Wampanoags' achievement: "There's nothing that I know of that's anything like the Wampanoag case. It would have been considered impossible. If I have been asked could it have been done, I would have taken for granted that it's impossible. It was gone." Today, it is here—indeed a documentary exploring the effort is accordingly titled *We Still Live Here—"Âs Nutayuneân."*

GETTING THERE

Red Line to Kendall Station, 0.3 mile (five-minute) walk.

TO LEARN MORE

Halle, Morris, and Norvin Richards. *Kenneth Locke Hale, 1934–2001: A Biographical Memo*, Washington, DC: National Academy of Sciences, 2007.

Makepeace, Anne (director). *We Still Live Here— "Âs Nutayuneân,"* Independent Television Service, 2011. https://www.pbs.org/independentlens/films/we-still-live-here/.

Wôpanâak Language Reclamation Project website: http://www.wlrp.org/

3.15 Harvard Square Public Toilet

Corner of Garden Street and Massachusetts Avenue

CAMBRIDGE

Beginning in 2013, a coalition of Harvard Square business people and Harvard University faculty and students partnered with

Harvard Square, 2018.

local homeless-service and advocacy organizations to address a basic human need and matter of hygiene—the availability of public toilet facilities. Although a popular and heavily trafficked venue, Harvard Square suffered from a dearth of public restrooms. Local businesses felt overwhelmed by requests to use their facilities and often had to remove waste and sanitize their building entrances each morning. Explaining that "all of us deserve access to a public restroom. Homeless especially," Richard Parker, a Harvard faculty member, pled the case before the Cambridge City Council. In response to his and the coalition's activism, the City of Cambridge subsequently conducted a study to understand the scale of the need and identify mechanisms to address it.

The City framed the problem narrowly as one of infrastructure and safety, choosing not to address broader concerns about homelessness and gentrification. Indeed, the coalition's name, Advocates for a Common Toilet, expressed its pragmatism and

limited goal. Subsequent debates centered on how to avoid "problems" experienced by other cities that have provided public restrooms: vandalism, drug use and abuse, sexual activities, occupation by homeless individuals, and high maintenance costs. Planners turned to Portland, Oregon, and Seattle for lessons. They settled on the "Portland Loo," a relatively low-cost public toilet designed and manufactured in the city for which it is named. Its design leaves patrons' feet visible to the outside and has running water for washing on the exterior. Its robust steel construction is coated with an antigraffiti surface.

In 2016, Cambridge installed a single Portland Loo in Harvard Square and a second one in Central Square in 2017, funded through the city's participatory budgeting process. The City of Cambridge thus joins a growing international consensus that access to safe, affordable, adequate sanitation is a basic human right.

TO LEARN MORE

Public Hygiene Lets Us Stay Human (PHLUSH). *Public Toilet Advocacy Toolkit*, 2013: http://toolkit.phlush.org/

GETTING THERE

Red Line to Harvard Square Station. The toilet is adjacent to the Cambridge Common.

Chelsea and Everett

Everett as seen from the Whidden Hospital, 2007.

Just across the Mystic River from Boston, the City of Chelsea occupies land once called *Winnisimmet* by its indigenous people. English settlement began with a fortified trading post established by Samuel Maverick (see **Maverick Square**) in 1626. Within a decade, disease decimated the area's indigenous population. Like Chelsea, Everett was part of the "Mystic core" of indigenous settlement. Seceding from **Charlestown**, Everett was incorporated in 1870. The cities remained sparsely settled until the mid-nineteenth century, when their populations exploded in tandem with the region's industrial, naval, and commercial activities.

Both cities are an integral part of the Boston-centered economy, functioning as warehousing and manufacturing hubs with a dense concentration of harbor, rail, highway, and road transportation nodes, in addition to airport-traffic and overflight roles. The resulting environmental concerns are aggravated by the cities' role as dormitories for a largely immigrant workforce serving Downtown Boston, **Logan Airport**, and the Seaport district—and beyond.

With thirty-six thousand residents, Chelsea is one of the country's most densely populated cities; 62 percent of its residents are of Latin American origin, consistent with Chelsea's history as an immigrant community. Beginning in the late 1800s, Chelsea became an important Jewish cultural hub and a center for labor organizing throughout the North Shore. Everett's forty-two thousand residents are majority white, largely of Italian descent, with significant Asian American and African American communities. In recent decades, Brazilian immigrants have played an increasing role in the city.

Prominent residents included Elizabeth Cady Stanton, the pioneering women's movement leader; Vannevar Bush, a Raytheon founder and MIT dean who played an important role in establishing the military-industrial complex; and Lewis Howard Latimer, a leading engineer. His father was George Latimer, also a Chelsea resident, whose 1842 "fugitive slave" case energized the abolitionist movement (see **Court House Square**). Present-day activism in both cities focuses on immigrant rights, gentrification, and environmental hazards.

3.16 Chelsea Naval Hospital

100 Commandants Way

CHELSEA

In 1918, as prospects for the Great War's end were in sight, another, deadlier catastrophe struck. In August, Boston, Freetown (Sierra Leone), and Brest (France) were nearly simultaneously hit with an influenza wave. Three sailors reported ill at Boston's Commonwealth Pier at the month's end; within days, the number of stricken grew exponentially. Initially the ill servicemen were treated at the Naval Hospital in Chelsea and at Camp Devens (northwest of Boston), overwhelming both facilities. With the transfer of the most critically ill patients to Chelsea, hospital personnel fell ill, and soon thereafter the disease spread to Boston proper.

By its end, the misleadingly named "Spanish flu" had infected a third of humanity, killing up to one hundred million people, one out of twenty then alive. In Massachusetts some eighty-five thousand individuals fell ill by the end of October. The virus strained the state's public-health infrastructure and highlighted the limits of its powers —its inability to order the closure of schools and the subway system, for example, and put a stop to public gatherings and church services. By year's end, the virus had claimed five thousand lives in Massachusetts.

The Spanish flu transformed scientific knowledge, leading to the recognition of viruses as distinct organisms. The most durable impact, however, was the eventual emergence of national health care and insurance systems in industrial countries. In the United States, it led to the growth of public health surveillance systems. It also deepened the recognition that global travel, especially the deployment of troops, enabled rapid spread of the disease.

The Naval Hospital, then known as the Marine Hospital, lay directly across the Mystic River from the **Charlestown Navy Yard**, somewhat removed from Commonwealth Pier, where the first cases were reported. Constructed in the 1830s in today's Admiral's Hill neighborhood— home for a period to nineteenth-century feminist leader Elizabeth Cady Stanton, then also very active in the abolitionist movement—the hospital was in continuous use until the 1970s. Most of the extant structures have been converted

Chelsea Naval Hospital, circa 1905–20.

to private, high-end condominiums and apartments.

GETTING THERE

MBTA bus from Downtown Boston or Commuter Rail (the Newport/Rockport line) to Chelsea Station, 1.0 mile (twenty-minute) walk.

NEARBY SITE

MARY O'MALLEY STATE PARK, Commandants Way, on the Mystic River, with great views of the Boston skyline and the Tobin Bridge.

TO LEARN MORE

Byerly, Carol R. "The U.S. Military and the Influenza Pandemic of 1918–1919," *Public Health Reports* 125 (Suppl 3, 2003): 82–91.

Spinney, Laura. *Pale Rider: The Spanish Flu of 1918 and How It Changed the World*, New York: Public Affairs, 2017.

3.17 Labor Lyceum

453 Broadway

CHELSEA

In the 1930s, as labor militancy and left-wing organizing rose in the face of the Great Depression and what many imagined to be capitalism's final crisis, the state of Massachusetts organized a "Special Commission to Investigate . . . Communistic, Fascist, Nazi and Other Subversive Organizations." Among the sites attracting their attention was the Labor Lyceum in Chelsea. It was a hub for union organizing in the leather and garment industries that extended well beyond its base among Jewish workers to include Italian, Armenian, and Irish laborers in factory towns north of Boston, especially in Peabody. The commission's reporting on

the Labor Lyceum included its outreach to Russian- and Armenian-language speakers, organizing workers in the building trades, conducting language classes, fielding a basketball team, and the operation of a mutual aid society. Most distressful to the commission, however, were the classes on Marxism Leninism and the maintenance of a library of related literature.

Evidence before the commission also suggested an active Jewish community with multiple institutions in Chelsea functioning largely in Yiddish, or what the commission referred to as "the racial language."

The local Workmen's Circle (headquartered in *Dorchester* and today Brookline) organized the multistory Lyceum. No longer standing, it was located directly across from Chelsea City Hall, its space now a bank parking lot.

GETTING THERE

MBTA Commuter Rail to Chelsea (Newburyport/Rockport Line), 0.2 mile (four-minute) walk.

TO LEARN MORE

Commonwealth of Massachusetts, Report of the Special Commission to Investigate the Activities within This Commonwealth of Communistic, Fascist, Nazi and Other Subversive Organizations, So Called. Under chapter 32, Resolves of 1937. May 27, 1938.

RELATED SITE

What was the local HEBREW SCHOOL building survived and today houses a private apartment complex. It is at 48 Washington Avenue, diagonally across from the Lyceum site.

Toxic salt pile at Marginal and Pearl Streets, May 2017.

3.18 Chelsea Salt Terminal

37 Marginal Street

CHELSEA

Entering Chelsea along one of its busiest routes, the Pearl Street Bridge, one encounters a number of human-made mountains of salt soaring some 50 feet over five acres along Chelsea Creek. Eight hundred thousand tons of salt pass through Eastern Salt Company's terminal each year en route to every Massachusetts municipality and highway as a de-icing agent in the winter. Most of the salt comes from Chile's Atacama Desert, although suppliers in Africa and Asia often supplement this. One hundred 18-wheeler trucks deliver the salt after diesel-powered equipment unloads and stores the freight.

Ever since the terminal opened in 2005, the associated traffic and noise have led to numerous complaints from the site's largely low-income Latino neighbors. As one resident explained to the *Boston Globe*, "There's a tunnel of sound and everything goes into my house - all of the noise and the diesel fumes . . . I have a lot of pain in my muscles and joints. I suspect it's from the salt." Both the Chelsea City Council and area non-profits have channeled these grievances and highlighted another more long-term danger: the salt pile incorporates a cyanide-based anti-caking agent with potentially disastrous consequences to both health and environment. It is for such reason that many municipalities are now trying to reduce their salt usage and the Canadian government (in contrast to the politically compromised U.S. Environmental Protection Agency) classifies the salt as a toxic agent.

Grassroots advocacy in Chelsea has produced some reforms. The salt pile is now covered for part of the year with industrial strength tarpaulins, for example, reducing airborne particulates. The corporation has also agreed to convert old oil tanks on the property into an urban park. Moreover, community resistance has thwarted Eastern Salt's plans to expand its facility across Chelsea Creek into East Boston. Larger safety questions, due to sea-level rise and storm surges, remain, however.

GETTING THERE

MBTA Commuter Rail to Chelsea, 0.6 mile (twelve-minute) walk. An MBTA bus from Maverick Square Station (Blue Line) passes very close to the site.

3.19 ExxonMobil Everett Terminal

42–148 Beacham Street

EVERETT

Roseann Bongiovanni, the future director of GreenRoots, an environmental-justice organization, was running along the bank of the Mystic River in early 2007 when she found it difficult to breathe. The stench of diesel fuel engulfed her. Some fifteen thousand gallons stored at the Everett Terminal had spilled into the Mystic and Island End Rivers, leading to an eventual $6 million settlement with ExxonMobil, the world's largest oil company. Despite subsequent agreements with the US Environmental Protection Agency and its Massachusetts counterpart, the pollution continued, prompting the Conservation Law Foundation to file suit in 2016.

In addition to addressing continuing pollution, the lawsuit calls attention to the corporation's failure to harden its facilities against the impacts of increased precipitation, sea-level rise, and wind-driven threats— all hazards closely related to the combustion of fossil fuels trafficked by the corporation. The lawsuit joins other state-level litigation over the corporation's alleged role in covering up the climate impacts of fossil fuel usage.

The company's facility is but one among several similar installations in the neighborhood. France- and Belgium-based transnational corporations operate the United States' oldest and largest liquified "natural" gas (LNG) terminals adjacent to ExxonMobil, for example, with just one site responsible for more than ten thousand truck trips each year.

The cluster of carbon emitters shares a haphazard maze of narrow roads, commuter rail lines, and waterways with the country's largest food processing and distribution center, the New England Produce Center, and a large metal recycling operation. Within a mile's radius of the center, well within the blast radius of potential gas explosions, are working- and middle-class neighborhoods in **Charlestown**, Everett, and Chelsea. Local and state environmental organizations, including GreenRoots, the Boston Climate Action Network, and Mass Power Forward have been organizing to connect local community needs with green energy generation and conversion infrastructure.

GETTING THERE

Commuter Rail to Chelsea Station (Newburyport/Rockport line), 0.75 mile (fifteen-minute) walk.

TO LEARN MORE

Conservation Law Foundation, "Putting Exxon-Mobil on Trial," 2017, https://www.clf.org/blog/putting-exxonmobil-trial/

4

North
of
Boston

Lowell

Mural (on Decatur Way Green Path) by Liz LaManche of "mill girl" Harriet Hanson Robinson, a writer for the *Lowell Offering*, book author, and leader in the women's rights movement, 2016.

Lowell sits at the Concord and Merrimack rivers' confluence, an area occupied by Pennacook Indians prior to colonization. English settlers began arriving in the area in the mid-1600s, but Lowell was not formally established until 1829 out of what had been East Chelmsford.

The city's name betrays its origins. Wealthy men that some call the Boston Associates (but who were never formally organized as such) provided the investment capital to establish water-powered textile mills along the Merrimack and build canals. Francis Cabot Lowell (d. 1817) had been a leading member of the group. By the 1850s, "Mill City" was the country's leading industrial center.

In addition to wealth accumulation, the Boston-based capitalists had a social mission. They wanted the United States to avoid England's industrial experience of filthy cities, urban poverty, and dire working conditions. They paid workers at levels higher than prevailing wages and owned matron-staffed boarding houses in which their female workers lived. To instill confidence in the rural families who sent their daughters to Lowell, the textile mills promised their good moral standing, enforcing standards of behavior and dress and requiring weekly attendance at church. While working conditions were better than those in factories elsewhere, they were still arduous—twelve-hour days, six days a week in rooms with lint-filled air—which helps explain why the "mill girls" often rebelled.

By the early 1900s, companies began to leave the polyglot city with its large populations of people of French Canadian, Greek, Portuguese, and Eastern European Jewish origins. By midcentury, high unemployment, empty factories, and heavily polluted waterways characterized Lowell. In recent decades, the creation of Lowell National Historical Park, the expansion of UMass Lowell and Middlesex Community College, and significant immigration—particularly from Cambodia—have helped to revitalize the city of approximately one hundred thousand residents.

Jack Kerouac, the great Beat writer is perhaps the city's most famous son. A Lowell Celebrates Kerouac Festival is held every October. There are numerous sites throughout Lowell associated with Kerouac's life.

GETTING THERE

Distances are provided from the Lowell National Park Visitor Center (246 Market Street), a 0.7 mile (fourteen-minute) walk from the Lowell Commuter Rail Station.

4.1 Wamesit

33 Walkway to Middlesex
Community College

LOWELL

The confluence of the Merrimack and Concord rivers was home to Wamesit, a "praying village" (see **Nonantum**) whose residents were nominally Christianized Pennacook Indians, part of a federation of Algonquian-speaking people. Archaeological evidence, including skeletal remains found at the UMass Lowell campus (which occupies part of the area that was Wamesit), and missionary accounts suggest that the confluence was important to the Pennacook for gatherings and for trade prior to Wamesit's founding in the 1640s. Rich in both fishing and horticultural resources, it also served as an economically productive space.

Despite this importance, Passaconaway, the Pennacook leader, consented to Wamesit's establishment. Analysts speculate that such consent was an attempt to contain

English influence, part of a complex strategy pursued by Passaconaway and his son, Wanalancet, to limit settler encroachment on Pennacook lands. Although some Pennacooks lived in Wamesit, the majority lived elsewhere, including Passaconaway himself, who retained his residence at Pawtucket Falls, a half mile away. It is thought that the Pennacook hoped that by agreeing to Wamesit and embracing a shared Christianity—even if only nominally in many cases—the English would respect Native land rights.

For most of the region's indigenous communities, the 1600s would prove calamitous as waves of smallpox decimated communities and European interest in timber expanded the colonial presence. Matters came to a head with King Philip's War in 1675 (see **Old Country House/1749 Court House**). This region-wide engagement ren-

Marker outside Eliot Church, 2018.

dered Passaconaway's strategy of accommodation unsustainable, especially after the colonists now defined even Christian converts as their enemy. After the war, the remaining Pennacook either fled north or were forcibly marched to Boston, from where they were later deported to the Caribbean and slavery.

A little more than a century later, with the establishment of textile mills in the same location, a Native presence animated Wamesit once again when several indigenous women from rural New Hampshire joined the workforce. They included Betsey Chamberlain, who became a writer for a local literary magazine, the *Lowell Offering*. Her biographer, Judith Ranta, suggests that Chamberlain's independent spirit and committed activism had their roots in her indigenous heritage. Ranta also suggests that Chamberlain was familiar with the early feminist abolitionists, "adding her voice to theirs" with her own writings.

The confluence of the Merrimack and Concord rivers is today home to Middlesex Community College, a successor in that location to the computer manufacturer Wang Laboratories.

GETTING THERE

From the NPS Visitor Center, 0.4 mile (eight-minute) walk.

RELATED SITE

273 Summer Street, Lowell, **ELIOT CHURCH MARKER**. In 1653 John Eliot, a missionary, erected a chapel here to preach to converted Pennacook, often referred to as Wamesit Indians.

TO LEARN MORE

Brooks, Lisa. *Our Beloved Kin: A New History of King Philip's War*, New Haven: Yale University Press, 2018.

Forrant, Robert, and Christoph Strobel. *Ethnicity in Lowell*, Boston: Northeast National Ethnography Program, National Park Service, 2011.

Mandell, Daniel R. *Behind the Frontier: Indians in Eighteenth-Century Eastern Massachusetts*, Lincoln: University of Nebraska Press, 1996.

Ranta, Judith. *The Life and Writings of Betsey Chamberlain: Native American Mill Worker*, Boston: Northeastern University Press, 2003.

4.2 Saint Paul's Methodist Episcopal Church/UTEC

35–41 Warren Street

LOWELL

UTEC's Bboy dance troupe at practice, 2011.

Lowell helped to perpetuate, and benefited significantly from, slavery—both by buying large amounts of cotton from slave states and producing low-quality textiles to clothe the enslaved. It also had a vibrant antislavery movement. Built in 1839, Saint Paul's was one of a number of Lowell churches that played an important role in that movement. In November 1841, Saint Paul's hosted a meeting with the members of the *Amistad* rebellion as they toured towns primarily in

New England to raise money to be able to return home. (In 1839 fifty-three captive Africans broke free of their chains and gained control of the slave ship transporting them. Eventually they ended up near Long Island, New York, where a US Navy brig took them into custody and then jailed them in Connecticut, then a slave state. After eighteen months of incarceration, a US Supreme Court decision forced their release while relieving US authorities of any responsibility for repatriating them. Eventually most settled in Sierra Leone with help from the abolitionist movement.) In all the venues, large, enthusiastic multiracial crowds received the *Amistad* Africans. While in Lowell, they also met with workers at the giant Boott Cotton Mills complex and inspected the machinery and textiles. Mostly young women from area farms, the workers spontaneously struck up a collection for their African guests and raised $58.50 (then equivalent to the weekly wages of about twenty-five workers).

Saint Paul's parish closed in 2005 and sold the building to UTEC (United Teen Equality Center), an acclaimed Lowell-based organization founded in 1999. UTEC works to decrease youth violence and gang activity and to provide enhanced economic opportunities for young people in the area. Among its activities is a "Streetworker Peacemaking Process" focusing on rival gangs, GED classes, and various workforce-development and social enterprises such as a catering business and Café UTEC, a popular lunchtime eatery, located in an addition to the church building. With a LEED platinum certification of its renovated home, UTEC

calls it the oldest "greenest" building in the United States.

GETTING THERE

From the NPS Visitor Center, 0.4 mile (seven-minute) walk.

NEARBY SITE

BOOTT COTTON MILLS MUSEUM (part of the Lowell National Historical Park), 304 Dutton Street.

TO LEARN MORE

Rediker, Marcus. *The Amistad Rebellion: An Atlantic Odyssey of Slavery and Freedom*, New York: Penguin Books, 2013.

4.3 *The Voice of Industry* and *Middlesex Standard*

76 Central Street

LOWELL

Many of the Mill City's nineteenth-century boosters claimed that relations between labor and capital were benign and harmonious. But the existence of the Lowell Female Labor Reform Association (LFLRA), founded in 1844 as the first union of working women in the United States, indicates otherwise. Increasingly onerous labor conditions catalyzed the union, and as mill owners endeavored to maintain their edge over competitors and grow their profits, Lowell's largely female workforce mounted strikes and protests.

In October 1845, *The Voice of Industry*, an independent worker-run newspaper established earlier that year in nearby Fitchburg by the New England Working-men's Association, moved its operations to

Masthead of *The Voice of Industry*.

Lowell. Sarah Bagley, a textile worker and the LFLRA's head, joined the three-person publishing committee of the newspaper. A counterweight to the more famous and corporate-friendly *Lowell Offering*, a monthly literary magazine, the four-page broadsheet dedicated itself to "the abolition of Mental, Moral and Physical Servitude, in all their complicated forms." *The Voice of Industry* had a "Female Department" that ran articles with a strong feminist bent written by and about women workers. With readership across New England, *The Voice* played a leading role in helping to organize female workers in the region, particularly in relation to the struggle for a ten-hour workday in Massachusetts.

In addition to publishing articles highly critical of the textile mills and their owners, *The Voice* also took strong stances opposing the US-Mexico War (1846–48) and slavery. Such positions, coupled with the fact that it briefly shared offices with the *Middlesex Standard* (1844–45), an antislavery newspaper (John Greenleaf Whittier, the famed poet and abolitionist from **Haverhill,** served as its editor in 1845), speak to the dynamic ties and blurry boundaries between activists and

Give me the money that has been spent in the war, and I will purchase every foot of land on the globe. I will clothe every man, woman and child in an attire that Kings and Queens might be proud of. I will build a school-house on every hill-side and every valley over the earth. I will supply that school-house with a competent teacher. I will build an academy in every town, and endow it—a college in every State, and fill it with able professors. I will crown every hill with a church, consecrated with the promulgation of the gospel of peace.

—Anonymous, "The Waste in War," April 3, 1846, *The Voice of Industry*; http://industrialrevolution.org/financing-war.html#wasteinwar

organizers involved in the leading social justice causes of the day.

In September 1847, *The Voice* began to publish simultaneously in Boston; by December of that year, it ceased publication in Lowell. On August 3, 1848, *The Voice* printed its last issue.

The building in which it was housed in Lowell, which sat on the bridge that crosses the Pawtucket Canal, no longer exists.

GETTING THERE

From the NPS Visitor Center, 0.2 mile (five-minute) walk.

RELATED SITES

166 CENTRAL AVENUE. *The Voice of Industry* was printed in this building.

SAINT ANNE'S EPISCOPAL CHURCH, which was Lowell's first church and a stop on the Underground Railroad, 8 Kirk Street.

TO LEARN MORE

Dublin, Thomas. *Women at Work: The Transformation of Work and Community in Lowell, Massachusetts, 1826–1860,* New York: Columbia University Press, 1993 (1979).

http://www.industrialrevolution.org/complete-issues.html

4.4 Saint Patrick Church

282 Suffolk Street

LOWELL

Saint Patrick was Lowell's first Catholic church. Opened in 1831, the church was built to serve the city's growing Irish Catholic population.

Among the earliest Irish immigrants to Lowell were a group of thirty men who, in 1822, walked from **Charlestown** to what would become the Mill City. There they worked by hand digging canals and helping construct the mills and worker housing. By 1830 there were five hundred Irish in Lowell. Relegated by the city's Yankee rulers to residing in "paddy camps" built on vacant land away from Lowell's center, the Irish lived in decrepit conditions. Saint Patrick's

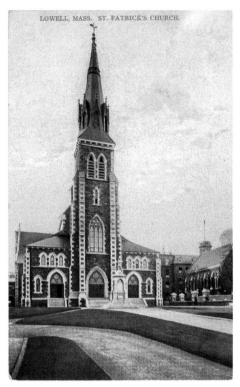

Postcard, circa 1900.

was built between the two main camps, "the Acre" and "the Half Acre," with the assistance of many of the inhabitants.

As in Boston, Lowell experienced an influx of impoverished Irish during the 1840s. By 1850, there were about eleven thousand Irish in Lowell (of a total population of a little more than thirty-three thousand).

A nativist undercurrent had been present in Lowell since the city's founding. It ratcheted up considerably with the establishment of a local Know-Nothing (see *Rainsford Island*) movement in 1851. In a context of growing local animosity toward what many characterized as "swarms of Irish poor" threatening the moral and socioeconomic wellbeing of Lowell, the opening of a Catholic school (seen by many as sectarian and undermining the community's intellectual development), and the building of a new, larger church building for Saint Patrick's, greatly intensified anti-Irish xenophobia.

Open conflict between Lowell's Yankee and Irish communities broke out in June 1854. The visit of John Orr, a well-known nativist campaigner who spoke before a large crowd on South Common, triggered the fracas. Soon after his speech, a gang of anti-immigrant, anti-Catholic Know-Nothings marched on Saint Patrick's. But Lowell's Irish were ready, "factory girls" having collected stones to defend their community and priests having organized dozens of men to protect a convent. As the Know-Nothings approached, Irish men and women—with women reportedly taking the lead—attacked the mob, with one "sinewy matron" throwing a gang leader over the railing of a canal into the water. The mob was repulsed.

By the late 1850s, Saint Patrick's was one of the largest Catholic parishes in New England, the Know-Nothings were discredited, and the Irish in Lowell were secure—their socioeconomic marginality notwithstanding.

Today Saint Patrick's characterizes itself as "a multi-cultural and multi-lingual Roman Catholic Community." Reflecting the great changes in Lowell's population, church services are held in five languages: Burmese, Cambodian, English, Spanish, and Vietnamese.

GETTING THERE

From the NPS Visitor Center, 0.4 mile (nine-minute) walk.

TO LEARN MORE

Forrant, Robert, and Christoph Strobel. *Ethnicity in Lowell*, Boston: Northeast National Ethnography Program, National Park Service, 2011.

Mitchell, Brian C. *The Paddy Camps: The Irish of Lowell, 1821–1861*, Urbana and Chicago: University of Illinois Press, 1988.

4.5 Socialist Hall

22 Middle Street

LOWELL

On the evening of January 2, 1920, and the following morning, federal agents and local police raided Socialist Hall and some private homes in an effort to rid Lowell of what authorities perceived of as dangerous "reds." They arrested some thirty men and women—all foreign born—brought them to a local police station, and interrogated them for about three hours. One newspaper reported that police had seized numerous books and pamphlets "printed in Russian, Finnish and Lithuanian" and "illustrated." The authorities released twenty-five suspected "radicals" and transferred the remaining five to a federal facility at Boston's *Deer Island* for imprisonment.

The arrests were part of the Palmer Raids. Named after President Woodrow Wilson's attorney general, A. Mitchell Palmer, and directed by FBI founder, J. Edgar Hoover, the raids took place in late 1919 and early 1920 during the first red scare in the United States. They involved the rounding up of thousands of suspected leftist radicals across the country, of whom more than five hundred were ultimately deported. About eight hundred of the arrests took place in New England, with most of them from the Greater Boston area—in municipalities such as Brockton, *Chelsea*, *Lawrence*, and *Lynn*. The raids reflected a polarized political context and elite fears of a "red revolution." Coming in the aftermath of World War I and the Russian Revolution, the fears were greatly heightened by escalating labor strife in the United States, May Day riots in many cities, and a series of bombings by alleged anarchists targeting government officials in 1919.

In this context, local officials, clergy, mill owners, and newspaper editors in Lowell railed against trade unionists and leftists, particularly "aliens." The Reverend Chauncey J. Hawkins of the First Congregational Church, for example, warned of the dangers of "hoodlums and radicals" to the United States and insisted that "they must be suppressed." Another minister, C. E. Fisher of the First Universalist Church, gave a sermon titled "The Red Flag or the Stars and Stripes— Which?" He implored churchgoers to reelect Calvin Coolidge as governor and to "be true to law, order, righteousness, and justice" and called for the deportation of immigrants "who come simply to cause unrest."

Lowell had a small but vibrant leftist population, especially in the city's Polish and Lithuanian communities. The first meeting of socialists took place in the 1880s, and the Socialist Party formally established itself in Lowell in the 1890s. By the early 1900s, it was able to field a slate for mayor and the city council but never received more than 4 percent of the vote as most of the city's voters in working-class areas remained loyal to the Democratic Party. A combination of the arrival of Russian and Eastern European immigrants in the 1910s and mill strikes in 1912—the Industrial Workers of the World (Wobblies) briefly had an office that year at 22 Hanover Street—had a radicalizing impact on Lowell's left, leading some to join the newly established Communist Party. Socialist Hall was the epicenter of the city's leftist activism. The arrests of January 2–3, 1920, and those of other suspected communists in subsequent weeks, however, seem to have had a chilling effect as Socialist Hall closed down soon thereafter.

Socialist Hall moved at least a few times in the early 1900s. The 22 Middle Street building in which Socialist Hall was housed during the Palmer Raids appears to have been torn down around 1980. An apartment building now occupies the site.

GETTING THERE

From the NPS Visitor Center, 0.2 mile (five-minute) walk.

TO LEARN MORE

Fitzsimons, Gregory. "Ethnic Entrepreneurs, Radical Politics, and Lowell's Red Scare: David A. Evpak, Ukrainian Shoe Repairer," essay produced for Lowell National Historical Park and published online at UMass Lowell's Center for Lowell History (now defunct) website on "Ethnicity and Enterprise," 2002.

Lawrence

Lawrence in Harmony choir in front of the monument to the 1912 strike, North Common. Bread and Roses Heritage Festival, 2017.

"designed by nature for the lovliest [sic] city in the world."

Lawrence changed tremendously, however, in subsequent decades. By 1912 it was a full-blown industrial city, the world's biggest producer of worsted wool, a city in which textile mills employed thirty-two thousand workers (out of about eighty-six thousand residents)—including many children—and no longer evoked bucolic imagery. Dense, slumlike housing in working-class areas, widespread poverty, and harsh working conditions in its factories characterized the city. It also became a site of militant labor organizing, including its famed strike in 1912 led by the radical Industrial Workers of the World (or "Wobblies") that resulted in significant gains for workers.

The City of Lawrence's birth is inseparable from the Essex Company's establishment. In 1843 wealthy Boston-based businessmen (organized as the Merrimack Water Power Association, MWPA) began to buy up land along the Merrimack River between Lowell and Haverhill. Acquiring tens of thousands of acres, the MWPA petitioned Massachusetts to build a dam and control and sell the river's water. This effort's success led to the chartering of the Essex Company (to which the MWPA sold all its property rights) in 1845 and to Lawrence's founding.

Lawrence reflected its Boston Brahmin founders' vision—combining what they saw as the best of the urban industrial and the rural. The highly planned city featured wide, tree-lined streets and many acres of land for public parks. Its location at the confluence of two rivers surrounded by lush farmland led many to praise its beauty. In 1846 the *Merrimack Courier* wrote that Lawrence was

Like many US cities, Lawrence was hard hit by deindustrialization, falling to the forces of capitalist competition and profiteering as well as new industrial technologies. Between 1920 and 1980, its population declined by one third. Today Lawrence is marked by significant poverty, among other challenges. However, Latino immigration (a Latino-majority city, it has the highest concentration of Dominicans outside of New

York City) as well as grassroots activism on various fronts and nonprofit organizations have energized the city in recent decades.

GETTING THERE

With the exception of the first site, distances/directions are provided from the Lawrence Heritage State Park, a 0.8 mile (sixteen-minute) walk from the Commuter Rail Station in Lawrence.

4.6 Lawrence Experiment Station/Ferrous Site Park

Zero Island Street, Confluence of Merrimack and Spicket rivers

LAWRENCE

The late 1800s saw a rising interest in the science of sanitation throughout much of the world. It was a time of mounting urban populations and increasing concerns about water pollution and sewage disposal, along with growing acceptance of the theory of waterborne disease (the notion that contact with, or consumption of, pathogen-tainted freshwater causes infections), and the advent of bacteriology. In this context, the State Board of Health of Massachusetts established the Lawrence Experiment Station in 1887 in a building and on land owned (and lent) by the Essex Company. The primary focus of the research laboratory, the predecessor of which the Essex Company established to refine the measurement of water, was on the purification of water, sewage, and industrial waste.

While such research had previously taken place in Europe, the importance of the Lawrence Experiment Station's research lay in its depth and scale. Innovations produced there brought about great advances in water purification and sewage-treatment methods and technologies, and helped to make Lawrence a pioneer among US cities in the filtration of public water (leading to a dramatic decrease in cases of typhoid in the city in the 1890s). As a result, scientists and engineers from countries around the world visited the station in the late nineteenth and early twentieth centuries to learn from its work.

When the station moved in the early 1950s to a larger, modern facility (now called the Senator William X. Wall Experiment Station, it is located on 37 Shattuck Street), the site became overgrown with dense vegetation. At the same time, industrial, often toxic waste from a steel foundry next door accumulated there.

In the 1990s discussions began about reclaiming and cleaning up the brownfield site and turning it into a park. It was not until after 2010, however, that work actually began. Spearheaded by Groundwork Lawrence, a nonprofit organization dedicated to improving distressed neighborhoods through environmental projects, the undertaking entailed environmental remediation and ecological restoration. The resulting approximately five-acre park/urban wilderness has green infrastructure—in the form of bioswales and a rain garden to filter storm water and limit its runoff into the river—as well as walking trails and sheltered picnic tables, while offering great views of the waterfront.

The public park, formally dedicated in June 2016, is part of the City of Lawrence's Spicket River Greenway, a 3.5 mile "emerald bracelet" that connects green spaces via walking paths that traverse various neighborhoods.

GETTING THERE

From the Lawrence Commuter Rail Station, the park entrance is a 0.6 mile (about a twelve-minute) walk.

NEARBY SITE

ESSEX ART CENTER (a community nonprofit "with a mission to inspire and nurture the diverse artistic potential of the Greater Lawrence community through classroom exploration and gallery exhibition—making the creation and enjoyment of art accessible to all"), 56 Island Street.

TO LEARN MORE

Clark, H. W. "An Outline of Sewage Purification Studies at the Lawrence Experiment Station," *Industrial and Engineering Chemistry* 19, no. 4 (1927): 448–52.

Cole, Donald B. *Immigrant City: Lawrence, Massachusetts, 1845–1921*, Chapel Hill: University of North Carolina Press, 2002.

Hearn, Mike. *The History of the Essex Company*, Lawrence, MA: Lawrence History Center, 2014.

Website of Groundwork Lawrence: http://www .groundworklawrence.org/

4.7 American Woolen Company

1 Mill Street

LAWRENCE

The American Woolen Company was founded in 1899 by William Wood and Frederick Ayer through the consolidation of the Washington Mills in Lawrence and seven mills throughout New England. As the heads of the Washington Mills, the largest

and most successful of the member mills, Ayer and Woods became the new company's president and treasurer, respectively. They were also among its largest investors. Despite Wood's nominally inferior position, he was the company's dominant force from its birth, later becoming president, until his retirement in 1924. The American Woolen building on Mill Street served as the company's local office.

With three mills in Lawrence, the company was the city's biggest employer of textile workers at the time of the 1912 strike. Wood, as the corporation's head, became the personification of greedy mill owners among striking workers and their supporters. From the work stoppage's outset he insisted that raising wages was impossible due to the intensely competitive nature of the woolen textile trade and his obligation to protect the best interests of company shareholders. Nonetheless, the intensely anti-union Wood eventually gave in to the workers' demands, granting raises ranging from 20 percent (for the lowest paid workers) to 5 percent (for the highest paid), with a 25 percent increase for all overtime work. He also pledged not to punish any workers who participated in the strike.

Emblematic of American Woolen Company's power and wealth as well as its Gilded Age origins was Wood's extreme compensation. The son of poor Portuguese immigrants, Wood received $1 million in compensation in 1924, equivalent to $13.6 million today, likely making him the second-highest-paid business executive in the United States at the time. The company owned sixty mills in eight states and had forty thousand employees, fifteen thousand of them in Lawrence. According to historian Edward Roddy, it was the "nation's largest woolen manufacturing concern" as well as "the world's greatest textile corporation."

From its headquarters in Boston, the American Woolen Company helped shape the lives of many in cities such as Lawrence and made Boston one of the world's leading wool markets. In the mid-1920s, the company's fortunes began to decline dramatically. While World War II and lucrative government contracts provided some respite, the decline resumed after the war. Sold in the 1950s, the American Woolen Company is today a small entity based in Stafford Springs, Connecticut. Having departed Lawrence long ago, its former office building now houses a bar on the first floor.

The American Woolen Company, Lawrence, circa 1912.

GETTING THERE

The building is next to the Lawrence Heritage State Park (along Canal Street).

RELATED SITES

THE NATIONAL SHAWMUT BANK BUILDING, 40 Water Street, Downtown Boston, housed the American Woolen Company's headquarters. (Around 1920, the company moved to 245 State Street.)

WILLIAM WOOD'S HOME, 21 Fairfield Street, Back Bay.

TO LEARN MORE

Roddy, Edward G. *Mills, Mansions, and Mergers: The Life of William M. Wood*, North Andover, MA: Merrimack Valley Textile Museum, 1982.

Rosenberg, Chaim M. *Goods for Sale: Products and Advertising in the Massachusetts Industrial Age*, Amherst: University of Massachusetts Press, 2007.

4.8 Franco-Belgian Hall

9 Mason Street

LAWRENCE

On June 19, 1905, eight Franco-Belgian immigrants living and working in Lawrence established the industrial city's L'Union Franco Belge, the Franco-Belgian Cooperative. Modeled after similar institutions in their homeland and grounded in a radical political tradition from the industrial borderlands of Belgium and France, the organization rejected the American Federation of Labor for its conservative politics and its refusal to embrace workers who were not white, male, and highly skilled. Operating on socialist principles, the cooperative had its own

You are the heart and soul of the working class. Single-handed you are helpless but united you can win everything. You have won over the opposed power of the city, state, and national administrations, against the opposition of the combined forces of capitalism, in face of the armed forces. You have won by your solidarity and brains and muscle. . . . You, the strikers of Lawrence, have won the most signal victory of any organized body of working men in the world. You have demonstrated that there is a common interest in the working class that can bring all its members together.

—William "Big Bill" Haywood
to the strikers on March 13, 1912,
at Franco-Belgian Hall

Franco-Belgian Hall, 1912.

grocery store and bakery. The cooperative dedicated 10 percent of its profits to a fund for strikes and for assistance to needy members, another 10 percent for the production and dissemination of socialist literature, and the rest to members at a level proportional to their annual purchases.

About five years after its founding, the cooperative purchased the building on Mason Street to serve as its headquarters. Intended as a space for both political work and for families to relax, the building had meeting rooms, a library, a gymnasium, a pool and billiards room, and a five-hundred-seat auditorium.

Franco-Belgian Hall served as the headquarters for the 1912 strike. Indeed, the day after it began on January 11, 1912, workers assembled at the building, formed a strike committee, and invited the leadership of

the IWW (the Industrial Workers of the World) to come to Lawrence. Ten days later the cooperative opened a soup kitchen at the hall, feeding thirteen hundred workers twice a day throughout the remainder of the strike. Consistent with its antiracist and internationalist principles, the cooperative served workers regardless of ethno-racial background and made the building available to them for meetings. And it was at the hall on March 13, 1912, where "Big Bill" Haywood, the head of the IWW, announced to an overflow crowd the terms of the agreement with the American Woolen Company that ended the strike.

That the hall played such a vital role attests to the success of the Franco-Belgian workers in Lawrence over the previous decade—both despite and because of their radical politics, which stressed building alliances while staying true to socialist principles. As historian Janelle Bourgeois writes, "They preached for revolution and the demise of capitalism,

North Lawrence Railroad Station, 1915 postcard.

but regularly lent their hall to any effort, conservative and radical alike."

The building that was Franco-Belgian Hall still stands. Today it is privately owned and used for receptions and other private gatherings.

GETTING THERE

From Lawrence Heritage State Park, 0.7 mile (fifteen-minute) walk.

TO LEARN MORE

Bourgeois, Janelle. 'Believe Comrades . . . the Day is Coming When Those at the End of Their Rope Will Require Struggle. It Will Be, Perhaps, Tomorrow.' Franco-Belgian Immigrants and the 1912 Strike," in *The Great Lawrence Textile Strike of 1912: New Scholarship on the Bread and Roses Strike*, ed. Robert Forrant and Jurg Siegenthaler, Amityville, NY: Baywood Publishing Company, 2014, 15–35.

Watson, Bruce. *Bread and Roses: Mills, Migrants, and the Struggle for the American Dream*, New York: Viking, 2005.

4.9 North Lawrence Railroad Station

Essex Street and Broadway

LAWRENCE

On Saturday, February 24, 1912—about six weeks into the woolen textile mill strike—40 or so children, along with some parents and chaperones, gathered in the waiting room at the North Lawrence train depot. They were part of the "children's exodus"—an effort by the Industrial Workers of the World (IWW) to lessen the social costs of the labor stoppage by sending workers' children to other cities to live with prostrike families and to win greater levels of sympathy from the broad public. A tactic borrowed from workers in Europe, the exodus had started two weeks earlier when 150 children and adults traveled to New York City to pass off Lawrence's young offspring. Throughout the strike, the IWW sent children to supportive, typically socialist, families in Barre, Vermont; Hoboken, New Jersey; Bridgeport,

Connecticut; and Philadelphia—among other cities.

Critics of the strike and the IWW quickly seized upon the exodus as an example of the Wobblies' ruthless willingness to coerce Lawrencians into giving up their children and to exploit them for crass political ends. In this context, elites in Lawrence determined to put a stop to it.

About twenty-five minutes before the early morning train to Boston was to arrive, Marshal John Sullivan, the head of the city's police, entered the station and proclaimed what he had announced in the preceding days: that police would engage in arrests if any attempts were made to export children from Lawrence. When the 7:11 a.m. train arrived, a large contingent of policemen was waiting, having formed a gauntlet between the waiting room and the train platform. Four militia companies and a cavalry squadron were also deployed around the station. Mothers began to march their children toward the platform nonetheless.

Eyewitness and press accounts reported that police responded by attacking the women and by forcibly separating them from their children. As the polyglot group of women cried out in protest in Lithuanian, Polish, Russian, and Yiddish and fought back, the police beat them with clubs, breaking several heads in the process, according to *The New York Times*. Not a single child was able to board the train. Police arrested 30–35 people that morning and throughout the day.

There is controversy over what exactly transpired at the depot and what the police did or did not do. It is clear, however, that the "children's affair" proved to be a major public relations victory for the IWW and helped make the 1912 strike one of the first in the United States to garner sympathetic coverage from national media outlets.

The North Lawrence train station first opened in 1849 and provided passenger service until 1918. The station, a Victorian Gothic brick structure (built in 1879), no longer exists.

GETTING THERE

From Lawrence Heritage State Park, 0.3 mile (seven-minute) walk. The station stood just west and north of the intersection of Essex and Broadway, on the Broadway side of the no-longer-used railroad tracks.

TO LEARN MORE

Cappello, Lawrence. "In Harm's Way: The Lawrence Textile Strike Children's Affair," in *The Great Lawrence Textile Strike of 1912: New Scholarship on the Bread and Roses Strike*, ed. Robert Forrant and Jurg Siegenthaler, Amityville, NY: Baywood Publishing Company, 2014, 59–78.

Watson, Bruce. *Bread and Roses: Mills, Migrants, and the Struggle for the American Dream*, New York: Viking, 2005.

4.10 Jonas Smolskas House

96 Lawrence Street

LAWRENCE

Jonas Smolskas was an immigrant from Lithuania who worked as a spinner in Lawrence's Arlington Mills. He was also an active supporter of the 1912 strike and a member of the IWW. On the evening of October 19, several months after the strike's end, there

Looking north on Lawrence Street at intersection with Elm Street, 1923. Smolskas's house would likely have been the structure just north of the corner building.

The murder reflects the relationship between violence and the effort by many in the Lawrence establishment to erase the memory of the strike, the incident having taken place soon after what later became known as the "God and Country" parade, an attempt to cleanse the city of radical political sentiment. One week after the killing, the police harassed Smolskas's funeral procession, a march of two thousand from the Lithuanian parish Saint Francis of Assisi (at 94 Bradford Street) to the Immaculate Conception Cemetery. Speaking to a violence of a different but related sort was the elimination of the sites associated with the killing—both the saloon and the house where Smolskas resided are gone, part of the eradication of entire streets and neighborhoods in the name of urban renewal from the late 1950s to the late 1970s.

was some sort of altercation at Riley's saloon on 249 Elm Street involving three of Smolskas's compatriots, resulting in their ejection from the premises. Three native-born men proceeded to chase the Lithuanian men, who fled to the alley in back of nearby Lawrence Street. At the time, Jonas Smolskas was returning to his home from the nearby Lithuanian food cooperative when he encountered the three men in pursuit. Seeing an IWW pin on his jacket, the trio accosted the twenty-seven-year-old in his backyard, with one of them, a boxer by the name of Kennedy, punching Smolskas and knocking him down. Smolskas's head struck a rock as he fell, fracturing his skull. Three days later, Smolskas, a husband and father of one son, died. At the gravesite ceremony, officiated by one of the IWW's leading organizers, Carlo Tresca, Wobblie head William "Big Bill" Haywood pronounced Smolskas the third and final fatality associated with the strike.

The stretch of Elm Street where the saloon stood is no longer; it is now part of the Amesbury Gardens apartment complex. As for the site of Smolskas's house, it would have stood a little north of where Elm Street used to intersect Lawrence Street (just in front of Saint Anthony's Maronite Church now), on the west side of the street roughly where Amesbury Street ends. Along with Anna LoPizzo and John Ramey—the two other individuals killed in strike-related violence—Jonas Smolskas is buried in Lawrence's Immaculate Conception Cemetery in the section near the last gate on Currant Hill Road.

GETTING THERE

From the Lawrence State Heritage Park, 0.5 mile (eleven-minute) walk.

NEARBY SITE

LAWRENCE PUBLIC LIBRARY, 51 Lawrence Street.

4.11 The Arlington Mills

550 Broadway

LAWRENCE

Police on horseback attacked a picket line of thousands of strikers and their supporters in front of the Arlington Mills on February 26, 1919. In the ensuing chaos, the crowd dispersed with the police in hot pursuit. Among the targets of the state violence was A. J. Muste, the head of the strike committee and a famed pacifist—he would later play important roles in the Civil Rights and anti–Vietnam War movements. Catching him in a nearby alley, police clubbed Muste on his body and legs until he could no longer stand. They then arrested him, charging the Christian minister with disturbing the peace and loitering. Workers quickly raised money for bail so that he was back on the picket line the following day.

The 1919 strike grew out of a campaign by unions in Lawrence—part of a national and worldwide effort—to cut the work week from fifty-four to forty-eight hours. On February 1, in the face of worker agitation and declining demand for textiles at the end of World War I, mill owners throughout Lawrence announced they would accept the demand but would not raise hourly wages. Given the conservative leadership of the national United Textile Workers, the vast majority of textile workers across the United States accepted similar offers. Lawrence textile unionists, however, did not, demanding fifty-four hours of pay for forty-eight hours of work. This demand—along with deep concerns regarding poor housing and heavy-handed discipline and discrimination in the

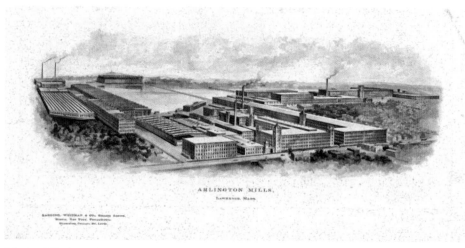

Arlington Mills, date unknown.

workplace—underlay the launch of the strike, one involving about twenty thousand of some thirty-five thousand local workers, on February 3.

The strike was characterized by aggressive police violence: Several weeks into it, the police escalated their opposition by mounting machine guns at major intersections. Lasting more than three months, the strike did not end until May 20, when mill owners accepted most of the workers' demands.

Muste's presence in Lawrence, and that of fellow radical pastors (Cedric Long and Harold Rotzel) from the Boston-based Comradeship, was driven by his left-wing politics—socialist and pacifist. It also spoke to the pragmatism of Lawrence's radical labor activists and the 1912 strike's enduring legacy. While many claim that Muste was needed to bring together the disparate elements of a polyglot, immigrant workforce and to have a strong English-speaker as the strike's public face, there were numerous English-speaking and highly skilled organizers among the workers' leadership. By allying themselves with prominent out-of-towners, Lawrence's workers sought to build their support base.

The Arlington Mills Company began operating on the site in 1865. Eventually it would grow to include twenty-three buildings on a seventy-five-acre site, becoming one of New England's largest textile production complexes. The great poet Robert Frost, after graduating from Lawrence High School, worked there in 1893 and 1894. The company closed its doors in 1952; Malden Mills subsequently took over the complex and later sold it to Polartec, which moved its operations to Tennessee in 2016. Now a smaller site called the Arlington Mills Historic District (it is listed on the National Register of Historic Places) occupies the Lawrence-Methuen border and is home to loft apartments. An industrial innovation hub is also reportedly in the works.

RELATED SITE

99 APPLETON WAY, South End (Boston). Muste lived at this address during 1918 and 1919; the rented house served as the Comradeship's headquarters. According to historian Leilah Danielson, the house "served as sort of alternative community for its members and for a hodgepodge of radicals who used it as a meeting place and safe haven."

TO LEARN MORE

Arnold, Dexter. *"A Row of Bricks": Worker Activism in the Merrimack Valley Textile Industry, 1912–1922*, PhD diss., Department of History, University of Wisconsin-Madison, 1985.

Arnold, Dexter. "Beyond the Bread and Roses Strike: Worker Militancy, Working-Class Realism, and Popular Memory in Lawrence, 1912–1937," unpublished paper.

Danielson, Leilah. *American Gandhi: A. J. Muste and the History of Radicalism in the Twentieth Century*, Philadelphia: University of Pennsylvania Press, 2014.

Snow, Ethan J. *Strike City: An Oral History of the Legacy of Labor Militancy in Lawrence, Massachusetts, 1912—1931*, MA thesis, Department of History, University of Massachusetts Lowell, 2012.

4.12 Schaake's Block

234 Essex Street

LAWRENCE

In the midst of a Depression-era strike in Lawrence's wool mills, the City's police

Original caption: "Edith Berkman being arrested at Red headquarters in Lawrence," 1931.

department and its political leaders showed once again whose side they were on in the battle between labor and capital. At noon on Thursday, February 26, 1931, police stormed Schaake's Block (also known as Post Office Block), a commercial building that housed the headquarters of the National Textile Workers Union (NTWU).

According to *The Evening Tribune* of Lawrence, city marshal Timothy J. O'Brien led a "spectacular" raid, part of an effort to arrest three "outside radicals who have been leading the local strikers." A "squad of plain-clothesmen and bluecoats . . . burst in the door of the room on the third floor where the strike committee was in session," the paper reported. They then arrested Edith Berkman and dragged her down the stairs. Facing "resistance," the police proceeded to

use their clubs to "split open" the heads of William Murdock (one of the other three "outside radicals" along with Berkman and Pat Devine, who had been arrested an hour earlier when he stepped outside) and one other, leading them outside "with blood streaming down their faces." Authorities charged Berkman and Devine with conspiracy to damage the ***American Woolen Company***'s property and to intimidate its workers, as well as with interference with police officers (a change levied against the other five arrestees as well).

Before the strike began on February 16, membership in the Communist Party–affiliated NWTU numbered in the hundreds in Lawrence as worker interest in radical expressions of unionism declined in the face of state persecution of leftists. As the mill owners tried to speed up and increase production (what was called a "stretch-out") and institute new "efficiency" measures, however, a small NWTU contingent staged a walkout, provoking a much larger work stoppage by thousands of laborers in the American Woolen Company's three mills.

The raid took place as the NWTU strike committee was meeting to discuss a proposed vote to end the strike, one involving about ten thousand workers, in light of the owners agreeing to end the "stretch-out" and withdraw their detested "efficiency experts" from the mills. Because of the arrests, and the federal government's piling on further charges and holding some of those arrested—most notably Berkman—on immigration charges as "undesirable aliens," that vote never took place. Instead, Lawrence's "Citizen's Committee" organized its own vote, one that unfolded in a context of fear and intimidation and in which only two thousand workers participated.

Although the workers approved the strike's end, it only led to a lull in labor unrest as the mill owners instituted a wage cut of 10 percent in early October, provoking a strike of twenty-four thousand workers. Edith Berkman, having been released on bail, returned to help head the work stoppage. However, the "Red Flame," as she was called, was soon re-arrested, on the pretext of speaking on the North Common without a permit, leaving the NTWU leaderless. This—combined with divisions between competing unions of differing political orientations, fear among workers that they would lose their jobs permanently

given the Depression, and a lack of relief funds for striking workers—led to the strike's fizzling out in mid-November. It would be the last gasp of radical unionism by Lawrence's mill workers in the twentieth century.

Edith Berkman, a Polish national, was imprisoned at the **East Boston Immigration Station** through much of 1932 but was eventually released. As for Schaake's Block, built in 1867–69, it was torn down at some point during the 1930s. The commercial building that now stands on the site was constructed in 1939.

GETTING THERE

MBTA Commuter Rail (Haverhill Line) to Lawrence Station. From Lawrence Heritage State Park, 0.2 mile (three-minute) walk.

NEARBY SITE

NORTH (OR CAMPAGNONE) COMMON, 200 Common Street. Important gatherings during the 1912 strike took place at North Common—including the occasion when fifteen thousand workers assembled on March 14, 1912, and voted to end the work stoppage. Today the Common hosts an annual Bread and Roses Heritage Festival ("Pro-Labor & Pro-Social Justice, Multi-cultural & Multi-ethnic") on Labor Day (the first Monday of September) to commemorate the strike. It is also the site (diagonally across from city hall) of a stone monument to the strike, which was unveiled in 2012.

TO LEARN MORE

Snow, Ethan J. *Strike City: An Oral History of the Legacy of Labor Militancy in Lawrence, Massachusetts, 1912—1931*, MA thesis, Department of History, University of Massachusetts Lowell, 2012.

4.13 The Essex Company Headquarters Compound/Lawrence History Center

6 Essex Street

LAWRENCE

In 1882–83, the Essex Company built the compound that now exists on Essex and Union (across from its old offices on the east side of Union Street). It contained the cashier's office and the engineering division, as

Lawrence History Center with Everett Mills structure in the background, 2018.

well as a stable and buildings for carpentry, blacksmithing, and equipment storage.

The company is today a subsidiary of Enel Green Power North America, Inc., but continues to own the Great Stone Dam and the canals that it built in the mid-1800s to power the textile mills, and a few properties in the city. It sold the compound to Immigrant City Archives (first founded in 1978) in 1992. What is now called the Lawrence History Center is a repository of a wide set of archives relating to the city's past. Its mission, according to the center's website, "is to collect, preserve, share, and interpret the history and heritage of Lawrence and its people." The center provides invaluable services to researchers while also engaging in public education through on-site and online exhibits as well as summer writing and multimedia workshops for local youth.

One can visit the center itself only by appointment. However, there are interpretative panels posted along the back wall of the compound (which one can access through

the gate on Essex Street) that provide a valuable history of the site.

GETTING THERE

From the Lawrence State Heritage Park, 0.3 mile (six-minute) walk.

NEARBY SITE

At the **INTERSECTION OF UNION AND GARDEN STREETS,** Anna LoPizzo, a thirty-four-year-old Italian immigrant mill worker was shot and killed on January 29, 1912, upon encountering a brawl between picketing workers and police. She was the 1912 strike's first casualty.

TO LEARN MORE

Hearn, Mike. *The History of the Essex Company,* Lawrence, MA: Lawrence History Center, 2014.

4.14 Bread and Roses Housing

210–212 Park Street

LAWRENCE

By the early 2000s, Park Street was known as the city's worst street. It was character-

Mural by David Fichter celebrating Lawrence's proud history of immigrant workers and commemorating the 1912 strike. Greater Lawrence Family Health Center, 150 Park Street, 2018.

needs of the city's poor and marginalized population. It did so through the provision of a free, full-course meal five evenings a week. As the numbers of families and individuals going to the center (at 58 Newbery Street) grew, it became clear that an underlying cause of their hunger was the large percentage of their incomes dedicated to housing.

The need for an afford-able housing program therefore became apparent, and Bread and Roses Housing was created in 1998, dedicated to the belief that housing is a human right rather than a commodity or something bought and sold with the intention of producing profit.

BRH is a combination land trust (a democratically run nonprofit entity owns the land on which the housing sits and holds it in perpetuity for the benefit of the community and its members) and limited equity housing program. Together they make the purchase of a home much more affordable than it would be otherwise, as the cost of the land is not included in the price. It also limits how much the value of the home can increase to ensure that it remains affordable for future buyers. Meanwhile, for a nominal monthly fee, families receive ninety-nine-year leases on the land where they reside.

As of mid-2019, BRH had developed forty-two units of housing (composed of eighteen duplexes and six single-family

ized by many poorly maintained tenements, trash-strewn empty lots, abandoned cars, and high levels of street crime. In 2003 Bread and Roses Housing (BRH), a "provider of sustainable homes and affordable home ownership opportunities," bought two vacant lots (at 210 and 212 Park Street)—both had been declared public nuisances—and constructed a six-bedroom duplex and sold each side separately to two local families. This played a significant role in revitalizing and stabilizing the neighborhood, one that has seen a marked increase in investment ever since BRH assumed control of the properties.

Based on principles of nonviolence and inspired by the teachings of Martin Luther King Jr. and radical Catholic activists Dorothy Day and Thomas Merton, Bread and Roses was founded in 1980 by a small group of volunteers and subsequently coordinated by six women. It was established as a hospitality center to respond to the basic homes) for low-income buyers, with all of them in Lawrence with the exception of six in neighboring North Andover (with active plans for expansion in **Haverhill**). In addition, BRH provides a variety of long-term support services to BRH homeowners and their children.

BRH now has eight housing units, all duplexes, on Park Street. Two of them (219–221) are diagonally across the street from 210–212. Built in 2012 with rooftop solar panels, and using energy efficient technologies and construction techniques, they reflect BRH's growing commitment to environmentally sustainable housing. BRH's office is located in the Everett Mills.

GETTING THERE

From the Lawrence State Heritage Park, 1.1 mile (twenty-minute) walk.

TO LEARN MORE

Hubbard, Kara Elizabeth. *Assessing the Community Land Trust Model: A Case Study of Bread & Roses Housing, Inc.*, MA thesis, Department of Urban and Environmental Policy and Planning, Tufts University, 2009.

Marra, Mary. *Affordable Housing: A Model*, MA thesis, Community Social Psychology Program, University of Lowell, 1989.

Website of Bread and Roses Housing: http://www.brhousing.org

4.15 1984 Riot Epicenter

Oxford and Haverhill Streets

LAWRENCE

Its considerable ethnic diversity notwithstanding, Lawrence was 99 percent white in the early decades of the 1900s. The Immigrant City's demographics began to change in the context of post–World War II deindustrialization, socioeconomic decline, and significant out-migration, which opened up housing and job opportunities for newcomers. Welcomed and sometimes recruited by the city's remaining manufacturers, Latinos—largely Puerto Ricans, but many Cubans and Dominicans as well—began to move to Lawrence in the 1960s and 1970s, many of them from New York City, in search of jobs and a better life, one seen as more possible in a small city.

Many in Lawrence did not welcome the city's new residents, however. As the Latino population increased, racial tensions grew as many white Lawrencians felt that "their" city was under siege and unjustly blamed Latinos for its decline. Outright expressions of racism toward Latinos were not uncommon, coupled with structural forms of exclusion and marginalization. The city's political class was insensitive at best to the challenges its Latino citizens faced, and its police force—with only two Latinos out of ninety-six officers—was often guilty of racialized abuse.

The Lower Tower Hill neighborhood, which prior to the 1970s had been made up largely of whites of French-Canadian descent, was about half Latino by the 1980s. It became a flash point for these tensions in the summer of 1984. For weeks, seemingly isolated acts of violence took place among local youth. These exploded on August 8 as hundreds of white and Latino youth clashed on Oxford Street. Throwing rocks and Molo-

A crowd chants during riots, August 9, 1984.

tov cocktails, and sometimes employing knives and guns, running battles took place over two long nights. Numerous houses and businesses were set on fire, with the police proving largely ineffective as both groups of rioters turned on them when they tried to intervene. Displaying the racism and xenophobia that underlay the violence, many whites taunted their Latino neighbors with chants of "USA! USA!" "Who's American? We're American," and "Go back to where you came from." Somewhat miraculously, no deaths resulted from the rioting, and the number of injuries was small.

Historian Llana Barber argues that ultimately the causes of the violence were multiple: "a Latino protest against racism and marginalization, a furious expression of white bigotry, a nativist protest against immigration, a working-class protest against urban economic decline and deindustrializa-

tion, and a popular protest against an out-of-touch city government." As for the outcomes, they too were multiple. In the short term, the rioting increased white flight from Lawrence. Over the longer term, the rioting led to intensified activism by Latino Lawrencians on various fronts, including efforts to gain access to the city's halls of power. These efforts have borne considerable fruit in recent years. One is that city government in Lawrence now reflects a city that is three-quarters Latino.

TO GET THERE

From the Lawrence State Heritage Park, 1.1 mile (twenty-one-minute) walk.

TO LEARN MORE

Barber, Llana. *Immigration and Urban Crisis in Lawrence, Massachusetts, 1945–2000*, Chapel Hill: University of North Carolina Press, 2017.

Haverhill

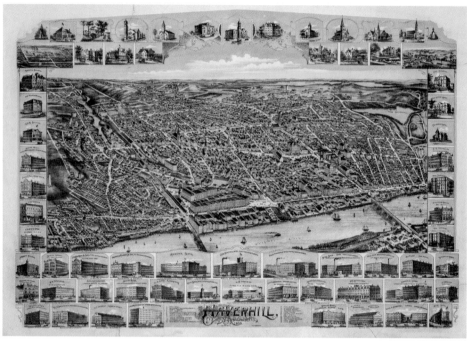

Haverhill, Massachusetts, 1893.

On the banks of the Merrimack River, land inhabited by indigenous bands affiliated with the Pennacook, of the Wabanaki Confederacy, an Algonquian-speaking community, English settlers established what is today the City of Haverhill. Early coexistence in the seventeenth century, however, did not last, and tension between the "frontier town" of Haverhill and the Native population escalated well into the 1700s and the French and Indian War (1754–63), which involved indigenous nations, the British, the French, and those countries' respective colonial subjects. Despite these difficult beginnings, nineteenth-century Haverhill joined its neighboring cities as an expanding industrial powerhouse. It also established itself as an unlikely seat of progressivism with a strong abolitionist tradition and later a municipal socialism associated with a militant labor movement. Its moniker, Queen Slipper City, reflects the centrality of its shoemaking industry.

Twentieth-century Haverhill saw its industrial base decline even while its cultural influence expanded as home to Archie Comics creator Bob Montana. His fictional Riverdale High is based on his own high school experience in Haverhill. Another city resident, Louis Mayer, would go on to found MGM Studios in Hollywood—several years after launching his own cinema and eventually owning all of his hometown's movie houses.

Today Haverhill styles itself a progressive city that is attentive to environmental concerns. Like many other former industrial towns, it is leveraging its former factories to lure higher-income young people with residential and small-business enterprise spaces. The city has sixty-three thousand residents, largely white and middle income, and a significant working-class population. Indigenous nations gather annually at Plug Pond in Haverhill for a powwow sponsored by the Massachusetts Center for Native American Awareness and the City of Haverhill.

The great poet and abolitionist John Greenleaf Whittier was born and raised in Haverhill. His home, now a museum, still stands on the city's outskirts.

4.16 Grand Army of the Republic Park

108 Main Street

HAVERHILL

Grand Army of the Republic Park is located in downtown Haverhill, close to City Hall. Among the six historical and war-related memorials that adorn the park, one stands out for both its age and its gory nature: a monument to Hannah Duston, erected in 1879.

In the early hours of a winter morning in 1697, Hannah Duston, her infant daughter, and a midwife were captured in Haverhill by an Abenaki band as part of a raid associated with the tensions between the colonies of New England and New France. In most tellings, the raid's first casualty was Duston's

Grand Army of the Republic Park, 2016.

newborn. Her response would come to define the mainstream frontier narrative.

Forced north and deep into New Hampshire, Duston and her midwife were placed in the custody of an Abenaki family, whose intentions remain unclear. At the time, following a century of pandemics and colonial warfare, decimated indigenous communities often raided one another and the settlements, taking hostages for trading and as replacements for lost family members.

Several days after her capture, Duston and two other English prisoners killed most of the Abenaki family while they slept. Ten individuals, including eight children, died; only two escaped. Leaving the camp, Duston paused and then returned to scalp her victims. She used an Abenaki canoe to navigate the Merrimack's turbulent waters. Reunited with her family, she was later welcomed by the Massachusetts General Assembly, which awarded her $45 for the scalps. In Boston, Cotton Mather interviewed Duston, later sermonizing about her—providing the primary source for her story's many retellings.

Duston's lore grew over the next two centuries, receding only as the West came to represent the "pioneer spirit." The erection of Duston statues in New Hampshire (at the purported site of the massacre) and in Haverhill suggest that her story received official imprimatur. The former is said to be the first publicly funded statue honoring a woman in the United States. The Duston story serves the colonial narrative well, rendering the indigenous people victimized by European expansion as aggressors. For Mather, Duston's reprisal represented the hand of divine retribution and the impossibility of any coexistence of settlers and indigenous peoples.

Haverhill still celebrates the Duston story. There are many Duston-related sites, including a surviving brick home funded by the bounty Duston received for the scalps that she took. The Buttonwoods Museum devotes exhibits to this story and includes a hatchet Duston is purported to have used. The monument in Grand Army Park features four friezes that recount elements of the original story.

GETTING THERE

MBTA Commuter Rail (Haverhill Line) to Haverhill, 0.7 mile (fourteen-minute) walk.

TO LEARN MORE

Atkinson, Jay. *Massacre on the Merrimack: Hannah Duston's Captivity and Revenge in Colonial America*, Guildford, CT: Rowman & Littlefield, 2015.

Grenier, John. *The First Way of War: American Warmaking on the Frontier*. Cambridge: Cambridge University Press, 2005.

Weidensaul, Scott. *The First Frontier: The Forgotten History of Struggle, Savagery, and Endurance in Early America*, Boston: Houghton Mifflin Harcourt Publishing, 2012.

4.17 Old Haverhill City Hall

1 Park Way

HAVERHILL

In 1899 John Calvin Chase, campaigning for reelection as Haverhill's mayor, predicted that he would win 3,500 votes. He was wrong: 3,542 voters returned him to city hall. Such was the organization of Haverhill-based socialists at the end of the nineteenth century that they could mobilize their voters with predictable results. On becoming the first openly socialist mayor in the United States in 1898, Chase had excited socialists throughout the country, generating hopes for a wave of similar outcomes elsewhere across the country. One cause for optimism was the fact that both Chase and his electorate were largely "native born," suggesting that socialism was no longer confined to immigrant circles.

Chase's electoral success was the fruit of years of organizing and ideological struggles. Beginning with a large, though unsuccessful, strike in 1893 by Haverhill shoe workers during an economic downturn, socialists established a close identification with working people, upending a then-widespread and technocratic vision of a socialism administered by elites. Instead, Haverhill socialists agitated about important local concerns, including unguarded railway

G 21541 City Hall, Haverhill, Mass.

Postcard, 1903.

favor of municipal ownership of the water department. Two years prior to Chase's reelection, Haverhill chose two socialists for both of their state legislative representatives.

By 1900, Chase and most Haverhill socialists faced huge challenges as the Catholic Church, local business leaders, rival trade union factions, and a united front of Republicans and Democrats together ousted Chase. Defeated in local government, with socialist factions divided against each other, Chase turned his attention to strengthening the Socialist Party by using statewide elections to educate the public. Later he moved to Pennsylvania, where he died in 1937.

The city hall that Chase occupied for two years, at the corner of Court and Main Streets, was closed down and its operations relocated in 1909. Today the original site is a parking lot for a local laboratory.

crossings, high heating-fuel costs, and the need for streetlights, while also addressing traditional working-class concerns over wages and the length of the workday.

During their campaigns, Haverhill socialists, who were loosely connected to broader, often competing, national currents around Daniel De Leon and Eugene V. Debs, gained credibility for their honesty and competence. Their activism and victories helped pull the entire public debate to the left. Competing against socialists, Haverhill Republicans declared that they too were in

GETTING THERE

MBTA Commuter Rail (Haverhill Line) to Haverhill, 0.6 mile (twelve-minute) walk.

TO LEARN MORE

Bedford, Henry F. *Socialism and the Workers in Massachusetts, 1886–1912*, Amherst: University of Massachusetts Press, 1966.

Newburyport

Brown Square; postcard, 1913.

Newburyport, a city of approximately seventeen thousand inhabitants, lies at the mouth of the Merrimack River, about forty miles north of Boston. Ceremonial mounds in the area indicate that it was long an area of importance to Native peoples. When English settlers first arrived there in 1635, it was part of the Newberry Plantation. In 1764 the General Court of Massachusetts created Newburyport as a separate entity.

The port city's most famous offspring is firebrand abolitionist William Lloyd Garrison, who was born there in 1805. It also played a role in the Underground Railroad as a number of residents helped those fleeing slavery find their way to freedom. However, like many places in Greater Boston, Newburyport's reputation as center of antislavery activism obscures its role in upholding, and benefiting from, the slave trade.

Although the total number of enslaved people in the area was small, many of New-buryport's wealthy families owned slaves—African and Native American—by the late 1600s. Ironically, some of the enslaved people were involved in the building of ships, a number of which were used to perpetuate the slave trade—either by transporting locally produced goods to the West Indies (dried cod, for example) in exchange for sugar and molasses and to the African continent (largely rum) in exchange for human beings. The labor of enslaved people helped make Newburyport the richest town (per capita) in late-colonial Massachusetts. According to local historian Susan Harvey, forty-seven ships built in Newburyport were used for slave voyages. Over a total of eighty-eight voyages, they were involved in the transport of 22,629 enslaved Africans, 3,582 of whom died in transit.

Accessible from Boston by Commuter Rail, Newburyport, with its quaint shops and historic architecture, attracts many tourists. Plum Island, which is part of New-buryport, is a popular vacation destination, particularly during the summer months. Much of the 4600-acre Parker River National Wildlife Refuge, a vital stopover for migratory birds, also sits in Newburyport.

4.18 William Lloyd Garrison House

3–5 School Street

NEWBURYPORT

William Lloyd Garrison House, 2016.

Born on December 10, 1805, in his family's modest home on School Street, William Lloyd Garrison was one of the US antislavery movement's most important figures. His childhood years in Newburyport were difficult. Because his family was poor, he often had to beg for leftover food at the homes of wealthy families on High Street and elsewhere in town. When he was eight, his father disappeared. Before he was ten, he was an apprentice to a shoemaker in **Lynn**. And prior to his eighteenth birthday, his mother passed away.

It was during his teenage years, when Garrison was around thirteen, that he began working as an apprentice (in 1818) to the editor of the *Newburyport Herald,* where he would remain until 1825. Despite little formal education, Garrison showed promise as a writer, penning anonymous pieces that he would surreptitiously submit to the *Herald,* which then published them. In 1826 Garrison became the editor of Newburyport's *Free*

Press. During this time, he befriended John Greenleaf Whittier (see **Haverhill**), whose writings he published and who would go on to become a famed poet and abolitionist.

In less than a year Garrison sold the *Free Press* and moved to Boston. Through his newspaper work and social circles, he increasingly engaged with reformist and radical political thought and became involved in the abolitionist movement. After a brief stint in Baltimore as the coeditor of a Quaker newspaper that advocated gradual emancipation, Garrison returned to Boston for good, cofounding (with Isaac Knapp) the newspaper *The Liberator.*

With financial assistance from the Philadelphia-based black businessman and abolitionist James Forten and influenced by Boston's David Walker, *The Liberator* took an uncompromising stance toward slavery. It played a central role in what is known as second-wave abolitionism, marked by a demand for immediate emancipation, racial

> I will be as harsh as truth, and as uncompromising as justice. On this subject, I do not wish to think, or speak, or write, with moderation. No! No! Tell a man whose house is on fire to give a moderate alarm; tell him to moderately rescue his wife from the hands of the ravisher; tell the mother to gradually extricate her babe from the fire into which it has fallen;—but urge me not to use moderation in a cause like the present. I am in earnest—I will not equivocate—I will not excuse—I will not retreat a single inch—*and I will be heard.*
>
> **—From the first issue of The Liberator, January 1, 1831**

integration, and full and equal rights for African Americans. Important abolitionist figures, both black and white, including Frederick Douglass and Maria W. Stewart, found expression in *The Liberator*'s pages. But Garrison's voice, infused

Masthead of *The Liberator*, including its motto: "Our Country is the World, our Countrymen are all Mankind."

with righteous indignation and a strong commitment to pacifism, dominated its pages, incurring the wrath of many in Boston and around the United States. Garrison also helped to found the New England Anti-Slavery Society and served as the president of the American Anti-Slavery Society.

The celebrated antislavery weekly endured until the Civil War's end, its last issue published on December 29, 1865. Despite the paper's demise, Garrison remained active until late in life, championing the causes of civil rights and women's rights. William Lloyd Garrison died in 1879. He is buried in **Jamaica Plain**'s Forest Hills Cemetery.

GETTING THERE

Commuter Rail from North Station to Newburyport.

NEARBY SITE

BROWN SQUARE (between Green Street and Titcomb Street) was the site of the first meeting of the Essex County Anti-Slavery Society (in 1836). Named after Moses Brown, Newburyport's largest property owner, the square features an imposing statue of William Lloyd Garrison (erected in 1893), on the base of which are engraved some of his most famous words. Brown was a merchant, shipbuilder, and an investor in the sugar, rum,

and molasses trade. Thus, as for many in Newburyport, his well-being was tied to slavery.

TO LEARN MORE

Hallett, William. *Newburyport and the Civil War*, Charleston, SC: The History Press, 2012.

Mayer, Henry. *All on Fire: William Lloyd Garrison and the Abolition of Slavery*, New York: St. Martin's Griffin, 1998.

Sinha, Manisha. *The Slave's Cause: A History of Abolition*, New Haven: Yale University Press, 2016.

4.19 Caleb Cushing Homes

98 and 63 High Street

NEWBURYPORT

Caleb Cushing was one of the most powerful and influential US politicians and diplomats of his era. Born in 1800 into a wealthy shipbuilding and merchant family, Cushing was raised in Newburyport. After graduating from Harvard College in 1817, he worked as a lawyer in Newburyport and went on to win election to the Massachusetts state legislature and later to the US Congress.

Cushing was one of the leading voices embracing US territorial and economic expansion. He was able to act on his vision when President John Tyler appointed him US envoy to China in 1843. Cushing's charge was to negotiate a treaty allowing US merchants the same privileges enjoyed by the British, privileges won through the first "Opium War" by which the British forced China's opening to trade and the ceding of Hong Kong. Militarily weak and eager to avoid war with another Western power, China agreed to US demands, granting the United States most-favored-nation status while ensuring, via the principle of "extraterritoriality," that US nationals working in China would never fall under Chinese jurisdiction.

After taking advantage of China's vulnerability to imperial power, Cushing returned to the United States in 1845 and became a champion of the annexation of what is today the US Southwest. A key desire of his was the acquisition of California and the port of San Francisco to expand trade with China and Asia. Driven by his belief in Anglo-Saxon superiority and Manifest Destiny, Cushing played a leading role in recruiting and organizing a regiment of soldiers from Massachusetts, one he would command, to fight in the Mexican-American War (1846–48). The war allowed the United States to take almost half of the territory that was then, at least officially, Mexico, gaining what now comprises all or part of ten US states.

Many in Massachusetts saw Cushing as a highly opportunistic and unprincipled politician. When he first ran for Congress, he was an opponent of slavery. He later switched political parties (from Whig to Democrat) and aligned himself with Southern anti-abolitionists. Such a position, combined with his conservative politics on women's rights and his support for the war against Mexico

(which was deeply unpopular in Massachusetts), helps explain why some referred to Cushing as the most disliked man in New England in the 1850s.

Caleb Cushing lived in the home at 98 High Street beginning in 1802. A national historic landmark, it serves now as the Museum of Old Newbury. In 1849 he acquired the house on 63 High Street and lived there until his death in 1879. A marker on the property, today a private residence, notes that Jefferson Davis, a close friend of his until the Civil War's outbreak (Cushing supported the Union side in the war), stayed there. It was Cushing who introduced Davis to the audience at *Faneuil Hall* in 1858 when the man who would lead the Confederacy tried to make the case for "state's rights" to Bostonians.

GETTING THERE

Commuter Rail from North Station to Newburyport.

NEARBY SITE

PLUMER FAMILY HOUSE (79 Federal Street) was the home of an abolitionist family and a station on the Underground Railroad.

TO LEARN MORE

Belohlavek, John M. *Broken Glass: Caleb Cushing and the Shattering of the Union*, Kent, OH: Kent State University Press, 2005.

Kuo, Ping Chia. "Caleb Cushing and the Treaty of Wanghia, 1844," *Journal of Modern History* 5, no. 1 (1933): 34–54.

Lazich, Michael C. "American Missionaries and the Opium Trade in Nineteenth-Century China, *Journal of World History* 17, no. 2 (2006): 197–223.

Salem

The House of Seven Gables, 1929.

An early settlement of the Massachusetts Bay Colony, Salem was established in 1626. With the arrival of European traders and English colonists, disease and dispossession helped to transform what had previously been a Native village and trading center. Salem quickly emerged as a key seaport and an important participant in the transatlantic slave economy, both through trade in enslaved persons and in goods for and from Caribbean slave plantations. (The House of Seven Gables, originally the Turner-Ingersoll Mansion, was partially financed in this manner.) It was the Salem-based *Desire* that first brought enslaved Africans to the Massachusetts colony in 1638.

During the Revolutionary War, many Salem ship owners became rich through privateering—using their own repurposed vessels to attack English ships, and keeping the resulting war booty. Following independence, Salem's size and wealth further expanded. By 1796, it was the country's sixth largest city (with ten thousand people); its Customs House generated about five percent of the national treasury's revenues. It was also reputed to be the New World's richest city per capita. Much of the wealth came from trade with Asia, with pepper, valuable as both a spice and a preservative, Salem's most lucrative import, and opium a valuable export.

The ongoing growth of Boston and New York City as shipping ports led to Salem's decline in the nineteenth century. Textiles, tanneries, and shoemaking helped to reenergize the city's economy. In the late 1800s, the now-defunct Parker Brothers company was founded in Salem; its most popular product was Monopoly, the capitalist game whose original version was a protest against monopoly capitalism and an effort to teach people to share wealth.

Salem is best known for the moral panic that resulted in the witch trials and executions of 1692. In the twentieth century, Salem began drawing on its history for various ends, both commercial and social-justice-oriented ones, and has become a popular tourist destination. Over a million people visit the city of approximately forty thousand each year—many of them coming on or near Halloween.

GETTING THERE

Directions are provided from the National Park Regional Visitor Center (2 New Liberty Street), a 0.3 mile (seven-minute) walk from the Salem Commuter Rail Station.

4.20 East India Marine Hall/ Peabody Essex Museum

161 Essex Street

SALEM

East India Marine Hall is one of the oldest gallery buildings of Salem's famed Peabody Essex Museum, among the top art museums in the United States and home to one of the country's largest collections of Asian art. When the building first opened on October 14, 1825—to help house the growing collection of "natural and artificial curiosities" of the East India Marine Society—it was with great fanfare. Attending the museum's opening banquet were Boston's mayor, Josiah Quincy, US Supreme Court Justice Joseph Story, US President John Quincy Adams, and John Thornton Kirkland, president of Harvard.

Their presence spoke to the prestige of the society—whose members were business agents ("supercargoes") and captains of ships that sailed beyond Cape Horn or the Cape of Good Hope to Asia—and to Salem's importance to the emerging US and global economies. The town's dominance in the South Pacific spice trade was such that many

referred to the region as the Salem East Indies. Ships from Salem and Boston were so prevalent in East Indian ports that the towns "were regarded as powerful countries," according to historian James Lindgren.

The "Pepper Coast" of Sumatra was a focus of much of Salem's trade. Between 1795 and 1831, there were about four hundred voyages by US ships—most out of Salem and Boston—to the area. In February 1831, a group of armed men attacked one such ship, the Salem-based *Friendship* (not to be confused with its namesake ship, a replica of which is today moored at Salem's Derby Wharf), and plundered most of its cargo off the shore of the village of Kuala Batu. The attackers killed at least three crew members and wounded several more. One year later, a US naval vessel, the *Potomac*, attacked Kuala Batu in response, killing hundreds, including children.

Obscured in the debate surrounding the US military's grossly disproportionate mission of revenge—while many in the press applauded it, some were heavily critical—was why the *Friendship* was assaulted in the first place. The aggressors, it turns out, were drug addicts—addicted to opium—which Salem-based vessels had for some time been carrying to the region to exchange for pepper. The ship's captain, Charles Moses Endicott, concluded that opium, $9,000 worth of which was on board, was the reason for the attack.

As a member of the East India Marine Society. Endicott, like others enriching Salem by sea-trafficking in opium, would likely have contributed to the holdings of its museum (then called a "cabinet"). It is to this that the Peabody Essex Museum traces its roots. The East India Marine Hall houses the original display cases and some of the early objects collected by the East India Marine Society.

GETTING THERE

MBTA Commuter Rail to Salem. From the NPS Regional Visitor Center, 350 feet away (a one-minute walk).

TO LEARN MORE

Booth, Robert. *Death of an Empire: The Rise and Murderous Fall of Salem, America's Richest City*, New York: St. Martin's Press, 2011.

Lindgren, James M. "'That Every Mariner May Possess the History of the World': A Cabinet for the East India Marine Society of Salem," *New England Quarterly* 68, no. 2 (1995): 179–205.

Long, David F. "'Martial Thunder': The First Official American Armed Intervention in Asia," *Pacific Historical Review* 42, no. 2 (1973): 143–62.

Morrison, Dane Anthony. "Salem as Citizen of the World," in *Salem: Place, Myth, and Memory*, ed. Dane Anthony Morrison and Nancy Lusignan Schultz, Boston; Northeastern University Press, 2004, 107–27.

Noor, Farish A. "America in Southeast Asia before the 'Pivot': The 'Battle of Quallah Battoo' in 1832," RSIS (Rajaratnam School of International Studies) Working Paper, no. 275, Singapore: Nanyang Technological University, 2014.

4.21 Lyceum Hall

43 Church Street

SALEM

Abolitionist siblings Charles Lenox Remond and Sarah Parker Remond tapped into a novel public forum to promote their cause. In the 1820s a burgeoning Lyceum movement—

public educational forums aimed at adults—spread across the United States. In 1831, with the construction of Lyceum Hall on Church Street, the movement came to Salem. Although the Lyceum hosted many types of events, contentious topics were often its focus. Lecturers included Frederick Douglass, Ralph Waldo Emerson, Susan B. Anthony, Oliver Wendell Holmes, and Henry David Thoreau. The Remonds were their distinguished local peers.

Their achievements manifest both their upbringing in cosmopolitan Salem and their family's active community presence. Their father, John Remond, arrived in Salem in 1798 as a free youth of African origin from Curacao. He became active in the local political scene while operating a successful catering and restaurant business for over fifty years. He also participated in the antislavery movement—fundraising for its "immediatist" wing, which demanded freedom and full citizenship for enslaved people without delay.

Remond married Nancy Lenox, a free-born African American Bostonian and a professional fancy-cake maker. Charles Lenox and Sarah Parker followed in their parents' footsteps, championing abolition and women's rights. Charles Lenox collaborated with Frederick Douglass and William Lloyd Garrison and was an agent for *The Liberator*—abolitionism's flagship publication. He was also a regular speaker on the Lyceum circuit.

Like her brother, Sarah Parker was an effective activist. In 1853 she challenged the segregation of the Howard Athenaeum in Boston. Injured as she was forced out of a whites-only section, she went on to sue the theater's owners and win its desegregation. She also mobilized support in Europe, particularly England. She remained there during the Civil War to forestall British intervention. As part of the successful movement to prevent British and French recognition of the Confederacy, she added her voice to those of European radicals, including Italy's Garibaldi and German exile Karl Marx.

Before the Salem Lyceum closed in 1898, Alexander Graham Bell, a Salem resident (1873–76), hosted the telephone's first public demonstration there. Lyceum Hall burned down in 1900. The building bearing its name was constructed soon thereafter; today it is home to a restaurant.

GETTING THERE

Eight hundred feet west of the National Park Service's Salem Maritime National Historic Visitor Center.

RELATED SITES

HAMILTON HALL, 9 Chestnut Street. Named for Alexander Hamilton, this assembly hall was the site of John Remond's catering business.

REMOND PARK, 1 Bridge Street. In June 2016 the City of Salem named this waterfront park in honor of the Remond family.

TO LEARN MORE

Porter, Dorothy Burnett. "The Remonds of Salem, Massachusetts: A Nineteenth Century Family Revisited," *Proceedings of the American Antiquarian Society* 95 (1985): 259–95.

4.22 Pequot Mill/ Shetland Industrial Park

Congress Street

SALEM

Spurning their elected leaders, eighteen hundred Pequot Mill workers, United Textile Workers union members, voted to strike on May 8, 1933. Ignoring a hasty telegram from their union's national president ordering them to remain at work and injunctions from Salem's mayor, they soon hit the streets. They also embraced outside support—especially from Anne Burlak, an organizer with the Communist Party–linked National Textile Workers Union. Eleven weeks later, the workers returned to work following what the *Boston Globe* hailed as "an almost complete victory."

Prior to the strike, academics, the American Federation of Labor (AFL), and business had heralded the mill a model of labor-

Anne Burlak in Fall River, 1934.

management cooperation. That cooperation yielded a "scientific approach" to the workforce, one that resulted in the local union's leadership playing a management role. This "efficiency"-driven cooperation facilitated increased layoffs, depressed wages, and speedups that ultimately spurred the strike.

The labor stoppage overcame many challenges: AFL betrayal, police repression, and severe resource constraints. It also surfaced important assets. Immigrant Polish and French-Canadian workers brought a combativeness somewhat lacking among their more settled Irish co-workers. Local institutions like the Polish-American Citizens Club offered meetings spaces denied by the City. Married women, who constituted half the plant's labor force and many of whom had been laid off because management did not respect their seniority, added to the workers' militancy and strengthened labor-community bonds.

Although Anne Burlak was a lightning rod for management's anticommunist propaganda, she gave substance to her organizing reputation through inspiring speeches (earning her nickname the Red Flame) and deft practical work; meanwhile, her organizing work throughout the region enabled her to focus solidarity efforts from other cities. The strikers also benefited from the advice of neighboring Peabody's socialist mayor. Furthermore, federal mediators provided a helpful framework for negotiations, signaling the 1930s' changing national labor environment.

By 1953, following decades of relocation threats aimed at tempering worker militancy, the mill closed and moved to South Carolina. Its Salem operations had begun 114 years earlier under the auspices of the Naumkeag Steam Cotton Company. Today Shetland Industrial Park owns the buildings. It operates the mixed-use site and is home to technology startups and state agencies' offices.

GETTING THERE

From the National Park Service's Salem Maritime National Historic Visitor Center, 0.4 mile (eight-minute) walk.

TO LEARN MORE

Chomsky, Aviva. *Linked Labor Histories: New England, Colombia and the Making of a Global Working Class*, Durham: Duke University Press, 2008.

4.23 Proctor's Ledge

7 Pope Street

SALEM

Approximately two hundred people gathered at Proctor's Ledge at noon on July 19, 2017, to dedicate a memorial to people who were hanged at the site in 1692 after having been convicted of witchcraft.

Accusations of, and convictions and executions for, witchcraft were not limited to Puritan Salem of 1692. Beginning in the 1640s, thirteen women, alleged witches, lost their lives in New England over a few decades. Additionally, numerous women— as well as some men—were banished from their communities for witchcraft. While there are multiple explanations for the moral panic that led to the accusations and killings, a dominant one focuses on the targeting of women who challenged society's patriarchal

Proctor's Ledge, 2017.

norms. Also significant were intensifying competition for arable land (in the face of population growth and the growing number of cattle), increasing disease, and challenging climatic conditions—from floods and cold, wet springs to summer droughts. In such a context, "witches" became scapegoats.

In Salem and its environs, the witchcraft panic exploded in 1692. Compounding environmental factors were the devastating impacts of King Philip's War, which had produced a postwar landscape throughout much of New England marked by "land hunger, pestilence, ravaged villages, refugees, war wounds, and nightmares" in historian Mark Fiege's words.

While the top of Gallows Hill had long been suspected as the site of the hangings, it was not until early 2016 that researchers pinpointed the location—Proctor's Ledge, at the hill's base. Soon thereafter, Salem began building the memorial.

A total of twenty-five accused witches (six of them men) lost their lives in Salem in 1692: one was crushed to death, five died in prison, and nineteen were hanged at Proctor's Ledge. The memorial dedication took place on the 325th anniversary of the first

witch trials–related mass execution, which claimed the lives of five women—Sarah Good, Elizabeth Howe, Susannah Martin, Rebecca Nurse, and Sarah Wildes.

GETTING THERE

MBTA Commuter Rail to Salem. From the National Park Service Regional Visitor Center, 1.1 mile (twenty-one-minute) walk.

TO LEARN MORE

Fiege, Mark. *The Republic of Nature: An Environmental History of the United States*, Seattle: University of Washington Press, 2013.

4.24 The Derby House

168 Derby Street

SALEM

Around 1762, Richard Derby, a sea merchant and one of Salem's richest men, built a house for his son (Elias) and wife-to-be (Elizabeth Crowninshield) as a wedding gift. It served as the home for the couple and their children for about two decades, before they moved to a bigger, more luxurious abode in Salem.

With his father, Elias worked as a privateer—a merchant ship owner who, with authorization from the government (the Continental Congress during the Revolution), reconfigured and equipped his vessels to be able to attack enemy ships—and as an investor in other privateering enterprises. Privateers helped to compensate for the lack of a naval force for George Washington's military. They were allowed to keep the spoils of their war-making, greatly enriching themselves in the process. At the same

The Derby House, 2016.

time, however, the profitability (and thus popularity) of privateering undercut the ability of the Revolutionary forces to acquire ships, weaponry, and sailors. Elias Derby did not hide his mercenary motivations, asserting, when asked to lease his ships to the state, "I shall be willing if the terms suit me, together with five percent commission."

Even though Elias died before Nathaniel Hawthorne was born, the famed author writes of him in *The Scarlet Letter*, derisively referring to him as "King Derby." The moniker speaks to not only Derby's great wealth, but the extent of his trading enterprise. Building on his father's trade endeavors along the Atlantic seaboard, Elias and his enormous fleet of ships began sailing to ports in the Baltic, Russia, southern Africa, the Indian Ocean—his ships were the first from the United States to reach Mauritius—India, Sumatra, and China in the years following the Revolutionary War.

Derby's enterprise was instrumental in making Salem one of the leading international trading ports in the United States, while helping to lay the foundation for global capitalism and the worldwide, militarized reach of the US state. When Derby

died in 1799, his wealth was worth a little more than $1 million, making him one of the very wealthiest men in the United States at the time.

The Derby House still stands; guided tours are provided.

GETTING THERE

From the National Park Service Regional Visitor Center, a 0.4 mile (eight-minute) walk.

NEARBY SITE

SAINT. JOSEPH'S HALL (a former Polish community center where a number of meetings of striking mill workers took place in 1933, now the site of the administrative offices of the National Park Service in Salem), 160 Derby Street.

TO LEARN MORE

Fichter, James R. *So Great a Proffit: How the East Indies Trade Transformed Anglo-American Capitalism*, Cambridge: Harvard University Press, 2010.
Patton, Robert H. *Patriot Pirates: The Privateer War for Freedom and Fortune in the American Revolution*, New York: Pantheon Books, 2009.

4.25 North Shore Community Development Coalition/Punto Urban Art Museum

96 Lafayette Street

SALEM

In November 2015, renowned Miami-based artist Ruben Ubiera returned to Salem, where he had attended high school in the early 1990s. His homecoming was part of a community-backed plan to invest in the Point neighborhood. The resulting, award-winning public art featured bold graffiti-style

Mural by Ruben Ubiera, 41–43 Ward Street, 2017.

portraits of neighborhood kids. The artwork expressed local hopes for "increasing neighborhood pride" and "civic engagement." In 2017, under the auspices of the North Shore Community Development Coalition, the project expanded, including many more artists and a growing collection of murals, which constitute the open-air Punto Urban Art Museum.

A major transformation in community demographics helps explain the cultural project's origins: Over the preceding half century, the Point saw immigrants from the Dominican Republic—precipitated by the 1965 US invasion of their country, which overthrew a democratically elected government—replacing a shrinking French-Canadian community. By the 1980s, the latter's upward mobility and low-income housing vacancies created a niche that the Dominican community came to fill.

As Salem resident and scholar Aviva Chomsky observes, early Dominican immigrants were rich in the skill sets needed by the local leather industry during the 1960s

and 1970s. As the community built new cultural institutions and networks, including an array of small grocery stores, bookstores, and independent churches, immigration expanded—even after the decline of the leather industry. Ubiera's family, for example, had originally emigrated in the 1980s and settled in the Bronx but soon thereafter relocated to Salem, attracted more by the sense of community than by employment prospects.

The North Shore CDC maintains more than two hundred affordable housing units in the Point, which is just south of Salem's traditional core. Many of the CDC's buildings serve as the canvas of its urban art museum. Bounded by Peabody, Congress, Chase, and Lafayette Streets, the Point neighborhood is on the National Register of Historic Places.

GETTING THERE

The neighborhood is 0.6 miles south of the National Park Service's Salem Maritime National Historic Visitor Center.

TO LEARN MORE

City of Salem. "Creating a Vision, Strengthening a Community: A Vision and Action Plan for the Point Neighborhood in Salem 2013–2020," http://www.mapc.org/salempointvision
Chomsky, Aviva. "Salem as a Global City, 1850–2004" in Salem: Place, Myth, and Memory, ed. Dane Anthony Morrison and Nancy Lusignan Schultz, Boston: Northeastern University Press, 2004, 222–48.

Lynn

"Doña Patria" by Angurria at 516 Washington Street, downtown Lynn, 2018.

1900s, becoming Lynn's largest employer. While GE remains in Lynn, its size is a fraction of what it once was.

In the nineteenth century, Lynn was the site of a vibrant antislavery movement. It was also home to radical labor organizers, giving rise to one of the first large strikes in the United States and helping to lay the foundation for the modern labor movement.

Settled by English colonists beginning in the late 1620s and early 1630s, the area that is today the city of Lynn was long a rural village, part of the town of Saugus. Lynn incorporated as an independent entity in 1850. By that time, Lynn was a major site of tanneries and (largely women's) shoe production. It was the latter that fueled Lynn's growth as immigrants flocked to the city to work in the shoe industry. By the turn of the twentieth century, Lynn was reputed to be the world's largest producer of shoes. Around that time, "Shoe City" (a moniker claimed by the City of Brockton as well) also became a home of General Electric (GE). As GE's industrial footprint grew, it eventually supplanted a declining shoe industry in the mid-

Lynn's largely working-class population (today about ninety-four thousand residents) is of diverse origins. The late 1800s and early 1900s saw the arrival of Greeks, Irish, Russian and Central European Jews, and French Canadians. More recent decades have seen the development of a large Latino community. Lynn also has sizable African American and LGBTQ communities and a growing Asian (particularly Cambodian) population.

GETTING THERE

Distances/directions are provided from the MBTA Commuter Rail station (Newburyport/Rockport Line) in Lynn.

4.26 Town Hall

54 South Common Street

LYNN

Lynn's Town Hall was the site of an "antislavery fair" on New Year's Day, 1839. Organized by the Lynn Female Anti-Slavery Society, the fair was most likely the time and place when the city's female abolitionists collected most of the 785 signatures on what became known as the Lynn Petition. Directed at the Massachusetts legislature, it called for the immediate repeal of "all laws in this State, which make any distinction among its inhabitants, on account of COLOR."

The petition grew out of a national effort launched by the American Anti-Slavery Society in 1837 to facilitate challenges to legislation concerning "distinctions of color." Part of a coordinated effort in Massachusetts, Lynn's appeal was one of four similarly worded petitions from local women's abolitionist organizations (the others coming from Brookfield, **Dorchester**, and **Plymouth**) presented to the state legislature when it opened in 1839. Their target was the state's ban on intermarriage between whites and people of color—specifically between a white person and "a negro, indian or mulatto."

The effort became synonymous with Lynn's petition, however, due to its large number of signatories, which dwarfed those of the other three. (The four totaled about thirteen hundred signatures.) The Lynn petitioners made clear that their concern was not simply opposition to legislation that helped spread slavery or that produced racial inequality—the chief interests of the American Anti-Slavery Society—but laws that rested on racial distinctions even if they did not result in inequity. Lynn's female abolitionists thus directly challenged the notion of "separate but equal," while showing that for many abolitionists, the movement was about not only ending slavery, but putting an end as well to all forms of what at the time was called "prejudice."

Many, particularly men, did not approve of the effort: In Lynn, 193 men submitted a counterpetition, sarcastically advocating that the city's 758 female signatories have the right "to marry, intermarry, or associate with any Negro, Indian Hottentot, or any other being in human shape, at their will and pleasure." Meanwhile the editor of Boston's *Morning Post* suggested that the women desired "the privilege of marrying black husbands" because they had failed to receive a *white* offer." Yet, despite such opposition, the movement in Lynn and statewide intensified their efforts and finally succeeded in 1843.

In addition to overturning the ban on interracial marriage, the victory gave Massachusetts abolitionists a sense of their power. It also helped to grow the movement and lay the basis for future wins—in combating segregation in railroads, churches, schools, and militias.

Lynn's Town Hall, built and opened in 1814, no longer exists. The seat of government, it originally stood at the center of the Lynn Commons (opposite Hanover Street) until 1832, when the building was moved to the eastern corner of South Common Street and Blossom Street. It burned down on

October 6, 1864. Today Saint George Greek Orthodox Church sits on the site.

TO LEARN MORE

Kull, Andrew. *The Color-Blind Constitution*, Cambridge: Harvard University Press, 1992.

Moulton, Amber D. *The Fight for Interracial Marriage Rights in Antebellum Massachusetts*, Cambridge: Harvard University Press, 2015.

Ruchames, Louis. "Race, Marriage, and Abolition in Massachusetts," *Journal of Negro History* 40, no. 3 (1955): 250–73.

Tracy, Cyrus M. *The City Hall of Lynn: Being a History of Events Leading to Its Erection and an Account of the Ceremonies at the Dedication of the Building*, Lynn: Thomas P. Nichols, Printer, 1869.

GETTING THERE

A 0.5 mile (ten-minute) walk.

4.27 Kimball and Butterfield/ *The Awl*

9 North Common Street

LYNN

Lynn Public Library, 2016.

Kimball and Butterfield was a printing business that sat directly across from the Lynn Commons. Among its customers was the Mutual Benefit Society of the Journeymen Cordwainers of Lynn. The shoemakers, who

> The division of society into the producing and the non-producing classes, and the fact of the unequal distribution of value between the two, introduces us at once to another distinction that of capital and labor . . . labor now becomes a commodity. . . . Antagonism and opposition of interest is introduced in the community; capital and labor stand opposed.
>
> —*The Awl*, 1844

had begun organizing in the 1830s, founded a newspaper called *The Awl* (a tool used by shoemakers to puncture and sew leather), Lynn's first labor newspaper, published weekly, starting on July 17, 1844.

The paper is noteworthy for the radical politics expressed in its pages, with a focus on anticapitalist analysis, class consciousness, and advocacy of worker solidarity. The paper thus helped lay the foundation for the 1860 strike by the city's shoemakers (see **Lyceum Hall**) .

For reasons that are unclear, *The Awl* ceased publication in a little less than two years. *The Pioneer*, another Lynn newspaper known for radical politics—particularly its strong abolitionist position—absorbed it. Other labor newspapers would follow in its wake.

The Lynn Public Library (at 5 North Common Street), built in 1898, now sits on the site where Kimball and Butterfield's office was located. The library has back issues of *The Awl* that one can view on microfilm.

GETTING THERE

A 0.5 mile (ten-minute) walk.

LYNN, SATURDAY, NOV. 23, 1844.

Masthead of *The Awl*.

TO LEARN MORE

Dawley, Alan. *Class and Community: The Industrial Revolution in Lynn*, Cambridge: Harvard University Press, 2000.

Mangan, J. J. *The Story of Lynn Newspapers* (Part 1), Lynn: Frank S. Whitten Printer, 1910.

4.28 **Frederick Douglass House**

Newhall Street

LYNN

Frederick Douglass escaped his enslavement in 1838. A few years later (on August 11, 1841), he gave an antislavery speech in Nantucket that greatly impressed his audience, a member of which was William Lloyd Garrison. This led to Douglass's employment as an agent for the Massachusetts Anti-Slavery Society.

Within weeks Douglass, his wife, Anna, and their two children moved to Lynn, drawn by the city's strong abolitionist community and its central location for his new job. They first resided in a house on Harrison Court (which stood near the corner of Broad and Market Streets), and then moved to a home on Baldwin Street (then called Pearl Street) near the intersection with High Street.

It was at his last home in Lynn, on Newhall Street, that the famed orator and antislavery activist wrote what is regarded by many to be one of the most important abolitionist pieces of literature of its time. During the winter of 1844–45, he penned *Narrative of the Life of Frederick Douglass, an American Slave.* Intended to counter critics who cast doubt on Douglass's claim that he had been enslaved

Frederick Douglass atop mural (detail by David Fichter) at 25 Exchange Street celebrating Lynn's history, 2018.

as well as abolitionists who tried to limit what he said in his speeches, the book greatly increased his credibility and visibility. It also spoke invaluably to the need for solidarity among the oppressed, for collaboration across racial divides, and of oppressed people's capacity to speak for themselves.

After the book's publication in 1845, Douglass, at age twenty-seven, fled to Britain and Ireland, fearful that his former "owner" would try to capture him. Anna and their children (by that time they numbered four) remained in Lynn until 1847 when Douglass returned to the United States. The family then moved to Rochester, New York.

As with the two previous Lynn residences (which no longer exist), where precisely the Douglass home stood on Newhall Street, other than between Sagamore and Amity Street, is unclear.

GETTING THERE

An 0.4 mile (eight-minute) walk.

NEARBY SITES

LYNN MUSEUM AND HISTORICAL SOCIETY, 590 Washington Street.

Former home of **FRAN'S PLACE,** 776 Washington Street. Established in the 1920s, it was until its closure in 2016 one of the oldest gay bars in Massachusetts. Originally called the Lighthouse Café, it moved to Washington Street in the mid-1970s.

High Rock Tower postcard, circa 1930–45.

4.29 High Rock Tower Reservation

Circuit Road

LYNN

A four-and-a-half-acre public park on top of a hill, High Rock Tower Reservation offers commanding views of much of Lynn, Boston, the coast, and the nearby peninsula town of Nahant. It is reputed to have once been a lookout point for Native Americans. John Hutchinson, who purchased the land in the 1840s, gave the summit of High Rock to the City of Lynn in the early 1900s for the construction of an observatory, thus laying the foundation for the park.

Along with three siblings (Abby, Asa, Judson), John was part of the Hutchinson Family Singers, among the most popular entertainers in the United States in the 1840s. The Hutchinson siblings moved to Lynn from New Hampshire in 1841, the same year that Frederick Douglass arrived in the city. Inspired by Christian (Baptist) beliefs and reformist politics, the Hutchinsons' music reflected the era's progressive causes—first that of temperance and then abolitionism, in no small part because of Lynn's vibrant antislavery community. Their song "Get Off the Track" (1844) served as the anthem of the Liberty Party, the first abolitionist political party in the United States.

The Hutchinson quartet performed in Europe and throughout much of the United States—to large, often interracial crowds, which the group openly encouraged. Their politics and their championing of racial integration won them great praise in abolitionist circles, but also incurred the wrath of many, earning them the moniker, among some, of "Nigger Minstrels." Many venues, including one in Philadelphia, refused to host them, and hostile anti-abolitionist mobs often threatened them. Frederick Douglass, a strong friend and ally of the Hutchinsons, asserted that the group "dared to sing for a cause first and for cash afterward."

With Abby's marriage and departure from the group in 1849, the Hutchinson Family Singers endured in various forms but would never achieve the same level of fame. Still, the remaining members stayed active in support of various causes on the national and local scene—from temperance and abolition to those of suffragettes, freedmen, and industrial workers.

John Hutchinson, the last surviving member of the quartet, died in Lynn in 1908. The family's stone cottage (built in 1858), surrounded by a fence given its decrepit state, stands at the edge of the park, below the tower. It served as a stop on the Underground Railroad.

GETTING THERE

A 0.8 mile (eighteen-minute) walk.

TO LEARN MORE

Gac, Scott. *Singing for Freedom: The Hutchinson Family Singers and the Nineteenth-Century Culture of Reform*, New Haven: Yale University Press, 2007.

Roberts, Brian. "'Slavery Would Have Died of That Music': The Hutchinson Family Singers and the Rise of Popular-Culture Abolitionism in Early Antebellum-Era America, 1842–1850," *Proceedings of the American Antiquarian Society* 114, no. 2 (2004): 301–68.

City of Lynn website: http://www.ci.lynn.ma.us/attractions_highrocktower.shtml

4.30 Lyceum Hall

Market Street, opposite Andrew Street

LYNN

Early in the morning of George Washington's birthday (February 22), 1860, thousands of shoemakers (then known as cordwainers) gathered at Lyceum Hall to begin what would become the largest pre–Civil War strike in the United States. Earlier that year, their newly formed Mechanics Association had held a mass meeting where they decided to demand higher wages and a regular wage schedule. The employers, however, refused to meet with their representatives to discuss their demands, thus the decision to strike.

Departing from Lyceum Hall that morning, the workers marched through the city's streets to the shops of their employers to hand in their work tools. At the height of the strike, twenty thousand shoemakers throughout Massachusetts—in cities and

At the outset, I am glad to see that a system of labor prevails in New England under which laborers can strike when they want to, where they are not obliged to work under all circumstances, and are not tied down and obliged to labor whether you pay them or not. I like the system which lets a man quit when he wants to, and wish it might prevail everywhere. One of the reasons why I am opposed to Slavery is just here.

—**Abraham Lincoln in reference to the Lynn strike, 1860**

Drawing of Lyceum Hall, 1852.

towns such as *Haverhill*, Natick, *Newburyport*, and *Salem*—and soon in Maine and New Hampshire as well, stopped working.

A combination of a depression in 1857 and technological innovations (particularly the introduction of Singer sewing machines) had led to a decrease in employment among those who worked out of their homes as well as to declining demand and overproduction of shoes, causing prices to plummet.

Manufacturers responded by drastically cutting wages—to as little at fifty cents per day at some Lynn establishments. It was in this context that Lynn's shoemakers launched their work stoppage.

Although most of the striking workers were US-born, the stoppage was noteworthy for strong solidarity among Yankee and Irish-descended laborers. In the realm of gender equality, however, the male-dominated strike was far less successful. Women shoebinders and stitchers played a key role in the strike but had specific concerns and demands, not least because they received wages far inferior to men's. The men, however, ignored the women's demands, which eventually led most women workers to abandon the strike. While the strike continued strong through much of March, male shoemakers also began returning to work at the month's end. By April, the employers had won.

The strike speaks to the great capacity of worker organizing during the period and the high levels of class consciousness among many workers, as well as the perils of not embracing equality among all workers. Despite the outcome, worker mobilizations throughout subsequent decades would show that the best of the radical spirit of Lynn's shoemakers did not die.

The Lynn Lyceum was built in 1841 but burned down in a huge blaze on Christmas Day in 1868. If one stands on Market Street at Andrew Street and looks across Market very slightly to the right, the Lyceum would have been located roughly where the Bank of America now sits.

A 0.2 mile (four-minute) walk.

TO LEARN MORE

Dawley, Alan. *Class and Community: The Industrial Revolution in Lynn*, Cambridge: Harvard University Press, 2000.

Juravich, Tom, William F. Hartford, James R. Green. *Commonwealth of Toil: Chapters in the History of Massachusetts Workers and Their Unions*, Amherst: University of Massachusetts Press, 1996.

4.31 River Works/General Electric

134 West Neptune Street

LYNN

River Works is an aircraft engine plant, part of General Electric (GE), and the City of Lynn's largest employer. The plant has its origins in the late 1800s when the Thomson-Houston Company was born. In 1892 the Lynn-based corporation merged with the Edison General Electric Company of Sche-

nectady, New York, to form General Electric. Building on Lynn's radical labor tradition, the workers at River Works became part of a new union in 1936, the left-wing United Electrical Workers (UE). In a climate of anticommunism within Massachusetts—with a Democratic Party egged on by the Catholic Church hierarchy leading the way—the UE and its members soon came under attack by red-scare forces.

Anti-left hysteria had significant roots in Massachusetts—on display particularly with Governor Calvin Coolidge's red-baiting during the Boston police strike of 1919 (see *Police Station 6/Patriot Homes*) and with the railroading and execution of Sacco and Vanzetti in the 1920s. Well before the US Congress established the infamous House Un-American Activities Committee (HUAC), Massachusetts set up its own "little HUAC" in 1937: the Special Commission to Investigate the Activities within this Commonwealth of Communistic, Fascistic, Nazi and Other Subversive Organizations. In 1949 the state also instituted a loyalty oath for all public employees. Two years later, in 1951, Massachusetts became the first state to outlaw the Communist Party—three years before Congress did so. University professors, civil libertarians, and radical labor activists became favorite scapegoats of anticommunist forces in the State House.

In the 1950s the state's red-scare politics dovetailed with those on the national level. In

Senator McCarthy in Boston, 1953.

this context, River Works and its left-leaning, unionized employees became the target of federal and state authorities—as well as of union-movement conservatives. By 1952 the FBI had set up a permanent office within the factory. The next year, James B. Carey, a fanatical anticommunist labor leader who had founded a rival union to the UE, the International Union of Electrical Workers (IUE), reported to Massachusetts's Bowker Commission on alleged communist leaders among the UE's leadership in Lynn. The redbaiting succeeded in narrowly preventing the UE from winning elections at River Works a few days later.

The anticommunist witch hunt culminated with Senator Joseph McCarthy coming to Boston in January 1954 and the subpoenaing of five current or former Lynn GE employees. In what the *Globe* described as "the most tumultuous Congressional sessions ever held in Boston," the infamous senator expelled two GE workers and a lawyer of one of them from the hearing room. One worker, Nathaniel Mills, accused McCarthy of trying to take jobs from GE workers and called him "a menace," leading to his forcible ejection.

In subsequent decades, worker militancy ebbed and flowed but, overall, endured to a significant degree as indicated by numerous strikes, the tensions between those who supported the UE or the IUE notwithstanding. That said, corporate restructuring and outsourcing had a huge, detrimental impact on the workforce. At World War II's height, there were approximately twenty thousand workers at the plant. In the mid-1980s there

were still about thirteen thousand. Today there are only around three thousand, half of them unionized. There is ongoing talk of GE's selling most of its seventy-seven-acre site to developers eager to profit from waterfront housing.

GETTING THERE

A 1.5 mile (thirty-minute) walk. An MBTA bus from the Lynn Commuter Rail busway in Central Square also passes very close to the site.

TO LEARN MORE

Crosby, Jeff. "It's Not the Water: Local 201 Fights to Survive in a Neo-Liberal World," unpublished paper, July 2008.

Heale, M. J. *McCarthy's Americans: Red Scare Politics in State and Nation, 1935–1965*, Athens: University of Georgia Press, 1998.

Schatz, Ronald W. *The Electrical Workers: A History of Labor at General Electric and Westinghouse, 1923–1960*, Urbana: University of Illinois Press, 1983.

4.32 Lynn Woods Reservation

106 Pennybrook Road

LYNN

Formally established in 1881, the Lynn Woods is one of the largest municipally owned, forested parks in the United States. Today at twenty-two hundred acres with about thirty miles of trails, it is more than two and a half times the size of New York City's Central Park.

The Lynn Woods has its origins in the years following the Civil War, a time when the populations of the City of Boston and nearby municipalities were growing dramatically and the destruction of area forests was rapidly unfolding.

During this time, Elizur Wright, a social reformer who had been a leading abolitionist and who later became the insurance commissioner for Massachusetts, began championing a hybrid approach to forests, one that embraced them as both working forests and wilderness. It allowed for selective harvesting of trees by commercial interests while preserving the larger natural system. Fearing for the future of US cities, Wright argued that extensive forests were needed to clean the air polluted by the burning of fossil fuels in the homes and factories of heavily urbanized areas, as well as to protect water supplies.

Inspired in part by Wright's ideas and enabled by two pieces of state legislation in 1882 (the Forest Law, which Wright's advocacy helped to bring about, and the Park Act), some citizens of Lynn came together to create the Lynn Woods. Private citizens as well as the City of Lynn purchased scores of land parcels to cobble together the forest.

Advocates presented the Woods' establishment as a rescue of the forest from private interests and its restoration to a public good, one that would provide open space to those who did not have access to privatized land. Yet Lynn's park commissioners also insisted that the Woods be a place for activities preferred by the middle and upper classes. As one of them wrote, the goal was "*not* to attract the multitudes to be amused by merry-go-round shows."

Today all are welcome in the Lynn Woods.

GETTING THERE

Take an MBTA bus from the Lynn Commuter Rail busway in Central Square to points along the Lynn Woods Reservation's edges.

TO LEARN MORE

Rawson, Michael. *Eden on the Charles: The Making of Boston*, Cambridge: Harvard University Press, 2010.

5

West
and
South
of
Boston

Waltham

Boston Manufacturing Company complex on the Charles River, Waltham, 2009.

Sited on the banks of the Charles River, Waltham, incorporated in 1738, is home to some sixty thousand residents and numerous corporations representative of the region's economic history. Settled by Europeans in the 1630s, Waltham had been continuously occupied, much like the rest of the Greater Boston, for nearly ten millennia, with the Charles helping to sustain life for indigenous peoples, particularly with their use of fish weirs.

Waltham is the site of the first factory of the US industrial revolution. Ironically, the shift to industrial production, predicated on the disruption of indigenous sovereignty, would depend on the river's power. In the course of subsequent economic development, Waltham earned its moniker "Watch City" as home to the American Watch Company. Although its operations tapered off

by the mid-1900s, the economy diversified. Today it includes two universities (Brandeis and Bentley), its largest employers, biotech companies, and the corporate offices of a large weapons manufacturer.

As with other former mill towns, Waltham has used its abandoned factory floor space to exhibit its industrial history and provide space for startups for its aspiring innovation economy. Largely white and middle class, Waltham also has a sizable immigrant population from Asia.

Since 2010, the city's industrial heritage and cultural presence have come together in an annual Watch City Steampunk Festival held on a spring weekend on the Waltham Common and at the Charles River Museum of Industry and Innovation. Reputed to be the largest outdoor festival of its type in the United States, it melds elements of the second industrial revolution–era aesthetics, "history and fashion with modern technology and fantastical fiction."

5.1 Walter E. Fernald State School

200 Trapelo Road

WALTHAM

Originally known as the Massachusetts School for the Feeble-Minded before its name change in 1924, the Walter E. Fernald State School was the Western Hemisphere's first institution for the care of developmentally disabled persons. Samuel Gridley Howe (husband of Julia Ward Howe) founded the school in Boston in 1848. In 1887, under Superintendent Walter E. Fernald's leadership, it relocated to Waltham. In what was then a rural setting, the institution's size exploded, growing to 196 acres of land, dozens of buildings, and, at its height in the 1960s, about twenty-six hundred students.

During the tenure of Walter Fernald, a prominent champion of eugenics who once advocated the sterilization of mentally disabled people, the school's mission shifted to one concerned with the pursuit of scientific knowledge. The eugenicist shift contributed to the effective incarceration of large numbers of individuals at the school who were not developmentally disabled, but were, for example, orphans or from poor families. In this context, many abuses took place.

Chief among them was something called the Science Club. Set up by scientists from the Massachusetts Institute of Technology in 1946, the "club" recruited unwitting boys,

luring them with promises of trips to the beach, baseball games, and gifts. The scientists then wrote to their parents asking that they agree to their sons' participation in a study involving their receiving a "special diet" with the aim of understanding how the human body absorbed cereals, iron, and vitamins. The experiment, the parents were told, would "cause no discomfort or change . . . other than possible improvement." What was not made known to them or the children was that the cereal-with-milk diet was laced with radioactive tracers. The Quaker Oats Company—which was interested in enhancing the nutritional quality of its cereal to gain an advantage over its main competitor, Cream of Wheat—along with the National Institutes of Health and the Atomic Energy Commission helped to fund the study.

Revelations in late 1993 of the radiation tests, which involved dozens of children over several years, led to investigations by the federal government and a lawsuit by former Fernald students. In 1998, MIT and Quaker Oats agreed to an out-of-court settlement of $1.85 million.

Following long political and legal battles, the Commonwealth of Massachusetts discharged the school's last resident and closed the facility in 2014, the same year the City of Waltham purchased the site. Deliberations about what to do with the campus are ongoing.

GETTING THERE

MBTA Commuter Rail (Fitchburg/South Acton Line) to Waverly Station, 1.0 mile (twenty-minute) walk.

Quakers outside of Raytheon facility, Cambridge, 2018.

5.2 Raytheon Corporate Headquarters

870 Winter Street

WALTHAM

Every third Sunday of the month, the Friends Meeting at Cambridge gathers to "bring . . . our Light to a barbaric assault on human dignity and life." Their Quaker meeting for worship takes place in front of a Raytheon research facility to bear witness to the activities of the Waltham-based corporation. Their specific concerns are Raytheon's missile production and sales promotion—a tragic twist for a corporation that named itself for the "light of the gods."

Launched in 1922 in Cambridge, Raytheon was originally a small manufacturer of radio batteries. It rose to prominence during World War II when it produced mag-netron tubes used in US and British radar systems. In the postwar period, however, Raytheon developed new missile technologies which, by 2017, made it the world's fourth-largest weapons contractor, with $22.3 billion in annual revenues. It is also the world's biggest missile manufacturer, producing the Tomahawk and Patriot missiles as well as cluster and bunker bombs that are consistently used against civilians.

Troubling to organizations like the American Friends Service Committee are the corporation's extensive lobbying efforts funded to the tune of an officially declared $5 million annually since 2006. In 2017 over 75 percent of Raytheon merchandise sold was to the United States government.

Raytheon is the target of numerous ongoing protests and boycotts. Among the

most recent is one organized by the Boycott, Divestment, and Sanctions movement
(BDS), which originated in a call from Palestinian civil society "to end international support for Israel's oppression of Palestinians
and pressure Israel to comply with international law." The movement calls attention to
the Israeli military's use of Raytheon mis-
siles and bombs against Palestinian civilians.
Another effort focuses on the company's
weapon sales to Saudi Arabia, which has put
them to deadly use in Yemen.

In 2010 the *Guardian* revealed that the
corporation had developed an "extreme-
scale analytics" system named Rapid Information Overlay Technology or RIOT, with
the capacity to monitor social media, including Facebook and related platforms. The
technology promised to predict an individual's movements and activities in real time.
Raytheon opaquely noted that it had not
sold the technology but "shared it with the
US Government and industry." In 2013 the
Electronic Privacy and Information Center
(EPIC) confirmed that Raytheon's program
was operational.

Beyond the corporation's sheer size and
influence peddling, its political power is
amplified by the seventy thousand relatively
well-paid workers it employs globally. Its
corporate philanthropy, often driven by
employee initiatives, provides the corporation with a benign face. Its research activities
are often tied into area universities, particularly the Massachusetts Institute of Technology. Its deep regional ties are suggested
by the fact that notwithstanding several
relocations over the decades, the corporation's headquarters moved *between* cities in
the Greater Boston area, from **Cambridge**, to
Lexington, Newton, and presently Waltham.

In June 2019, Raytheon and United Technologies (a manufacturer of aircraft engines,
aerospace systems, and military technologies) announced their merger. The new
company, Raytheon Technologies, will be
headquartered in the Boston area.

GETTING THERE

MBTA buses and Commuter Rail bring passengers to within two miles or so of the headquarters.

Concord

Reenactment of the Battle at Concord Bridge, 1928.

About eighteen miles west of Boston, the Town of Concord is best known as the site of the "shot heard around the world," the opening salvo of the April 19, 1775, battle that marks the Revolutionary War's beginning, and of Walden Pond. The Native people of the area referred to the area as *Muskataquid*, a term meaning the grassy plain. Situated along the principal road to Boston, Concord was the Massachusetts Bay Colony's first inland settlement. It quickly grew into a prosperous farming community and a regional center of trade.

In the mid-1800s, Concord became a literary, intellectual, and activist center. Reflecting the presence of a strong antislavery and Transcendentalist community, the town served as a station on the Underground Railroad for enslaved persons fleeing to freedom in Canada. Louisa May Alcott, Ralph Waldo Emerson, Nathaniel Hawthorne, and Henry David Thoreau were among Concord's most famous denizens during this time.

Today's Concord is a generally high-income commuter suburb of about seventeen thousand residents, with many well-preserved historic sites, and is home to the Great Meadows National Wildlife Refuge. In 2012 it became the first municipality in the United States to ban the sale of water in single-serving plastic bottles of one liter or less.

5.3 The Robbins House

320 Monument Street

CONCORD

Located on the grounds of the Minute Man National Historical Park, the Robbins House was built around 1823. At the time, it stood on the edge of Concord's Great Meadow on thirteen acres of land. The first occupants were the families of siblings Susan and Peter Robbins, freeborn black residents of Concord. Their father, Caesar Robbins, was enslaved at birth but emancipated after he served as a soldier in the Revolutionary War.

Peter Robbins, who owned the house, lost it in 1837 because of debt. A relative of his wife Fatima bought the house and farm in 1852 and then sold it and moved away in 1868.

Susan and her husband, Jack Garrison, who had escaped slavery in New Jersey, lived on one side of the house. Susan was a founding member of the Concord Female Antislavery Society and its only black member. The organization met in the Robbins House at least once.

Among Susan and Jack's children was Ellen Garrison. Born in 1823, she was heavily influenced by the activism of her mother and those around her. Ellen and Susan were among two hundred Concord women who signed a petition in 1838 protesting the US government's removal of the Cherokee people.

Ellen moved to Boston around 1841, shortly after her mother's death, and became active in antislavery circles, joining the First African Baptist Church on Beacon Hill (see *Abiel Smith School/Museum of African American History*). In the 1860s she moved to Maryland, where she worked as a teacher. While there, she tested the Reconstruction Era's Civil Rights Act of 1866. On May 5 of that year—almost a century before Rosa Parks sat in the front of a bus in Montgomery, Alabama—Ellen and a fellow teacher sat in the ladies waiting room at a Baltimore train station and were forcibly ejected by a train officer. With the support of local civil rights activists, Ellen filed a suit against the railroad. Despite the Civil Rights Act's promise of equal protection under the law for all citizens, a Baltimore grand jury dismissed the case.

The Robbins House is also the name of a Concord nonprofit organization that seeks to uncover and raise awareness of the town's African, African American, and antislavery history—offering an excellent walking tour—and to connect it with contemporary social justice endeavors. The Robbins family's former home serves as the center for its educational activities.

GETTING THERE

MBTA Commuter Rail to Concord Depot (Fitchburg Line), 1.3 mile (twenty-five-minute) walk.

TO LEARN MORE

The Robbins House website: http://www.robbinshouse.org/

5.4 Brister's Hill
Walden Woods/Hapgood Wright Town Forest
CONCORD

Brister's Hill is named after Brister Freeman, a freed slave who, until his death in 1822, lived there with his wife, Fenda. Enslaved in Concord for the first thirty or so years of his life (see *MCI-Concord / The Concord Reformatory*), he gained his freedom after a nine-month enlistment in the US army (1779–80). Soon thereafter he purchased an acre of land in what is now the Hapgood Wright Town Forest, a few hundred feet from Walden Pond, near the edge of which Henry David Thoreau later famously took up residence (in 1845) in an effort to reject industrial life and embrace simple living. Much of chapter 4 of Thoreau's *Walden*, an account of his time there, discusses many of the formerly

Path to the Brister Freeman house site, 2018.

enslaved individuals, including Brister Freeman, who had lived nearby.

What made the Walden Pond area available to formerly enslaved persons was its
sandy soil, which made it less than ideal
for agriculture (which contributed to the
malnutrition and premature death suffered
by many in the black enclave), thus less
expensive and free of most whites. These
characteristics also made it attractive to others who lived on the sociopolitical-economic
margins, such as Thoreau.

Today the site of the Freeman home is
marked by an engraved granite boulder.
Close by (walking from Walden Street, to
the right just as one enters the grassland
section along Thoreau's Path on Brister's
Hill) is a bench—part of the Toni Morrison
Society Bench by the Road project—to commemorate Brister Freeman and Concord's
slavery survivors.

GETTING THERE

MBTA Commuter Rail to Concord Depot (Fitchburg Line). Near downtown Concord, take the

Emerson-Thoreau Amble through woods and
fields that leads to Brister's Hill. (Approximately a
1.7 mile walk.)

TO LEARN MORE

Lemire, Elise. *Black Walden: Slavery and Its Aftermath in Concord, Massachusetts*, Philadelphia:
University of Pennsylvania Press, 2009.
The Robbins House website: http://www.rob
binshouse.org/projects/brister-freeman-family
-home-site/

5.5 Concord Jail

Monument Square/Lexington Road

CONCORD

One day in 1846 (July 23), Henry David Thoreau left his temporary home near Walden
Pond and walked to Concord town to do
some errands. While there, he ran into Sam
Staples, the town's constable and tax collec-
tor. Staples asked Thoreau to pay his back
taxes, ones he had refused to pay for six
years in protest of the institution of slavery.
(Thoreau's mother and sisters were active
members of the Concord Female Anti-

> Down the road . . . on Brister's Hill, lived Brister Freeman, 'a handy Negro,' slave of Squire Cummings once,—there where grow still the apple-trees which Brister planted and tended; large old trees now, but their fruit still wild and ciderish to my taste.
>
> **—Thoreau, *Walden* (1854)**

> I think that we should be men first, and subjects afterward. It is not desirable to cultivate a respect for the law, so much as for the right.
>
> The law will never make men free; it is men who have got to make the law free.
>
> **—Thoreau**

Slavery Society , and his family had hosted and hidden many individuals fleeing from slavery. Henry himself had often escorted these individuals to safe houses farther along the Underground Railroad.)

His determination intensified by his strong opposition to the recent US-provoked war with and invasion of Mexico, Thoreau refused to make payment. Staples thus arrested and jailed him.

While imprisoned, he received a visit from Ralph Waldo Emerson. When Emerson asked him why he was in jail, Thoreau reportedly replied, "Waldo, the question is what are you doing out there?"

An unidentified person paid the back taxes—much to Thoreau's chagrin—so Staples released him the next morning. Thoreau's experience, however, was quite forma-

tive and served as the basis for his renowned essay "Civil Disobedience," in which he famously argued that one should respect not the law, but what is right. The essay proved highly influential on political figures such as Gandhi and Martin Luther King.

A small marker commemorates the site where the jail once stood.

GETTING THERE

Commuter Rail from North Station (Fitchburg line) to Concord Station. Just before Main Street enters Monument Square, there is a war memorial on the left side. Behind it is a parking lot, on the far side of which is a grassy strip and the marker, 0.6 mile (twelve-minute) walk.

TO LEARN MORE

Thoreau, Henry D., and William Rossi, ed. *Walden, Civil Disobedience, and Other Writings*, New York: W. W. Norton, 2008.

Zinn, Howard. "Henry David Thoreau," in *A Power Governments Cannot Suppress*, San Francisco: City Lights Books, 2006, 121–41.

5.6 MCI-Concord/ The Concord Reformatory

965 Elm Street

CONCORD

In 1961–63, a group of Harvard University researchers led by Dr. Timothy Leary conducted what became known as the Concord Prison Experiment. Based on the hypothesis that use of psilocybin (also known as "magic mushrooms"), a naturally occurring psychedelic drug, would lead to long-term, positive behavioral change, Leary and his team worked with thirty-two male prisoners at the Massachusetts Correctional Institute-

Concord, a medium-security prison. The experiment involved administering the drug to the prisoners, all volunteers approaching their parole dates, as part of a group psychotherapy effort.

Old Concord Reformatory building, 2010.

Leary initially touted the results as leading to dramatic reductions in recidivism. But follow-up studies questioned the findings and led to the conclusion that the experiment contributed to only a small improvement in postrelease behavior of incarcerated men. Leary ultimately concluded that a combination of psilocybin-assisted group psychotherapy combined with comprehensive postrelease programs modeled after Alcoholics Anonymous would lead to long-term reductions in recidivism.

Opened in 1878 as the New State Prison, its name was changed to the Concord Reformatory in 1884. For fifteen months in 1947–48, Malcolm X was incarcerated there. The prison, renamed MCI-Concord in 1955, sits on what was the property of John Cuming, a wealthy landowner and doctor, as well as the "owner" for twenty-five years of Brister Freeman (see **Brister's Hill**), who would have likely farmed the land. Cuming's former house now serves as a prison office building.

GETTING THERE

MBTA Commuter Rail to Concord Depot (Fitchburg Line). About 2.1 miles by foot from station, 2.7 miles by car.

TO LEARN MORE

Doblin, Rick. "Dr. Leary's Concord Prison Experiment: A 34-Year Follow-up Study," *Bulletin of the Multidisciplinary Association for Psychedelic Studies* 9, no. 4 (1999–2000): 10–18.

Hendrick, Peter S., et al. "Hallucinogen-use Predicts Reduced Recidivism among Substance-involved Offenders under Community Corrections Supervision," *Journal of Psychopharmacology* 28, no. 1 (2014): 62–66.

Lemire, Elise. *Black Walden: Slavery and Its Aftermath in Concord, Massachusetts*, Philadelphia: University of Pennsylvania Press, 2009.

Plymouth and the South Shore

Statue of Massasoit, overlooking Cole's Hill at dawn, 2010.

waves of Brazilian immigration have shifted the demographics somewhat. Plymouth, especially its downtown economy, trades largely on its historical past.

Quincy and Weymouth, two other cities on the South Shore, as the region is known—

Home to the Pokanoket members of the Wampanoag nation and located on their land, Plymouth is at the heart of the US national story, styling itself "America's Hometown." It is best known for the early cooperation and later conflict between a burgeoning settler population and indigenous people, but its eighteenth-century and later history is less well known. While Plymouth revels in the Mayflower mystique or engages awkwardly with its debt to the indigenous people, subsequent immigration, especially from Italy, grew Plymouth as an industrial center and largely defined its present-day population. For most of the nineteenth and early twentieth centuries, Plymouth's industrial activities related to its seafaring origins. It cordage factory grew to be the largest in the world. While the population remains largely white, more recent

stretching from Boston to Cape Code, with a population of about half a million—are also deeply connected to early developments in Plymouth. The sites described here refer to their seventeenth-century pasts. As with Plymouth, these cities exhibit a patchwork of economic dynamism and stagnation overlaid by related ethnoracial and immigrant diversity.

5.7 Cole's Hill

35 Carver Street

PLYMOUTH

In 1970, for the 350th anniversary of the 1620 arrival of English settlers in Plymouth, the Commonwealth of Massachusetts invited Frank James, a leader of the Aquinnah Wampanoag nation, to address that year's Thanksgiving celebration. Also known as Wamsutta, James prepared a speech and sub-

Day of Mourning, Cole's Hill, 2018.

> What is this you call property? It cannot be the Earth for the land is our Mother nourishing all her children, beasts, birds, fish, and all men. The woods, the streams, everything on it belong to everybody and is for the use of all. How can one man say it belongs to him?
>
> —Massasoit, circa 1630s

pride and militancy, James reviewed the history of indigenous-settler relations. Noting that the hospitality exemplified by the first "thanksgiving" dinner of 1621 was to be "the beginning of the end," he observed that "before 50 years were to pass, the Wampanoag would no longer be a free people." In a related set of actions earlier that day, Russell Means and Dennis Banks, prominent national leaders of the American Indian Movement, led protestors to briefly take over the *Mayflower II* site, cover Plymouth Rock with sand, and disrupt the town-sponsored Thanksgiving parade.

mitted it to the feast's organizers. On reading the text, the organizers presented James with an ultimatum: Read a radically revised speech written by the organizers or the invitation would be retracted. James chose his own words.

On the appointed day, James delivered his original speech before a gathering of hundreds of indigenous people on Cole's Hill, inaugurating the first annual Day of Mourning. He did so in the shadow of a statue depicting the 1600s Wampanoag sachem Massasoit and directly across from the fabled Plymouth Rock. In his speech, reflecting the period's national reawakening of Indian

Every year since, the United American Indians of New England have rallied at noon on the fourth Thursday of November on Cole's Hill before marching through Plymouth Village Historical District and hosting a potluck lunch at the nearby First Parish Plymouth Church. Adding historical import to the meal is the fact that the church is built on the site of the original Plymouth Plantation and fort (built in 1621). Today the rally draws indigenous activists and allies from all over the Americas.

Cole's Hill overlooks Plymouth Harbor, home to the *Mayflower II,* a replica of the original Pilgrim vessel. It also features a town-sponsored plaque with a tersely worded statement explaining the significance of the National Day of Mourning as

> We forfeited our country. Our lands have fallen into the hands of the aggressor. We have allowed the white man to keep us on our knees. What has happened cannot be changed, but today we must work towards a more humane America, a more Indian America, where men and nature once again are important; where the Indian values of honor, truth, and brotherhood prevail.
>
> —Frank James, 1970

a "protest of the racism and oppression which Native Americans continue to experience."

GETTING THERE

Cole's Hill, also the site of the first Pilgrim burial ground, is two miles south of the Commuter Rail station in Plymouth. There is an hourly bus between the station and the downtown area.

TO LEARN MORE

United American Indians of New England (2017). "National Day of Mourning" website: http://uaine.org

5.8 Old Country House/1749 Court House

1 Town Square

PLYMOUTH

Old Country House, 2017.

On June 8, 1675, following a brief trial at the Country House, Plymouth Colony executed three indigenous men for the killing of John Sassamon, a Christianized indigenous person. The three men—Mattashunannamo, Tobias, and Tobias's son, Wampapaquan—were all associated with the Wampanoag sachem Metacom (also known as King Philip). The executions triggered a catastrophic, region-wide conflict known as King Philip's War. Lasting fourteen months, it united mainly Wampanoag, Narragansett, and Nipmuc nations as well as several other indigenous bands and communities against the English colonies. Despite numerous battlefield victories for Metacom, indigenous support provided to the English by the Mohegan and Mohawk nations inflicted debilitating losses, leading ultimately to his defeat.

It was the deadliest North American war on a per capita basis, and broadly destructive. Among the colonists, three thousand settlers were killed, thirteen towns destroyed, more than half of the ninety settlements damaged, and the colonies' treasuries depleted. The Native population saw its numbers halved and their networks decimated. For the Narragansett, military defeat resulted in their near annihilation.

The war definitively established settler military supremacy and redefined the participants in conflict. Whereas before the war, conflicts took place between particular colonies and indigenous polities, thereafter antagonists faced each other as two polarized forces, colonists versus "Indians." Moreover, the conflict marked the formal end of indigenous polities in Massachusetts, although armed resistance, especially to the north of Boston, persisted well into the next century.

That the trial triggered a war would have been unsurprising to both sides. It was the first colonial prosecution of an alleged Indian-on-Indian murder, representing a blatant challenge to Metacom's authority, especially since it had occurred outside the colony. In contrast to the 1620s, when the Wampanoag had assisted the early settlers, relations had changed radically over the intervening fifty years. Indigenous sovereignty, which had been guaranteed by custom, was being progressively subverted by deeds and treaties, expanding colonial settlements, farming practices, and illicit land deals between settlers and individual Native persons.

As the 1670s approached, Governor Josiah Winslow, who presided over the trial that precipitated the war, was attempting to build alliances to acquire more land. He even sought an alliance with Weetamoo, Metacom's sister-in-law, who commanded a significant fighting force and much land. The alleged murder of John Sassamon—there is a dispute as to whether he died accidently, expired from natural causes, or was actually murdered—provided an opportunity to extend the colony's power.

The 1749 Court House, built on the same site, replaced the Old Country House. Today it is a museum at the head of Leyden Street, the country's oldest paved road. Adjacent is the site where Metacom's head was displayed for many years following the war.

GETTING THERE

Two miles south of the Commuter Rail station in Plymouth.

TO LEARN MORE

Brooks, Lisa. *Our Beloved Kin: A New History of King Philip's War*, New Haven: Yale University Press, 2018.

Lepore, Jill. *The Name of War: King Philip's War and the Origins of American Identity*, New York: Alfred A. Knopf, 1998.

5.9 Plimoth Plantation

137 Warren Avenue

PLYMOUTH

Founded in 1947 to celebrate the struggles of the Pilgrims after their 1620 landing in Plymouth, Plimoth Plantation has evolved to represent "two cultures." A living museum, it is a replica of the original Plymouth settlement and a Wampanoag homesite. Although the bicultural relationship is often described as "a complex one," the representation of such complexity is the outcome of struggles at the museum.

Wampanoag young people employed at the museum as historical interpreters redefined both their roles and the narratives they presented. For one of them, Nanepashemet, known in his youth as Anthony Pollard, the work became a project of recovery and redemption of the Wampanoag and more generally of the indigenous experience. Deeply influenced by 1970s-era indigenous movements, the self-taught historian helped uncover and retell the story of Hobbomock, a Wampanoag leader who lived next to the actual Pilgrim settlement in the 1620s.

Nanepashemet also helped reframe the entire Plimoth narrative, creating space for indigenous peoples to tell their stories and more accurately represent the injustices, challenges, and survival experiences of the Wampanoag. Widely hailed as a substantial contributor to indigenous historiography as well as contemporary struggles, Nanepashemet passed away at age forty-one of diabetes complications in 1995. By that time, he had become the plantation's research director.

The plantation is located on a hill alongside the Eel River, replicating the original Plymouth Village, which sat on Town Brook's banks, 2.2 miles northeast.

The Society of Allied Museum Professions/UAW2320 has organized the museum's historical interpreters, but management refuses to recognize the union. In 2018 the Trump administration's National Labor Relations Board upheld management's position. The union local is supportive of Wampanoag sovereignty, having adopted a resolution in favor of federal recognition of Mashpee territory as a reservation.

GETTING THERE

There are hourly buses from downtown Plymouth to the plantation (2.9 miles away). Plimoth Planation is closed during the winter months.

TO LEARN MORE

Dempsey, Jack. "Nani: A Native New England Story," 2011, www.youtube.com/watch?v=4d_svvlLIoQ&t=2925s

Society of Allied Museum Professionals: https://www.facebook.com/plimothunion/

5.10 Maypole Hill Park

90 Samoset Avenue

QUINCY

The maypole likely originated in sixteenth-century folk festivals in Germany and Austria and has roots in pagan rituals. Its first use in what became the United States was on May 1, 1627, in what is today Quincy. On that date, Thomas Morton and his men set up an eighty-foot-long pine pole in the midst of their small trading post and settlement called Merry Mount, drinking and dancing around it with Native women invited to join them. Morton was a free-thinking and -acting English settler who had arrived in the region only two years earlier as a partner in a private colonization effort led by Captain Wollaston (after whom part of Quincy is named).

Morton's settlement numbered only seven individuals. Nonetheless, the Pilgrims of Plymouth Colony saw it as threat. They arrested him in 1628—officially for selling weapons and gun powder to local Indians—cut down the maypole, and deported him to England. A little more than a year later, Morton returned to the area only to have the Puritans of the newly established Massachusetts Bay Colony arrest him on spurious charges, confiscate his property, and banish him again to England. More than a decade later, Morton returned a second time and was imprisoned—under brutal conditions. Upon release a year later, he was in very poor health and died soon thereafter.

Whatever the official justifications for arresting, jailing, and exiling Morton, the true reasons concerned his refusal to con-

Morris dancers carry the maypole up Maypole Hill in Quincy, 2008.

form to the conservative social, religious, ecological, and sexual mores of the English colonists. Whereas the English tended to see the land as uninteresting, barren, or threatening and in need of conquest, Morton, who wrote the first natural history of the colony, celebrated its wildness and abundance. Similarly, he rejected the dominant perception of his Indian neighbors as cruel and barbarous, characterizing them instead as "full of humanity" and "more friendly" than his fellow colonists. At the same time, Morton was a sexual libertine who had little respect for colonial orthodoxy. In addition to embracing relations outside of marriage, he also celebrated sexual liaisons between Native people and the English, while suggesting openness to same-sex relationships. Indeed, the English castigated Morton for engaging in "sodomy" and "buggery."

The City of Quincy's official seal commemorates Thomas Morton's trading post site. A marker in Maypole Hill Park in Quincy's Merrymount neighborhood indicates the location of Morton's maypole. In recent years, revelers have gathered there annually around May Day to celebrate Morton's memory and freewheeling ways.

GETTING THERE

Red Line to Quincy Center Station. MBTA buses pass a few blocks away from the site.

TO LEARN MORE

Drinnon, Richard. "The Maypole of Merry Mount: Thomas Morton and the Puritan Patriarchs," *Massachusetts Review* 21, no. 2 (1980): 382–410.

Zuckerman, Richard. "Pilgrims in the Wilderness: Community, Modernity, and the Maypole at Merry Mount," *New England Quarterly* 50, no. 2 (1977): 255–77.

5.11 Wessagusset Memorial Garden

230 Sea Street

NORTH WEYMOUTH

On October 21, 2001, descendants of some of the area's first English settlers and representatives of the Massachusett Indians gathered near the bottom of Sea Street for the dedication of a memorial garden. The ceremony symbolized the reconciliation of opponents who had engaged in violent conflict nearly four centuries earlier. In 1830 workers had discovered the remains of two decapitated Indians there.

The site of the garden was part of Wessagussett (today the name of a Weymouth neighborhood), the second English settlement in Massachusetts. Established in 1622 by about sixty male settlers, most of them indentured servants sent by a wealthy English merchant named Thomas Weston (who had helped to fund the Plymouth colony), Wessagussett ran into difficulties soon after they arrived. Running out of provisions, they began stealing corn from their Native neighbors.

According to Edward Winslow of Plymouth Colony, Massasoit (aka Ousemequin), a Wompanoag sachem, told him in the winter of 1622–23 that the Massachusett Indians were planning to attack Wessagussett and Plymouth. On the basis of this information, the Plymouth colonists, rather than trying to ascertain if the information was true or negotiate with the Massachusett, decided to launch a preemptive attack.

Led by Myles Standish, Plymouth Colony's military leader, several colonists traveled to Wessagussett and, on April 6, 1623, killed seven Massachusett men outside the settlement. Then they cut off the head of one of the victims, carried it to Plymouth, and mounted it on a pole to serve as a warning to any would-be adversaries. In response, the Massachusett killed three Wessagussett colonists who were living among them to obtain food.

The colony dissolved soon thereafter. Most of the men returned to England, while some rejoined Plymouth Colony. Despite the colony's collapse, other colonists would follow, including many from Weymouth, England, and settle the area. Among them were William Blackstone (or Blaxton), who moved to the Shawmut Peninsula and claimed land that would later become the **Boston Common**. Another, Samuel Maverick, settled on Noddle's Island (now part of **East Boston**), and became the namesake for **Maverick Square**.

GETTING THERE

Red Line to Quincy Center Station. MBTA buses to and from the station stop within a few blocks of the site.

TO LEARN MORE

Wisecup, Kelly, ed. *"Good News from New England" by Edward Winslow: A Scholarly Edition*, Amherst: University of Massachusetts Press, 2014.

6

Thematic
Tours

Native Greater Boston Tour

In today's Greater Boston, the historical presence of Native people is manifest
in myriad ways—from statues and place
names to the depiction of an Indian on the
Massachusetts state flag. As living people
still engaged with the world around them,
however, the area's indigenous population
seems invisible to many. This tour seeks to
help rectify this.

To speak of "Native Greater Boston" is
not simply to harken back to a past when
the area's indigenous population engaged
and shaped the land (and waterways),
made it their home, and held collective
rights to it through custom and membership in political communities. It is also to
highlight how contemporary Native-led
endeavors remind us that Greater Boston
and eastern Massachusetts more broadly
remain Indian land in various manners.

As the tour covers a considerable
amount of space, we divide it into three
sections: the cities of Boston, Cambridge,
and Somerville; north of Boston—in
Haverhill and Lowell; and the South Shore,
encompassing Quincy, Weymouth, and
Plymouth. Site names in **bold and italics**
are discussed elsewhere in the book. Those
also in **CAPITAL LETTERS** are shown on the
map accompanying this tour.

Begin by going to Orient Heights Station
(Blue Line) in East Boston. From there, take
an MBTA bus to **DEER ISLAND**, the site of a
concentration camp for Native Americans
during King Philip's War in the late 1600s.

Prior to European settlement, Native peoples lived seasonally on the island.

Upon returning to Orient Heights Station,
take the Blue Line to State Street Station.
Nearby, at 1 Federal Street, is the former site
of the **ODEON THEATRE**, where William Apess,
a Native American (Pequot) minister, activist,
and intellectual spoke in 1836 to denounce US
government "removal" of indigenous peoples.

Close by is where the **ANNE HUTCHINSON
HOUSE** once stood (283 Washington Street).
There, dozens of women and men gathered regularly in the late 1630s to engage
Hutchinson's alternative readings of the
Bible. Many of the men who gathered were
among those who refused to participate in
the first major war between English settlers
and Indians, the so-called Pequot War.

From there, go to Park Street Station and
catch the Green Line to Arlington Street Station, or walk across the **Boston Common** and
the Public Garden. At 501 Boylston Street
(enter from the Newbury Street side), you'll
find **THE NEWBRY**, a mixed-use building in
the lobby of which is a diorama that models
Native American fish weirs found in the area
in the early 1900s, evidencing Native presence going back thousands of years.

Getting back on the Green Line, go to
Kenmore Square Station. An MBTA bus from
there stops within walking distance of two
sites—one at **Brighton**'s Oak Square, the other
at Magnolia Avenue and Eliot Memorial Road
in Newton—associated with **NONANTUM**, a
"praying town" of Christianized Indians established by the Reverend John Eliot in the 1640s.

From Oak Square, an MBTA bus goes
to **Cambridge**'s Harvard Square, home of

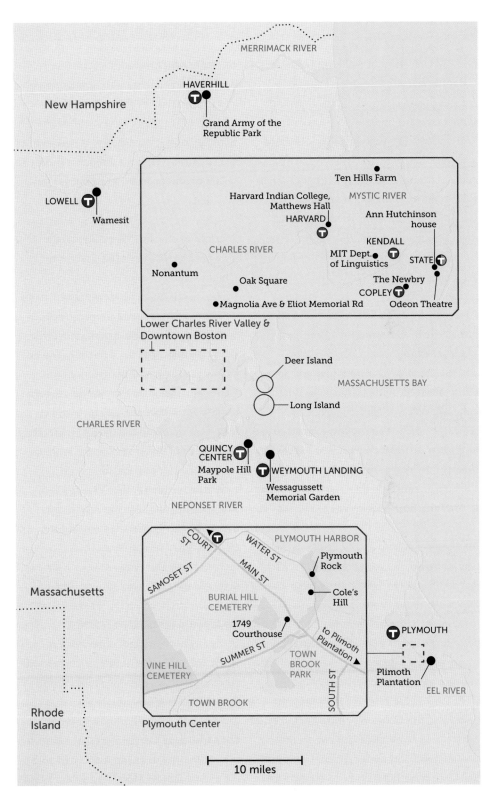

MERRIMACK RIVER

New Hampshire

HAVERHILL
🚇
Grand Army of the
Republic Park

LOWELL 🚇
Wamesit

Ten Hills Farm

MYSTIC RIVER

Harvard Indian College,
Matthews Hall
HARVARD 🚇

Ann Hutchinson
house

KENDALL
MIT Dept. 🚇
of Linguistics
STATE 🚇

CHARLES RIVER

Nonantum

Oak Square

The Newbry
COPLEY 🚇
Odeon Theatre

● Magnolia Ave & Eliot Memorial Rd

Lower Charles River Valley &
Downtown Boston

Deer Island

Long Island

MASSACHUSETTS BAY

CHARLES RIVER

QUINCY
CENTER 🚇
Maypole Hill
Park

WEYMOUTH LANDING
🚇
Wessagussett
Memorial Garden

NEPONSET RIVER

COURT ST
🚇

WATER ST

PLYMOUTH HARBOR

Plymouth
Rock

SAMOSET ST

MAIN ST

BURIAL HILL
CEMETERY

Cole's
Hill

Massachusetts

1749
Courthouse

to Plimoth
Plantation

🚇 PLYMOUTH

VINE HILL
CEMETERY

SUMMER ST

TOWN
BROOK
PARK

SOUTH ST

Plimoth
Plantation

EEL RIVER

Rhode
Island

TOWN BROOK

Plymouth Center

10 miles

Native Greater Boston Tour

Harvard University, in the "yard" of which is **MATTHEW HALL**. A plaque on the building indicates that it is where the **HARVARD INDIAN COLLEGE**, built in 1655, once stood.

Two stops from the Red Line's Harvard Station (Kendall/MIT Station) is the Massachusetts Institute of Technology. It is a short walk to the **RAY AND MARIA STATA CENTER** (32 Vassar Street), home to MIT's Department of Linguistics and Philosophy. There, a Native scholar worked with an MIT linguist beginning in the 1990s to resurrect the Wampanoag language.

About two and a half miles away is the former site of Governor John Winthrop's **TEN HILLS FARM** (indicated by a marker where Governor Winthrop Road and Shore Drive intersect). In the early 1600s, Winthrop employed enslaved Native individuals—captives from the Pequot War—on his large farmstead. To get there, it is best to take the subway into Downtown Boston (Downtown Crossing Station) and then the Orange Line to Assembly Square Station.

About thirty miles north of Boston is the City of *Lowell*, home to **WAMESIT** (33 Walkway to Middlesex Community College), an important site of Pennacook gatherings and trade prior to English settlement. It later became the site of a "praying village," one whose existence ended in the context of the violence associated with King Philip's War.

Just as you can reach Lowell via Commuter Rail from Boston's North Station, you can travel to *Haverhill* (about twenty miles east of Lowell, but on a different Commuter Rail line). Haverhill is home to **GRAND ARMY OF THE REPUBLIC PARK** (108 Main Street). A statue there uncritically commemorates a horrific massacre of Abenaki Indians. The monument thus serves as a disturbing reminder of the violence associated with settler colonialism and the dominant society's failure to acknowledge and atone for the violence.

South of Boston are five additional sites. Two are accessible by MBTA bus from Quincy Center Station (Red Line).

The first is Quincy's **MAYPOLE HILL PARK** (90 Samoset Avenue). In the early 1600s, it was the site of a small English settlement led by Thomas Morton, a freethinker who challenged the Pilgrims' depictions of the Native population and worked to establish respectful relations with them. There in 1627, Morton organized the first maypole celebration in the Americas, one in which Native women participated.

A little further south is Wessagussett, a neighborhood in Weymouth that was the site of a Pilgrim settlement. In 1623, Pilgrims killed several Massachusett men there. Almost four hundred years later, descendants of the two groups gathered to reconcile and establish the **WESSAGUSSETT MEMORIAL GARDEN** (230 Sea Street).

Go back to Quincy Center Station, where an MBTA Commuter Rail train will take you to *Plymouth*. Two miles from the station is the downtown area. Located there, across from Plymouth Rock, is **COLE'S HILL** (35 Carver Street), the launch site, since 1970, of events associated with the annual Day of Mourning, a Native-led effort to redefine what is known as Thanksgiving Day.

Nearby, a four-minute walk away, is the **OLD COUNTRY HOUSE/1749 COURT HOUSE** (1 Town Square). It was there in 1675 that the Plymouth Colony convicted three Native men for murder and then executed them. This was the event that triggered King Philip's War, a devastating and bloody conflict that lasted fourteen months.

Finally, about three miles away (via a bus from the downtown area), is *PLIMOTH PLANTATION* (137 Warren Avenue). Closed during winter months, it is a "living museum" and a replica of the original Plymouth settlement and a Wampanoag village. Thanks to the efforts of area Native peoples and their allies, the stories told there now reflect multiple viewpoints and the complex nature of Native-colonist relations.

Malcolm and Martin Tour

In the struggle for racial justice and human rights, Greater Bostonians—most born and raised in the area, some relative newcomers—have long played important roles, whether in challenging racism at "home" or working to contest it elsewhere in the United States or abroad. Two such Greater Bostonians (at least for some portion of their lives) were Malcolm X and Martin Luther King Jr. Their time in the area was formative to who they were and who they became, and to their work. This tour highlights sites that were central to their Greater Boston years. Only four of the sites have entries associated with them. Addresses are provided for sites when not indicated in the accompanying maps. Sites that are in **BOLD CAPITAL LETTERS** are shown on the map accompanying this tour. Sites that are *italicized* have entries that discuss them elsewhere in the book.

Malcolm Little first came to Boston at the age of fifteen (in 1940–1941) and stayed at the now-demolished house of his half-sister, Ella Little-Collins—whom he characterized as "the first really proud black woman" he knew—near the corner of Waumbeck and Humboldt Avenue in *Roxbury*. At some point in 1941, Little-Collins bought a house (which still stands) nearby at **72 DALE STREET,** where Malcolm frequently stayed for the next several years.

Malcolm held many different jobs during this time. He worked in the "**AUTO PARK**" (a parking lot) of an in-law of Little-Collins (whose last name was Walker) in *Chinatown* at what was 75 Beach Street, roughly where the Chinatown Gate now stands. He also worked as a soda jerk at **TOWNSEND DRUG STORE**, which no longer exists, at the intersection of Townsend Street and Humboldt Avenue in Roxbury, as a busboy in Downtown's *PARKER HOUSE* hotel (60 School Street), as a shoe shiner in the **ROSELAND STATE BALLROOM** (it stood on Massachusetts Avenue, at about what is now no. 245, across from the Christian Science church), and in the **WAREHOUSE OF THE SEARS-ROEBUCK** building (now

Malcolm Little at Franklin Park, with Ella Little-Collins (far right) and two friends, 1941.

the Landmark Center at Park Drive and Brookline Avenue) in the *Fenway*. In addition, he worked out of **SOUTH STATION** as a Pullman porter for the New Haven Railroad and, later, the Seaboard Railroad. In his spare time, he frequented the **SAVOY CAFÉ**, a jazz club that once stood in the *South End*. He also became involved in a burglary gang, one that often hung out in an apartment building on the edge of Harvard Yard called **THE AMBASSADOR**. Torn down in 2002, it is now the site of Harvard's Knafel Center for Government and International Studies.

Police arrested Malcolm in 1946. He was convicted of larceny and breaking and entering, and sentenced to eight to ten years. He spent his time in three prisons: **CHARLESTOWN STATE PRISON** (where Massachusetts executed Sacco and Vanzetti in 1927, and today is the site of Bunker Hill Community College, 250 Rutherford Street, *Charlestown*); ***CONCORD REFORMATORY*** (today MCI-Concord—965 Elm Street, Concord); and **NORFOLK STATE PRISON** (2 Clark Street, Norfolk), an experimental facil-

ity where—because of his sister's efforts to effect his transfer—Malcolm had access to its considerable library. Malcolm was a member of the Norfolk Debating Society, which he credited with sparking his passion for public speaking. It was during his incarceration that Malcolm learned about the Muslim religion, joined the Nation of Islam, and changed his name to Malcolm X. He was paroled in 1952.

There are four other noteworthy sites. The first is a **MONUMENT ON THE *BOSTON COMMON*** to those killed in the Boston Massacre of 1770 (near Tremont Street, between Avery and West Streets). In his autobiography, Malcolm X states that he was astonished to learn that the first person killed was "a Negro named Crispus Attucks. I had never known anything like that." Second is **MUHAMMAD'S MOSQUE NO. 11** in *Dorchester*. Some claim that Malcolm founded the mosque; what is certain is that he visited and spoke there on a number of occasions as part of his duties as a regional minister for the Nation. Formerly a Jewish synagogue, the building is now known as Masjid Al-Qur'aan. Third, when in Boston beginning

MLK at Freedom
House, 1958.

in the late 1950s, Malcolm was a frequent guest on the late-night talk show of **WMEX 1510** radio in the Fenway. Finally, on March 18, 1964, Malcolm spoke at **LEVERETT HOUSE** in Harvard Yard (across from Harvard Station on the Red Line) in *Cambridge*, giving one of his first speeches after breaking with the Nation of Islam and starting a new group, the Organization of Afro-American Unity.

Martin Luther King arrived in Boston in 1951 to enroll in a PhD program in the **SCHOOL OF THEOLOGY** at Boston University. He first resided in BU's **MYLES STANDISH HALL** in Kenmore Square. In 1952–53, he lived in what was likely a boarding house on **MASSACHUSETTS AVENUE** in the *South End*. MLK's apartment served as the meeting place for the Dialectical Society, a club dedicated to discussing matters of philosophy and theology and composed largely of African American male graduate students. At some point, he moved nearby to an apartment on **SAINT BOTOLPH STREET**. His future wife, Coretta Scott (whom he met in early 1952), lived nearby (in a building

owned by the **LEAGUE OF WOMEN FOR COMMUNITY SERVICE**) while a student at the **NEW ENGLAND CONSERVATORY OF MUSIC** and occasionally participated in the group's meetings. Upon marriage, they lived briefly on Northampton Street, on a stretch of the street that no longer exists (it is part of the *SOUTHWEST CORRIDOR PARK*). While a student at BU, MLK often attended services, taught religion classes, and preached at **TWELFTH BAPTIST CHURCH** (which relocated to its present site in 1957).

After leaving Boston in June 1954, and moving to Atlanta, MLK returned to the city on at least two occasions. On March 20, 1958, he attended a reception held in his honor at *Roxbury*'s **FREEDOM HOUSE**, the center of civil rights advocacy in Boston's African American community. Upon the invitation of three black state representatives, MLK, having recently won the Nobel Peace Prize, addressed a joint session of the Massachusetts legislature at the State House on April 21, 1965. Following the speech, he visited the **PATRICK CAMPBELL SCHOOL** (today the Martin Luther King Jr. School)

Malcolm and Martin Tour

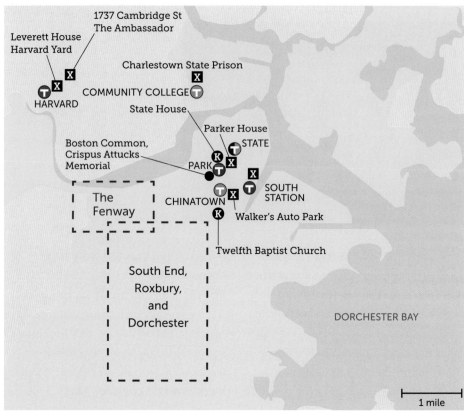

1737 Cambridge St
The Ambassador

Leverett House
Harvard Yard

Charlestown State Prison

COMMUNITY COLLEGE

HARVARD

State House

Parker House

STATE

Boston Common,
Crispus Attucks
Memorial

PARK

The
Fenway

CHINATOWN

SOUTH
STATION

Walker's Auto Park

South End,
Roxbury,
and
Dorchester

Twelfth Baptist Church

DORCHESTER BAY

1 mile

City of Boston

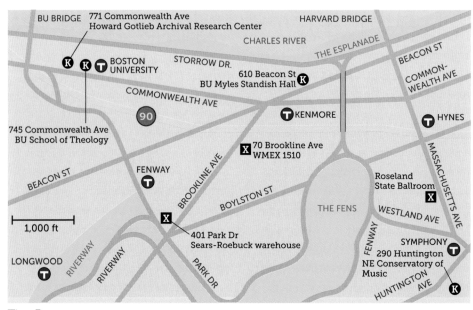

BU BRIDGE   771 Commonwealth Ave
Howard Gotlieb Archival Research Center

HARVARD BRIDGE

CHARLES RIVER

STORROW DR.

THE ESPLANADE

BEACON ST

BOSTON
UNIVERSITY

610 Beacon St
BU Myles Standish Hall

COMMON-
WEALTH AVE

COMMONWEALTH AVE

90

KENMORE

HYNES

745 Commonwealth Ave
BU School of Theology

70 Brookline Ave
WMEX 1510

MASSACHUSETTS AVE

BEACON ST

FENWAY

Roseland
State Ballroom

BOYLSTON ST

THE FENS

WESTLAND AVE

1,000 ft

401 Park Dr
Sears-Roebuck warehouse

SYMPHONY
290 Huntington
NE Conservatory of
Music

LONGWOOD

RIVERWAY

RIVERWAY

PARK DR

FENWAY

HUNTINGTON
AVE

The Fenway

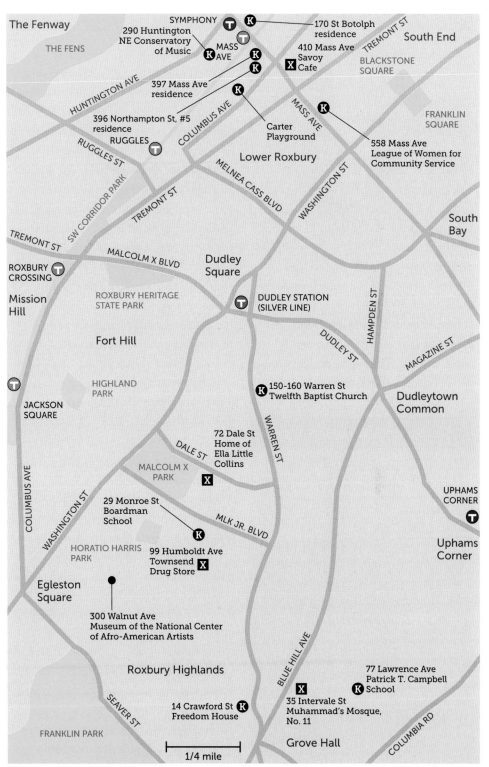

The Fenway

THE FENS

SYMPHONY Ⓣ Ⓚ ──────── 170 St Botolph
                              residence

290 Huntington
NE Conservatory   Ⓣ
of Music   MASS   410 Mass Ave   TREMONT ST   South End
          Ⓚ AVE   Savoy
                          Ⓚ Ⓧ Cafe   BLACKSTONE
                          Ⓚ   SQUARE

HUNTINGTON AVE

397 Mass Ave   Ⓚ
residence

396 Northampton St, #5
residence   Ⓚ   FRANKLIN
                                               SQUARE
RUGGLES   COLUMBUS AVE   MASS AVE
RUGGLES ST Ⓣ
                                 Carter
                 Lower Roxbury   Playground   558 Mass Ave
                                               League of Women for
            MELNEA CASS BLVD   Community Service

                                  WASHINGTON ST

SW CORRIDOR PARK   South
TREMONT ST   Bay
TREMONT ST
                 MALCOLM X BLVD   Dudley
ROXBURY Ⓣ   Square
CROSSING

Mission   ROXBURY HERITAGE
Hill   STATE PARK   Ⓣ DUDLEY STATION   HAMPDEN ST
                                      (SILVER LINE)

                 Fort Hill   DUDLEY ST   MAGAZINE ST

         Ⓣ   HIGHLAND
                 PARK   Ⓚ 150-160 Warren St   Dudleytown
JACKSON   Twelfth Baptist Church Common
SQUARE
                                                    UPHAMS
                 72 Dale St   CORNER
         DALE ST Home of
                 Ella Little   WARREN ST   Ⓣ
COLUMBUS AVE   Collins
                 MALCOLM X   Uphams
         WASHINGTON ST PARK Ⓧ   Corner

                 29 Monroe St
                 Boardman
                 School   MLK JR. BLVD
                         Ⓚ
         HORATIO HARRIS 99 Humboldt Ave
         PARK   Townsend Ⓧ
                        Drug Store
Egleston
Square   ●

         300 Walnut Ave
         Museum of the National Center
         of Afro-American Artists
                                      BLUE HILL AVE
                 Roxbury Highlands   77 Lawrence Ave
                                                    Patrick T. Campbell
                                      Ⓧ   Ⓚ School
         SEAVER ST 14 Crawford St Ⓚ 35 Intervale St
                    Freedom House   Muhammad's Mosque,   COLUMBIA RD
FRANKLIN PARK   No. 11

         ├──────────┤
            1/4 mile   Grove Hall

Roxbury, and parts of the South End and Dorchester

and the **WILLIAM BOARDMAN SCHOOL** (on a section of Monroe Street, east of Humboldt, which no longer exists) to support parents working to rectify inadequate educational opportunities, overcrowded, unsafe conditions, and racial segregation. Outside both buildings, he spoke to large crowds. The next day, MLK led a march protesting racial segregation in Boston schools and housing from the **CARTER PLAYGROUND** (Columbus Avenue at Camden Street) in the South End to the **BOSTON COMMON**. There he spoke to a crowd estimated at more than twenty thousand people.

The **HOWARD GOTLIEB ARCHIVAL RESEARCH CENTER** at Boston University today houses a collection of MLK's personal papers and others items from 1947 to 1963.

Sacco and Vanzetti Tour

Nicola Sacco and Bartolomeo Vanzetti were born in Italy in 1891 and 1888, respectively, and immigrated to Greater Boston in 1908. A little more than a decade after their arrival, the men, left-wing political activists, would become two of the world's most famous people. This tour highlights sites that were central to their Greater Boston years.

Apart from *MAVERICK SQUARE*, none of the sites have entries associated with them. Addresses are provided for sites when not indicated in the accompanying maps. Sites and municipalities that are in **BOLD CAPITAL LETTERS** are shown on the map accompanying this tour. Sites that are *italicized* are discussed elsewhere in the book.

Sacco and Vanzetti were involved in anarchist politics in eastern Massachusetts, where they eventually met, and both were involved in labor organizing. Sacco worked briefly at the Draper Company, a maker of power textile looms, in the town of **HOPEDALE** (24 Hopedale Street); he was part of a support group for a strike there in 1913, about which he wrote (the first of many articles) for an Italian-language anarchist weekly, the then-**LYNN**-based *Cronaca Sovversiva* (located at 32 Oxford Street, now a parking lot). For several years, he also worked at the Milford Shoe Company (177 Central Street, Milford) and was active in an anarchist group in **MILFORD** called the Circolo di Studi Sociali. Vanzetti was a part of a 1916 strike at the Plymouth Cordage Company (a rope- and twine-making entity in **PLYMOUTH**—today the location of a retail and office center with a small museum dedicated to the company—at 10 Cordage Park Circle).

In a context of numerous politically motivated bombings in the United States in 1919—bombings attributed to anarchists— Sacco and Vanzetti, like many of their political comrades, came under government surveillance. Local authorities suspected them of robbery and the murder of a guard (Alessandro Berardelli) and a paymaster (Frederick Parmenter) outside the **SLATER AND MORILL SHOE FACTORY** (on Pearl Street) in South Braintree on April 15, 1920. Tipped off that the pair was traveling on a streetcar from West Bridgewater, police arrested them soon after it entered **BROCKTON** on Montello Street, near the intersection with

Sacco and Vanzetti demonstration, Boston, March 1, 1925.

East Chestnut Street, on May 5. A little more than a year later, on July 14, 1921, a jury at the **COURTHOUSE IN DEDHAM** (621 High Street) convicted Sacco, a leather trimmer in a shoe factory, and Vanzetti, a fish peddler, of armed robbery and first-degree murder, the punishment for which was death by electric chair.

Many across the country and throughout the world perceived the convictions as politically motivated and informed by anti-Italian sentiment that was pervasive in the United States at the time. While there was no question of Sacco and Vanzetti's political beliefs—and membership in an anarchist cell, *Gruppo Autonomo*, that met in and around *East Boston*'s **MAVERICK SQUARE**—the trial was marked by many irregularities, and the jury's decision was highly questionable given the flimsy evidence.

Despite massive opposition in Boston and throughout much of the world, opposition coordinated by the **SACCO AND VANZETTI DEFENSE COMMITTEE** in the *North End*, the

Commonwealth of Massachusetts executed Nicola Sacco and Bartolomeo Vanzetti at **CHARLESTOWN STATE PRISON** (250 New Rutherford Avenue, *Charlestown*—now the site of Bunker Hill Community College) on August 22, 1927. Their execution led to protests—both peaceful and violent—across the world: from Bueno Aires and Bucharest to Johannesburg and Tokyo, from Athens and Rome to Marrakech and Sydney. In Boston, about two hundred thousand people lined the streets as the funeral cortege, accompanied by tens of thousands, proceeded from the **LANGONE FUNERAL HOME** in the North End to **FOREST HILLS CEMETERY** in *Jamaica Plain*. The *Boston Globe* called the procession "one of the most tremendous funerals of modern times."

The **BOSTON PUBLIC LIBRARY** at Copley Square houses the Aldino Felicani Sacco-Vanzetti Defense Committee Collection, one of the library's most utilized archives; on the third floor of the library's McKim building, there is a plaster cast commemorating Sacco and Vanzetti attached to a wall near Special Collections. Very nearby, the **COMMUNITY CHURCH OF BOSTON** (565 Boylston Street), a politically left congregation, gives out an annual Sacco-Vanzetti Memorial Award for Social Justice "to outstanding activists in the peoples' struggles." In South Braintree, at Pearl Street and French Avenue, a **MEMORIAL** commemorates Berardelli and Parmenter, and has a placard that discusses the case.

In 1977, Massachusetts Governor Michael Dukakis signed a proclamation on the execution's fiftieth anniversary, declaring it Sacco and Vanzetti Memorial Day and asserting that "any stigma and disgrace should be forever removed from the names of Nicola Sacco and Bartolomeo Vanzetti."

Sacco and Vanzetti Tour

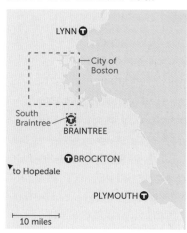

Eastern Massachusetts

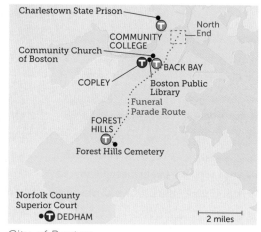

City of Boston

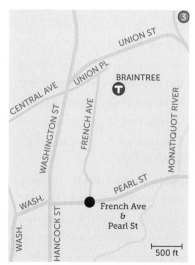

South Braintree

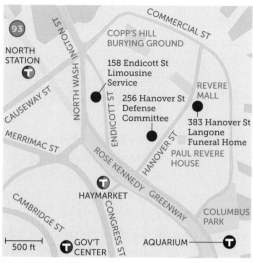

North End, Boston

Bread and Roses and More Tour

What some have referred to as "Strike City," Lawrence is home to one of the most famous labor actions in US history: the so-called (after the fact) Bread and Roses Strike. The 1912 work stoppage saw more than twenty thousand mill workers, mostly immigrants, withhold their labor for two months during a bitterly cold winter, effectively shutting down the world's largest complex of worsted wool factories. In the face of high levels of intimidation, repression, and violence on the part of the city's police, state militia, and mill owners, a multiethnic, polyglot group of workers—under the leadership of the radical Industrial Workers of the World (the "Wobblies")—ultimately prevailed.

While the tour focuses on sites associated with the strike of 1912, it includes sites associated with subsequent large-scale labor actions in 1919 and 1931. Also, because Lawrence is more than struggles between workers, capital, and its allies in the state apparatus, the tour takes you to a few other important sites in this largely working-class city.

Most are located within central Lawrence—within easy walking distance of the downtown area. A small number are close to a mile or more away. If walking (or bicycling) is not an option, Merrimack Valley Regional Transit Authority buses are available, as are taxis. Site names in **bold and italics** are discussed elsewhere in the book. Those also in **CAPITAL LETTERS** are shown on the map accompanying this tour.

If you're coming from outside the city, the MBTA Commuter Rail Lawrence Station serves as your launching point. From there, walk north on Union Street and the Duck Bridge across the Merrimack River to the **ESSEX COMPANY HEADQUARTERS COMPOUND** (6 Essex Street). The Essex Company planned and oversaw the construction of Lawrence as an industrial city. It is today home to the **LAWRENCE HISTORY CENTER**, an important community institution.

Across Union Street where it intersects with Essex is the former **EVERETT MILL** (15 Union Street). There, on January 11, 1912, the strike began when a group of Polish women workers walked out upon discovering that the mill owners had reduced their wages.

Near the northern edge of the building is the **INTERSECTION OF UNION AND GARDEN STREETS,** where Anna LoPizzo, a thirty-four-year-old Italian immigrant and mill worker, was shot and killed on January 29, 1912, when she came upon a brawl between picketing workers and the police.

Backtrack a bit and walk west on Canal Street. At the corner of Mill Street, you will come upon what was the office building of the **AMERICAN WOOLEN COMPANY**. With three mills, the Boston–based company was by far the biggest employer of textile workers in "Immigrant City" at the time of the 1912 strike. William Wood, the corporation's head, became the personification of greedy mill owners among striking workers and their supporters.

Behind it is the **LAWRENCE HERITAGE STATE PARK** (1 Jackson Street), an excellent, state-run museum that focuses on the history of industrialization in Lawrence and the 1912 textile strike. It is housed in a former boarding house, built around 1847, for textile mill workers.

Two streets north and one west is the site of where **SCHAAKE'S BLOCK** (234 Essex Street) used to stand. Torn down in the 1930s, the building contained the headquarters of the National Textile Workers Union. On February 26, 1931, police raided the NTWU headquarters during a major textile mill strike and beat up and arrested key leaders in an effort to undermine the union.

One block north (on Common Street, between Jackson and Haverhill Streets) is the **NORTH (OR CAMPAGNONE) COMMON**. An estimated twenty thousand Lawrencians gathered there to hear IWW leader William "Big Bill" Haywood speak on January 24, 1912. Another fifteen thousand assembled on the Common almost two months later, on March 14, where they voted to end the strike. On the southern edge of the Common, diagonally across the street from City Hall, is a fifteen-ton granite **MONUMENT TO THE 1912 STRIKE**, unveiled in 2012.

A few blocks northwest—you'll pass the **LAWRENCE PUBLIC LIBRARY** (51 Lawrence Street) on the way—is **JONAS SMOLSKAS'S HOUSE** site (at what was 96 Lawrence Street but is now in front of where Saint Anthony's Maronite Church stands). A Lithuanian immigrant and member of the IWW, Smolskas was killed several months after the 1912 strike's end. His murder demonstrates how strike-related tensions endured. Big Bill Haywood pronounced Smolskas the third and final fatality associated with the strike.

Continuing to head northwest, you will reach the site (210–212 Park Street) of homes associated with **BREAD AND ROSES HOUSING**, an organization that endeavors to democratize land ownership by way of a community land trust and to provide affordable and secure housing for low-income folks in and around Lawrence. Its offices are located in the **EVERETT MILL**.

A little west, at the end of Park Street, is the **ARLINGTON MILLS** (550 Broadway). Jonas Smolskas worked there, as did the famed poet Robert Frost—as a clerical assistant in the 1890s after graduating from Lawrence High School. Now home to loft apartments, it was a key site associated with a huge strike (and police violence) in 1919, one that lasted more than three months.

Southwest, about a half-mile away, is the **IMMACULATE CONCEPTION CEMETERY**. If you enter at Barker Street and Currant Hill Road, you'll find nearby the graves of Anna LoPizzo, John Ramey (the second worker killed during the strike of 1912), and Jonas Smolskas.

Another half-mile or so away from the cemetery, heading south, is the intersection of Oxford and Haverhill Streets, the **1984 RIOT EPICENTER**. The riot reflected the violent opposition of many white Lawrencians in what was then a declining industrial city to its growing Latino population. Its aftermath contributed to the emergence of a Latino-dominated Lawrence.

Seven-tenths of a mile from the cemetery (moving southwest) is what use to be **FRANCO-BELGIAN HALL** (9 Mason Street), the headquarters of the Franco-Belgian Cooper-

Bread and Roses and More Tour

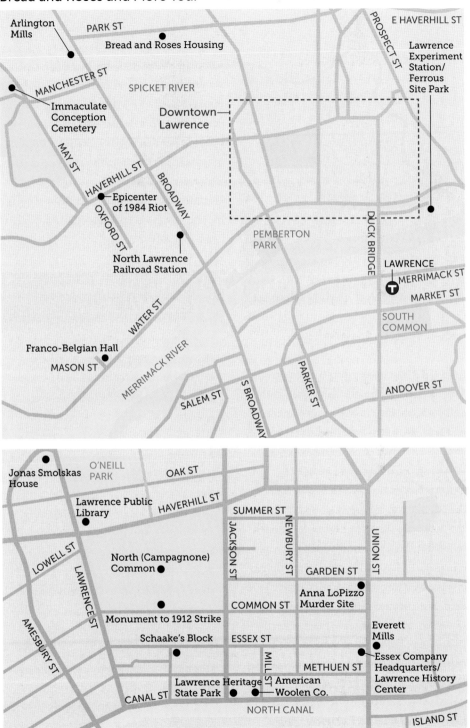

Arlington Mills

PARK ST

Bread and Roses Housing

PROSPECT ST

E HAVERHILL ST

Lawrence Experiment Station/ Ferrous Site Park

MANCHESTER ST

SPICKET RIVER

Immaculate Conception Cemetery

Downtown Lawrence

MAY ST

HAVERHILL ST

OXFORD ST

BROADWAY

Epicenter of 1984 Riot

North Lawrence Railroad Station

PEMBERTON PARK

DUCK BRIDGE

LAWRENCE

MERRIMACK ST

MARKET ST

SOUTH COMMON

WATER ST

Franco-Belgian Hall

MASON ST

MERRIMACK RIVER

SALEM ST

S BROADWAY

PARKER ST

ANDOVER ST

Jonas Smolskas House

O'NEILL PARK

OAK ST

Lawrence Public Library

HAVERHILL ST

SUMMER ST

JACKSON ST

NEWBURY ST

UNION ST

North (Campagnone) Common

GARDEN ST

Anna LoPizzo Murder Site

COMMON ST

Monument to 1912 Strike

Everett Mills

Schaake's Block

ESSEX ST

MILL ST

Essex Company Headquarters/ Lawrence History Center

METHUEN ST

AMESBURY ST

LAWRENCE ST

LOWELL ST

Lawrence Heritage State Park

American Woolen Co.

CANAL ST

NORTH CANAL

ISLAND ST

Downtown Lawrence

Massachusetts militiamen with fixed bayonets surround striking workers, Lawrence, 1912.

Street, confluence of Merrimack and Spicket rivers). The Experiment Station, a research laboratory focused on the purification of water, sewage, and industrial waste, helped to make Lawrence a pioneer among US cities and a world leader in the filtration of public water (leading to a dramatic decrease in typhoid in the city in the 1890s). A steel foundry caused the surrounding land to become toxic. Reclaimed and cleaned up, the site now hosts Ferrous Site Park, which opened in 2016.

ative, a socialist enterprise. Today a privately owned events venue, the hall served as the IWW's headquarters for the 1919 strike.

Heading back toward the downtown area, seven-tenths of a mile away, is the former site of the **NORTH LAWRENCE RAILROAD DEPOT** (just west and north of the intersection of Essex and Broadway, on the Broadway side of the decommissioned railroad tracks). One of the highest-profile events during the 1912 strike—some contend it was a turning point in shifting public opinion across the United States in favor of the workers—took place there when the Lawrence police attacked mothers attempting to help their children board a train.

Before you return to the Commuter Rail Station, stop at the former site of the **LAWRENCE EXPERIMENT STATION**, now known as **FERROUS SITE PARK** (Zero Island

The One Percent of Greater Boston Tour

A term popularized during the "Occupy" movement in 2011, "the One Percent" highlights the small number of wealthy and powerful people who dominate decision making over the organization of society and the allocation of its resources. They do so in a manner that perpetuates and enhances their power while often marginalizing and harming many of those lower in the socio-economic hierarchy. In the case of Greater Boston, its One Percent has its roots in the early 1600s and a precapitalist colonial economy. Over four centuries, the area's ruling class has successfully adapted to and shaped waves of capitalist development, bringing about new forms of property and power, reproducing and often intensifying inequality in the process. Throughout, the One Percent has helped to legitimate these outcomes through legal, political, and intellectual institutions. Greater Boston's One Percent has done so not only through its control of capital and its associated practices, but also through the ideas it has championed.

This tour takes you to sites within the Boston, Cambridge, and Salem, illustrating the diverse activities of the region's One Percent and how those activities, the actors, and their geographies have shifted over time. Site names in **bold and italics** are discussed elsewhere in the book. Those also in **CAPITAL LETTERS** are shown on the map accompanying this tour.

Start the tour at Boston's **FANEUIL HALL** (a short walk from both Government Center and State Stations on the Blue, Green, and Orange Lines). Peter Faneuil, a wealthy merchant who was active in the triangular trade linking the West Indies, the Atlantic colonies, Europe, and Africa, donated the building, which opened in 1742, to serve as a centralized marketplace. Much of Faneuil's wealth was derived from his trafficking in enslaved Africans.

Nearby, about one block away, is **EXCHANGE PLACE** (53 State Street). The birthplace of the xenophobic **IMMIGRATION RESTRICTION LEAGUE** in 1894, it is today the home of various corporate entities, including the headquarters of *The Boston Globe*, owned by John Henry. One of the Boston area's wealthiest individuals, Henry is also the owner of the Boston Red Sox baseball team and **FENWAY PARK.**

Walk 0.3 miles from the State Street site to **CENTRAL WHARF**, once the home of **JAMES AND THOMAS H. PERKINS AND COMPANY**.

Thomas Perkins and his nephew John became two of Boston's wealthiest individuals in the mid-1800s—largely through the company's smuggling of opium into China, proceeds from which helped to establish leading Boston-area institutions, including the Massachusetts General Hospital.

About a half-mile walk from the wharf (or a quick subway ride on the Blue Line from Aquarium Station to State Station) in Downtown is the **BOSTON SAFE DEPOSIT AND TRUST COMPANY/THE VAULT** (100 Franklin Street). It was the meeting place of what was called the Coordinating Committee and known more popularly as the Vault. Seeing themselves as the saviors of a financially precarious city, members of the Vault, established in 1959, were the heads of Boston's major corporate and financial entities. Over more than three decades, they played a major role in transforming Boston into a city increasingly welcoming to the interests of national and international capital.

From there, take a four-minute (0.2 mile) walk to 40 Water Street, site of the former National Shawmut Bank Building and, at the time of the 1912 textile strike in *Lawrence*, the headquarters of the **AMERICAN WOOLEN COMPANY.**

A few blocks farther is Park Street Station, where you can get the Green Line (B, C, D, or E) to Arlington Station (two stops away). Upon exiting, first go to 15 Arlington Street (at the corner of Newbury Street) to the **TAJ BOSTON**. A high-end, luxury hotel, it was until 2006 the Ritz-Carlton, Boston. In the early- to mid-twentieth century, the hotel served as the home of Samuel Zemurray, the head of the **UNITED FRUIT COMPANY**, a politically infamous, Boston-based corporation that was the world's largest agricultural enterprise. It is said that Zemurray had to rent a suite at the hotel because as a Jewish man—albeit a very rich one—he was not welcome to acquire or rent property in Boston's wealthy areas.

About two blocks away, at 535 Boylston Street (at the corner of Clarendon Street), are the offices of the **MASSACHUSETTS COMPETITIVE PARTNERSHIP**. Sometimes referred to as "the new Vault," it is the most powerful business group in Massachusetts. In an effort to make the state more economically "competitive," it champions neoliberal polices aimed at deregulation and austerity.

Just a block down Clarendon Street, in the John Hancock Tower, is the headquarters of **BAIN CAPITAL**. Founded by former Massachusetts governor and Republican presidential candidate Mitt Romney, it is a global investment firm that plays an outsized role in corporate restructuring. The company also illustrates the bipartisan nature of the area's One Percent: one of its principals is Deval Patrick, a Democrat who succeeded Romney as governor.

After heading back on the Green Line to Park Street Station, catch the Red Line to **Cambridge**, getting off at Kendall/MIT Station. Three-tenths of a mile away is **TECHNOLOGY SQUARE**. Formerly the home of **POLAROID**, a target of a successful local effort in the 1970s to force corporations to ends their complicity with apartheid in South Africa, it is now an epicenter of ven-

ture capital and high-tech research and production businesses focused on weaponry, big pharma, biotech, and information technology. This is an increasingly powerful sector of the area's ruling class.

Returning to the Red Line, go to Harvard Station. From there, either walk (about 0.6 miles) or catch a bus down North Harvard Street just across the line into Boston's **Allston** neighborhood. There you'll find the campus of the **HARVARD BUSINESS SCHOOL** (HBS), where leading members of the area's One Percent—including Mitt Romney and Abigail Johnson (the head of Fidelity Investments and a member of the **MASSACHUSETTS COMPETITIVE PARTNERSHIP**, she is Boston's wealthiest person)—received their training in advanced capitalism. Through its graduate programs, executive training and online programs, and publications, the school's importance for the global One Percent is perhaps even greater.

If you go back to Harvard Square, you can either walk one mile or catch an MBTA bus that will leave you near 33 Elmwood Avenue, the site of **ELMWOOD**, an almost three-acre estate that is home of the president of Harvard University. In the late 1700s, it was the home of Britain's lieutenant colonial governor, Thomas Oliver, son of a wealthy sugar-plantation and slaveholding family. In 1774, an uprising of "the people" forced Oliver and his family to abandon the estate.

A short day trip outside of Boston and Cambridge will bring you to **Salem** (via MBTA Commuter Rail from North Station, Newburyport/Rockport Line). Reputed to be the

The One Percent of Greater Boston Tour

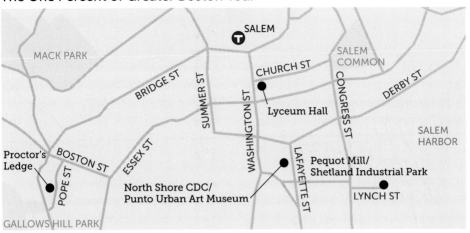

Salem

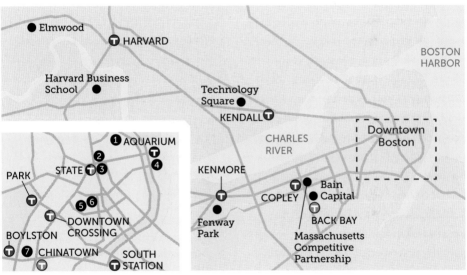

Boston and Cambridge

Downtown Boston Sites

1. Faneuil Hall
2. United Fruit Co.
3. Immigration Restriction League, Exchange Place
4. Central Wharf, James & Thomas H Perkins & Company
5. Boston Safe Deposit & Trust Co. / The Vault
6. American Woolen Company
7. Taj Boston

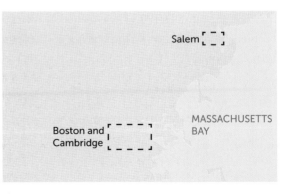

New World's wealthiest city per capita in the early nineteenth century, Salem was an important maritime trading city. In this regard, two sites stand out.

First is **THE DERBY HOUSE** (168 Derby Street). It was the home of Elias Haskert Derby, a merchant who enriched himself as a privateer during the Revolutionary War, attacking British ships and keeping the booty for himself. Subsequently his fleet of ships sailed to ports across the world, particularly to Asia, helping to lay the foundation for Salem's emergence as a global shipping power. When Derby died in 1799, he was among the richest people in the United States.

Three-tenths of a mile away, you will find a result of Salem's sea-trade wealth: **EAST INDIA MARINE HALL/PEABODY ESSEX MUSEUM** (161 Essex Street). One of the top art museums in the United States and home to one of the country's largest collections of Asian art, its roots lie with Salem's East Indian Marine Society. The group's members— local ship captains and business agents— enriched themselves through trade with Asia and collected objects for what eventually became the museum. Some of the trade was in opium. It was a business that both led to addiction abroad and relied, at least on one occasion involving Salem, on the violence of US militarism.

The Nature of Greater Boston Tour

Nature—the foundation of all places—is inevitably the object of contention when competing socioeconomic forces, ideological differences, and disparities in wealth collide. There is certainly true in Greater Boston where the region's longstanding inequities associated with class, gender, and race—among other social and geographical categories—have long been reflected in the treatment, uses, and transformations of the natural environment. It is an environment not limited to the region in light of the transformation and appropriations of nature some of its most powerful people and institutions have helped to bring about across the globe.

In exploring Greater Boston's multifaceted relationship to nature, we have necessarily limited our focus to the City of Boston, the neighboring cities of Chelsea and Everett, and, farther away, Concord and Lynn. Site names in **bold and italics** are discussed elsewhere in the book. Those also in **CAPITAL LETTERS** are shown on the map accompanying this tour.

Start in East Boston by taking the Blue Line to Wood Island Station. Named after a park that fell victim to the expansion of Logan Airport in the 1960s, the station is next to **NEPTUNE ROAD EDGE BUFFER PARK** (Neptune Road between Frankfurt and Bennington Streets). Opened in 2015, the park commemorates a neighborhood that was destroyed in subsequent decades to accommodate the airport's land-hungry ways.

From Wood Island Station, get back on the Blue Line and go one stop (inbound) to Airport Station, and then take a free shuttle bus to **BOSTON LOGAN INTERNATIONAL AIRPORT**. Comprising two-thirds of the *East Boston* neighborhood's land, the airport is a testament to land-making that involved the joining of a number of small islands. It is also a testament to air travel's heavy use of fossil fuels. A major producer of air pollution, Logan is Boston's largest source of CO2 emissions. Flights from Logan and their greenhouse gas emissions contribute more to climate change than some countries do.

From Airport Station, continue inbound on the Blue Line and get off at Maverick Station. From there, catch an MBTA bus (on Meridian Street) to the first stop in *Chelsea*, after crossing the bridge into the predominantly working-class and Latino city. Very close by is the **CHELSEA SALT TERMINAL** (37 Marginal Street), where all the salt for de-icing the roads of the entire state of Massachusetts arrives. The very operation of the terminal—with its heavy truck traffic—and the presence of cyanide-laced salt present significant threats to the surrounding households.

A little more than a one-mile walk away is another example—the **EXXON MOBIL EVERETT TERMINAL** (42–148 Beacham Street, *Everett*)—of the way the location of environmental hazards is tied to vulnerable communities. Sited along waterways, it is a major storage site for diesel fuels and a source of toxic pollution. Area environmental and environmental justice

organizations have thus focused their energies on the terminal.

After heading back to Maverick Station, take the Blue Line inbound to Downtown Boston's State Street Station. Very close by is the site where the original headquarters (60 State Street) of the **UNITED FRUIT COMPANY** once stood. Just as **NEPTUNE ROAD EDGE BUFFER PARK** (as well as myriad sites associated with the **NATIVE GREATER BOSTON TOUR**) manifests the centrality of domestic land struggles in Greater Boston's history, the United Fruit Company illustrates how much of Boston's wealth is tied to the taking of land and environmental resources abroad, and to the transformation of landscapes. At its height in the mid-1900s, the United Fruit Company was the world's largest agricultural enterprise. In Guatemala, it owned the majority of the country's private land, ownership the company maintained through horrific violence in alliance with the US Central Intelligence Agency and the Guatemalan military.

About ten minutes away by foot is the **BOSTON COMMON** (Tremont Street, between Park and Boylston Streets). The first public park in the United States, the Common, since its founding, has been a contested space reflecting divisions of various sorts, particularly those of class.

At Park Street Station, take the Red Line to JFK/UMass Station. From there, it is a half-mile to *South Boston*'s **CARSON BEACH** (William Day Boulevard). In the mid- to late-1970s, it was an intensely contested space when African American and Latino residents of the nearby Columbia Point

Housing Project asserted their rights of access to the beach.

From there, heading to *Dorchester*, go to the former site of the *LAURA ANN EWING HOME/COLUMBIA POINT HOUSING PROJECT* (260 Mount Vernon Street). The killing of Laura Ann Ewing by a City of Boston truck in 1962—due to the siting of city dumps on the small peninsula—highlighted the ties between matters of race and class and unequal exposure to environmental detriments and its life-diminishing consequences. It also led to a successful effort to relocate the dumps, an effort that, ironically, contributed to the gentrification of the neighborhood, one whose low-income, working-class population is today markedly smaller.

At JFK/UMass Station, catch an MBTA bus to Dudley Street, home to the offices (550 Dudley Street) of the *DUDLEY STREET NEIGHBORHOOD INITIATIVE* (DSNI). If the commodification of land is a key reason why so many in Greater Boston suffer from housing insecurity and have inadequate access to environmental resources, DSNI's work points to a remedy. A community land trust, DSNI has democratized control of land in one of Boston's lowest-income areas and stabilized its housing market, while greatly increasing the quality of life of its residents.

An MBTA bus from Dudley Street will take you to the Orange Line, at one end of which is Forest Hills Station. From there, catch another bus to the former site of historic *BROOK FARM* (670 Baker Street), a utopian experiment in communal living in the 1840s. Based on simple living and cooperation, the agricultural community's

legacy lives on today in part through the New Brook Farm—which describes itself as "a sustainable agricultural, educational, and environmental initiative"—based at the site.

The tour takes you to two municipalities beyond the City of Boston and its immediate neighbors to give you a chance to experience nature's beauty on walking trails.

The first is in the City of *LYNN*, home to the *LYNN WOODS RESERVATION* (106 Pennybrook Road). (MBTA Commuter Rail or a bus from East Boston will take you to downtown Lynn, from where another bus passes close to an entrance to the park.) It is one of the largest municipally owned forested parks in the United States and has about thirty miles of walking trails. Its establishment in the late 1800s reflected dominant views among Greater Boston's middle and upper classes of nature as a place for leisure, recreation, and contemplation.

The largest body of water in the Lynn Woods is Walden Pond. This is not to be confused with the more famous, eponymous pond in *CONCORD*, the focus of the second destination municipality on this tour. You can get to Concord by MBTA Commuter Rail to Concord Depot (Fitchburg Line). If you like to bike, the Minuteman Commuter Bikeway, from just outside the MBTA's Alewife Station (Red Line), connects to the Reformatory Branch Trail, which brings you to Concord (about a fifteen-mile ride total). Along the way, you'll pass by the *GREAT MEADOWS NATIONAL WILDLIFE REFUGE*, a largely freshwater wetlands area where animals—particularly migratory birds—nest, rest, and feed.

The Nature of Greater Boston Tour

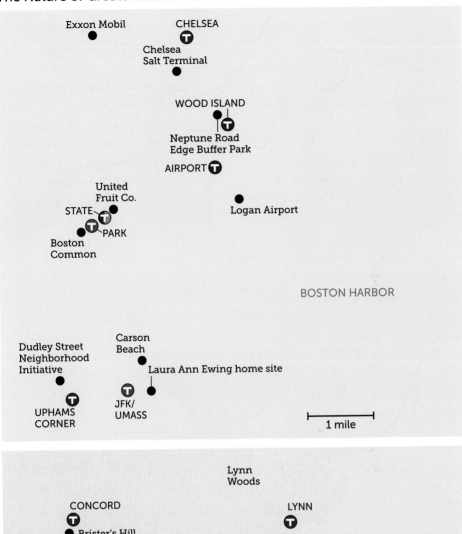

Exxon Mobil

CHELSEA

Chelsea
Salt Terminal

WOOD ISLAND

Neptune Road
Edge Buffer Park

AIRPORT

United
Fruit Co.

STATE

PARK

Logan Airport

Boston
Common

BOSTON HARBOR

Carson
Beach

Dudley Street
Neighborhood
Initiative

Laura Ann Ewing home site

UPHAMS
CORNER

JFK/
UMASS

1 mile

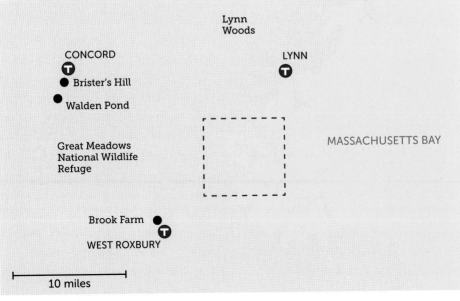

Lynn
Woods

CONCORD

LYNN

Brister's Hill

Walden Pond

MASSACHUSETTS BAY

Great Meadows
National Wildlife
Refuge

Brook Farm

WEST ROXBURY

10 miles

From near the center of Concord, take the Emerson-Thoreau Amble, through woods and fields, that leads to **BRISTER'S HILL** (about a 1.7-mile walk.) Once the home and farming site of Brister Freeman, the area's sandy soil made it less than ideal for agriculture and thus less desirable for most whites. It became an area of settlement for the formerly enslaved of Concord, including Brister Freeman. As with other sites on this tour, it speaks to the interrelationship of nature and class and race—not least in terms of the quality of land to which one has access.

Nearby is **WALDEN POND**, close to Henry David Thoreau's famous retreat (the former site of his cabin is marked), where he lived from 1845 to 1847 to concentrate on his writing and to experiment with living simply. A classic in environmental writing, *Walden; Or, Life in the Woods* is a result of his time there.

Public Transportation via the MBTA
Subway, Silver Lines & Commuter Rail

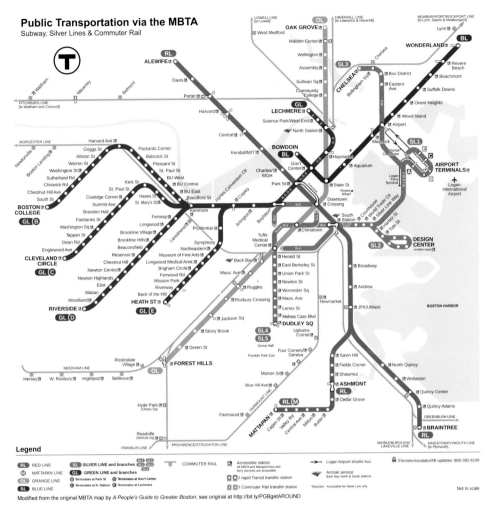

Legend

Modified from the original MBTA map by *A People's Guide to Greater Boston*; see original at http://bit.ly/PGBgetAROUND

MBTA Subway and Commuter Rail System

Acknowledgments

When we started the research for this book in 2014, none of us imagined how much work the project would involve. Nor did we anticipate how much we would learn in the process—not least the profound limitations of our own knowledge of things Greater Boston and the larger world of which it is part and that it has helped to produce.

If no person is an island, no book is the work of only those credited with authorship. In our case, to the extent that we have made headway in understanding and illuminating the region, it is due to an immeasurable degree to the many individuals who have helped us. This book is the result of many conversations, real and imagined, direct and indirect, with people past and present. That the Greater Boston area enjoys so many insightful and generous individuals—many of whom have shared their knowledge through their writings, others through their speech, still others through the organizing and activism (and via a combination of these different activities)—speaks to the region's great dynamism and wealth (of a sort far beyond that associated with capital).

While there are many people to thank in Greater Boston, we'd like to highlight a small number who helped us in myriad ways over the course of the project. Jim Beauchesne, Nick Brown, Aviva Chomsky, Bob Forrant, and Tunney Lee stand out for their multiple forms of support. They answered our countless questions, suggested things to read and people to contact, read drafts of entries and entire sections, and offered helpful feedback. The book is much richer than it would have been otherwise.

In the early stages of our research and writing, we reached out to a number of people to interview them about their experiences and areas of expertise and help us brainstorm about what *A People's Guide to Greater Boston* might or should look like. In addition to the individuals mentioned above, they include Michael Bronski, Jeff Crosby, Marilyn Frankenstein, Jim Kaplan, Mel King, Penn Loh, Dorotea Manuela, Jason Pramas;

Sandra Ruiz-Harris, Fred Salvucci, Paul Shannon, John Trumpbour, Chuck Turner, and Ann Withorn. They were all generous with their time, memories, and insights. Moreover, some of them read and constructively commented on components of the manuscript.

We also benefited greatly from the resources of libraries, archives, and historical societies throughout Greater Boston and beyond. They include the A. J. Muste Memorial Institute; Boston Public Library (and its Norman B. Leventhal Map Center and various branch libraries); Brighton-Allston Historical Society; Brockton Public Library; Cambridge Historical Commission; Cambridge Public Library; Chinese Historical Society of New England; City of Boston Archive; City of Chelsea Public Library; Countway Harvard Center for the History of Medicine; Dorchester Historical Society; Harvard University Archives; Historic New England; The History Project; Lawrence History Center; Lawrence Public Library; Lynn Public Library; Massachusetts Historical Society; New York Public Library; North End Historical Society; Pollard Memorial Library (Lowell); South Boston Historical Society; Archives and Special Collections, Snell Library at Northeastern University; W.E.B. DuBois Special Collections and Archives, and Special Collections and University Archives, University of Massachusetts Amherst Libraries; UMass Boston Archives, and Wellesley College Archives.

While there are many people at these institutions who assisted us in countless ways, a few deserve special mention. At the Lawrence History Center, Kathy Flynn and Amita Kiley were always very generous with their time, insights, and good humor. The knowledge and resources that they shared with us were invaluable in helping us gain appreciation for the richness (and nuances) of Lawrence.

For the images in this book, we called upon Aaron Schmidt of the Boston Public Library's Print Division, Molly Brown at Northeastern University's Snell Library, Archives and Special Collections, and Marta Crilly of the Boston City Archives on many occasions, and they came through for us—almost invariably.

And then there's Chris Glass, a research librarian at the Boston Public Library in Copley Square, where we spent an inordinate amount of time combing through the stacks and archives, collaborating and writing. From the first time we asked Chris for assistance, he expressed great support for the project and exhibited it through his efforts to track down information for us—information that we were often convinced was not findable, but, more often than not, he proved otherwise. Chris undertook many tasks—big and small—for us in his professional capacity and did so with great skill and generosity. We are in his debt.

Many others provided various forms of assistance, big and small—by, for example, suggesting topics to pursue or sites to explore, providing information or resources, making themselves available for an interview, or providing feedback on entries. We thank them (and apologize to anyone we have forgotten to include) and list them here in alphabetical order: Hal Abelson; Emily Achtenberg; Frank Ackerman; Joshua Alba; Vicente Alba-Panama; Michael Albert; José Aleman; Alistair Towesland Allen; Matt Andrews; Dexter Arnold; Che Arraj; Katherine Asuncion; Christine Bachman-Sanders; Jose Barros; Jane Becker; Dawn Belkin-Martinez; Alison Bell; Marcella Bencivenni; Michele Berger; Will Blum; Christopher Bonanos; Libby Bouvier; Natalie Brady; John Broderick; Nino Brown; Irene Bruce; Doug Brugge; Lauren "Tess" Bundy; Ed Cafasso; Michael Cane; Ross Caputi; Daniel Casieri; Evan Casper-Futterman; Karen Chen; Jonathan Chenette; Susan Chin-sen; Noam Chomsky; Chuck Collins; Rodnell P. Collins; Pasqualino Colombaro; Donald Coloumbe; Mary Jo Connolly; Bridget Cooley; Karilyn Crockett; Jeff Crosby; Bob Cullum; Robert D'Attilio; Leilah Danielson; Russ Davis; Ben Day; Barbara Deck; Christine M. DeLucia; Charlie Derber; Tim Devin; David Dinklage; Diane Dujon; Jack Eckert; Andrew Elder; Neena Estrella Luna; Chris Faraone; David Fichter; Marisa Figueiredo; Lorenz Finison; Britta Fischer; Gail Fithian; Kate Flaherty; Susan Fleischmann; Robin Fleming; Gabrielle Flohr; Lorraine Fowlkes; Herb Fox; Kaitlyn Fox; Marilyn Frankenstein; Demita Frazier; Christopher Fung; Siobhan Gallagher; Laura Gang; Jack Geiger; Ted German; Michael Gerry; Livia Gershon; Yesenia Gil; Mike Godbe; Brian Godfrey; Rebecca Goldman; David Goodman; Susan Goodwin; David Grosser; Shep Gurwitz; Robert Hannan; John Harris; Cole Harrison; Dan Hawkins; Loie Hayes; David Himmelstein; Rachel Hock; Amy Hoffman; Bill Hoynes; Caroline Hunter; Cassie Hurd; Susan Jacoby; Dave Jenkins; Chuck Jones; Mimi Jones; Paula Jones; Rick Jones; Peter Kadzis; Don Kales; Michael Kane; Jerry Kaplan; Jim Kaplan; Natasha Karunaratne; Dylan Kaufman-Obstler; Nancy Kearns; Joe Kebartas; Joyce Kelly; Martin Kessler; Amita Kiley; Gavin Kleespies; Mariel Klein; Richard Knight; Dan "the Bagel Man" Kontoff; Kathy Kottaridis; Lisa Kulyk-Bourque; Brian Kwoba; Jasmine Laietmark; Alisa LaSotnik; Jerry Lembcke; Charles Levenstein; Richard Levins; Elaine Lewinnek; Penny Lewis; Mike Leyba; Juan Leyton; Michael Liu; Lydia Lowe; Jason Lydon; Joel Mackall; Duncan MacLaury; Paul Malachi; Mary Marra; Homefries Matthews; Olivia May; Arthur McEwan; Kevin McHenry; Julie McVay; Liz Mestres; John Miller; Derek Mitchell; Emily T. Molina; Kate Moore; Samantha Muller; Myrna Morales; Robert Morris; Mahtowin Munro; Carol Nevins; Judy Norsigian; Brian O'Connell; Tom O'Connell; Lisa Owens; Cole Palatini; Alex Papali; Ronald Patkus; Monica Pelayo; Cynthia Peters; Linda Pinkow; Michael Prokosch; Brynne Quinlan; Joseph Ramsey; Marcia Rasmussen; Kathleen (Kit) Rawlins; Marcus Rediker; Kaitlin Reed; Mary Regan; Sergio Reyes; Kimberly Reynolds; Celeste Ribeiro Myers; Alessandra Rico; Dan Rico; Simon Rios; Jeanette Roach; Marilynne Roach; Michelle Romero; David Rubin; Greg Ruggiero; David Russo; Laura Russo; Anthony Sammarco; Louise Sandberg; Conrado Santos; Pat Scanlon; Sigrid Schmalzer; Jill Schneiderman; Juliet Schor; Gerry Scoppettuolo; Fred Seavey; Paul Shannon; Jennifer Siegel; Isaac Simon Hodes;

Manisha Sinha; Lydia Sisson; Karen Slater; Nathanial Smith; Ethan Snow; Mark Solomon; Fred Sperounis; Dean Stevens; Dottie Stevens; Heather Stevenson; Jonas Stundza; Chris Sturr; Charles Sullivan; Felicia Sullivan; Abha Sur; Mike Tamulis; Earl Taylor; Weimin Tchen; Felipe Cupertino Teixeira; Evan Thornberry; Chris Tilly; Roberto Torres-Collazo; Wen-ti Tsen; Yanni Tsipis; Moriah Tumbleson-Shaw; Pavel Uranga; Karen Valentino; Tony Van Der Meer; Charlie Vasiliades; Jim Wallace; Victor Wallis; Charlie Welch; Jessy Wheeler; Janine Whitcomb; Caroline White; Greg Williams; Ann Withorn; Catherine T. Wood; Steffie Woolhandler; Charles Yancey; and Liza Zayas.

In addition, there were many Greater Bostonians to whom we are grateful for engaging us in conversations—often at their initiative—when we were visiting sites, for sharing information and sometimes telling us about other sites we did not know about.

At Vassar College, Adele Birkenes, Richard Bryenton, and Kaitlin Reed provided valuable research assistance at various stages of the project. Funding from the college's Committee on Research was vital in allowing us to employ a research assistant based in Greater Boston and to purchase rights to numerous images.

This book is part of a series. For that reason alone, we'd be remiss if we did not thank the editors of the "People's Guide" series—Laura Barraclough; Wendy Cheng; and Laura Pulido (in Laura Pulido's case not least for taking seriously our immodest suggestion that we write the book after she asked if we knew anyone who might be capable of doing so). Throughout the process, Wendy Cheng served as our editor and did so admirably, patiently addressing our concerns and questions and providing very helpful feedback throughout the process.

We are also grateful to the University of California Press for publishing the book, to Kim Robinson, our editor at the press, for her support, Benjy Malings for his help with matters related to the images we use here, Peter Perez and Jolene Torr for their work on the publicity front, and to Summer Farah for her editorial assistance. In addition, we thank Francisco Reinking for overseeing the production process at the press, Holly Bridges for her skilled copyediting, Nicole Hayward for designing the book, and Jim O'Brien for putting together the index.

External reviewers solicited by the press provided a lot of helpful feedback on our original manuscript—Aviva Chomsky, Marie Kennedy, and Fred Sperounis. We thank them for their reviews and for having follow-up discussions with us.

Neil Horsky produced all but one of the maps contained in this book. We deeply appreciate his artistry and creativity and thank him for sharing his skills and knowledge of Greater Boston with us—as well as for his support throughout the project.

Finally, our families and loved ones supported us (and put up with us) in too many ways to mention. So big thanks are due to Mizue Aizeki; Amina and Sayako Aizeki-Nevins; Charlie Klemmer, Stavros Macrakis, Kira Moodliar, Carol Nevins, Francesca Pignoni, and Dominique Stassart.

Bibliography

Adams, Catherine, and Elizabeth H. Peck. *Love of Freedom: Black Women in Colonial and Revolutionary New England.* Oxford and New York: Oxford University Press, 2010.

Allison, Robert. *A Short History of Boston.* Beverly, MA: Commonwealth Editions, 2004.

Altshuler, Alan A., and David Luberoff. *Mega-Projects: The Changing Politics of Urban Public Investment.* Washington, DC: Brookings Institution Press, 2003.

Archer, Richard. *As If an Enemy's Country: The British Occupation of Boston and the Origins of Revolution.* New York: Oxford University Press, 2010.

Arnold, Dexter. "'A Row of Bricks': Worker Activism in the Merrimack Valley Textile Industry, 1912–1922." PhD diss., Department of History, University of Wisconsin-Madison, 1985.

Basso, Keith H. *Wisdom Sits in Places: Landscape and Language among the Western Apache.* Albuquerque: University of New Mexico Press, 1996.

Beckert, Sven. *Empire of Cotton: A Global History.* New York: Vintage, 2015.

Bedford, Henry F. *Socialism and the Workers in Massachusetts, 1886–1912.* Amherst: University of Massachusetts Press, 1966.

Beito, David T. *From Mutual Aid to the Welfare State: Fraternal Societies and the Welfare State, 1890–1967.* Chapel Hill: University of North Carolina Press, 2000.

Blumrosen, Alfred W., and Ruth G. Blumrosen. *Slave Nation: How Slavery United the Colonies and Sparked the American Revolution.* New York: Barnes and Noble, 2005.

Booth, Robert. *Death of an Empire: The Rise and Murderous Fall of Salem, America's Richest City.* New York: St. Martin's Press, 2011.

Bradley, Patricia. *Slavery, Propaganda, and the American Revolution.* Jackson: University of Mississippi Press, 1999.

Bressler, Ann Lee. *The Universalist Movement in America, 1770–1880.* New York: Oxford University Press, 2001.

Brooks, Lisa. *Our Beloved Kin: A New History of King Philip's War.* New Haven: Yale University Press, 2018.

Brown, Nicholas. "Experiments in Regional Settler-Colonization: Pursuing Justice and Producing Scale through the Montana Study," in *Settler Colonialism and the Urban Prairie West.* David Hugill, Tyler McCreary, Julie Tomiak, and Heather Dorries, eds. Winnipeg: University of Manitoba Press, 2019.

Bryant, Howard. *Shut Out: A Story of Race and Baseball in Boston*. Boston: Beacon Press, 2002.

Chomsky, Aviva. *Linked Labor Histories: New England, Colombia, and the Making of a Global Working Class*. Durham, NC: Duke University Press, 2008.

Cole, Donald B. *Immigrant City: Lawrence, Massachusetts, 1845–1921*. Chapel Hill: University of North Carolina Press, 2002.

Cronon, William. *Changes in the Land: Indians, Colonists, and the Ecology of New England*. New York: Hill and Wang, 2003.

Dawley, Alan. *Class and Community: The Industrial Revolution in Lynn*. Cambridge: Harvard University Press, 2000.

DeLucia, Christine M. *Memory Lands: King Philip's War and the Place of Violence in the Northeast*. New Haven: Yale University Press: 2018.

Deutsch, Sarah. *Women and the City: Gender, Space, and Power in Boston, 1870–1940*. New York: Oxford University Press, 2000.

Domosh, Mona. *Invented Cities: The Creation of Landscape in Nineteenth-Century New York and Boston*. New Haven: Yale University Press, 1996.

Fields, Gary. *Enclosure: Palestinian Landscapes in a Historical Mirror*. Berkeley: University of California Press, 2017.

Formisano, Ronald. *Boston Against Busing: Race, Class, and Ethnicity in the 1960s and 1970s*. Chapel Hill, NC: University of North Carolina Press, 1991.

Forrant, Robert, and Christoph Strobel. *Ethnicity in Lowell*. Boston: Northeast National Ethnography Program, National Park Service, 2011.

Forrant, Robert, and Jurg Siegenthaler, eds. *The Great Lawrence Textile Strike of 1912: New Scholarship on the Bread and Roses Strike*. Amityville, NY: Baywood Publishing Company, 2014.

Fowler, William M., Jr. *Empires at War: The French and Indian War and the Struggle for North America, 1754–1763*. New York: Walker Publishing Company, 2005.

Frank, Thomas. *Listen, Liberal, or, What Ever Happened to the Party of the People?* New York: Metropolitan Books, 2016.

Fraser, Rebecca. *The Mayflower: The Families, the Voyage, and the Founding of America*. New York: St. Martin's Press, 2017.

Ghent, W. J., ed. *Socialism and Government: Working Programs and Records of Socialists in Office*. Girard, KS: Appeal to Reason, 1916.

Handlin, Oscar. *Boston's Immigrants, 1790–1880*. New York: Atheneum, 1975.

Harvey, Susan M. "Slavery in Massachusetts: A Descendent of Early Settlers Investigates the Connections in Newburyport, Massachusetts." Master's thesis, Fitchburg State University, June 2011.

Hayden, Dolores. *The Power of Place: Urban Landscapes as Public History*. Cambridge: MIT Press, 1997.

Higham, John. *Strangers in the Land: Patterns of American Nativism, 1860–1925*. New Brunswick, NJ: Rutgers University Press, 2002.

History Project. *Improper Bostonians. Lesbian and Gay History from the Puritans to Playland*. Boston: Beacon Press, 1998.

Hodson, Christopher. *The Acadian Diaspora: An Eighteenth-Century History*. Oxford: Oxford University Press, 2012.

Horne, Gerald, *The Counter-Revolution of 1776: Slave Resistance and the Origins of the United States of America*. New York: NYU Press, 2014.

Isenberg, Nancy. *White Trash: The Four-Hundred-Year Untold History of Class in America*. New York: Penguin Books, 2016.

Juravich, Tom, William F. Hartford, James R. Green, *Commonwealth of Toil: Chapters in the History of Massachusetts Workers and Their Unions*. Amherst: University of Massachusetts Press, 1996.

Kantrowitz, Stephen. *More Than Freedom: Fighting for Black Citizenship in a White Republic, 1829–1889*. New York: Penguin Books, 2013.

Kennedy, Lawrence W. *Planning the City upon a Hill: Boston Since 1630.* Amherst: University of Massachusetts Press, 1994.

Kendrick, Stephen, and Paul Kendrick. *Sarah's Long Walk: The Free Blacks of Boston and How Their Struggle for Equality Changed America.* Boston: Beacon Hill Press, 2004.

King, Mel. *Chain of Change.* Boston: South End Press, 1981.

Lepore, Jill. *The Name of War: King Philip's War and the Origins of American Identity.* New York: Alfred A. Knopf, 1998.

Lukas, J. Anthony. *Common Ground: A Turbulent Decade in the Lives of Three American Families.* New York: Knopf, 1985.

Lupo, Alan Frank Colcord, and Edmund P. Fowler. *Rites of Way: The Politics of Transportation in Boston and the U.S. City.* Boston: Little, Brown and Company, 1971.

MacDonald, Michael Patrick. *All Souls: A Family Story from Southie.* Boston: Beacon Press, 2007.

Mandell, Daniel R. *Behind the Frontier: Indians in Eighteenth-Century Eastern Massachusetts.* Lincoln: University of Nebraska Press, 1996.

———. *Tribe, Race, History: Native Americans in Southern New England, 1780–1880.* Baltimore: Johns Hopkins University Press, 2008.

Mangold, C. S. *Ten Hills Farm: The Forgotten History of Slavery in the North.* Princeton: Princeton University Press, 2010.

Marchione, William P. *Allston-Brighton in Transition: From Cattle Town to Streetcar Suburb.* Charleston, SC: The History Press, 2007.

Massey, Doreen. "Power-Geometry and a Progressive Sense of Place." In J. Bird, B. Curtis, T. Putnam, and L. Tickner, eds., *Mapping the Futures: Local Cultures, Global Change.* London, Routledge, 1993, 59–69.

Medoff, Peter, and Holly Sklar. *Streets of Hope: The Fall and Rise of an Urban Neighborhood.* Boston: South End Press, 1994.

Mitchell, Don. *The Lie of the Land: Migrant Workers and California Landscape.* Minneapolis, London: University of Minnesota Press, 1996.

Morrison, Dane Anthony, and Nancy Lusignan Schultz, eds. *Salem: Place, Myth, and Memory.* Boston: Northeastern University Press, 2004.

Newell, Margaret Ellen. *Brethren by Nature: New England Indians, Colonists, and the Origins of American Slavery.* Ithaca: Cornell University Press, 2015.

O'Brien, Jean. *Firsting and Lasting: Writing Indians out of Existence in New England.* Minneapolis: University of Minnesota Press, 2010.

O'Connell, James C. *The Hub's Metropolis: Greater Boston's Development from Railroad Suburbs to Smart Growth.* Cambridge: MIT Press, 2013.

O'Connor, Thomas H. *Boston Catholics: A History of the Church and Its People.* Boston: Northeastern University Press, 1998.

———. *South Boston, My Home Town: The History of an Ethnic Neighborhood.* Boston: Quinlan Press, 1988.

Penna, Anthony N., and Conrad Edick Wright, eds. *Remaking Boston: An Environmental History of the City and Its Surroundings.* Pittsburgh: University of Pittsburgh Press, 2013.

Peterson, Mark. *The City-State of Boston: The Rise and Fall of an Atlantic Power, 1630–1865,* Princeton, NJ: Princeton University Press, 2019.

Puleo, Stephen. *A City So Grand: The Rise of an American Metropolis, Boston 1850–1900.* Boston: Beacon Press, 2010.

———. *Dark Tide: The Great Boston Molasses Flood of 1919.* Boston: Beacon Press, 2003.

Pulido, Laura, Laura R. Barraclough, and Wendy Cheng. *A People's Guide to Los Angeles,* Berkeley: University of California Press, 2012.

Rawson, Michael. *Eden on the Charles: The Making of Boston.* Cambridge: Harvard University Press, 2010.

Richter, Daniel. *Facing East from Indian Country: A Native History of Early America.* Cambridge: Harvard University Press, 2001.

Russell, Francis. *A City in Terror: Calvin Coolidge and the 1919 Boston Police Strike*. Boston: Beacon Press, 2005 (1975).

Schneider, Mark R. *Boston Confronts Jim Crow, 1890–1920*. Boston: Northeastern University Press, 1997.

Schorow, Stephanie. *East of Boston: Notes from the Harbor Islands*. Charleston. SC: The History Press, 2008.

Seasholes, Nancy S. *Gaining Ground: A History of Landmaking in Boston*. Cambridge: MIT Press, 2003.

Sinha, Manisha. *The Slave's Cause: A History of Abolition*. New Haven: Yale University Press, 2016.

Small, Mario Luis. *Villa Victoria: The Transformation of Social Capital in a Boston Barrio*. Chicago and London: University of Chicago Press, 2004.

Sweetser, M. F. *King's Handbook of Boston Harbor*. Cambridge: Moses King, Publisher, 1882.

Tager, Jack. *Boston Riots: Three Centuries of Social Violence*. Boston: Northeastern University Press, 2001.

Taylor, Steven J. L. *Desegregation in Boston and Buffalo: The Influence of Local Leaders*. Albany: State University of New York Press, 1998.

To, Wing-kai. *Chinese in Boston: 1870–1965*. Charleston, SC: Arcadia, 2008.

Thrush, Coll. *Native Seattle: Histories from the Crossing-over Place*. 2nd ed. Seattle: University of Washington Press, 2017.

Vrabel, Jim. *A People's History of the New Boston*. Amherst and Boston: University of Massachusetts Press, 2014.

Warren, Wendy. *New England Bound: Slavery and Colonization in Early America*. New York: Liveright Publishing Corporation, 2016.

Watson, Bruce. *Bread and Roses: Mills, Migrants, and the Struggle for the American Dream*. New York: Viking, 2005.

———. *Sacco and Vanzetti: The Men, the Murders, and the Judgment of Mankind*. New York: Viking, 2007.

Weiner, Mark S. *Black Trials: Citizenship from the Beginnings of Slavery to the End of Caste*. New York: Knopf Doubleday, 2004.

Whitehill, Walter Muir, and Lawrence W. Kennedy. *Boston: A Topographical History*. Cambridge: Belknap Press of Harvard University Press, 2000.

Wilder, Craig Steven. *Ebony and Ivy: Race, Slavery, and the Troubled History of America's Universities*. New York: Bloomsbury Press, 2013.

Winship, J. P. C. *Historical Brighton: An Illustrated History of Brighton and Its Citizens*. Vol. 1. Boston: George A. Warren Publishers, 1899.

Winsor, Justin, ed. *The Memorial History of Boston, Including Suffolk County, Massachusetts, 1630–1880*. Vol. 1. Boston: James R. Osgood and Company, 1881.

Wise, Steven M. *Though the Heavens May Fall: The Landmark Trial That Led to the End of Human Slavery*. Boston: Da Capo Press, 2005.

Worthy, William. *The Rape of Our Neighborhoods: And How Communities Are Resisting Take-overs by Colleges, Hospitals, Churches, Businesses, and Public Agencies*. New York: William Morrow and Company, 1976.

Yuhl, Stephanie E. "Sculpted Radicals: The Problem of Sacco and Vanzetti in Boston's Public Memory." *Public Historian* 32, no. 2 (2010): 9–30.

Zinn, Howard. *A People's History of the United States*. New York: Harper Perennial, 2015.

Journalistic sources

Associated Press

The Bay State Banner

BINJ Reports

Boston.com

Boston Daily Globe

The Boston Globe

The Boston Globe Sunday Magazine

The Boston Herald

Boston Magazine

The Boston Phoenix

The Boston Pilot

Boston Post

The Daily Free Press (Boston University)

Daily Kos

Daily News (Newburyport)

DemocracyNow!

DigBoston

Dorchester Reporter

East Boston Times-Free Press

ESPN.com

The Evening Tribune (Lawrence)

The Fenway News

Friends Journal

Harper's Weekly

Harvard Business Review

The Harvard Crimson

Harvard Magazine

Indian Country Today

The Jamaica Plain Gazette

Jewish Advocate

Lawrence Telegram

The MetroWest Daily News

Mother Jones

NationalGeographic.com

The Nationalist

The New England Magazine

The New York Times

The New Yorker

The Patriot Ledger

Priceonomics

Radical America

The Rainbow Times

ReVista: Harvard Review of Latin America

The Salem News

The San Francisco Bay Guardian

Spare Change News

The Tech (MIT)

The Telegraph (Nashua, NH)

The Tufts Daily

TomDispatch.com

Universal Hub

UU World

WBUR.org

WGBH.org

Credits

Page 161 (below): Courtesy of Boston City Archives.

Page 162: Photo by Spencer Grant.

Page 163: Created by Chinese Progressive Association. Courtesy of Northeastern University Libraries, Archives and Special Collections Department.

Page 168: Photo by Spencer Grant.

Page 169: Photo by Eleni Macrakis.

Page 171: Courtesy of the *Harvard Crimson*.

Page 172: Photo by Midnightdreary.

Page 173: Courtesy of the Trustees of the Boston Public Library.

Page 175: Courtesy of the Peter Simon Collection, Special Collections and University Archives, University of Massachusetts Amherst Libraries.

Page 176 (above): Courtesy of African Activist Archive Project, Michigan State University.

Page 176 (below): Courtesy of African Activist Archive Project, Michigan State University.

Page 177: Courtesy of Jeff Albertson Photograph Collection, Special Collections and University Archives, University of Massachusetts Amherst Libraries.

Page 178: Public domain.

Page 179: Courtesy of Dollars and Sense.

Page 180: Photo by Spencer Grant.

Page 182 (above): Public domain.

Page 182 (below): Courtesy of Food Not Bombs.

Page 183: Photo by David Goodman.

Page 185: Photo by Tony Webster.

Page 186: Photo by Eleni Macrakis.

Page 187: Public domain.

Page 188: Courtesy of Chelsea Public Library Archive Collection.

Page 190: Photo by Suren Moodliar.

Page 194: Photo by Liz LaManche.

Page 195: Photo by Eleni Macrakis.

Page 196: Photo by UTEC.

Page 198: Public domain.

Page 199: Courtesy of the Lowell Historical Society.

Page 202: Photo by Steve Osemwenkhae for the Bread and Roses Heritage Committee.

Page 205: Courtesy of the Library of Congress.

Page 206: Courtesy of the Lawrence History Center.

Page 207: Courtesy of the Lawrence History Center.

Page 209: Courtesy of the Lawrence Public Library.

Page 210: Courtesy of the Lawrence History Center.

Page 212: Courtesy of the Boston Public Library, Leslie Jones Collection.

Page 214: Photo by Eleni Macrakis.

Page 215: Photo by Eleni Macrakis.

Page 217: Photo by John Tlumacki / *Boston Globe* via Getty Images.

Page 218: Public domain.

Page 219: Photo by Suren Moodliar.

Page 221: Public domain.

Page 222: Public domain.

Page 223: Photo by Joseph Nevins.

Page 224: Public domain.

Page 226: Courtesy of the Trustees of the Boston Public Library.

Page 229: Courtesy of Everett Collection Inc., Alamy.

Page 231: Photo by Joseph Nevins.

Page 232: Photo by Joseph Nevins.

Page 233: Photo by Joseph Nevins.

Page 234: Photo by Eleni Macrakis.

Page 236: Photo by Mizue Aizeki.

Page 237 (above): Public domain.

Page 237 (below): Photo by Eleni Macrakis.

Page 238: Tichnor Brothers Collection. Courtesy of the Trustees of the Boston Public Library.

Page 240: Drawing by Henry McIntyre. Public domain.

Page 241: Courtesy of the Boston Public Library, Leslie Jones Collection.

Page 246: Public domain.

Page 248: Photo by Eleni Macrakis.

Page 250: Courtesy of the Boston Public Library, Leslie Jones Collection.

Page 252: Photo by Suren Moodliar.

Page 254: Photo by John Phelan.

Page 255: Photo by Andrew Todd Phillips.

Page 256: Photo by Brynne Quinlan.

Page 257: Photo by Suren Moodliar.

Page 260: Courtesy of the *Patriot Ledger*.

Page 268: Courtesy of Rodnell Collins.

Page 269: Courtesy of Freedom House Collection, Northeastern University Libraries, Archives and Special Collections Department.

Page 273: Public domain.

Page 278: Courtesy of the Lawrence History Center.

Index

wharves, 10, 11*map*; 13, 14, 16–19, 43*fig.*, 44, 94, 279, 285*map*
Wheatley, Phillis, 13–14
White, Kevin, 78*fig.*
Whittier, John Greenleaf, 33, 198, 219, 223
Wildes, Sarah, 231
William Monroe Trotter House, 131–32
Williams, Daryl, 97–98
Williams, Ken, 175–76
Wilson, Woodrow, 131
Wincumbone, 169
Winslow, Edward, 261
Winslow, Josiah, 258

Winthrop, John, 3–4, 94, 169, 170, 266; and slavery, 3, 169, 266
Winthrop, Mass., 13, 23*map*
witch trials, 230–31. *See also* Salem witch trials
Womble, Mike, 119i
Women's Center in Cambridge, 145, 177–78
Women's Trade Union League, 40, 63, 65
Wood, William, 204, 275
Wood Island Park, 103
Worcester, Noah, 159, 160
Workmen's Circle, 189
World War I, 52

World War II, 101, 110, 137, 205, 242, 248
Wright, Elizur, 243
WS Development, 118

Y
Yawkey, Tom, 85
Youth's Companion, The, 83–84
Youth's Companion Building, 25*map*(#36), 83–84

Z
Z Magazine, 75
Zemurray, Samuel, 279–80
ZNet, 75

Founded in 1893,
UNIVERSITY OF CALIFORNIA PRESS
publishes bold, progressive books and journals
on topics in the arts, humanities, social sciences,
and natural sciences—with a focus on social
justice issues—that inspire thought and action
among readers worldwide.

The UC PRESS FOUNDATION
raises funds to uphold the press's vital role
as an independent, nonprofit publisher, and
receives philanthropic support from a wide
range of individuals and institutions—and from
committed readers like you. To learn more, visit
ucpress.edu/supportus.